The Crucible Concept

The Crucible Concept

Thematic and Narrative Patterns in
Cervantes's *Novelas ejemplares*

E. T. Aylward

Madison • Teaneck
Fairleigh Dickinson University Press
London: Associated University Presses

© 1999 by Associated University Presses, Inc.

All rights reserved. Authorization to photocopy items for internal or personal use, or the internal or personal use of specific clients, is granted by the copyright owner, provided that a base fee of $10.00, plus eight cents per page, per copy is paid directly to the Copyright Clearance Center, 222 Rosewood Dr., Danvers, Massachusetts 01923. [0-8386-3777-9/99 $10.00 + 8¢ pp, pc.]

Associated University Presses
440 Forsgate Drive
Cranbury, NJ 08512

Associated University Presses
16 Barter Street
London WC1A 2AH, England

Associated University Presses
P.O. Box 338, Port Credit
Mississauga, Ontario
Canada L5G 4L8

The paper used in this publication meets the requirements
of the American National Standard for Permanence of Paper
for Printed Library Materials Z39.48-1984.]

Library of Congress Cataloging-in-Publication Data

Aylward, E. T.
   The crucible concept : thematic and narrative patterns in
Cervantes's Novelas exemplares / E. T. Aylward
     p.   cm.
   Includes bibliographical references (p.   ) and index.
   ISBN 0-8386-3777-9 (alk. paper)
   1. Cervantes Saavedra, Miguel de, 1547–1616. Novelas exemplares.
I. Title.
PQ6324.Z5A95   1999
863'.3—dc21   98-7694
                                                          CIP

PRINTED IN THE UNITED STATES OF AMERICA

Contents

Acknowledgments	7
Introduction	11
1. Cervantes and the Crucible of Love: Thematic and Structural Affinities in *La gitanilla* and *La ilustre fregona*	41
2. Patterns of Symmetrical Design in *El amante liberal, La fuerza de la sangre,* and *La española inglesa*	94
3. Porras's Manuscript and the Curious Configuration of *Rinconete y Cortadillo, El celoso extremeño,* and *El licenciado Vidriera*	152
4. *Las dos doncellas* and *La señora Cornelia:* Dramatic Echoes of *Don Quixote,* Part One	206
5. The Enigmatic Layered Structure of *El casamiento engañoso* and *El coloquio de los perros*	240
Conclusion: The Arrangement of the *Novelas exemplares*	274
Notes	289
Works Cited	309
Index of Critics Cited	322

Acknowledgments

This seven-year project could never have been brought to a successful conclusion without the support and cooperation of those who assisted me during that period. First and foremost, I would like to thank Prof. Rita Gardiol, chair of the Department of Spanish, Italian, and Portuguese at the University of South Carolina, for the unwavering support and encouragement she always offered as I labored over this task. My thanks also are extended to a distinguished group of graduate students whose research efforts often provided me with valuable new insights into Cervantes's *Novelas:* Catherine Davis Vinel, whose doctoral dissertation on Cervantes's entire collection of *novelas* will, I hope, be published in the near future; Sharon Knight, whose work on the Greek romance provided me with a firm critical background for my studies of *El amante liberal* and *La española inglesa;* Devon Hanahan, whose analysis of the structure of *La señora Cornelia* did much to sharpen my focus on that work; and María Zabala-Peña, who rendered the same valuable service with regard to *Las dos doncellas*.

The Crucible Concept

Introduction

A few years before her death, Ruth El Saffar offered a radically different perspective from which to evaluate Cervantes's late works: the alchemical view. Unfortunately, the thesis she offered was directed only to the posthumously published *Persiles* (1617). In my opinion, however, her perspective works equally well with the dozen *Novelas ejemplares* Cervantes published a few years earlier. El Saffar proposes studying Cervantes's late narratives as literary experiments in character development that parallel the purgative process of the alchemists (i.e., the chemical bath or *solutio*) "by which base matter—the *prima materia*—is cleansed of its dross so that the essential perfection hidden within it may be freed."[1]

Viewed from this angle, Cervantes's *Novelas* can be seen to represent life as a sentimental crucible in which the protagonists' inflated egos undergo a process of psychological dissolution and coagulation in a series of harrowing and sometimes near-miraculous occurrences. The effect of these events on the individuation of these characters, male and female alike, is remarkably comparable to the sustained stripping away of false values that El Saffar notes in the cases of Persiles and Sigismunda. Consequently, I have designated this "crucible concept" as the overriding thematic element that manages to hold together an otherwise curious and incongruous collection of fictional exercises concocted by Cervantes and served up in 1613.

Keeping in mind the theoretical proposition that each tale will include some remarkable event or series of key occurrences that will alter the destiny of one or more protagonists, let us summarize the contents of these dozen tales.

1. *La gitanilla*. A bildungsroman about a young nobleman named Juan de Cárcamo whose fate is radically changed by his decision to live among a band of Gypsies (where he is known as Andrés) in order to win the hand of the lovely Gypsy maiden, Preciosa, who is eventually found to be of noble lineage, too. Primary theme: *jealousy* (in the process, Juan/Andrés

gradually learns to overcome his intensely jealous nature). Secondary theme: *freedom* (the contrast between Gypsy and conventional social customs; the role of the nonconforming artist in society).

2. *El amante liberal*. The central characters, a pair of egotistical lovers named Ricardo and Leonisa, are catapulted into adulthood—and eventually marriage—by the traumatic experience of having been captured by Turkish pirates and sold into slavery in Cyprus. Primary theme: *freedom* (love cannot be coerced; it must be given freely). Secondary theme: *jealousy* (Ricardo learns to overcome his romantic insecurities). Thematically, this story is practically a duplicate of the first one, except that the emphasis on primary and secondary themes is reversed. Structurally, however, the two stories are radically different.

3. *Rinconete y Cortadillo*. The maturation of the two teenage protagonists is rapidly advanced by their unusual experiences with the Sevillian underworld. The key event is their visit to the house of Monipodio, reigning godfather of the *hampa*, and the strange occurrences they witness there. Theme: *freedom* again, but now it is seen as an illusion (there are as many silly rules in the underworld as there are in the normal, "straight" world). The boys, we are told, eventually get their lives in order and return to society.

4. *La española inglesa*. The theme changes in the fourth story as *constancy*, not freedom or jealousy, becomes the overriding issue. The seemingly star-crossed lovers, Ricaredo and Isabela, undergo a series of misfortunes designed to test the strength of their romantic commitment to each other. The most serious of these trials occurs when a jealous woman administers to Isabela a powerful potion that horribly—but only temporarily—disfigures the young girl's face and threatens to drive a permanent wedge between the sweethearts. Virtue and constancy win out in the end, however, and harmony is restored with their eventual marriage.

5. *El licenciado Vidriera*. A philter again figures as the pivot point in this biographical sketch of the life of an intellectual young man named Tomás Rodaja/Rueda who aspires to greatness as a jurist. A jealous lover's potion turns the brilliant student Rodaja into the eccentric, apothegm-spouting Licenciado Vidriera, a popular court celebrity despite his declaration that he's made of glass and his refusal to let the public approach or touch him. The ending is supremely ironic: upon recovering his sanity, Tomás discovers that his services as a legal consultant are not nearly as much in demand as were his mad alter ego's; he is forced to abandon his practice at the royal court in favor of the military career that he had originally spurned but that ultimately gains him the fame he had always been seeking. *Constancy* is again the principal theme. Like the faithful suitor Ricaredo who pursued his beloved Isabela in the preceding story, Tomás is unwavering in his devotion to the pursuit of truth and knowledge. The denouement is

sobering because Rueda's final reward, i.e., the longed-for fame that had always eluded his grasp, is finally earned only by his heroic demise on the battlefields of Flanders. The ambitious Tomás is never allowed to bask in the glow of his ultimate achievement.

6. *La fuerza de la sangre*. Although *honor* appears to be the central issue here, the real social virtues being emphasized are those of *constancy* (as demonstrated by Leocadia's firm faith in God's justice and mercy) and *personal responsibility* (i.e., Rodolfo must make amends for his rape of Leocadia in the opening scene). The structural and thematic pivot point is the near-fatal trampling of little Luisico, the living product of Rodolfo's sexual assault upon Leocadia. This potentially tragic event precipitates a chain of events that culminates in a powerful climactic scene: the confrontation—and ultimate union in matrimony—of the violator and his victim.

7. *El celoso extremeño*. As can be gathered from the title here, the popular *jealousy* theme we saw in the first two stories of the collection is brought back in the seventh tale in tandem with the ever-popular *honor* theme. Less obvious but of even greater significance here is the issue of *personal responsibility* that is also reprised in the disgraceful conduct of old Carrizales, who attempts to lock his young bride away from the world. The final traumatic event in this case is the apparent seduction of Carrizales's young bride by the crafty and lustful Loaysa, who has successfully triumphed over the jealous old man's elaborate security system for defending his home against intruders. Once the old man realizes that the defenses of his supposedly impregnable convent-fortress have been penetrated, he is forced to reexamine his values and come to grips with the inevitable consequences of his foolish actions. The acceptance of his own responsibility ultimately enables Carrizales to forgive his wife's youthful indiscretion.

8. *La ilustre fregona*. Many have noted the common thematic similarities shared by this, the eighth story in the collection, and the opening tale, *La gitanilla*. This narrative, however, is considerably more complex in its structure than its predecessor. Practically every important plot element we find in *Gitanilla* is doubled in *Fregona*. For example, instead of a single male protagonist, there are a pair of heroes whose adventures are recounted here, sometimes together, sometimes separately. Predictably enough, each protagonist undergoes his own personal trial. The reckless Carriazo needs to sow his wild oats through a series of risky picaresque adventures, culminating in a near-disastrous encounter with some professional gamblers. His less rebellious cohort Avendaño must merely become more experienced in the ways of love and learn how to woo and win the woman of his dreams, the lovely scullery maid Costanza, despite the presence of a rich and powerful rival, the corregidor's son. The duplication technique is extended to the introduction of twin blocking agents in the form of two unsavory

wenches, la Argüello and la Gallega, whose narrative function is essentially the same as Juana Carducha's in the Gypsy tale. Thematically, this story manages to summarize and bring to a close the cycle of topics introduced in the earlier novellas. In this single narrative Cervantes manages to deal simultaneously with all the major themes treated in the preceding seven stories: *freedom, jealousy, honor, constancy,* and *personal responsibility.* This story, therefore, can be said to close the first section of the *Novelas ejemplares.*

9. *Las dos doncellas.* The final narrative section of the collection focuses almost exclusively upon the problem of *honor.* In *Las dos doncellas* and the following story, Cervantes turns his attention to the plight of virtuous maidens who find themselves seduced and abandoned by inconstant lovers. There are obvious similarities between the cases of Teodosia and Leocadia, the two trusting maidens to which the title refers, and the plucky Dorotea of *Don Quixote,* Part One, who had to labor mightily to convince her fickle suitor, Fernando, to make an honest woman of her in matrimony. Despite the fact that we have two protagonists instead of one, the narrative structure of this tale is relatively simple. Both complainants pursue the irresponsible Marco Antonio to Barcelona, where Marco Antonio is discovered near death from an accidental blow to the head. If the bold Leocadia can be said to replicate the aggressive determination of Dorotea, the reticent Teodosia appears to follow instead the passive example of the timid Cardenio. Upon regaining his senses, Marco Antonio surprisingly chooses the quiet and ladylike Teodosia over her more aggressive competitor.[2]

10. *La señora Cornelia.* This story echoes *Las dos doncellas* in the same fashion that *La ilustre fregona* reprises the action of *La gitanilla*: it focuses on the same general theme *(honor)* while doubling both the action and the intrigue. Once again, the pivotal event around which the solution revolves is a life-threatening one, in this case the premature birth, out of wedlock, of Lady Cornelia's baby. Through the efforts of two young Spanish gentlemen, the Gordian knot of complications is eventually severed; in the end, mother and baby are reunited with the child's father, the duke of Ferrara, who is persuaded to keep his promise to wed his longtime (and secret) fiancée.

11. *El casamiento engañoso.* The major theme is again that of reputation, but now seen from the other side: all of the characters portrayed here are sleazy social types who operate on the basis of a *total lack of honorability.* As a consequence, the story comes off as nothing more than a dreary representation of what life would be like in a society devoid of honor. The trauma of having been lured into a bogus marriage and then fleeced of all his worldly possessions by an unscrupulous female con-artist forces the chary Campuzano, himself something of a shady character up to this point, to

reevaluate his life. Cervantes joins this story thematically and structurally to the next one,

12. *El coloquio de los perros*. A descent into a picaresque nether world *totally devoid of honorability* and therefore dominated by elements of fraud, corruption, and witchcraft. This is a virtuoso performance on the part of Cervantes as we observe the narration taking place on four distinct levels, each one commenting on the layer immediately below it. The topmost layer is actually located in the preceding *Casamiento engañoso*, from which point the narration enters the colloquy itself and then spirals down in stages to the core episode of the witch Cañizares's bizarre, drug-induced reverie. This is, structurally, the most complex of all Cervantes's novellas and serves as the perfect vehicle with which to conclude the collection and return the reader to the prologue.[3]

We see, then, that there exists a broad but discernible spectrum of thematic material in the *Novelas ejemplares*: the themes of jealousy and freedom dominate in the first three stories, but these soon yield to the more sophisticated issues of constancy and personal responsibility in the next triad, after which we find the full roster of themes reprised in the seventh and eighth entries. The final four stories move on to a new central theme, honor, which treated in terms of either its supreme importance in the lives of the characters or its total absence in certain pockets of human society. What these twelve stories have in common is the narrative technique by which Cervantes repeatedly subjects his protagonists' lives to a painful purification process that I call the crucible concept: a *solutio* or acid bath that strips away all the tangential negative elements of the human psyche and ultimately yields a pure nugget of psychological and spiritual integrity.

Novel versus Romance

Among Cervantists there is an ongoing debate regarding the great writer's attitude toward these two competing, and seemingly incompatible, fictional modes. Ruth El Saffar (1974) was the first to note an apparently anachronistic movement in Cervantes's short fiction, a pulling back from what we now consider the "modern" (i.e., seemingly autonomous, highly mimetic) storytelling techniques he exhibited so expertly in *Don Quixote*, in favor of a return to the traditional, archetypal narrative forms of the more narrator-controlled medieval romance.[4] On the other hand, Gonzalo Sobejano (1978) and E. C. Riley (1981) see no such drift in Cervantes's poetics; Riley goes so far as to state that "to the end of his days [he] was liable to write in either vein or in some combination of the two."[5]

Sobejano lists the principal points of differentiation between these two fictional modes, which may be summarized as follows:

Romance	*Novel*
Offers a transcendental vision of the world.	Has an alienated vision of the world.
The narrator maintains his distance from his characters.	The narrator attempts to be very close to his characters.
An atmosphere of certainty.	A world of great uncertainty.
Omniscience.	Ambiguity.
Contrast of good and evil characters.	Perspectivism regarding human actions.
Protagonist is sheltered by the author.	Protagonist is complex; creates his/her own character.
Hero escapes from fiction through reason or *desengaño* (rude awakening).	Hero escapes from reality through madness or *engaño* (trickery or deception).
Goal: integration of the individual into the social milieu.	Goal: separation of the individual from the rest of society.
An orderly cosmos.	A chaotic universe.
A unified work.	Lack of unity in the work.
A happy ending.	An unsatisfying ending.
Preference for vague abstraction over the particular detail, often with a broken or interrupted chronology.	Preference for precise historical detail and a strictly chronological ordering of events.
The marital union of lovers is the ultimate prize.	Single independence is prized above marital commitment.
Usually ends in triumph.	Frequently ends in failure.
Conformity to social norms is expected and usually rewarded.	Criticism of and nonconformity to social conventions often result in exile or punishment.[6]

E. Michael Gerli (1986) follows Sobejano and Riley in viewing *La gitanilla* as a curious mix of romance and novel characteristics, i.e., a notable Cervantine attempt to reconcile the conflict of these two opposing styles in a single work. Gerli considers the story of the little Gypsy girl a literary experiment where "the plots, characters, landscape, and motifs of romance are ironically subverted through contrast with a subtly crafted vision of a cynical world presided over by the type of petty passion, abuse of privilege, and prosaic venality we associate with the realm of the novel."[7] In other words, Cervantes harks back to the romance form solely in order to attack it by infusing his narrative with novelistic elements that will eventually contradict the romance's archetypal elements. As we shall see, I wholeheartedly share Gerli's view, but would extend the experimental classification to the entire collection. But before moving forward with this argument, let me clarify my terminology.

Romance. The fictional mode par excellence for incurable optimists and true believers. This blissfully myopic mind-set dates from the Middle Ages and reflects both the early Christian worldview and the sociopolitical values of the feudal aristocracy that controlled European society before the Renaissance. It is a narrative form that was cultivated by writers (and readers) who fervently clung to the following tenets:
1. that God or some sort of divine providence is in total control of the universe and all human destiny;
2. that this Deity is omnipotent;
3. that he is just and fair; and
4. that the world—including our lives—ultimately makes perfect sense, since it is all part of the Great Plan. As a consequence, good deeds are ultimately rewarded and evil ones punished.[8]

Novel. The preferred fictional form of skeptics and doubters, hence the unmistakable sense of *irony* that tends to permeate the great novels. The novel responds to the desire of writers to portray the baser part of the human psyche, the part that the prose romance had consciously suppressed. The result in Cervantes's time was a taste for the new picaresque mode, an uncompromising examination of contemporary social reality that was coincidental with the Renaissance period's spirit of scientific inquiry and the development of new, empirical methods of discovery. The rise of the novel is also connected with the emergence of the capitalist economic system in the West. Largely as a result of their exposure to the pagan philosophy of ancient Greece and Rome, European Christians soon began to cast off the cultural restraints that had been imposed upon them for centuries by Christian asceticism and embrace the material prosperity and pleasure that could be derived from and justified through the classical (i.e., non-Christian) worldview. Given all of the above, it should not surprise us to note that the new, "realistic" form of fiction that emerged during the Renaissance shared a great affinity with the classical tragedy.

With regard to point (1) above, the novelist and his intended reader do not necessarily have to be atheists or agnostics, but they should at least be harboring some grave doubts vis-à-vis the traditional Christian explanations of the universe and man's place in it. As for points (2) and (3) about God's omnipotence and supreme fairness, they are essentially moot issues. Even if the novelist should accept the idea of a Supreme Being, he or she probably rejects one or both of these secondary notions, which explains why we so rarely find the concept of poetic justice at work in the modern novel. Consequently, the world represented in the novel—point (4) above—often appears to be both chaotic and unstructured, as are the pointless lives of the characters who tend to inhabit it.

What Cervantes recognized is that the reading public was not monolithic; readers will, at different times and for totally different reasons, be attracted to one or the other—perhaps both—of these fictional modes, depending upon their particular worldview. What the author was seeking was a way to appeal to both audiences in the same collection, perhaps even in the same narrative unit.

Cervantes's fondness for irony and the fact that he may have been experimenting with a curious juxtaposition and blending of romance and novelistic conventions in this collection of short narratives is hinted at in the mysterious references he makes to the conde de Lemos in the prologue and dedication of the *Novelas ejemplares*. Towards the end of the prologue Cervantes mentions that he has *dared to* ("he tenido osadía") dedicate the volume to the "great" Lemos. But then he immediately cautions that his stories contain some hidden mystery that elevates them ("algún misterio tienen escondido que las levanta") (1:53).[9] Not a word is added to clarify the hidden element. In the formal dedication that follows, Cervantes employs the classical rhetorical device of paraleipsis to draw attention to Lemos's genealogy and achievements by pretending to leave to others the task of memorializing the many accomplishments and titles of the count's ancestors, an infinite number of virtues "así naturales como adquiridas" (1:54) [both innate and acquired]. We note that both the prologue and the dedication are most unconventional in both their style and their tone, a strong indication of the innovative and revolutionary literary products that were to follow. As such, Cervantes's prefatory pages to the *Novelas* are a harbinger of the dedication (again, to Lemos) that he would pen a couple of years later for the Second Part of *Don Quixote*, a composition that Elias L. Rivers has called "a most informal mixture of *burlas* and *veras*."[10]

Gerli observes that "the juxtaposition of the ideal and the real is central to the structure and narrative technique of *La gitanilla*," pointing to the key that is skillfully furnished by the narrator in the very first word of his text: "Parece" [It appears].[11] I would like to expand upon Gerli's thesis by suggesting that the theme established in the opening lines of *La gitanilla* should, in fact, be applied to the entire collection of novellas. Each of these stories subjects its protagonist(s)—sometimes there is more than a single central figure—to at least one harrowing experience or perilous adventure that will shake that person or persons to the core of their being and bring about a much-needed beneficial alteration of their system of values.

The El Saffar and Sobejano-Riley camps are both correct, in my opinion. El Saffar's assertion that Cervantes was powerfully attracted to the archetypal presentation associated with the medieval romance in his late works seems incontrovertible. Toward the end—and the *Persiles* is the final proof of this—the great writer clearly appears to have discerned an underlying, comprehensive divine plan for the universe, an ultimate design that would explain and give shape to the seemingly random events that make up our collective human experience. In the rest his literary output, however—and the *Novelas ejemplares* are the best example of this phenomenon, as I shall show—he chose to demonstrate his thesis by alternating novelistic and romantic treatments of the same theme in consecutive stories, or, as Sobejano and Riley assert and Gerli has demonstrated in at least one case, by successfully combining the two seemingly contrasting modes in the same tale.

To Cervantes, life makes perfect sense in the long run (which is why he generally prefers the romantic mode), but on the surface it frequently appears to be totally chaotic, which explains the novelistic qualities of so many episodes and/or tales. From God's superior vantage point, human life is a romance; it merely *appears* to be a novel when seen up close by the characters themselves. The proper perspective can be gained, but only through some sort of transcendental experience. And, as I said earlier, transcendental experiences are precisely what the twelve *Exemplary Novels* have in common. Cervantes begins his lesson about the deceptive nature of human existence with the very first word of the opening tale ("Parece" [It appears]); he then leads us through a dozen exemplary cases, the last of which points right back to the beginning.

Like the collection of stories Cervantes has arranged in this circular pattern, the road of life is often a winding, convoluted one where there seems to be no plan or organizing principle behind our earthly existence. Eventually, however, if we live according to Christian principles, the plan will manifest itself to us. In its own way, each of the *Novelas ejemplares* is Cervantes's attempt to demonstrate how God works in mysterious ways, often through near-catastrophic events and semimiraculous anagnorises, to jolt individuals back to reality so that they may fulfill their destiny. This is what I call the crucible concept.

The Critics and the *Novelas ejemplares*

Those who have preceded me along this trail have generally proceeded deductively: they have attempted to analyze both the collection itself as well as each of the individual stories according to a preconceived theoretical construct; each one of these critics has attempted to chop and stretch Cervantes's material to fit the critic's own special Procrustean bed. I, on the other hand, prefer to let the thematic and structural peculiarities of the twelve stories—both individually and collectively—determine the path of my conclusions.

With regard to theories about the arrangement and ordering of the *Novelas ejemplares* themselves, we begin with Francisco Rodríguez Marín's 1917 edition of *La ilustre fregona*. In the prologue of this edition Rodríguez Marín divided Cervantes's *Novelas* into three distinct groups.[12]

A. The Realistic "Novelas vividas":
   3. *Rinconete y Cortadillo*
   5. *El licenciado Vidriera*
   7. *El celoso extremeño*
   8. *La ilustre fregona*
  11. *El casamiento engañoso*
  12. *El coloquio de los perros*

B. The Imaginative "Novelas de pura invención":
   2. *El amante liberal*
   6. *La fuerza de la sangre*
  10. *La señora Cornelia*

C. Mixed Narratives (combinations of the experienced and the imagined):
   1. *La gitanilla*
   4. *La española inglesa*
   9. *Las dos doncellas*

While Rodríguez Marín must be credited with a sincere attempt to make sense of the unusual nature and peculiar arrangement of Cervantes's collection of short narratives, the critic's very traditional division of the stories into "realistic," imaginative," and "mixed" groups is no longer considered very helpful.

The next important effort to categorize the *Novelas* came in 1948, when William C. Atkinson noted in the collection an almost perfect design of alternating idealistic and realistic stories, broken only by the reversal of the pattern with *La ilustre fregona* and *Las dos doncellas*, an incongruity that he attributed to the printer rather than to the author.[13] The principal objection raised against Atkinson's system for ordering the stories in Cervantes's collection was that the terms "realistic" and "idealistic" as applied there are a relatively modern construct that would have had no literary or critical significance in Cervantes's time, and thus were virtually worthless as organizing principles for the *Novelas*.

In his *Sentido y forma de las Novelas ejemplares* (1962) Joaquín Casalduero attempted to remedy the situation by reworking Atkinson's imaginative construct along new lines, reclassifying Cervantes's short fiction this time according to baroque aesthetic principles, while still maintaining the basic idealistic-realistic dichotomy. Casalduero gave special attention to the principles of contrariety and antithesis and placed strong emphasis on the notion of symmetry and balance that dominated the arts in seventeenth-century Europe.[14]

In Casalduero's scheme of things, the individual works are grouped according to the amount of attraction they exhibit toward the baroque poetic constructs that informed and dominated Spanish letters in the early seventeenth century. For Casalduero certain polar oppositions and contradictions are encountered in abundance and wide variety in Cervantes's short fiction, among them:

thesis-antithesis	virtue-vice
theme-form	purity-baseness
light-darkness	beauty-ugliness
loyalty-treachery	blonde-brunette
masculine-feminine	primary-secondary
musicality-plasticity	generosity-selfishness
aggressiveness-passivity	spirituality-materialism
nobility-vulgarity	intellectual-sensual
enslavement-freedom	friendship-rivalry
dynamism-stasis	centrality-marginality

Given Casalduero's declared critical bias, it is not surprising that he would find examples of baroque polarity at every turn, even in cases when there was scant or negligible evidence to support such a claim. This methodology serves Casalduero well in the majority of cases, but it occasionally causes him to follow a false trail, as we note in his much-too-tidy theoretical construct for grouping the dozen very different items in Cervantes's collection. Casalduero arranges the stories into a trio of four-story clusters, the first four standing in absolute opposition—as we might well expect in a baroque anthology—to the final four, while the middle four are conveniently split into opposing pairs (25–28).

A. Opposing Clusters:
1. *La gitanilla*
2. *El amante liberal*
3. *Rinconete y Cortadillo*
4. *La española inglesa*

12. *El coloquio de los perros*
11. *El casamiento engañoso*
10. *La señora Cornelia*
9. *Las dos doncellas*

B. Opposing Pairs:
5. *El licenciado Vidriera*
7. *El celoso extremeño*

6. *La fuerza de la sangre*
8. *La ilustre fregona*

Some of Casalduero's insights hit the mark squarely, in which cases the oppositions he posits are rightly and properly bracketed. For example, he notes that the idealism, generosity, and moral righteousness portrayed in *La gitanilla* and *El amante liberal* are perfectly counterbalanced by the egotism, moral depravity, and avarice exhibited in the *Coloquio* and the *Casamiento engañoso*. Also insightful is Casalduero's pairing of the concept of intellectual hubris shown in *El licenciado Vidriera* with the more sensual sort of moral transgression portrayed in *La fuerza de la sangre*.

The Spanish critic comes up short, however, in his other pairings. To link the lightweight, semipicaresque tableau presented in *Rinconete y Cortadillo* with the serious social theme (honor) examined in *La señora Cornelia* is to stretch the notion of counterbalancing beyond the limits of plausibility. More serious evidence is needed to forge this link than merely the idea of equalizing the weight of the lady's *nobleza* (nobility) with that of the ruffians' *bajeza* (baseness).

Similarly, Casalduero's attempt to forge a bond between *La española inglesa* and *Las dos doncellas* simply on the basis of the pilgrimages to religious shrines taken in them is indeed weak and superficial. In the former, the star-crossed lover Ricaredo's journey to Rome is one of several key complications that conspire to keep him and Isabela apart for an extended period of time. The journey to Santiago de Compostela made by the two pairs of lovers at the close of *Las dos doncellas* takes place after all the early romantic complications have been resolved and has more symbolic than real meaning within the story.

And finally there is Casalduero's feeble attempt to pair *El celoso extremeño* with *La ilustre fregona*. This is seen as simply Cervantes's attempt to contrast the claustrophobic atmosphere of Carrizales's prisonlike house with the openness and freedom enjoyed by the lovely scullery maid. The usually perspicacious Casalduero's overly zealous pursuit of a perfectly balanced scheme that would serve to ratify his preconceived arrangement of the twelve novellas leads the Spanish critic to ignore the obvious thematic similarities *Fregona* shares with the preceding *Gitanilla*, which he had already paired with the *Coloquio*. This obliges the uncompromising Casalduero to marry, seemingly on the basis of spatial factors alone, the lighthearted, upbeat story about the courtship of a lovely scullery maid with the dark, ominous *Celoso extremeño*, a totally unique unit within the collection and one that cannot be joined, at least on the basis of narrative form, with any of the other tales. Casalduero's unfortunate obsession with finding a totally balanced package of contrasting baroque narratives leads him down a blind alley on more than one occasion.

Still another theoretical arrangement emerged in 1974 when Ruth El Saffar reworked the conventional idealistic-realistic dichotomy in *Novel to Romance* by proposing a different principle of alternation: early versus late compositions. In El Saffar's theoretical construct, Cervantes's early stories, those which modern critics have generally referred to as "realistic," tend to present characters plagued by an irreconcilable psychological opposition between their own ego and the real world (cf. Don Quixote), which accounts for the tendency of these stories to have inconclusive or unhappy endings. These are surrounded in the collection by later compositions, often called "idealistic," that more closely resemble the optimistic tone Cervantes's final work, the *Persiles*. These stories are characterized by sudden and fortuitous turns of events, near-miraculous resolutions for seemingly insurmountable problems, and improbable reconciliations between antagonists in the final paragraphs.

In El Saffar's view, Cervantes begins his collection with a pair of stories (*La gitanilla* and *El amante liberal*) that establish the general theme of the work: a happy resolution of the self/others problem. The next grouping consists of three opposing pairs of narratives: in each tandem the first tale (an early work) presents a vision of life as untranscendable opposition; this is immediately followed by a late story that responds to the first one by repeating the original theme of harmonious resolution. For El Saffar, *Rinconete y Cortadillo*'s pessimism is quickly countered by the upbeat theme of *La española inglesa*, the sad irony of *El licenciado Vidriera* by the optimism *La fuerza de la sangre*, and the depressing fate of *El celoso extremeño* by the hopeful outlook of *La ilustre fregona*. Cervantes finishes the cycle by reprising his opening theme in the felicitous conclusions of *Las dos doncellas* and *La señora Cornelia*. The final entry, the curious combination of the late *Casamiento* and the early *Coloquio*, serves as the perfect coda to a collection built upon the notion of pairing seemingly contradictory and offsetting stories.[15]

A. Opening Statement of Harmonious Resolution:
   1. *La gitanilla* (Late)
   2. *El amante liberal* (Late)

B. Core Collection of Contrasting Narratives:
   3. *Rinconete y Cortadillo* (Early)
   4. *La española inglesa* (Late)
   5. *El licenciado Vidriera* (Early)
   6. *La fuerza de la sangre* (Late)
   7. *El celoso extremeño* (Early)
   8. *La ilustre fregona* (Late)

C. Closing Statement of Harmonious Resolution:
   9. Las dos doncellas (Late)
   10. *La señora Cornelia* (Late)

D. Coda:
   11. *El casamiento engañoso* (Late)
   12. *El coloquio de los perros* (Early)

Gonzalo Sobejano's 1978 review of El Saffar's book, while accepting the author's general division of the twelve Cervantine novellas into clusters of early versus late works, nonetheless rejected the notion of the Spanish author's gradual evolution away from the blunt realism of the novel and toward the idealistic, stylized form of the romance. Sobejano maintains that Cervantes continued throughout his writing career to cultivate both the realistic and idealistic forms of prose narrative. For Cervantes, the novel and the romance were surprisingly compatible and even capable of coexistence within a single work.[16] In his 1981 article E. C. Riley echoed the sentiments of Sobejano and offered the same three-tiered arrangement for the twelve *Novelas ejemplares*:[17]

A. Predominantly "Romance":
   2. *El amante liberal*
   4. *La española inglesa*
   6. *La fuerza de la sangre*
   9. *Las dos doncellas*
   10. *La señora Cornelia*

B. Predominantly "Novel":
   3. *Rinconete y Cortadillo*
   5. *El licenciado Vidriera*
   7. *El celoso extremeño*
   11. *El casamiento engañoso*
   12. *El coloquio de los perros*

C. Mixed
   1. *La gitanilla*
   8. *La ilustre fregona*

In *Cervantes and the Humanist Vision* (1982) and *Cervantes and the Mystery of Lawlessness* (1984), Alban K. Forcione offered little opinion about the arrangement or ordering of Cervantes's *Novelas* (Forcione limited himself to a discussion of only half the stories in the collection), but he added a great deal to our understanding of the thematic content and latent symbolism contained in the half-dozen stories he examined. In Forcione's view, the *Novelas ejemplares* assume a much less subversive attitude toward literary traditions than did the *Quijote*, particularly Part One, but they do confront, in an original and subtle manner, the issue of generic codes. Forcione's intention is to present Cervantes as "an experimenter in literary forms."[18] As such, the author of the *Novelas ejemplares* is seen to employ a variety of clever techniques for adapting the traditional genre forms to modern fiction. Forcione cites four methods in particular (28):

Hybridization: a combination of traditional forms of disorder *(El casamiento engañoso* and *El coloquio de los perros)*;
Accommodation: a complex fusion of ideas and romance conventions *(La gitanilla);*
Unraveling and reconstitution: critical engagement with a prestigious hagiographic form *(La fuerza de la sangre);*
Violent deconstruction: unexpected formal disarticulation *(El celoso extremeño).*

The Princeton scholar asserts that Cervantes uses dialectical, ironic and paradoxical modes to explore the complexities of truth, with the result that the discourse in the *Novelas* is frequently deceptive, particularly with regard to Cervantes's creative use of freedom as a theme (29). No serious analysis of *La gitanilla, El licenciado Vidriera, La fuerza de la sangre, El celoso extremeño, El casamiento engañoso,* or *El coloquio de los perros* can afford to fail to take Forcione's seminal investigations into account.

In his *Novedad y ejemplo* (1980), Julio Rodríguez-Luis divides the twelve *novelas* of Cervantes's collection into four groups.[19]

A. Of Italian Inspiration (the most stylized):
   2. *El amante liberal*
   4. *La española inglesa*
   6. *La fuerza de la sangre*
   9. *Las dos doncellas*
   10. *La señora Cornelia*

B. The Theme of Separation of a Young Girl from Her Parents:
   1. *La gitanilla*
   8. *La ilustre fregona*

C. The Picaresque Overview:
   3. *Rinconete y Cortadillo*
   5. *El licenciado Vidriera*
   12. *El coloquio de los perros*

D. Stories with Dramatic Intensity and Psychological Veracity:
   7. *El celoso extremeño*
   11. *El casamiento engañoso*

The clusters suggested by Rodríguez-Luis strive to avoid the old realistic/idealistic dichotomy in favor of other groupings: openly fantastic narratives descended from the Italian tradition; a pair of stories based on the theme of a young girl's separation from her parents (although one wonders why he does not include *La española inglesa* in this category); picaresque tableaus and dialogues that allow Cervantes to comment on the peculiar and often amusing behavior of various social types; and finally, works that allow the author to display his talent for dramatic suspense and keen psychological insight.

Theorizing about the order and configuration of the individual novellas in Cervantes's collection continued in Albert A. Sicroff's 1988 article.[20] In Sicroff's view, the collection is characterized by a sharply declining line of development that begins at the summit of exemplarity *(La gitanilla)* and moves steadily downward until it reaches its nadir in the *Coloquio*, where exemplarity is totally annihilated. According to Sicroff, only the first four *novelas* are truly exemplary. The fifth story, *El licenciado Vidriera*, marks the appearance of negative themes in the collection; he notes that the stories that follow *LV* take place mostly in the darkness of night and "appear to be marked with a sort of 'original sin' without possibility of a redemption that is more than illusory" (358).

L. A. Murillo offered still another tentative grouping for the *Novelas ejemplares* in a 1988 article.[21] Murillo divides the dozen stories into four distinctly labeled groups, which he calls "structures." The most prominent of these is the romance structure, which embraces a total of five stories in three variations; second in importance is the biographic structure, comprising four stories in three variations. The final groupings are the legendary structure (only two titles) and the dialogic (one) (232).

  A. Romance Structure:
    Idealized Betrothal
      1. *La gitanilla*
      4. *La española inglesa*
    Imperiled Courtship
      2. *El amante liberal*
      9. *Las dos doncellas*
    Betrothal as Reward
      8. *La ilustre fregona*

  B. Biographic Structure:
    Variation #1
      3. *Rinconete y Cortadillo*
    Variation #2
      5. *El licenciado Vidriera*
    Variation #3
      7. *El celoso extremeño*
      11. *El casamiento engañoso*

C. Legendary Structure:
    6. *La fuerza de la sangre*
    10. *La señora Cornelia*

D. Dialogic Structure:
    12. *El coloquio de los perros*

    My objections to Murillo's groupings are several. To begin with, Murillo declares that the major organizing principle for the romance structure is the fact that all the heroines in these stories are both beautiful and chaste, a special quality that Murillo calls "a spiritualized *eros*" (233). This theory works especially well in the cases of Preciosa *(Gitanilla)*, Leonisa *(Amante)*, Isabela *(Española)*, and Costanza *(Fregona)*, but it clearly cannot be applied to the sexually experienced Teodosia *(Doncellas)*. Murillo fudges his categorical distinctions here by proceeding to make an essentially pointless distinction between what he calls "the maximum degree of idealization" (virginity preserved, as in the first four cases) and a minor degree of the same (virginity exchanged for a promise of marriage), which is said to apply only to Teodosia (233).

    From the standpoint of the issue of honor/virginity lost and regained, Teodosia would seem to fit more comfortably in the same category with Leocadia *(Fuerza)* and Cornelia *(Cornelia)*, women who strive against overwhelming odds and ultimately succeed in achieving marital union with the men who seduced and abandoned them. For some reason, Murillo finds this very logical and obvious grouping to be inadequate and unappealing. His preference is to link Teodosia's case with those of the four virgins who clearly belong in the first category. On the other hand, the histories of Leocadia and Cornelia, simply because they involve the birth of a child before marriage, are elevated to a new category (and a higher reward) within what Murillo calls the legendary structure, the name of which derives from the Christian legends of saints, with their characteristic note of "divine intervention in favor of an elect protagonist" (245).

    In the matter of Cervantes's having his protagonists become separated from, then finally reintegrated with, their natural social environment, Murillo posits two different kinds of separation: imaginative separation (e.g., Preciosa) and procreative separation (e.g., Costanza or Cornelia's baby). The distinction is not terribly clear, but to Murillo it would seem that the latter category has something to do with separation *at birth* (235).

    Murillo's categories also appear to ignore the ironic (i.e., unsettling and antiromance) undertones that can be found in the "happy" endings of some of Cervantes's *novelas* and that consequently cast grave doubt as to how complete and rewarding the protagonists' social reintegration is going to be. A notable example of this phenomenon is Preciosa's final decision to abandon the artistic freedom of her former Gypsy lifestyle in order to marry the aristocratic Don Juan at the end of *La gitanilla*. Her decision represents a considerable personal sacrifice for the free-spirited heroine, one that is skillfully counterbalanced in the final paragraphs by the actions of her artistic soul mate, the poet-page Clemente, who opts instead to escape to Italy, where he knows he will be allowed to continue to follow the bohemian lifestyle. Murillo is absolutely silent with regard to these significant last-minute narrative developments, perhaps because they do not correspond neatly with the "romance" interpretation of the story to which he has already committed himself.

The same sort of rigidity is seen in Murillo's realistic biographic structure, but here the movement is *away from* social reintegration. The critic charges that in these stories the marginalized "biographic" protagonists' use or misuse of nonconformity and freedom serves only to lead them to self-deception and moral defeat. This analysis works well for *El celoso extremeño* and *El casamiento engañoso*, but flies completely in the face of reality when applied to *Rinconete y Cortadillo* and *El Licenciado Vidriera*, two works that close on a distinctly high moral note. In the final paragraph of the former story we are told that the elder *pícaro*, Rinconete, remains undeceived by the ridiculous facade erected by Monipodio and his minions and that he planned to advise his companion to abandon "aquella vida tan perdida y tan mala" (1:240) ['that God-forsaken way of life'] (1:229). And although *El licenciado Vidriera* ends with Tomás Rueda's unfortunate demise, we learn that he fully recovered both his sanity and his moral compass before leaving the world of academe to embark upon the military career that would ultimately bring to him on the battlefields of Flanders a hero's death, plus the fame that had always managed to elude his grasp in the past—"dejando fama en su muerte de prudente y valentísimo soldado" (2:74) ['leaving behind him, when he died, the reputation of having been a wise and most valiant soldier'] (2:97).

Ultimately, then, Murillo's categories fall short because they are too rigid: his romance structure demands a totally positive resolution of all plot complications while making no provision whatsoever for the notably subversive elements that are unmistakably present in some of these stories. Conversely, his biographic structure simply refuses to recognize the optimistic tone we find at the close of certain works. Murillo's scheme is ambitious but serves only to point out the need for a different method of categorization whose viability will not be imperiled by Cervantes's maddening penchant for mixing contrasting elements (e.g., realism and idealism, optimism and pessimism) in the same work.

In their essay "Cervantes and the Dialogic World" (1989), Nicholas Spadaccini and Jenaro Talens advanced the cause of a new perspective for judging Cervantes's *Novelas* by proposing strong stylistic and thematic bonds among a number of individual stories that had never been grouped before. They envision the *Coloquio* as the final link in a chain of reality-based narratives beginning with *Rinconete y Cortadillo*, stretching through the *Celoso extremeño,* and culminating in the *Casamiento engañoso.* As Spadaccini and Talens see it, this thread of "realistic" elements is intercalated among other, nonverisimilar ones that abound in the rest of the collection. Only at the end, with the *Coloquio*, does Cervantes manage to unify both lines by combining a superrealistic narration with a highly nonverisimilar pretext: a dog that speaks.[22]

Other methods of grouping Cervantes's novellas continue to emerge. For example, in his biography of the great Spanish writer, *Cervantes* (1990), Jean Canavaggio viewed the 1613 collection of short works as a combination of traditional motifs and conventional situations that have existed since antiquity. Canavaggio's list features three classic categories:[23]

A. Long-thwarted Love Finds a Way:
   1. *La gitanilla*
   2. *El amante liberal*
   4. *La española inglesa*
   8. *La ilustre fregona*

B. Marriage as Reparation for a Sin Born of Desire:
   6. *La fuerza de la sangre*
   9. *Las dos doncellas*
   10. *La señora Cornelia*

C. Frustration of Sinful Designs against Nature:
   7. *El celoso extremeño*
   11. *El casamiento engañoso*

Not unsurprisingly, Canavaggio's catalog neglects to include *Rinconete y Cortadillo, El licenciado Vidriera,* or *El coloquio de los perros*, a trio of stories that simply do not fit the classical mold. As I shall demonstrate at a later point, it is no coincidence that at least two of these very unconventional narratives have a documented or theoretically possible connection with the Porras manuscript, and therefore with origins other than Cervantine.

A New Approach

As Dana B. Drake has so thoroughly documented in his *Critical Bibliography*, the vast majority of scholarship concerning the *Novelas ejemplares* published in the past three centuries has tended to concentrate on a number of general questions or long-range problems that seem to defy definitive resolution, to wit:

• The sources of Cervantes's material and the influence on him of earlier classical and/or Italian authors like Lucian or Boccaccio (M. Fernández de Navarrete, Menéndez y Pelayo, Fitzmaurice-Kelly, Pierce).
• The influence of Cervantes's short fiction on subsequent literature in other European nations like France, Italy, Holland, Germany, and Russia (Crooks, Schevill, Hainsworth, Turkevich).
• The chronology of the twelve *novelas* in Cervantes's collection; or the approximate/actual date of composition of one or more of the tales in that compilation (Pellicer, Icaza, Schevill and Bonilla, Meregalli).
• The classification of Cervantes's stories, usually into opposing categories like realistic versus idealistic (Menéndez y Pelayo, Entwistle, Atkinson) or embellished versus unembellished (Ortega y Gasset, Castro).
• The question of whether Cervantes's style and themes are akin to those of the Erasmists of the Renaissance period (Castro), to writers of the baroque period (Bataillon, Hatzfeld, Casalduero), or somewhere in-between (Díaz-Plaja).
• The exemplariness—real or merely feigned—of the *novelas* in general or of specific stories therein (Fernández de Avellaneda, Tieck, Apráiz, Entwistle).
• Specific biographical and/or historical events portrayed in various *novelas* (Icaza, Apráiz).
• The theatricality or dramatic quality of certain tales in the collection (Avellaneda, Hainsworth, Schevill and Bonilla, Crooks, Herrero-García).

Still others have chosen to debate at length over narrower, more specific issues:

• The identity of the supposed real-life models for the bizarre protagonists of *El licenciado Vidriera* and *El celoso extremeño* (M. Fernández de Navarrete, Foulché-Delbosc, Fitzmaurice-Kelly, Rodríguez-Marín, Hainsworth, Singer, Green).
• What, if any, symbolism should be attached to the Licenciado Vidriera's illness? (Schevill, Azorín).
• Whether the alterations Cervantes made in his published version of *El celoso extremeño*, especially the young bride's last-minute decision not to cuckold her unconscious old husband by sleeping with Loaysa, was a positive or negative change vis-à-vis the original Porras version (Castro versus Spitzer; Rodríguez-Marín, Fitzmaurice-Kelly, Pfandl, Sordo, Atkinson, Amezúa y Mayo, McLean).

I find it highly ironic that although, over the years, so much has been written about Cervantes's short fiction, generally from a thematic standpoint, one can remain fundamentally unsatisfied by the conclusions and observations reached. Despite so many valuable comments proffered by the above-mentioned critics and others, I myself have continued to search for some unifying principle or plan in Cervantes's mind to fuse the dozen independent entries into an artistic whole. It finally occurred to me that the elusive unifying factor might lie in the area of narrative structure rather than theme. A study of the artistic design of the twelve *Novelas ejemplares*, I reasoned, could yield exciting and surprising insights into the how and why of Cervantes's literary endeavor.

What I propose in the present study, then, is to put aside the traditional views about the *Novelas* while taking a slightly different approach to Cervantes's short fiction. My proposal is to treat these tales as a dozen imaginative experiments in narrative design (a theoretical construct, by the way, that speaks directly to Cervantes's bold claim in the prologue of this collection that he is the first to write *novelas* in Castilian).

My methodology is based upon an objective reading of each story, eliminating all preconceptions about what Cervantes may have had in mind when he penned it; this is followed by a linear diagram of the structure of each tale as it unfolds in the text. Phase two involves internal and external confrontations of these structural designs. As we shall see, a side-by-side comparison of the narrative with the chronological order of the events portrayed in the same story frequently yields valuable insight into Cervantes's preferred storytelling strategies, particularly his pronounced fondness for using flashback summaries and other analeptic devices. Still other interesting observations can be made between two or more tales that clearly exhibit the very same or remarkably similar narrative designs. The final step is an attempt to classify or categorize the results of my investigations and formulate a theoretical statement about Cervantes's general artistic plan for this unique collection of short narratives.

At this point perhaps a few general statements about what I have concluded would be in order. In a limited number of cases *(Rinconete y Cortadillo, El celoso extremeño,* and *El licenciado Vidriera)* Cervantes's technical innovations are elaborated upon the skeleton of documents he discovered during his residence in Seville. These tend to be "realistic" tales that do not conform to the Italian model, each one featuring its own special Cervantine experiment. Another group of tales, the ones critics have preferred to call "idealistic," adhere more closely to the traditional Italian norms, but Cervantes has essayed distinctly "modern" technical innovations in the telling, e.g., relating the events in a nonchronological order. Among the stories in this group are *La gitanilla, El amante liberal, La española inglesa, La fuerza de la sangre,* and *La ilustre fregona.*

Separate classifications are needed for the final four tales in the collection. *Las dos doncellas* and *La señora Cornelia*, works that commence in highly dramatic situations, might easily be categorized as dramas in narrative disguise. Their plot structure, featuring many changes of scene, is precisely what seventeenth-century audiences were accustomed to find in a dramatic piece. The collection closes with the unique blending of the dramatic and the narrative modes in *El casamiento engañoso* and *El coloquio de los perros*. Here we have two very different literary narrative forms fused into a complex, four-layered artistic unit. The great Spanish writer clearly intended to save the best for last, and I intend to demonstrate that this final literary experiment in layered narrative was Cervantes's most daring and successful one.

In my discussion and analysis of these dozen works I have found it fruitful to employ a formal/structural approach to Cervantes's storytelling art. With regard to the concept of duration (i.e., narrative time versus story time), I have chosen to adopt the terms coined and defined by Seymour Chatman.[24] According to the scheme proposed by Chatman, all narrative discourse can be reduced to one of five possible categories, based on the relationship that is established between the events of a story (story time) and the artistic representation of those events (narrative time):

Ellipsis: [NT = 0]. Here time passes extremely rapidly, so quickly that *no narration* is possible or necessary. This automatically creates a time gap in the narration, but the events that take place during the unrelated time period are not important, or they will be filled in at a later point. Very popular in modern literature as a substitute for the traditional summary. In film, this is represented by the sharp cut between unconnected scenes.

Summary: [NT < ST]. Time passes quickly, but not as briskly as in ellipsis, and there is *some form of capsulized narration* present. Either the narrator or one of the characters provides a brief resumé (exposition) of events that have already taken place, either once (the usual case) or repeatedly (called the iterative). A technique as old as the epic, this is the standard "flashback" technique—the device Gérard Genette has called *analepse*[25]—that is made necessary by any in medias res beginning and was used with great success by Cervantes. Considered difficult and awkward in film, it has been replaced by Ellipsis.

Scene: [NT = ST]. Both the narration and the story move at an *identical pace*. Often alternating with summary, this has been and continues to be the most commonly used narrative mode in fiction, even in film. Because it tends to grow monotonous, scene is difficult to maintain for any considerable length of time, especially in film. There is, however, one full-length movie classic whose narrative and story times remain constant from beginning to end: *High Noon.*

Stretch: [NT > ST]. Here the action appears to be taking place in *slow motion.* The narration of what is happening actually takes up more time than the events themselves, generally because the narrator opts to prolong the moment with a detailed description or explanation. Very popular among nineteenth-century realist writers, this technique is less commonly employed today. From time to time we see this motif resurrected in violent action films through the use of slow-motion camera work.

Pause: [ST = 0]. This is a *"freeze-frame"* technique in which (story) time actually stands still, while the narrator's voice rambles on. It has perhaps been most effectively used in the interior monologues of James Joyce's *Ulysses.* Also very popular in films, usually combining the freeze-frame with the voice-over device.

Most of Cervantes's novellas feature a combination of scenes and expository summaries; he often disrupts the flow of his main action with anachronous "flashback" narratives designed to recall previous events. Consequently, a few words need to be said about the various ways in which such analeptic narratives can be integrated into the text.[26]

Partial Analepsis. The retrospective narrative (B) begins in the distant past and moves forward to a point in the recent past; however, it does *not* bring the action all the way up to the starting point of the main narrative (A). The narrator leaves a gap—to be bridged by an ellipsis—between the analeptic exposition and the first or principal narrative. The purpose here is usually to bring the reader an important but isolated piece of information (see schema 1).

Schema 1

Complete Analepsis. The flashback (B) begins in the past and carries the reader right up to the moment at which the principal narrative began. In effect, the two narratives fit flush against each other. This is the technique most often associated with the traditional epic practice of beginning in medias res; its aim is to retrieve all the antecedents necessary to an understanding of the main narrative (schema 2).

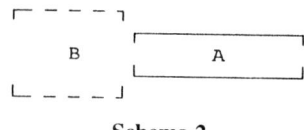

Schema 2

Mixed Analepsis. The retrospective narration (B) actually *overlaps* the principal story (A) by carrying the reader past the moment when the main narrative began, all the way up to the point at which the flashback itself was introduced (schema 3).

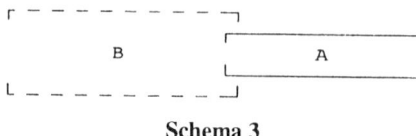

Schema 3

As we shall note in the structural diagrams that follow, each of the *Novelas ejemplares* can be reduced to one of several storytelling strategies. The first narrative plan, of which the opening tale of *La gitanilla* is perhaps the best illustration, features a series of scenes generally separated by ellipses (^); toward the end of the story, however, there will be one or more informative flashbacks, revealing analeptic summaries, either partial or complete, that will provide all the important information necessary to overturn or reverse the action of the plot.

The story of *La gitanilla* consists of six major scenes, lettered A, B, C, D, E, and G, with two analeptic summaries, F and H. The first four scenes occur in rapid sequential order, with no interruption. Scene E, however, is cleft by analeptic summary F (Clemente's flashback account of how and why he has come to be a fugitive from the law in Madrid); likewise, scene G is interrupted by a second complete analepsis (H), the reading of a written confession explaining the noble origins of the little Gypsy girl. The schematic arrangement of the narrative components of this story can be represented by a diagram (schema 4).

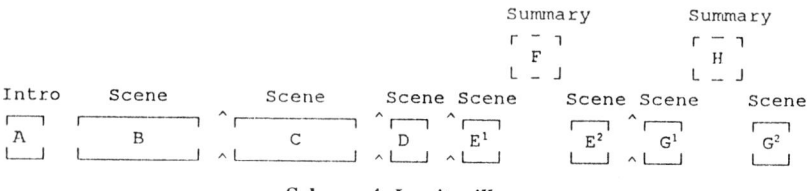

Schema 4. *La gitanilla*

The same basic pattern is seen again in the eighth story of the collection, *La ilustre fregona*, but now on a much larger scale, principally because Cervantes breaks the lengthy Scene C into two separate (but simultaneous) channels that alternate in the printed text as the parallel adventures of the story's two protagonists, Tomás de Avendaño (C^1) and Diego de Carriazo (C^2). Additionally, there are two analeptic Summaries: the innkeeper's story (F) of how baby Costanza came to be raised in his home; and the elder Carriazo's confession (H) that he fathered the child. These must be considered partial or incomplete analepses in the sense that neither one conveys a complete set of details about Costanza's origins. Taken together, however, these narrative sections constitute a complete analepsis (schema 5).

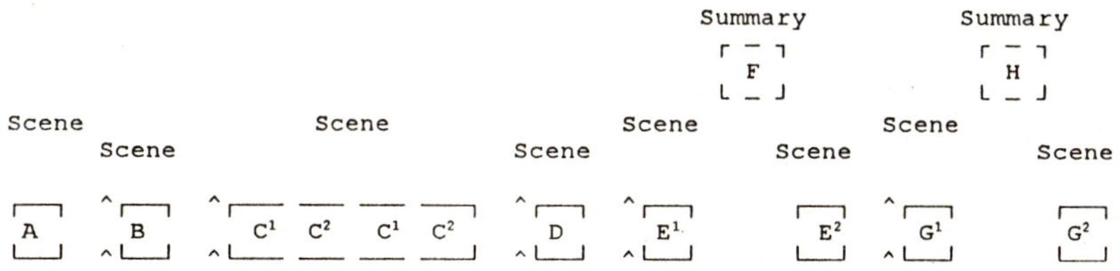

Schema 5. *La ilustra fregona*

The second tale in the collection, *El amante liberal*, recounts a story remarkably similar in theme to *La gitanilla*, but in this account Cervantes utilizes the second of his storytelling strategies: varying the pace of his narrative by alternating blocks of scene and summary. The four principal sections of the main narrative (A, C, E, and G) are separated, not by ellipses, but by three separate flashback summaries, two partial (B, D) and one complete (F) (see schema 6).

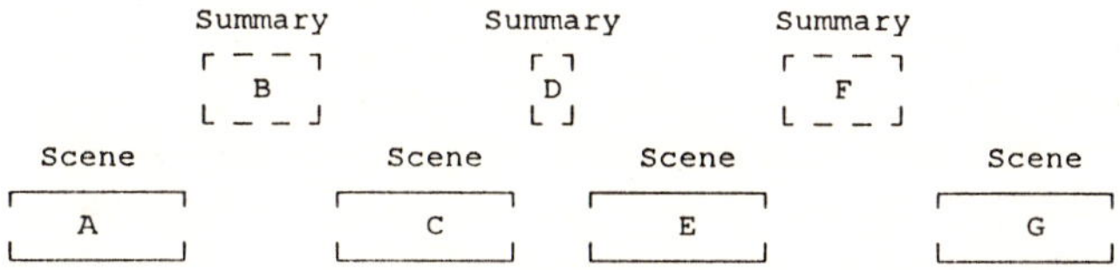

Schema 6. *El amante liberal*

A similar pattern of juxtaposing units of scene and summary is reprised toward the end of the collection in *Las dos doncellas* and *La señora Cornelia*, but here the analeptic blocks serve as interruptions within a single long scene, not wedges inserted between different episodes. While the first of these tales features a simple intrigue recounted in a relatively straightforward manner, the more complex *La señora Cornelia* virtually doubles the number of narrative elements in the story.

Avid readers of Cervantes would hardly be surprised by the fact that both tales deal with the special problems of women in Spanish society, in this case the stigma borne by women who have been seduced and abandoned by sweet-talking but inconstant lovers. Some readers might, however, be surprised to discover that these two stories actually share the same narrative plan, one on a small scale, the other painted on a more panoramic canvas. As the diagrams below indicate, Cervantes's plan for each tale is twofold: (1) to divide the story into three distinct narrative blocks, each separated from the preceding one by an ellipsis; (2) to introduce plot complications early on by weaving alternating sections of scene and summary until some sort of climactic moment is reached. At this point the narrative suddenly streamlines itself and the denouement and epilogue follow in rapid succession (schemas 7 and 8).

Still another narrative strategy is at work in the third, fifth, and seventh entries in the 1613 collection. *Rinconete y Cortadillo, El licenciado Vidriera,* and *El celoso extremeño* share several interesting and provocative characteristics, among them a lack of analeptic elements. These stories employ only combinations of scene and ellipsis, eschewing summary entirely. For example, the story of two mischievous urchins named Rincón and Cortado is told in its entirety using only two long scenes, one taking place at an inn outside Seville, the other within the city. These two major narrative blocks are separated by a single brief ellipsis (^), which accounts for the time the boys spent on the road between these events (schema 9).

The unusual and ironic biography of Tomás Rodaja, more commonly known as The Man of Glass *(El licenciado Vidriera),* is told in four scenes: the first two are devoted to his early formal education at the University in Salamanca (A) and his experiences in the company of Captain Valdivia on the European continent (B); these are followed by the parts that treat his strange madness and sudden cure (C) and his eventual heroic death in battle on the fields of Flanders (D). Scenes A, B, and D move very rapidly as they condense months and years of activity into a single paragraph. The major events in Rodaja's life are summarized in chronological order, connected only by ellipses, without any retrospective analepses. Only the long section that deals with the licenciado's period of insanity (C) seems to move at a normal narrative pace, but even this is deceptive. The string of pithy utterances recorded in this portion of the text has been accumulated, we are told, over a two-year period, but the narration itself is presented as if the events were taking place in a single day (schema 10).

INTRODUCTION

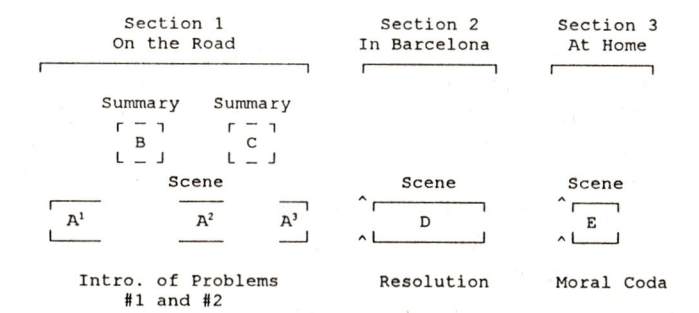

```
        Section 1              Section 2          Section 3
       On the Road            In Barcelona         At Home

      Summary    Summary
       ┌ ─ ┐      ┌ ─ ┐
         B          C
       └ ─ ┘      └ ─ ┘
            Scene                 Scene              Scene
      ┌─────────────────┐      ┌───────┐          ┌───────┐
      │ A¹   A²    A³  │      │   D   │          │   E   │
      └─────────────────┘      └───────┘          └───────┘

     Intro. of Problems       Resolution        Moral Coda
          #1 and #2
```

Schema 7. *Los dos doncellas*

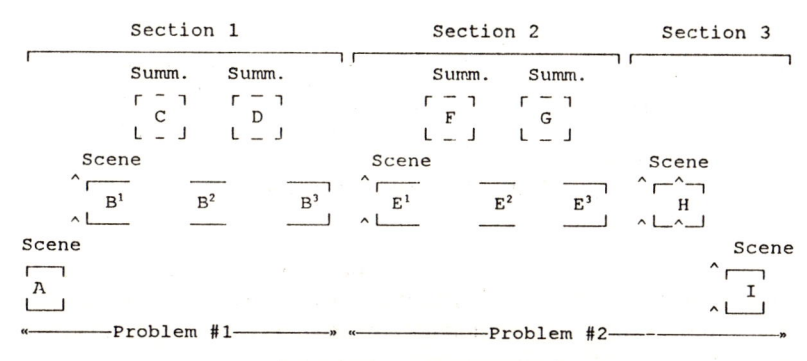

```
           Section 1                    Section 2              Section 3

         Summ.    Summ.              Summ.    Summ.
         ┌ ─ ┐    ┌ ─ ┐              ┌ ─ ┐    ┌ ─ ┐
           C        D                  F        G
         └ ─ ┘    └ ─ ┘              └ ─ ┘    └ ─ ┘
              Scene                       Scene                Scene
         ┌──────────────────┐        ┌──────────────────┐    ┌───────┐
         │ B¹    B²    B³  │        │ E¹    E²    E³  │    │   H   │
         └──────────────────┘        └──────────────────┘    └───────┘
   Scene                                                              Scene
   ┌───┐                                                             ┌───┐
   │ A │                                                             │ I │
   └───┘                                                             └───┘
   «────── Problem #1 ──────» «────────── Problem #2 ──────────»
```

Schema 8. *La señora Cornelia*

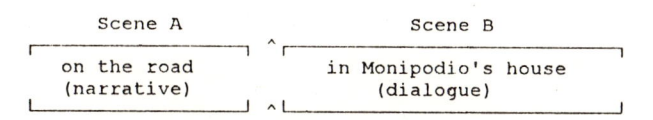

```
              Scene A                        Scene B
         ┌─────────────────┐          ┌──────────────────────┐
         │   on the road   │          │  in Monipodio's house│
         │   (narrative)   │          │      (dialogue)      │
         └─────────────────┘          └──────────────────────┘
```

Schema 9. *Rinconete y Cortadillo*

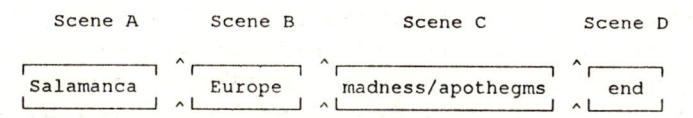

```
         Scene A         Scene B           Scene C              Scene D
      ┌───────────┐   ┌───────────┐   ┌──────────────────┐   ┌───────┐
      │ Salamanca │   │  Europe   │   │ madness/apothegms│   │  end  │
      └───────────┘   └───────────┘   └──────────────────┘   └───────┘
```

Schema 10. *El licenciado Vidriera*

Like *Rinconete y Cortadillo* (with which it is so often linked by virtue of the two stories' appearance in the Porras manuscript), *El celoso extremeño* consists of only two major scenes: (A) a prehistory dealing with the early life of the aged and jealous bridegroom Felipo Carrizales; and (B) the step-by-step description of an ingenious plan devised by a young Sevillian rogue named Loaysa to penetrate the elaborate security system around Carrizales's house and seduce the old man's teenage bride. The prehistory is, in effect, a complete analepsis and has many of the properties of a narrative summary. But since there is no flashback-type interruption of the main narrative, it will be treated here as scene (schema 11).

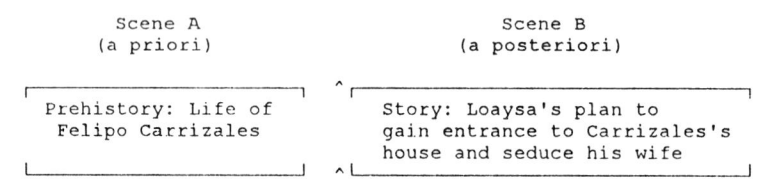

```
        Scene A                          Scene B
       (a priori)                     (a posteriori)
                              ^
┌─────────────────────────┐    ┌──────────────────────────────┐
│ Prehistory: Life of     │    │ Story: Loaysa's plan to      │
│ Felipo Carrizales       │    │ gain entrance to Carrizales's│
│                         │    │ house and seduce his wife    │
└─────────────────────────┘  ^ └──────────────────────────────┘
```

Schema 11. *El celoso extremeño*

With *La española inglesa*, the fourth tale in the collection, comes still another innovative narrative scheme: the construction of a story told in two identical and perfectly balanced halves, each of which is made up of three scenes and a summary, with ellipses (^) separating scenes A and B, D and E, and E and F (schema 12).

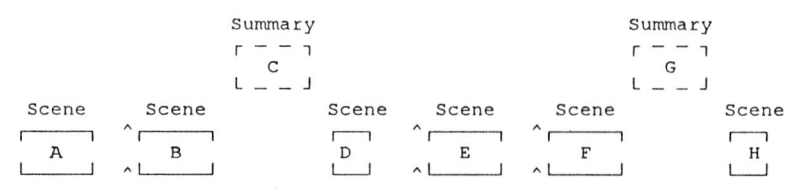

```
                Summary                              Summary
               ┌ ─ ─ ┐                              ┌ ─ ─ ┐
                  C                                    G
               └ ─ ─ ┘                              └ ─ ─ ┘
  Scene     Scene        Scene    Scene    Scene          Scene
 ┌─────┐  ^ ┌─────┐     ┌───┐  ^ ┌─────┐ ^ ┌───┐         ┌───┐
 │  A  │    │  B  │     │ D │    │  E  │   │ F │         │ H │
 └─────┘  ^ └─────┘     └───┘  ^ └─────┘ ^ └───┘         └───┘
```

Schema 12. *La española inglesa*

The same sort of balanced structure is evident in *La fuerza de la sangre*, the sixth story in the series, but here the two halves are not identical but rather mirror images of each other pivoting on the fulcrum of one central scene: Luisico's near-fatal accident (D). The story, which covers about seven years in time, is told without resorting to a formal ellipsis. The rapid compression of time is accomplished instead through analeptic passages B and

INTRODUCTION 39

F, which effectively condense and summarize the events of Rodolfo's self-imposed exile in Italy, occurrences that run parallel to the happenings of the main action in Toledo (schema 13).

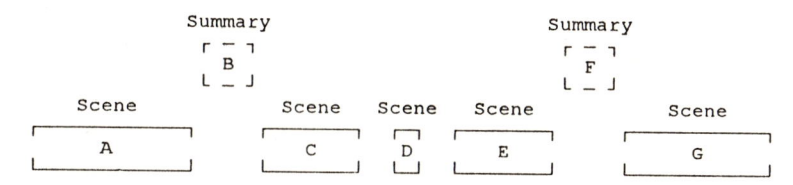

```
              Summary                    Summary
              ┌ ─ ┐                      ┌ ─ ┐
                B                          F
              └ ─ ┘                      └ ─ ┘
  Scene         Scene    Scene   Scene              Scene
┌─────────┐   ┌──────┐  ┌───┐  ┌──────┐           ┌──────┐
│    A    │   │   C  │  │ D │  │  E   │           │   G  │
└─────────┘   └──────┘  └───┘  └──────┘           └──────┘
```

Schema 13. *La fuerza de la sangre*

Fortunately, Cervantes saved the best of his narrative tricks for the end. The final two tales of the collection, *El casamiento engañoso* and *El coloquio de los perros*, need to be treated as a single entity because Cervantes decided, for purely aesthetic reasons, to close out his collection of novellas by fusing two otherwise completely independent narratives into a new, hybrid literary unit.

The story of Campuzano's deceitful marriage (B) is introduced by his chance meeting with his old friend Peralta outside the hospital where he has been undergoing treatment for syphilis (A). Upon completing the unhappy tale of his painful involvement with the crafty Estefanía, Campuzano begins to tell Peralta about his encounter one night in the hospital with two dogs who had miraculously been endowed with human speech (C). The text of the dogs' colloquy forms the next section (D), and the story closes with a critique of Campuzano's manuscript by Peralta (E) (see schema 14).

```
            Summary                Summary
         ┌ ─ ─ ─ ─ ┐            ┌ ─ ─ ─ ─ ┐
              B                       D
         └ ─ ─ ─ ─ ┘            └ ─ ─ ─ ─ ┘
  Scene              Scene                  Scene
┌───────┐          ┌───────┐              ┌───────┐
│   A   │          │   C   │              │   E   │
└───────┘          └───────┘              └───────┘
```

Schema 14. *El casamiento engañoso + El coloquio de los perros*

This design gives the erroneous impression of conforming to the second narrative pattern of alternating blocks of Scene and Summary represented in *El amante liberal, Las dos doncellas,* and *La señora Cornelia,* but it does not. In each of those preceding tales the strategy was to interrupt the main thread of narrative periodically to inject information from the past that would help the reader understand the situation at hand. In the combined *Casamiento engañoso/Coloquio* Cervantes turns the normal storytelling conventions inside out: he moves the two main blocks of narrative one step further away from the reader to have them appear in the form of analeptic summaries; at the same time he creates a totally new present-time narrative plane (scene) solely to serve as a frame around the two stories that will hold them in place. Because of this new arrangement, there is no need for any ellipsis.

For too many years Cervantes has been considered a kind of unschooled genius, an *ingenio lego* whose otherwise impressive oeuvre is maddeningly plagued by a careless style and a notorious inattention to detail. Cervantes's occasional *descuidos* notwithstanding, nothing could be farther from the truth, in my opinion. The structural diagrams I have made in this study of the *Novelas ejemplares* uncover several deliberate and carefully conceived artistic patterns in Cervantes's short fiction and point to an underlying concern with narrative technique.

I may not win many immediate converts to my particular conceptualization of the *Novelas ejemplares*, but I can reasonably hope to plant the seeds of a fruitful new insight into the plan behind Cervantes's most singular collection of experimental narratives. If I can accomplish that goal, I will consider my efforts here a success.

1
Cervantes and the Crucible of Love: Thematic and Structural Affinities in *La gitanilla* and *La ilustre fregona*

As is most appropriate for the initial story in a literary potpourri, *La gitanilla* bears a very strong thematic resemblance to a number of other stories contained in Cervantes's *Novelas ejemplares*. This is especially true in the case of the eighth entry, *La ilustre fregona*, which presents a remarkably similar story and make essentially the same point as the aforesaid *Gitanilla* about how an individual's inherent moral qualities can survive among and eventually overcome even the most unsavory childhood and adolescent experiences. Secondarily, both stories also manage to link the social themes of jealousy and individual freedom. With regard to structure, we note that both stories culminate in a dramatic recognition scene that almost miraculously calms the troubled waters of moral upheaval and brings about the restoration of the delicate social balance that in some manner has been seriously threatened by previous events.[1]

In the end, both of these tales are designed to oblige the reader to confront the enormous problem of sex and marriage in a well-ordered society. An important part of this scenario are the many difficulties attendant on the selection of an appropriate mate, a favorite Cervantine theme that is treated seriously and at length in every one of his novels. We should begin by closely examining the peculiar structure of each of these stories.

LA GITANILLA

This is a story about whose genre critics are still unable to reach agreement. Over the centuries, because so much of the story treats the Gypsies and their culture, many critics have categorized *La gitanilla* as a picaresque work. The movement away from this tradition begins with Juan Bautista

Avalle-Arce, who declares that it is only superficially roguish. On the other side of the question we have Frank Pierce and Thomas R. Hart, who place the story of young Preciosa squarely within the pastoral tradition. There are certain undeniable parallels shared with Alemán's *Guzmán de Alfarache*, as Robert Ter Horst has noted, but ultimately this critic opts to classify Cervantes's opening novella as a "fallen pastoral." E. Michael Gerli sees it as an artful combination of both picaresque and pastoral elements.[2]

The narrative design of Cervantes's first *novela* features a brief introductory section (A) that paints for the reader the incongruous fusion of Preciosa's various noble qualities with the decidedly ignoble atmosphere of the Gypsy society in which she is raised. The introduction is followed by a series of five distinct scenes, B, C, D, E, and G, which take place in four different locales and are separated by temporal ellipses. The total number of narrative sections is five, however, since still another ellipsis is used to divide into equal halves the extensive scene in Madrid. Furthermore, at strategic points along this trajectory Cervantes interrupts certain scenes to inject analeptic summaries, i.e., a pair of retrospective interludes, the first (F) to recapitulate Clemente's misadventures back in Madrid, the second (H) providing us with some invaluable and previously suppressed information regarding Preciosa's noble birth.

- (A) Introduction: Preciosa versus Gypsy society
- (B) Madrid I: Preciosa and the page-poet
- (C) Madrid II: Preciosa and Juan/Andrés
- (D) En route to Toledo: The apprenticeship of Andrés Caballero
- (E) Extremadura: Jealousy erupts: Clemente at the Gypsy camp
  (F) = Clemente's story
- (G) Murcia: Jealousy overcome; Anagnorisis and restoration of Identities; Clemente's escape to Italy
  (H) = The Old Gypsy's story

See schema 15 for a representation of the narrative order of these various parts.

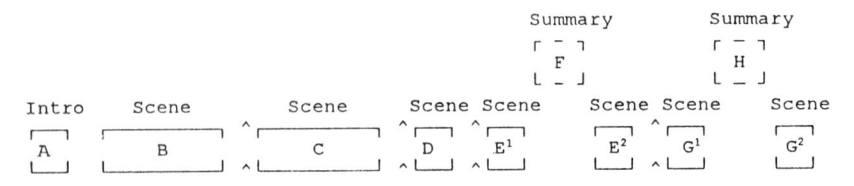

Schema 15. *La gitanilla*

One notes from this schematic representation that the story is almost schizophrenic in its structure, consisting of two halves, each with its own peculiar style and structure. It should be noted that the first two scenes (B and C), which both take place in Madrid, constitute almost one-half of the total text. This portion is dedicated almost entirely to sketching the particular personality traits of the three principal characters, which gives them a somewhat static, novelistic tone. There is very little in the way of genuine plot movement. On the other hand, the second half of the story, which begins with the Gypsies' departure from Madrid for Toledo in section D, conforms to the much more dynamic romance pattern. Because there is so much more emphasis here on physical action and plot complication, the narrative pace quickens remarkably, as sections D, E and G are recounted in rapid succession, the latter two supplemented by brief analeptic interludes F and H.

With regard to these two "flashback" sequences, Clemente's account of his scrape with the law in Madrid (F) is of considerably less importance to the development of the plot; it occupies only about a page and a half of text during the Gypsies' sojourn in Extremadura (E). Viewed chronologically, this brief section moves us slightly back in time to the events in narrative section D. The second—and clearly more significant—analeptic section, the long-awaited anagnorisis that reveals the identity of Preciosa's real parents (H), conforms to the standard in medias res romance pattern. The account of Preciosa's origins happens to be embedded in the final narrative block (G), but it transports the reader all the way back to events that antedate the main action of this story.

We should now examine in closer detail the six major narrative divisions of *La gitanilla*.

(A) Introduction: Preciosa versus Gypsy Society

The initial description focuses on the lovely Gypsy girl and the picaresque environment in which her beauty, charm, and grace bloom. From the very start the reader is presented with a social incongruity: the refreshing wholesomeness of the sprightly Preciosa, as contrasted with the markedly unsavory ambience of the Gypsy camp. An ample number of additional hints and indications of the young maiden's secret aristocratic bloodlines are carefully planted throughout the narration. This contrast of ideal and realistic elements in the opening paragraph serves two purposes: to arouse a sense of *admiratio* in the reader, and to provide us with a vital key to understanding the rest of this sometimes strange and self-contradictory narrative.[3]

The opening paragraph, to be sure, is one of the finest examples to be found of studied ambivalence on the part of a narrator toward his subject. From the opening word ("Parece"), Cervantes is determined to becloud the issue of Preciosa's strange history sufficiently so as to befuddle even the most careful reader, while completely defrauding the careless one.[4] Although the narrating voice appears to be adhering to all the conventions of the fictional romance, he manages at the same time to subvert his text and create the desired ambiguity by slyly inserting enough contradicting details about the harsh reality of Gypsy life to bring the narration down to a more prosaic, novelistic level.[5]

Both Woodward and Martínez-Bonati have observed a decided ambivalence in the movement from the universal to the particular in the story's opening paragraph. For example, Cervantes's narrator begins by parroting the general consensus of Spanish citizens about the unsavory Gypsy population in their midst:

> Parece que los gitanos y gitanas solamente nacieron en el mundo para ser ladrones: nacen de padres ladrones, críanse con ladrones, estudian para ladrones, y, finalmente, salen con ser ladrones corrientes y molientes a todo ruedo, y la gana del hurtar y el hurtar son en ellos como ac[c]identes inseparables, que no se quitan sino con la muerte. (1:61)[6]

> [It seems that gypsies, both male and female, were born into this world to be thieves; they are born of thieving parents, they are brought up with thieves, they study to be thieves, and finally they become fully qualified thieves and the desire to steal and stealing itself are in them essential characteristics, which they lose only in death.] (1:13)

But in his very next utterance the narrator, through the insertion of the discrediting qualifier "pues" ['then'], obliges the reader to question the reliability of the original disparaging assertion:[7]

> Una, pues, desta nación, gitana vieja, que podía ser jubilada en la ciencia de Caco, crió una muchacha en nombre de nieta suya, a quien puso [por] nombre Preciosa, y a quien enseñó todas sus gitanerías, y modos de embelecos, y trazas de hurtar. (1:61)

> [A member of this race, then, an old gypsy woman who could be regarded as a complete expert in the science of thievery, brought up a young girl, as a granddaughter of hers; she gave her the name of Preciosa, and taught her all her gypsy lore, methods of deceit and tricks of stealing.] (1:13)

The narrator's attempt to emphasize his initial sweeping judgment on Gypsy customs by enumerating some of the particulars tends to provide a light and humorous inflection (comic idealization), rather than the serious tone the reader would ordinarily expect. The example he cites here to support his position, the case of the old Gypsy woman, seems to support the opening statement about that marginal group's innate venality. However, a subsequent reference to the special physical and intellectual attributes ("hermosa y discreta" ['beautiful and shrewd']) of the fair Preciosa actually weakens the case against the Gypsies by only partially confirming the original general thesis.[8]

> Salió la tal Preciosa la más única bailadora que se hallaba en todo el gitanismo, y la más hermosa y discreta que pudiera hallarse, no entre los gitanos, sino entre cuantas hermosas y discretas pudiera pregonar la fama. (1:61)

> [Preciosa turned out to be the most outstanding and exceptional dancer in the whole of gypsydom and the most beautiful and shrewd young woman you could find, not only among gypsies but also among the most beautiful and intelligent girls known to Fame.] (1:13)

To summarize, the narrator begins by informing us that all Gypsies are born thieves; next he tells us that a certain old Gypsy woman taught her granddaughter her entire repertoire of cons, frauds, and scams, as a result of which young Preciosa blossomed into a gifted dancer. A *dancer??!!* This simply is not a reasonable expectation. The reader immediately begins to suspect that he has been victimized by the narrator's skillful verbal legerdemain.[9] The result: growing confusion in the reader's mind about the validity of the opening statement and an invitation to rethink the stereotypical Gypsy image.[10]

We also note that the narrator's comments have suddenly acquired an unexpected ascendent tone. This upward movement continues in the next sentence, where we are informed that the remarkable Preciosa seems totally unaffected by the physical harshness and moral deprivations of her Gypsy upbringing and has emerged as if she were a person of an entirely different heritage ("en extremo cortés y bien razonada" ['extremely courteous and well-spoken']):

> Ni los soles, ni los aires, ni todas las inclemencias del cielo a quien más que otras gentes están sujetos los gitanos, pudieron deslustrar su rostro ni curtir las manos; y lo que es más, que la crianza tosca en que se criaba no descubría en ella sino ser nacida de mayores prendas que de gitana, porque era en extremo cortés y bien razonada. (1:61–62)

> [Neither the sun, the winds, nor any inclemency of weather, to which gypsies are more exposed than are other people, could spoil her face or

roughen her hands; and furthermore, the coarse upbringing she had had only revealed that she had been born of better stock than that of the gypsies, because she was extremely courteous and well-spoken.] (1:13)

The narrator's soaring description of the Gypsy beauty begins to level off as he informs us that Preciosa was perhaps a bit too shameless and impudent ("desenvuelta") for her own good, although this apparent shortcoming was not serious enough to raise any doubts about her chastity or modesty. She is, in fact, so *honesta* that no Gypsy woman would dare to utter a lascivious word in her presence.

> Y, con todo esto, era algo desenvuelta; pero no de modo que descubriese algún género de deshonestidad; antes, con ser aguda, era tan honesta, que en su presencia no osaba alguna gitana, vieja ni moza, cantar cantares lascivos ni decir palabras no buenas. (1:62)

> [And yet, with all this she was a little cheeky, but not in any way that might reveal any sort of unchaste behaviour; rather, although she was sharp, she was so virtuous that no gypsy woman, young or old, dared to sing dirty songs or use bad language when she was present.] (1:13)

The preliminary comments then conclude by descending once again to the original level of discourse with the revelation that the old woman was determined to make Preciosa as tough and "street-smart" as any Gypsy.

> Y, finalmente, la abuela conoció el tesoro que en la nieta tenía, y así, determinó el águila vieja sacar a volar su aguilucho y enseñarle a vivir por sus uñas. (1:62)

> [And, finally, her grandmother became aware of the treasure she had in her granddaughter, and this old eagle decided to teach her chick to fly and to live by her claws.] (1:13)

The opening paragraph, then, is an emotional roller-coaster ride for the reader: it begins at ground level with its characterization of Gypsy society in general and portrayal of a certain wily old Gypsy grandmother; but then the narrative suddenly ascends to unexpected heights with a psychological portrait of the lovely and talented Preciosa, only to finish with a return to the harsh reality of Gypsy life. Cervantes is toying with his readers here, consciously undermining all our preconceptions about the central figure of this story and the world in which she lives.

The remainder of the introductory section is used to prepare the reader for the events he is about to witness and the characters he is about to meet in the story being told. The narrator makes reference to the fact that Preciosa

1 / Cervantes and the Crucible of Love

earns her living by giving public performances of an estimable repertoire of songs and dances:

> Salió Preciosa rica de villancicos, de coplas, seguidillas y zarabandas, y de otros versos, especialmente de romances, que los cantaba con especial donaire. (1:62)

> [Preciosa has a rich repertoire of songs, sarabands, *seguidillas* and other verses, especially ballads, which she sang with special grace.] (1:13)

In order to be assured a fresh supply of suitable material, however, she must rely upon the contributions of both professional and amateur poets, who are always at hand:

> y no faltó poeta que se los diese; que también hay poetas que se acomodan con gitanos, y les venden sus obras, como los hay para ciegos, que les fingen milagros y van a la parte de la ganancia. (1:62)

> [and there was no lack of poets to supply them, because there are also poets who work for gypsies, and sell them their works, just as there are for blind men; they make up miracle lyrics for them and share in the proceeds.] (1:13)

With these words the narrator is preparing the reader for Preciosa's impending encounter with the mysterious page-poet of many names, but who will be principally remembered as Clemente.

Cervantes's narrator also makes no real attempt to conceal the fact that Preciosa may not actually be a Gypsy, but rather a descendant of clearly superior, probably aristocratic, bloodlines. Early references are made to her being "born of better stock than that of the gypsies" and to the fact that the old Gypsy woman had "brought [her] up . . . *as* a granddaughter" (emphasis added). In the early scenes Cervantes will hint no further than to inform us that the old woman "llamábala nieta, y ella la tenía por abuela" (1:66) ['called her "granddaughter," and Preciosa regarded her as her grandmother'] (1:17). Any discerning reader should already have a firm idea as to what will eventually be discovered about Preciosa's true lineage.

(B) Madrid I: Preciosa and the page-poet

The first actual occasion on which the talented little Gypsy puts her singing and dancing skills on display is at the feast of St. Anne in Madrid, when she recites, to great critical acclaim, a *romance* in honor of the revered mother of the Blessed Virgin. That triumph is followed a fortnight later by another vocal performance in praise of a more contemporary maternal icon, Philip III's young wife, Margarita de Austria, who has recently given birth to a royal heir. Joaquín Casalduero and Alban K. Forcione share the same favorable opinion about these verses: they represent twin examples, one celestial and the other terrestrial, of the ideal Christian marriage to which Preciosa aspires. Joseph V. Ricapito, on the other hand, interprets *La gitanilla* strictly in terms of the story's portrayal of social and historical realities. He rejects Forcione's contention that the story is about the theme of ideal Christian marriage. Ricapito posits a totally different purpose: "to expose the vacuity of the concept of *honra*" and "to examine and reveal the inhumane treatment of one of Spain's minorities."[11]

A slightly different view is offered by Gerli, who considers St. Anne a model of spiritual nobility amidst rustic simplicity and the popular Queen Margarita a paragon of Christian ideals in an otherwise corrupt social environment. Still another interpretation—interesting for its total lack of aesthetic principles—is Joan Ramón Resina's Marxist reading of these verses: St. Anne's blessed motherhood is compared in function to that of the die used to cast the royal coinage; Margarita, in turn, is symbolic of Spain's precapitalist economy. Francisco J. Sánchez prefers to interpret Preciosa's role here as that of an actress transformed into the figure of the Virgin, complete with seignorial attributes; the reader is expected to relate this performance to the comment in the opening paragraph of the story about how Gypsies seem to be *born* thieves. Cervantes, he asserts, wishes to link the issues of birth (or rebirth, in the case of Preciosa/Costanza), money, and a hierarchical concept of justice.[12]

Julio Rodríguez-Luis notes that these two opening scenes—especially in the verses she recites on each occasion—are designed to underscore, respectively, the two most important aspects of Preciosa's character: her wholesomeness *(honestidad)* and innate astuteness in dealing with the public *(discreción).*[13]

During this second visit to the Spanish capital, Preciosa comes in contact with some rather peculiar aristocratic types, namely the Teniente and his wife Doña Clara, who remind us of Lazarillo de Tormes's penurious squire *(escudero)* in their hypocritical attempt to maintain the false appearances of nobility and wealth. They do not have even pocket change with which to reward the young entertainer for her singing, dancing, and fortune-telling. This encounter becomes lesson number one in the disabusement *(desengaño)* of Preciosa: the pervasiveness of hypocrisy in high social circles. The Teniente and Doña Clara, not unlike the duke and duchess in *Don Quixote*, Part Two, represent the degradation (both moral and political), corruption, and arrogance of Spanish officials in Cervantes's time. It is in their home that the two Spains—high and low society—confront each other. This is especially noticeable in the scene in which Preciosa offers a clever and carefully worded fortune-telling performance.[14]

S. F. Boyd suggests that the Gypsy girl's physical attractiveness is a sign of her innate spiritual beauty, and that these moral qualities are the result of her free practice of virtue, not characteristics derived from her noble birth. In Boyd's view, the Teniente and the Gypsies stand at opposite ends of the political seesaw that has always attempted to balance society's need for order with the individual's need for greater personal freedom; Preciosa stands at the midpoint, refusing to define herself by the conventions of either world.[15]

A second adventure in the capital city will have even more serious and long-lasting implications for the sprightly protagonist. Preciosa is approached by a well-dressed young man in the guise of a page who offers her a *romance* (actually, it's a *redondilla*) that he assures her is "honesto," with the promise of more to come. (He has also included a gold escudo in the package, which causes Preciosa to suspect that this is not your average penniless amateur poet.) The verses constitute a verbal portrait of the beautiful maid (whose humble Gypsy origins the poet seriously questions) and describe the bewitching charm she seems to exercise over men; the poem closes with a profession of love from one who calls himself a poor and humble admirer ("pobre . . . humilde amador") (1:76). At this point the narrator is deliberately contrasting the virtues of Gypsy life with the obvious vices and moral defects of those who have chosen to live amidst the corruption of the royal court. The page-poet, then, is introduced as the perfect incarnation of these two very distinct lifestyles.[16] The same mysterious young wordsmith will reappear on several other occasions in the course of the story and will ultimately play a pivotal role in the development of the relationship between the two principal characters.[17]

Finally, a few words are in order concerning what is presented in the introductory section as Preciosa's single character flaw: her carefree sexuality and willingness to flirt with her male admirers *(desenvoltura)*. The naive openness she exhibits in dealing with total strangers would appear to be on a collision course with her strong and oft-expressed desire to maintain her *honestidad*. During her first visit to Madrid, for example, she is seen accepting a poem from a total stranger whose motives are unknown to her, then carelessly allowing that poem to be snatched from her bosom and read aloud by yet another unfamiliar male. We also observe her entering a gambling establishment filled with less-than-wholesome men and giving a rather vulgar fortune-telling performance at the house of the Teniente. It is clear that Preciosa must learn to be more circumspect in her dealings with men, especially marriageable ones, and the remainder of the story will be concerned, at least in part, with her apprenticeship along those lines.

(C) Madrid II: Preciosa and Juan/Andrés

On still another occasion just outside the city, Preciosa is unexpectedly confronted by a handsome and elegantly dressed young nobleman who approaches her with a proposal of marriage, an offer that will elevate greatly her social status. Instead of thanking him for his generous offer, Preciosa scolds him for his effrontery in thinking that she would barter her virginity so casually for mere promises or gifts. Her virtue cannot be bought or sold, she declares, and she goes on to stipulate that she will be his only after he has served a two-year apprenticeship among the Gypsies. Surprisingly, he accepts her challenge and promises to join the Gypsy band within the week, after he has made certain arrangements at home to deceive his parents into believing that he is going off to serve with the king's forces in Flanders.

At this point the principal theme of the story, jealousy, is injected when the young man—who at this point is known only by the name he will adopt as a Gypsy, Andrés—begs Preciosa in the meantime not to return to Madrid so as to avoid the occasions of sin there. This strange request brings from the young Gypsy girl a second rebuke: she will have none of his silly ideas about restricting her freedom, nor will she stand for carrying the weight of someone else's jealous feelings. As we shall see, this issue of *celos* is destined to be resurrected on more than one occasion in the remaining pages of this romance.

Almost immediately after taking leave of Andrés, Preciosa comes upon the young page-poet again; on this second occasion their conversation turns to the nature of poetry and poets. In response to her inquiry, he declares that he is not a professional poet, but rather an amateur who treats poetry as one would a precious jewel, i.e., as something to be worn or used only on special occasions. The next image he conjures up is even more interesting, for it is precisely the one the reader has already been given of Preciosa herself: he refers to poetry as

> una bellísima doncella, casta, honesta, discreta, aguda, retirada, y que se contiene en los límites de la discreción más alta. Es amiga de la soledad. Las fuentes la entretienen, los prados la consuelan, los árboles la desenojan, las flores la alegran, y, finalmente, deleita y enseña a cuantos con ella comunican. (1:91)

> [a beautiful young girl, chaste, pure, sensible, acute, retiring, inclined to keep herself within the bounds of the highest good sense. She loves solitude. Streams please her, meadows console her, trees make her feel tranquil, flowers make her happy, and, in conclusion, she teaches and delights all who have to do with her.] (1:45)

The correspondence between Dame Poetry and the young Gypsy maid could not be more clearly drawn than it is in this scene. When the page-poet offers her another of his verses and a second escudo, she moves quickly to accept them, although she professes to esteem him more for his art/poetry than for his generosity. When the young poet challenges her to demonstrate the sincerity of her remark by returning his pecuniary offering, she gladly surrenders the coin, thereby establishing poetry, not money, as the basis for the enduring friendship she hopes they will have: "y desta manera tendremos amistad que dure" (1:91).

Several critics, including Karl-Ludwig Selig and Joaquín Casalduero, have commented on Preciosa's embodiment of all the qualities the page-poet attributes to Dame Poetry. Georges Güntert noted that the figure of the poet was essential to the structure of this novella, and concluded that Preciosa was a symbol of poetry itself. Ruth El Saffar agrees, but comments that the page-poet's attitude toward Preciosa seems to be one of indifference, as if he were not capable of making a complete commitment either to her or to his poetry. As Frank Pierce notes, Cervantes seems to associate Preciosa with poetry from the very beginning; Ann E. Wiltrout says she "personifies poetry from the onset." Joseph B. Spieker goes even further; for him, Preciosa represents a living incarnation of Dame Poetry. An entirely different opinion is held by Alban K. Forcione, who cites continual and clear references to the Gypsy girl's all-too-human frailties ("shrewdness, worldliness and mischievous boldness . . . degenerating into . . . caustic cynicism and acerbity"), flaws that Forcione says make Preciosa totally incompatible with the image of Dame Poetry; instead, he considers Preciosa to be simply the artistic surrogate of Cervantes himself.[18]

We see here that Preciosa's ambivalence regarding the relationship of poetry and money reflects her very special identity problem. As one critic has noted, when Preciosa pockets the page-poet's first coin, she is clearly allowing her Gypsy upbringing to determine her conduct. Later, however, when she rejects his second monetary offering she is opting to follow her higher—and natural—aristocratic instincts, which traditionally include an indifference to material and financial concerns.[19] To put it another way, Preciosa is shown here to be moving away from the purely materialistic values of the Gypsy society in which she has been raised and toward the overwhelmingly spiritual values of the amateur poet whose siren call she has begun to heed.[20]

At this point the triangular relationship among the Gypsy girl, the amateur poet, and the jealous young noble begins to take shape. The romantic intrigue is heightened shortly thereafter when Preciosa arrives at the house of Andrés's parents. After she pretends to read the young man's fortune in a cleverly veiled reference to his secret plan to join the Gypsy band, she goes on to counsel him to stay at home with his parents until he has matured enough to think about marriage. Shortly thereafter during a dance she is performing, Preciosa accidentally drops the second poem she recently received from the page-poet. One of the guests seizes the paper and then rudely reads the sonnet aloud, much to the embarrassment of the Gypsy girl, since the verses sing unabashedly about her great beauty and talent. The reaction of Andrés is predictable: his complexion turns ashen and he falls into a swoon. At this point the page-poet seems to be portrayed as Andrés's most formidable rival for the affections of Preciosa.

The true nature of the page-poet and his function within the story have been the subject of much debate. Alban K. Forcione offers some original and persuasive insights into the unusual psyche of this character, referring to him as a subversive figure (cf. Pedro de Urdemalas) living on the edge of society.[21] Forcione views the aspiring poet as Juan's double, a character whose initial role is linked with the principal theme of the romance: the conventional discourse of love and the distortion of judgment it produces. In the second half of the story, however, Clemente's function changes and the page-poet becomes a rival for Preciosa's affections (149–50). Frank Pierce would appear to agree; he notes that Clemente, once he has exhausted his utility as Juan/Andrés's rival, fades out of the picture even more suddenly than he had appeared earlier.[22] A slightly different view is expressed by Robert Ter Horst, who accepts the first part of Forcione's thesis but squarely rejects the second, i.e., he denies the existence of any romantic attraction between Preciosa and the page-poet.[23]

Ann E. Wiltrout, on the other hand, views the Andrés-Clemente relationship as that of master and servant: "Andrés leads, Clemente follows. Andrés actively falls in love with Preciosa and Clemente admires her from afar with his songs. Andrés chooses to join the gypsies and Clemente joins them by accident when he stumbles onto the camp. . . . Clemente and his master are criminals, forced to flee from society and seek redemption or death in the military."[24] Wiltrout posits three separate functions for Clemente's character: (1) the second-banana to Andrés's lead role; (2) a companion and confidant for the romantic lead; and (3) a convenient foil to Andrés's history by providing a contrasting tale of love, death, and flight from prosecution (395). In the end, Andrés wins the heart and hand of Preciosa because he manages to put his ideals into action; conversely, Clemente's inability to move beyond the artistic expression of his ideals leaves him unfulfilled, with no choice but to slink away unrewarded (399).

The newest and most intriguing interpretation of Clemente's role is Lesley Lipson's. This commentator rejects the notion of the page-poet as Juan's double; Clemente is linked instead with Preciosa—and, ultimately, with Pedro de Urdemalas.[25] As Lipson sees it, Preciosa is the consummate professional poet, which is to say, an inveterate liar. Clemente, on the other hand, is only a novice, an awkward fabricator of falsehoods who never manages to advance beyond amateur status. The Gypsy girl actually *performs* poetry; the page-poet merely manufactures it (41). At the close of the story Preciosa happily renounces her career as a Gypsy performer to marry Juan, while Clemente opts for exile in Italy where he hopes to pursue his dream of becoming a professional poet. He will fail, of course, because he "is a non-achiever . . . committed to neither truth nor fiction, an aimless, naïve talent" (49). In a more realistic sense, Clemente is removed from the scene because he does not lie well enough and becomes a victim of his own illusions when he takes his art—and himself—too seriously (50–51).

As I view it, the rivalry between these handsome males is simply an illusion Cervantes has fabricated to distract, albeit temporarily, the reader's attention from the more serious real themes of this work: the need for Christian mercy and the portrayal of the artist as a social outcast. While it is true that both male protagonists can be said to descend into the nefarious Gypsy underworld in *La gitanilla*, I would maintain that only Andrés can be seen as Preciosa's intended savior or redeemer, an agent sent to rescue the lost maiden and return her to her rightful social status as his bride. Clemente, conversely, should be viewed as Preciosa's spiritual double; together they function as twin representatives of poetry and the artistic community. In the early scenes he is clearly portrayed as the novice page-poet, continually inspired to polish his noble craft by the worldly-wise beauty of Preciosa, his personal muse. In the final scenes, however, their respective roles will be radically altered: Preciosa will opt to abandon the uninhibited lifestyle of the Gypsy/artistic community in order to return to the comfortable aristocratic world from which she came; Clemente, having become a polished poet as a result of his Gypsy experience, will be required to remain in the underworld in the role of a restless vagabond poet.

In a sense, then, Preciosa's rescue is accomplished through the combined and coordinated efforts of the two heroes. Andrés is cast in the role of a hero who descends into the underworld of Gypsy society in order to carry the captive damsel back up to the civilized world. Clemente's role is complementary: he will serve as a hostage to ensure Preciosa's freedom; he will exchange his fate for hers so that she may be permitted to return to the comfort and security of her aristocratic birthright. This is why Clemente is not allowed to be reintegrated into society along with Andrés and Preciosa at the close of the adventure. It also explains the importance of the final word of the story as it relates to the missing protagonist and the real theme of *La gitanilla*: "clemencia."

Let us return to the critical juncture at which the page-poet's unexpectedly appears at the Gypsy camp and causes Andrés's swoon. At this point the narrator, heretofore invisible, suddenly intervenes—an infrequent occurrence in

Cervantes's short fiction—to speak directly to his main character, informing her of Andrés's genuine pain and counseling her to speak words into his ear that will revive him:

> (Mirad lo que habéis dicho, Preciosa, y lo que vais a decir; que ésas no son alabanzas del paje, sino lanzas que traspasan el corazón de Andrés, que las escucha. ¿Queréislo ver, niña? Pues volved los ojos y veréisle desmayado encima de la silla, con un trasudor de muerte; no penséis, doncella, que os ama tan de burlas Andrés que no le hiera y sobresalte el menor de vuestros descuidos. Llegaos a él enhorabuena, decilde algunas palabras al oído, que vayan derechas al corazón y le vuelvan de su desmayo. ¡No, sino andaos a traer sonetos cada día en vuestra alabanza, y veréis cuál os le ponen!) (1:96–97)

> [(Look at what you've said, Preciosa, and what you are about to say; these are not compliments to the page, but lances piercing the heart of Andrés, who is listening to you! Do you want proof, child? Well, look around, and you'll see him fainting on a chair, with mortal sweat; do not think, girl, that the slightest bit of carelessness from you does not upset and wound him. Go up to him, for goodness' sake, and say into his ear a few words which will go straight to the heart and bring him out of his faint. Or, go ahead, and bring sonnets in your praise every day, and see what effect they have on him!)] (1:53)

Preciosa moves forward to perform the act requested, but here again Cervantes seems to be playing with the reader's expectations. To begin with, we learn here that Juan/Andrés has not actually fainted; he has merely lost some of his color. And Preciosa's words are quite different from those which the narrator has just urged her to say. The maiden's utterances into the ear of her would-be husband are hardly words of consolation; she reproves him sharply for his childish reaction to the poem and seriously questions his ability to withstand the proposed two-year apprenticeship in the company of her Gypsy family. Shortly thereafter the Gypsies take their leave of their hosts, and Preciosa's final words to the young suitor encourage him to join her at the Gypsy camp at his earliest convenience.

(D) En route to Toledo: The apprenticeship of Andrés Caballero

From a structural standpoint, it is interesting to note that Andrés's apprenticeship in the Gypsy way of life begins at the virtual midpoint of the story. The entire first half of the narrative has been devoted to establishing a romantic triangle in which two young noblemen—the first a poet of some merit, the other a jealous, pampered, and callow scion of a wealthy family—will vie for the attention of a lovely Gypsy girl who exhibits some very surprising "noble" qualities. The second part of the story will be quite different; it will be more concerned with plot complication and intrigue than with the slow and careful character development we witnessed in the opening half.

The fourth section of narrative, Andrés's induction into Gypsy society, is more important for its symbolic ceremonials than for any small contribution it may make to the advancement of the plot. This narrative block begins with the young nobleman's arrival at the Gypsy camp and the ensuing debate as to what ought to be done with Andrés's handsome rented mule. The sly Gypsies immediately make plans to disguise the beast's true markings and sell it to some unsuspecting trader. Andrés, on the other hand, insists that the animal be killed and its carcass buried where no one will ever find it. Here Cervantes devotes an inordinate amount of narrative and dialogue to a matter that, at least on the surface, appears to be rather trivial: the fate of a dumb animal. On a symbolic level, however, the episode carries more weight. It is injected to provide a vivid demonstration of the sincerity of Andrés's commitment to his new lifestyle. As such, it symbolizes the complete break he has chosen to make with the conventional values of his aristocratic upbringing.

The next important occurrence in this narrative block is the induction ceremony that Andrés must undergo. With the possible exception of occasional reflections upon his personal experiences as a soldier and prisoner of war in Algiers, Cervantes's fiction has never been noted for the strict historical or empirical accuracy of the data it contains. Therefore, the Gypsy rites he describes here so vividly should not be considered anything more than a fanciful re-creation of what many or most Spaniards of the 1600s would have been willing to accept as the bona fide Gypsy code of conduct.

The only item of the Gypsy code that requires our attention here is the matter of *celos*, jealousy being labeled a bitter pestilence ("una amarga pestilencia") (1:101) that has infected the rest of Spanish society and from which the Gypsies wish to remain free. The overall picture of the Gypsy way of life presented here is a decidedly negative one. The only positive aspect of the Gypsy code that Cervantes describes—and, again, there is no documentation to support the representation of such a casual approach to carnal relations in Gypsy society—is their peculiar method of obviating violent and uncontrolled reactions to adulterous romantic entanglements. As one old Gypsy explains it:

> Entre nosotros, aunque hay muchos incestos, no hay ningún adulterio; y cuando le hay en la mujer propia, o alguna bellaquería en la amiga, no vamos a la justicia a pedir castigo; nosotros somos los jueces y los verdugos de nuestras esposas o amigas; con la misma facilidad las matamos y las enterramos por las montañas y desiertos como si fueran animales nocivos;

no hay pariente que las vengue, ni padres que nos pidan su muerte. Con este temor y miedo ellas procuran ser castas, y nosotros, como ya he dicho, vivimos seguros. Pocas cosas tenemos que no sean comunes a todos, excepto la mujer o la amiga, que queremos que cada una sea del que le cupo en suerte. Entre nosotros así hace divorcio la vejez como la muerte. El que quisiere, puede dejar la mujer vieja, como él sea mozo, y escoger otra que corresponda al gusto de sus años. (1:101)

[Among us, although there is a lot of incest, there is no adultery; and if there is any with one's wife or any naughty behaviour in a mistress, we do not complain to the law; we are the judges and the executioners of our wives or our mistresses; we kill them or bury them in the mountains or the deserts as if they were harmful animals; there are no relations to avenge them, nor parents to charge us with their deaths. With this fear and terror they see to it that they remain chaste, and we, as I said, live secure. We have few things that are not common to all, except for wife or mistress, as regards to whom we want each one to belong to the man fate chose for her. Among us old age and death are the causes of divorce. Anyone who wants to can leave an old wife, if he is young, and choose another who suits the taste of his years.] (1:59)

The narrator makes it quite clear that Andrés is entering here into a picaresque underworld governed by a code of conduct some 180 degrees removed from the polite chivalric value system of the aristocratic society in which he was raised. It will be left to Andrés, as part of the individuation process, to mediate between two completely opposite societies as he forges a value system of his own. Preciosa will assist and accompany him in his quest, for she declares that she has already rejected "la bárbara e insolente licencia que estos mis parientes se han tomado de dejar las mujeres, o castigarlas, cuando se les antoja" (1:104) ['The barbarous and insolent freedom which these kindsmen of mine have adopted, to abandon or punish their womenfolk whenever they like'] (1:61). She wants no part of hollow promises or flowery vows; *experience*—two years of carefully observing Andrés's conduct—will be her only guide.

In the city of Toledo Andrés is scheduled to undergo his first lesson in the art of thievery, but his aristocratic values—Cervantes attributes it to his "buena sangre" (1:107) [good blood]—prevent him from behaving like a true Gypsy. We are told that he is greatly disturbed ("se le arrancaba a él el alma") (1:107) by the many larcenies committed by his cohorts and is moved by the tears of their victims, so much so, in fact, that he makes restitution to the victims out of his own pocket. The Gypsies censure him for having too much concern for his victims *(caridad),* which they consider a direct threat to their traditional way of life. He eventually demands to be allowed to work alone so that he may purchase items that he will pass off as stolen

1 / Cervantes and the Crucible of Love 57

when he returns to the camp, a practice at which he becomes so proficient that he soon begins to enjoy the reputation of a first-rate thief, not to mention the admiration of the fair Preciosa. All appears to be proceeding according plan for Andrés and Preciosa at the end of the third section as the Gypsy band moves to Extremadura for the onset of autumn.

(E^1) Extremadura: Jealousy erupts: Clemente arrives at the Gypsy camp

In the idyllic pastoral setting near the Portuguese border the relationship between Andrés and Preciosa grows stronger; he is more captivated than ever by her charms and she actually begins to experience feelings of love for him and his gentle ways. The Gypsies prosper there and Andrés Caballero gains wide fame for his athletic prowess and "gallarda disposición," [gallant disposition] but all of that is threatened by the sudden appearance one evening of a wounded stranger dressed in white, as if he were a miller. Preciosa recognizes him as the page-poet she met back in Madrid and—foolishly, as it turns out—mentions this to Andrés, along with the remark that she found the poet to be sensible, well-spoken, and extremely honorable ("discreto, y bien razonado, y sobremanera honesto") (1:110). Andrés, predictably enough, reacts in a childishly jealous manner; he concludes that the poet could have arrived at the Gypsy camp for only one reason: to steal the heart of Preciosa. He also accuses the girl of enjoying the flattery of having two men captivated by her beauty.

Preciosa will have none of this. She immediately chides him for his boorish and petty behavior, for allowing his jealousy to becloud his better judgment *(discreción)*. Her final remark summarizes perfectly her objection:

Mira, Andrés, no me pesa a mí de verte celoso; pero pesarme ha mucho si te veo indiscreto. (1:110)

[Look, Andrés, I'm not grieved to see you are jealous, but I'd be grieved to see you unwise.] (1:69)

Preciosa's strong and eloquently stated objections notwithstanding, Andrés remains curious as to how and why the handsome and talented page-poet has suddenly appeared in their midst, if not to woo Preciosa.

Shortly thereafter Andrés begins to grill the newcomer, who attempts to palm off an obviously phony story to explain his sudden and unexpected appearance. Andrés next confronts the stranger with his suspicions and, posing as a relative of Preciosa, offers to sell the Gypsy beauty—to be either his wife or his mistress, depending upon the price—to the man in white. He receives a potentially devastating shock when he learns that the stranger has four hundred gold escudos in his possession, a price more than sufficient to pry even the lovely Preciosa away from the Gypsies. But then the newcomer declares that, despite Preciosa's abundant beauty, wit, and charm, he has absolutely no romantic interest in her; it has been a case of misfortune, not love, that brings him their camp.

(F) Analeptic summary #1

At this point the stranger proceeds to narrate a flashback account of an unfortunate incident in Madrid that has caused him to flee the capital: he has become the principal suspect in a homicide case and has been obliged to take refuge in the countryside to escape prosecution. His goal is to make his way to Seville, then Cartagena, and eventually to Italy to escape the Spanish authorities who are looking for him.

(E^2) Extremadura

Moved by the stranger's story, Andrés convinces the Gypsies to help the young stranger and offer him shelter in their camp until they can work their way into Murcia, from which point he will be able to escape on his own. Strangely enough, Preciosa is the only listener to oppose the plan, but she is overruled by the elders and the young fugitive is welcomed into Gypsy society as "Clemente." Andrés, for his part, still has serious reservations about Clemente's true intentions, especially in light of the poet's former relationship with Preciosa (as indicated in his verses) and the ease with which the fugitive was persuaded to alter his escape plans in order to remain near her in the Gypsy camp. But he does not oppose the newcomer's joining the troupe. He decides instead to observe Clemente closely and try to fathom the poet's actual intentions by becoming Clemente's closest comrade. The poet, still naively ignorant of Andrés's gnawing jealousy and less-than-selfless ulterior motives, accepts the proffered friendship as if it were some great honor. They soon become inseparable friends and even achieve a certain amount of renown for their athletic achievements.

(G^1) Murcia: Jealousy overcome; Anagnorisis and restoration of identities; Clemente escapes to Italy

In Murcia the matter of Andrés's jealousy will be resolved, but one further complication—and a life-threatening one, at that—will be introduced before Preciosa and Andrés's love will be allowed to triumph. The overland trek to that city is a journey of some six or seven weeks' duration, and we are told that in the course of the journey not even once does Clemente attempt to speak to Preciosa. At the same time Andrés has fully informed the poet about the peculiar bargain he has struck with the beautiful Gypsy girl. Finally, however, the three principal characters have a discussion that is intended to clear the air about their unique triangular relationship. Preciosa begins by asking Clemente not to think ill of Andrés's decision to live as a Gypsy for two years to win her love; Clemente replies that he is fully aware of the effects that great beauty such as hers can have on a man and that he thinks no less of Andrés for agreeing to her terms. He wishes them only happiness, a long life together, and many beautiful offspring.

But Andrés is still plagued by doubts about the lush romantic verses Clemente had composed months earlier in praise of Preciosa's charms. Were his words merely a polite poetic convention, or was he really in love with her at the time? It is obvious that Andrés has not yet overcome what the narrator refers to as "la infernal enfermedad celosa" (1:118) [the infernal sickness of jealousy].

Matters come to a head just outside of Murcia one evening when the two friends exchange a series of verses *(canto amebeo)* in honor of the Gypsy beauty, each poet beginning a new strophe by picking up and building upon the final verse of his rival. Perhaps the most notable aspect of these verses—which are quite conventional and not especially noteworthy outside the context of this particular story—is the fact that Clemente sings the praises of Preciosa from a respectful distance while Andrés makes it clear that he is singing of a beautiful woman who belongs to him ("dulce regalo mío") (1:120). The contest ends when Preciosa suddenly interrupts with some verses of her own in praise of integrity *(honestidad)* over beauty *(hermosura)*. The parallel between this scene and the romantic triangle Cervantes presented earlier in his *Galatea* is unmistakable. Philip Krummrich has succinctly summarized the relationship of the three protagonists at this point: "Andrés becomes Elicio, an Elicio who has a real chance to attain his ends through service and devotion. Clemente fills the shoes of Erastro, minus his quirks and his love. Preciosa emerges as a *pastora* [shepherdess], but much more mature than Galatea."[26]

Somewhere in the three-way exchange of verses and subsequent conversation Andrés learns to conquer his own jealousy. But before the Gypsy lovers will be permitted to achieve a blissful relationship, they must share one great and final test of their love: the false accusations made against Andrés by a rich and jealous teenager named Juana Carducha, who is described as more sexually free and easy than beautiful ("más desenvuelta que hermosa") (1:122). It is curious to note that Juana Carducha's extreme forwardness in dealing with Juan/Andrés should turn out to be precisely the same—and indeed the only—negative trait attributed to the otherwise perfect Preciosa in the early part of the story. On the one hand, it would seem that the Carducha character is intended to symbolize the negative side of Preciosa's sexual aggressiveness *(desenvoltura),* i.e., she is the kind of wanton female that a less righteous Preciosa might be. On the other hand, an even stronger argument can be made for casting Juana in the role of Juan/Andrés's doppelgänger (and for far more serious reasons than the mere coincidence of their names). The young gentleman-turned-Gypsy is forced to confront in the obsessive Carducha a personality even more given to jealous excess than he. Cervantes's plan calls for Juan/Andrés to come to grips here with the darker side of his own psyche and immediately resolve to overcome his only serious character flaw.

After her amorous advances toward the handsome Gypsy have been rebuffed, Juana vindictively accuses Andrés of robbery (after having planted some incriminating evidence among his belongings); charges and insults are quickly exchanged, and in a matter of moments Andrés/Don Juan's noble bloodlines reach the boiling point and he slays an ill-tempered soldier who foolishly strikes him across the face. Thomas R. Hart notes that the disguised aristocrat's violent reaction in *chaude colle* is proof of both his innocence and his innate nobility.[27] But since Andrés's true lineage has not yet been revealed, the authorities seize Andrés and take most of other Gypsies into custody. As the officials are escorting the prisoners into Murcia, Doña Guiomar, the wife of the corregidor, is stunned by the beauty of Preciosa (just as so many before her had been) and orders that the Gypsy maiden be brought before her.

(H) Analeptic summary #2

At this point, while Preciosa is pleading for Andrés's life, her putative grandmother takes the corregidor and his wife aside and confesses, in an analeptic aside, that Preciosa is really the child she had stolen from them some fifteen years before. The old hag also explains how and why the young man known as "Andrés" is really Juan de Cárcamo, son of a famous knight in the Order of Santiago.

(G^2) Murcia

Having heard this extraordinary testimony, the corregidor might now be expected to order the immediate release of Andrés/Don Juan, but he opts instead to allow the unsuspecting prisoner to believe that he is about to be executed in order to surprise him at the last moment with his freedom. It would appear that Cervantes had at least two additional points he wished to make.

First of all, he wanted to show that Andrés had at long last learned to control his proclivity for jealous reactions. When the corregidor first appears in his jail cell and asks if Preciosa is his wife, the young man's initial reaction is to suspect that the old official simply lusts after her. As the narrator explains, jealous feelings are subtle and penetrate other bodies without causing any apparent physical damage ("los celos son de cuerpos sutiles y se entran por otros cuerpos sin romperlos, apartarlos ni dividirlos") (1:130). But this time he holds himself in check, calmly refusing either to confirm or deny the assertion.

The second point is made with regard to Preciosa. When asked by Doña Guiomar and the corregidor if she loves Andrés/Don Juan, the discreet young girl replies on two separate occasions that she is grateful for the sacrifice he has made in her honor, and that she has felt some affection for him because of his innate honesty, but that her wishes (with regard to the selection of a husband) will be whatever her newly discovered parents decide. This is a point that is made time and again in Cervantes's fiction: children, especially daughters, must ultimately defer to the wishes of their parents in the selection of a mate.

In the general spirit of goodwill that emerges at the close of the story with the planned nuptials for Preciosa and Andrés (now restored to their original identities as Costanza and Juan), all past transgressions on the part of certain characters are either pardoned or conveniently ignored. Both the old Gypsy and Juana Carducha are forgiven for having kidnapped the young Costanza and for having pressed false charges against the disguised Juan, respectively. The uncle of the murdered soldier is easily persuaded to drop the charges against Don Juan in exchange for the sum of two thousand *ducados*.

As for Clemente, the narrator tells us that he was occupied elsewhere when his friend Andrés ran afoul of the law in Murcia and that, upon learning what unpleasantness had befallen his comrade, he decided to beat a hasty retreat. We learn at a later point that he succeeded in reaching Cartagena, from which port he was able to book passage to Genoa and make good his escape from the Spanish authorities who were searching for him. From a purely technical standpoint, Clemente is allowed to disappear from the narration because he has completed his assigned role: the catalyst for bringing Costanza/Preciosa and Juan/Andrés to a full realization of their mutual destiny.

One critic has viewed Andrés's "victory" here over Clemente as a triumph of the active principle over the passive, of arms over letters. The daring Andrés fearlessly opts to convert his lofty ideals into acts of great consequence, gaining Preciosa as his eventual reward. The more intellectual Clemente, however, limits himself merely to the lyric expression of his sentiments and is (justly) left unrewarded at the end.[28]

In the case of Preciosa and Juan/Andrés we see that, largely through their interaction with the page-poet, they have been fundamentally transformed. The Gypsy girl has learned to temper her careless *desenvoltura;* at the same time the shallow and materialistic young scion now has the required aesthetic qualities, formerly lacking in his character, of a mature and cultured gentleman. As Krummrich notes, "All that remains is to dispense with the disguise and put the two in their native sphere."[29]

What is to be made, then, of the fundamental antagonism that has seemed to exist throughout the story between Juan/Andrés and Clemente? As the various problems begin to reach resolution toward the end of the narrative, the reader begins to sense that the surface-level "rivalry" between Clemente and Andrés for Preciosa's affections has actually been masking a more serious and significant relationship. One critic has argued that when the two young men join their voices in a *canto amebeo* to sing the praises of Preciosa at the Gypsy camp, Cervantes makes it evident that the outsider Clemente's real role has not been that of a competitor against Juan/Andrés, but rather that of a complementary character, a projection and amplification of Don Juan himself.[30]

Another critic claims that the page-poet's function is predominantly a contrastive one: he serves as a link or bridge between the sexually restrictive atmosphere of the royal court and the more loosely structured marital conventions of the Gypsy *aduar*. Clemente's role is that of a unique mediating agent who has witnessed/experienced both the "amores livianos e inconstantes" [fickle and inconstant love-affairs] of the Spanish capital city (i.e., relationships characterized by violent outbursts of jealousy, such as the one which obliged him to flee for his life from the capital) as well as the firm and perfect love engendered by the free love philosophy of Gypsy society.[31] In other words, the page-poet is an indispensable catalytic element in the process of uniting Preciosa and Juan/Andrés.

Many critics, Casalduero being perhaps the first among them, have observed that the beautiful and seductive Gypsy girl seems to be a symbol of Poetry itself.[32] However, such an interpretation requires further elaboration regarding the characters that surround her and interact with her. El Saffar accepts Casalduero's basic premise but then rejects the notion that the chameleon-like page-poet (who uses the names Alonso Hurtado, Don Sancho, and Clemente in the course of the story) might represent the Poet. She says the page-poet's attitude toward Preciosa is one of indifference, i.e., he can admire poetry only in the abstract, while she is very concrete. The slippery Clemente can be neither a poet nor Preciosa's lover because he is incapable of a full commitment to anyone or anything. The true Poet in this story is Andrés, says El Saffar, because he dedicates his life exclusively to Preciosa.[33]

In *Cervantes and the Humanist Vision*, Alban K. Forcione puts a very different spin on this puzzling triangular relationship. For him, Preciosa is indeed "Dame Poetry, a beautiful, chaste maiden";[34] furthermore, she should be considered an alter ego of no one but Cervantes himself, because both are ironists (219). Alonso Hurtado/Don Sancho/Clemente, on the other hand, is an elusive figure with a variety of functions in the narration; he is both Juan's double and his rival for Preciosa's love. In his initial appearance the page-poet represents "a flawed experience of love which to some extent marks Juan's early courtship" (129). But before long Clemente begins to emerge as a romantic rival; he becomes the "courtly" lover and "courtly" love poet whose function is to test the jealous nature of Juan/Andrés (129, 149–50).

My own view is based on a pair of distinct but complementary arguments recently presented by J. R. Resina and Julio Rodríguez-Luis. Resina, echoing Casalduero's earlier observation,[35] insists that it is the emotionally unstable Juana Carducha, not the noble Clemente, who appears to have been designed to serve as Juan/Andrés's baser spiritual counterpart in this story.[36] What, then, do we make of Clemente? Here I am inclined to accept the reasoning of Rodríguez-Luis, who finds the page's wisdom comparable only to that of Preciosa; it is Clemente, not Juan/Andrés, who represents the spiritual balance and serenity of a person who truly knows himself ("el equilibrio y la serenidad espirituales de quien se conoce a sí mismo").[37] If we leave aside Clemente's catalytic role in bringing the two lovers together, it can be seen that the main function of the highly aesthetic page-poet is to mirror the attitudes and values of Preciosa by serving as her spiritual doppelgänger. In the matter of "doubles," then, the real pairings would be these:

Don Juan/Andrés   {———}   Juana Carducha
Don Sancho/Clemente   {———}   Preciosa

In support of this spiritual bond between Clemente and Preciosa, let us consider the psychological profiles that are offered for these characters in Cervantes's story. The initial description of the sprightly Gypsy girl paints her as the most beautiful and shrewd young woman one could find ("la más hermosa y discreta que pudiera hallarse") (1:61) as well as extremely courteous and well-spoken ("en extremo cortés y bien razonada") (1:62). These words are virtually echoed at the story's midpoint when Preciosa herself provides her Gypsy companions with an appraisal of the character of the newly arrived Clemente: "que el mozo es discreto, y bien razonado, y sobremanera honesto" (1:110) ['the young man is sensible, well-spoken, and extremely honourable'] (1:69).

This parallel is no casual coincidence. In portraying the close bond between such similar yet distinct characters, Cervantes is also representing, I feel, the peculiar relationship he perceived to exist between the traditional form of narrative fiction (the prose romance) and the innovative narrative form he created in his *Don Quixote*, which we now call the novel.[38]

What makes *La gitanilla* special is the fact that it is designed to appeal simultaneously to two distinct reading audiences: (1) the admirers of the traditional romance genre, readers who expect goodness to be rewarded and evil punished in a universe that ultimately makes perfect sense; and (2) the more sophisticated skeptical readers who are capable of appreciating the supremely ironic nature of human existence, the frustrating unpredictability of fate and the frustrating lack of tidiness in our day-to-day existence.

This peculiar kind of double discourse is borne out in the final paragraphs of the story itself. Toward the end of the narration it becomes apparent that the Gypsy girl and the admiring page-poet have turned out to be quite different from what each one appeared to be when they first met in Madrid. In time each has discovered and been forced to deal with a "dark side" of his or her own personality. The uplifting account of Preciosa's reunion with her parents and her courtship and marriage to Don Juan clearly conforms to the traditional romance formula, which is to say, it draws to a tidy and satisfying conclusion, despite the many vicissitudes of the plot, in the final sentences of Cervantes's text. Most critics have been content to analyze only this part of the story, conveniently refraining from offering any comment at all regarding Clemente's fate, an equally important subject alluded to in those same final paragraphs.

What should be obvious to all is that the "romance" format used to relate the trials and tribulations of Preciosa (her separation from and reintegration with her real family; her strange courtship by Don Juan) coexists and contrasts sharply with an intertwining "novelistic" account of the page-poet Clemente's equally difficult search for artistic freedom. His is an open-ended, unpredictable, and much darker history, one that we are led to believe will be played out in Italy as a kind of narrative coda extending far beyond the closing sentence of *La gitanilla*. A very different view is offered by Francisco J. Sánchez, who considers the stories of Clemente and Juana Carducha to be simply variations on the peripatetic Byzantine model.[39]

Another interesting interpretation of the relationship between Preciosa and Clemente—and the conflicting genres through which their respective stories are told—has been advanced by Catherine Vinel. Vinel's interpretation is somewhat allegorical: Clemente represents the poet as creator, while Preciosa symbolizes poetry itself, the product of the creative impulse, the performance or expression of the poetic muse. His initial role is to furnish the songs she sings, but he also reminds her continually of her obligation to employ her beauty and seductive talents in the service of art. As the story progresses, however, both the reader and the page-poet observe Preciosa moving gradually away from the idealistic purity of her poetic calling and toward the prosaic reality of her destiny as an aristocratic wife and daughter. In the end, says Vinel, Preciosa must be considered a failure as the embodiment of poetry; when she opts to return to her birth family and marry Don Juan, she is also abandoning her artistic calling in favor of material wealth and social comfort. And so, when Preciosa, now called Costanza, submits to her parents' will and agrees to a very conventional and stultifying—in comparison with her previous Gypsy lifestyle, at least—marriage, the poet Clemente is left without a voice. Self-imposed exile in Italy, where he hopes to rekindle his muse, is his only logical recourse.[40]

This double-genre concept helps to explain the two major schools of critical interpretation Lesley Lipson discerns when it comes to *La gitanilla*.[41] Those who focus on the ideal elements of the story (e.g., Casalduero and El Saffar) are reading it as a romance; the more skeptical critics like Avalle-Arce, Forcione, and Gerli are concentrating on the novelistic elements. As I see it, both groups have valid interpretations of *La gitanilla* because Cervantes's genius enabled him to conceive that particular *novela* with both audiences in mind.

Carroll B. Johnson has offered a slightly different interpretation of the Preciosa-Clemente bond: a purely economic scenario. According to Johnson's theory, the Gypsy girl and the page-poet are linked, not by their common interest in poetry and art, but rather as twin harbingers of the new, dynamic economic order of bourgeois capitalists that Cervantes believed would soon supplant the stagnant aristocratic system that had controlled the Spanish economy since feudal times. In Johnson's mercantile paradigm, the raw material of the economic enterprise is language itself, from which the clever page-poet manufactures a series of entertaining verses; he then transfers these valuable verbal artifacts to the lovely Gypsy girl, who proceeds to polish them to perfection and sell them at their optimum value as part of her street performances.[42]

Johnson's economic model fits easily within my proposal for a double-sided denouement for *La gitanilla*. The same bifurcated ending can be seen whether the poetry generated by Preciosa and Clemente is viewed as a creative work of art or as a symbol of the emerging capitalistic system that in Cervantes's time was threatening the tired old feudal economy. We note once again that in the "romance" ending Cervantes presents Preciosa as the dutiful daughter who accedes to the wishes of her high-born parents by abandoning the economically precarious Gypsy life in order to return the security of her aristocratic roots. Here the young woman not only submits to the repressive patriarchal social order but also sacrifices the promise of her nascent capitalistic enterprise in favor of the archaic but comfortable economic system of her forefathers. In the alternative (i.e., "novelistic") ending Cervantes allows the other half of the economic equation, the enterprising Clemente, to skip off to Italy, where he will presumably be allowed to pursue his craft and his entrepreneurial dreams without hindrance from the Spanish authorities.

As a final note I would add an observation about Cervantes's symbolic use of proper names in *La gitanilla*. Johnson cogently observes that the name Preciosa given by the child's putative grandmother points to the old Gypsy's accurate estimation of the talented little girl as a potential cash cow.[43] Even when it is discovered late in the story that the beautiful entertainer's baptismal name is Costanza, the new/old appellation suddenly seems perfectly suited for the highly conventional role she is preparing to assume at that point: the constant and conforming daughter who, having been restored to her true identity, is prepared to accept unquestioningly her parents' choice of a husband for her.[44]

A similar notation can be made in the case of the unlucky page-poet. This character adopts a variety of names in the course of the story (Don Sancho and Alonso Hurtado being the first two), but as he races for the port of Cartagena to make his escape to Italy with the Spanish authorities in hot pursuit, the appellation by which he is most vividly remembered is Clemente. I believe that it is no mere coincidence that *clemencia* is both the final word of Cervantes's story and the spiritual value for which this character has an especially desperate need at this point.

LA ILUSTRE FREGONA

As was the case in the opening story, *Fregona* begins with an introductory section (A) that presents the family background of the twin protagonists of the story, two would-be *pícaros* named Diego de Carriazo and Tomás de Avendaño; this prologue is followed by five distinct narrative divisions (B, C, D, E, and G), with two analeptic recapitulations (F and H) inserted into the final two scenes. The plan for *La ilustre fregona* includes eight separate sections:

(A) Introduction: Family background of Carriazo and Avendaño
(B) Transition I: Conversation overheard at the gates of Illescas
(C) Bifurcated narrative
    (C^1) = Courtship of Costanza by Avendaño at the inn
    (C^2) = Adventures of Carriazo in town as a water seller
(D) Transition II: Six days without incident

1 / Cervantes and the Crucible of Love

(E) Arrival of the corregidor
   (F) = Innkeeper's story
(G) Arrival of the elder Carriazo and Avendaño; Denouement
   (H) = Don Diego's story;

I shall reserve for a later moment my comments on the various thematic parallels that can be noted between the respective histories of the Gypsy dancer, Preciosa, and the illustrious scullery maid, Costanza. My primary objective at this point is to point out the striking structural affinities that exist between these two very similar novellas (schemas 16 and 17).

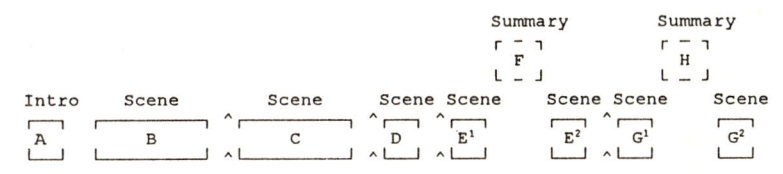

Schema 16. *La gitanilla*

Schema 17. *La ilustra fregona*

We immediately notice that they share virtually identical narrative patterns, with only minor formal differences. The structure of *Fregona*, for example, takes the form of a long chain of brief scenes, while *Gitanilla*'s narrative units tend to be fewer in number but longer in duration. The major structural difference between the two—and the element that I believe raises *La ilustre fregona* a notch above its more celebrated predecessor in the area of technical artistry—is Cervantes's decision to split the central narrative section (C) into two separate but parallel plotlines; the narrator repeatedly switches his focus from the purely comic adventures of Avendaño at the inn (C^1) to the more serious issues being faced by Carriazo in town (C^2), and back again. As I shall explain at a later point, Cervantes is not introducing this potentially disruptive device in a frivolous manner, but rather as part of a bold literary experiment in narrative form.

Before proceeding with my analysis of each of the narrative sections of *Fregona*, I would like, as so many others have done before me, to note the several points of correspondence—as well as a few of the significant differences—that can be cited when comparing *La gitanilla* and *La ilustre fregona*.

The most obvious parallel is found in the name and family origins of the two eponymous heroines. To begin with, both girls have been baptized with the name Costanza, although the one in *La gitanilla* is universally called by her Gypsy name, Preciosa. Secondly, each girl's title is artfully misleading: from the outset the narrator leaves a string of clues pointing to Preciosa's non-Gypsy bloodlines; likewise, it is quickly made clear that Costanza has never scrubbed a pot or plate. Each girl turns out to be, in fact, the long-lost daughter of Spanish aristocrats, a child separated shortly after birth from her natural parents, then raised in humble circumstances by a surrogate family.

Curiously enough, while Cervantes has named each of these novellas for the pivotal female love interest around whom the action happens to revolve, the major focus of *Gitanilla* and *Fregona* lies with the (mis)adventures of one or more male coprotagonists. To some degree then, the female character's recovery of her true identity is merely an ancillary plot point, an interesting secondary issue designed to complement and enhance the male lead's more glamorous quest.

The respective male suitors, Don Juan/Andrés in *La gitanilla* and Tomás de Avendaño in *La ilustre fregona*, are, predictably, also the progeny of noble forebears. These males are portrayed as heroic and worthy of literary celebration because they decide to shed their real identities and "rescue" their ladyloves by descending voluntarily to the social nether world and embracing the same fate that has been imposed by others upon their female counterparts. Both novellas end with the belated discovery of the heroine's hidden noble origins by the local corregidor (whose wife also plays a role in the discovery), an event that permits the lovers to be restored at last to their proper social position and united in matrimony. Ann Wiltrout has terms these "rites of passage," at the completion of which the males *resume* their proper social station and the females *assume* theirs.[45]

Thematically speaking, each story indeed demonstrates the need for a test, a trial, a purification rite of some sort, to strengthen and temper the emotional maturity of the young lovers before their marriage. This is especially necessary for the male partners, who must shed certain adolescent emotional baggage in order to learn new adult attitudes and behaviors. The process requires each suitor to eliminate an obvious character flaw that has heretofore impeded his maturation—feelings of jealousy in the case of Don Juan/Andrés, excessive shyness for Avendaño—before undertaking the

1 / Cervantes and the Crucible of Love

serious business of contracting matrimony. At least one critic has recently suggested the possibility that "the similarity between the two stories is intentional and meant to be noticed by the reader."[46]

Of even greater interest than these affinities, however, are the subtle ways in which these two stories differ, and it is in this latter area that I will concentrate in the present chapter. For example, in *La gitanilla* Don Juan/Andrés and Preciosa are the central focus of the narration; the entire story—including a secondary plot that features the fascinating presence of the amateur poet Clemente—revolves around their slow-developing relationship. In *La ilustre fregona*, on the other hand, the would-be lovers Tomás and Costanza are certainly conceived as two affable, virtually flawless youngsters, but they are essentially passive figures who generate little excitement or interest in the reader. They have only one noteworthy conversation and that exchange ends with the extremely shy Tomás's having his hopes of winning her temporarily dashed. The most interesting events that take place in the story have nothing at all to do with their budding romance, but are concerned instead with the simultaneous picaresque adventures of Tomás's friend Carriazo as a water seller in Toledo.

We should recall that Don Juan in *La gitanilla* is already quite smitten with Preciosa when he makes his first appearance. In the opening paragraphs of *Fregona*, however, Avendaño remains totally ignorant of Costanza's existence; one of the main threads of the narrative will be devoted to tracing the *process* by which Tomás falls in love with and courts Costanza.[47] The narrator takes us through every step, starting with the overheard remarks about her great beauty by two *mozos de mulas* in Illescas; we subsequently witness the first moment of Tomás's ardor when he spies her at the inn, their first verbal exchange, the young man's pangs of jealousy upon hearing the moonlight serenade in her honor by the corregidor's son, and Avendaño's own heavy-handed attempts at poetry and love letters. The principal obstacle to Tomás's success is his acute shyness and lack of experience in these matters. But even with Avendaño's inability to get his stumbling courtship under way, the sophisticated reader knows from the start that it is simply a matter of time until fate will bring these two attractive young people together.

Unlike the problem-fraught courtship in *La gitanilla* in which Preciosa imposes a platonic two-year probationary period upon Don Juan's courtship and in which the young man's excessive jealousy comes to be a real impediment to their happiness, there is no great obstacle for the lovers to surmount in *La ilustre fregona*. Consequently, no observable growth of affection or mutual understanding can be said to take place while Costanza and her suitor are becoming better acquainted, as is the case with Don Juan and Preciosa in *La gitanilla*. Instead, Tomás and the comely kitchen maid are simply yoked together at the end by the timely intervention of a deus ex machina.[48]

Over the years readers have come to esteem the spunky Preciosa because she plays such an active role in controlling her own destiny, i.e., selecting a mate on her own terms. The passive Costanza has fared less well in the critics' judgment because she is perceived as neither having nor wanting any role in determining the outcome of her life. Because of its more sophisticated characterization, then, *La gitanilla* is generally considered the superior work and has understandably enjoyed much greater popularity in modern times.

With regard to the construction of the plot, here again the critics have tended to favor *La gitanilla*. In the Gypsy tale we also have the mysterious figure of Clemente, the page-poet who appears at one point to be a serious rival for the affections of Preciosa but develops instead into Andrés's good friend and confidant, not to mention an important influence in helping his friend recognize and overcome his strong penchant for jealous reactions. No comparable figure exists in *La ilustre fregona*. The rivalry posed by the verse-spouting son of the corregidor is weak and unconvincing in comparison with the Clemente figure who continually stalks Preciosa in *La gitanilla*. This so-called rival in *La ilustre fregona* is easily disposed of by means of a quick-fix marriage to Avendaño's sister at the very end. Tomás Avendaño's friend Carriazo might normally have served as a convincing blocking agent for Tomás, but Cervantes has another plan in mind. Young Carriazo remains strangely impervious to the beauty and natural charm of Costanza from the start. And with good reason, as it turns out, for it is later revealed that he and the lovely maid are actually half-brother and sister. In Cervantes's fictional universe heredity generally tends to overcome the effects of external social factors; bloodlines often tell us as much about the characters and how they will react as the people themselves do through their conscious utterances, a factor that occasionally renders the characterization weak and somewhat predictable in his works.

Let us now turn our attention to the narrative structure of *La ilustre fregona*.

(A) Introduction: Family background of Carriazo and Avendaño

One of the most interesting aspects of *La ilustre fregona* is the fact that the opening paragraphs of this novella depart radically from the pattern normally found in Cervantes's short fiction. The Spanish writer generally likes to begin each story by presenting his protagonist(s) in action, as we note, for instance, in *Rinconete y Cortadillo* and *La gitanilla*. In the case of

La ilustre fregona, however, the story does not begin with a reference to the title character, nor does it introduce the two boys who will ultimately emerge as the protagonists of the tale. It opens instead by focusing on the comfortable lifestyle of the well-to-do fathers of the two major characters.

> En Burgos, ciudad ilustre y famosa, no ha muchos años que en ella vivían dos caballeros principales y ricos: el uno se llamaba don Diego de Carriazo, y el otro, don Juan de Avendaño. El don Diego tuvo un hijo, a quien llamó de su mismo nombre, y el don Juan otro, a quien puso don Tomás de Avendaño. A estos dos caballeros mozos, como quien [*sic*] han de ser las principales personas deste cuento, por escusar y ahorrar letras, les llamaremos con solos los nombres de Carriazo y Avendaño. (2:139)

> [Not long ago in Burgos, that city of great renown, there lived two noble, wealthy gentlemen. The first of these was called Don Diego de Carriazo, the other Don Juan de Avendaño. Both had sons: Don Diego named his son after himself and Don Juan called his Don Tomás de Avendaño. Since these two young gentlemen are to be the heroes of this story, we shall call them simply Carriazo and Avendaño, to be thrifty with words.] (3:63)

This is unusual because, although these two parental figures are destined to play an important role toward the end of the story, at this early point they have no real function in the narrative scheme; they vanish immediately after their introduction. This, too, is a departure from the Cervantine norm, because this author is not inclined in his other short works to introduce characters until the moment they are needed, on some occasions to advance the action of the plot, on others to clarify some obscure or forgotten issue. I believe Cervantes introduces the fathers in the opening paragraph because he has a totally different narrative plan in mind for *La ilustre fregona*. B. W. Ife would appear to agree. He considers the first two sentences of *Fregona* to be an artistic triumph for Cervantes, who skillfully establishes here a circular plot pattern that will culminate in the denouement, when the two father figures will suddenly emerge from the shadows to make their significance perfectly clear.[49] It is no mere coincidence that the young *pícaro*, Diego de Carriazo, should inherit both the name and the licentious disposition of his father; nor that Tomás de Avendaño is *not* named for his father, Juan. At the close of the story we learn that young Diego will raise three virtuous and studious sons, none of whom will bear his baptismal name. The implication is that, at least in this novella, the name "Diego" is the equivalent of "libertine." Carriazo's half of the story, therefore, is about his laying to rest the family curse.[50]

We need to note the many subtle ways in which the opening of *Fregona* departs from the pattern Cervantes established earlier in *La gitanilla*. Immediately following the opening account of the comfortable home life of the two protagonists in Burgos, the narrator begins his account of the artificially created picaresque adventures of one of the boys, Diego de Carriazo. If it had been Cervantes's intention to create a typical picaresque character in Carriazo, he certainly did not follow the pattern established by the original *pícaro*, Lazarillo de Tormes, or that of the even more celebrated creation of Mateo Alemán. From the outset Carriazo is presented as a curiously well-bred and aristocratic sort of ruffian:

> era generoso y bien partido con sus camaradas. Visitaba pocas veces las ermitas de Baco, y aunque bebía vino, era tan poco, que nunca pudo entrar en el número de los que llaman desgraciados.... En fin, en Carriazo vio el mundo un pícaro virtuoso, limpio, bien criado y más que medianamente discreto. (2:140)
>
> [he was generous and unselfish with his companions. He rarely worshipped at the altar of Bacchus, and although he drank wine, this was in such small quantities that he could never be counted among those unfortunate people who, when they overindulge, turn as red as if they had painted their faces with vermilion and ochre. In short, to the world Carriazo was a virtuous *pícaro*, unsullied by that life, well bred and with more than his fair share of wisdom.] (3:63)

The picaresque lifestyle of Carriazo, as described in the opening section of this story, is clearly nothing more than a literary pose designed to draw the reader's attention to the comfortable manorial upbringing behind Carriazo's phony *pícaro* mask. This should be contrasted with the case of *La gitanilla*, where the narrative begins with the focus on the real-life picaresque ambience of the Gypsy camp and Preciosa's life among the riffraff.

In both stories Cervantes likes to toy with the reader's expectations. By introducing the figure of the page-poet (originally called Don Sancho, then Alonso Hurtado, later Clemente) prior to the appearance of Don Juan/Andrés, the author leads the reader—at least temporarily—to believe that the poet may be the one destined to win the heart of the beautiful Gypsy girl. A similar deception is carried out in *La ilustre fregona* by offering a great deal of information about the bold Carriazo's picaresque adventures, but relatively little regarding the less colorful Avendaño. As a consequence, the reader is initially led to believe—again, falsely—that Carriazo will play the romantic lead in this piece.

On the surface, there are certain obvious parallels that can be drawn between the female leads in *Gitanilla* and *Fregona* and their male suitors.

But this apparent simplicity is deceiving. Preciosa's is a strong and complex personality, a fascinating combination of beauty and talent; Costanza can also boast of great physical attractiveness, but she has no discernible talent at all; she is simply a figurine, a passive character virtually devoid of personality.[51] The only things they really have in common are their remarkable pulchritude and the fact that they are both children of aristocratic parents who have been raised in a low socioeconomic environment. As for their male suitors, Don Juan de Cárcamo and Tomás de Avendaño have in common only their willingness to assume roles beneath their social station in order to win the hand of the object of their desire. However, as we shall see, even stronger resemblances exist between Preciosa's Don Juan and young Diego de Carriazo, who is a decidedly nonromantic character in *Fregona*.

It would seem, then, that the opening of *La ilustre fregona* is conceived to be the obverse of that of *La gitanilla*. In the story of the little Gypsy girl we are introduced immediately to the heroine but must bide our time until the male romantic lead makes his belated appearance. In *La ilustre fregona*, while the male partner is introduced early on, the heroine's appearance is delayed until the story is well under way.

I would take the previous observation one step further and state that the opening paragraphs of *La ilustre fregona* were specifically composed with *La gitanilla* in mind, and that they were carefully and deliberately designed by Cervantes to mislead any careless reader who might be tempted to make certain assumptions here based on what he or she had read in the earlier story. Consider the following: the first characters we meet, the boys' fathers, are not of any importance at the time and will not become significant until the very end of the story. The next personality presented, the younger Carriazo, although the most vibrant figure in the entire novella, will *not* be the romantic lead, contrary to what the reader might expect. The character who will emerge unexpectedly as Costanza's successful suitor is Tomás de Avendaño, who at first glance seems much too bland and colorless to be able to carry the story's action on his own callow shoulders. Given this radically different configuration in the design of the story, one soon begins to wonder what, exactly, Cervantes has in mind for this story. Even the critics cannot agree on this matter.

In his edition of the *Novelas ejemplares*, Harry Sieber has observed that, structurally speaking, *La ilustre fregona* is really two stories in one; what at first appears to be a purely picaresque narrative picks up a new, romantic thread once the two protagonists decide to remain in Toledo.[52] Each of the boys then becomes the protagonist of a separate, but equal, story. On the one hand we have a typical romantic intrigue: the timid Tomás de Avendaño's efforts to woo and win the heart of the fetching scullery maid, Costanza. This is complemented by a parallel picaresque narrative: the slow and painful maturation process at work in the life of Diego de Carriazo, who must eventually abandon his adolescent pursuit of the *pícaro*'s life and prepare himself to assume the duties and responsibilities of the high social station to which he was born.

J. B. Avalle-Arce, on the other hand, finds a distinct imbalance with regard to the relative importance of each of these two narrative threads. In his introduction to *Fregona*, Avalle-Arce states that this story is nothing less than Cervantes's formal response to Mateo Alemán's pessimistic definition of the picaresque.[53] While the parallel romantic adventures of Avendaño in pursuit of Costanza are a pleasant diversion, the real focus of the story is on Carriazo's picaresque adventures as a water seller in Toledo. Avendaño, once he has fulfilled his narrative function of falling in love with Costanza, is quietly pushed offstage ("como personaje es colocado entre bambalinas"); Carriazo's personality and his dangerous scrapes with various underworld figures are clearly intended to be the dominant element in the second half of the story[54]

A slightly different interpretation is offered by Javier Herrero, who views this story as a parody of the classic romance and comedic motif of the hero's descent from the Edenic to the Infernal World and back again.[55] In *Fregona* Cervantes draws clear lines between the pagan world of the *almadrabas* (tuna fisheries) of Cádiz and the water sellers of Toledo—a world marked by an atmosphere of unrestrained freedom, violence, and lascivious dances like the *chacona*—and the virtuous "straight" society of the aristocracy and bourgeoisie, where liberality, chastity, and wisdom (as personified by Costanza) are the norm. Cervantes's message is ironic insofar as he allows both of his aristocratic "heroes" to find spiritual renewal in the crucible of the unsavory underworld.[56]

Thomas R. Hart's interpretation is remarkably similar to Herrero's, with one major exception: he views the boys' self-renewing period of exile as a pastoral "sojourn in a natural setting," not a heroic "descent" to some sort of Hades. The *almadrabas*, for Hart, should be interpreted less as a symbol of the picaresque underworld than as a recasting of the shepherd's life as it appears within the pastoral tradition.[57]

Perhaps the most accurate and useful analysis of what is actually taking place in *Fregona* is that of Robert M. Johnston, whose interpretation is similar to Hart's but more broadly conceived. Johnston asserts that while the inn's setting appears to be picaresque, the general movement and form of the story are more comparable to that of the pastoral romance.[58] In many ways the inn at Toledo resembles the world of *La Galatea;* it is a place that overflows with poetry, music and dance. The common element shared by both the picaresque and pastoral genres—and, therefore, that which en-

1 / Cervantes and the Crucible of Love

ables Cervantes to combine them experimentally in the same story—is the freedom these modes afford their protagonists to live apart from the restrictions of ordinary society (172). Cervantes recognized that the picaresque and the pastoral were not necessarily antithetical literary forms and that they could conceivably be blended into a single narrative by an able artist. *Fregona*, then, represents the Spanish writer's attempt to do just that, which explains the curious bifurcation of the plot in section C to which I alluded earlier.

The romantic/pastoral portion of the story line (Avendaño and Costanza's courtship) is nowhere in evidence at the opening of the action. As one reads the first three or four paragraphs, one cannot be blamed for wondering what this particular story has to do with a scullery maid, illustrious or otherwise. It appears instead to deal with the adventures of a teenage boy from a wealthy family who has a strange taste for life down at the other end of the social spectrum among the low-lifes living and working at the tuna fisheries at Zahara. There can be no doubt as to Cervantes's negative opinion of the lifestyle of those who worked in the *almadrabas*, particularly in view of his sarcastic diatribe in the fourth paragraph of the story.

> ¡Oh pícaros de cocina, sucios, gordos y lucios, pobres fingidos, tullidos falsos, cicateruelos de Zocodover y de la plaza de Madrid, vistosos oracioneros, esportilleros de Sevilla, mandilejos de la hampa, con toda la caterva innumerable que se encierra debajo deste nombre *pícaro*! Bajad el toldo, amainad el brío, no os llaméis pícaros si no habéis cursado dos cursos en la academia de la pesca de los atunes. ¡Allí, allí, que está en su centro el trabajo junto con la poltronería! Allí está la suciedad limpia, la gordura rolliza, la hambre prompta, la hartura abundante, sin disfraz el vicio, el juego siempre, las pendencias por momentos, las muertes por puntos, las pullas a cada paso, los bailes como en bodas, las seguidillas como en estampa, los romances con estribos, la poesía sin acciones. Aquí se canta, allí se reniega, acullá se riñe, acá se juega, y por todo se hurta. Allí se campea la libertad y luce el trabajo; allí van, o envían, muchos padres principales a buscar a sus hijos, y los hallan; y tanto sienten sacarlos de aquella vida como si los llevaran a dar la muerte. (2:141)

> [Oh, you kitchen *pícaros*, filthy, fat and sleek, fake beggars, false cripples, pickpockets of Zocodover and the main square of Madrid, gaudy prayer-mongers, Sevillian carriers, serving boys of the underworld, with that whole numberless throng of those who are included under the name *pícaro*. Lower your sails, moderate your jaunty ways, and don't call yourselves *pícaros* unless you've studied for two years in the academy at the tunny fisheries. Yes, that's the place where industry and idleness go hand in hand! There the squalour is unmitigated, obesity is rife, hunger is round every corner, surfeit is rampant, vice undisguised, gambling ceaseless,

brawling constant; deaths may occur at any moment, there is swearing wherever you turn, dancing like at weddings; you hear *seguidillas* of the kind they publish, ballads that have refrains and poems that do not. Here they sing, there they curse, there they quarrel, here they gamble, and everywhere they steal. There freedom reigns and work is the exception. There many noble fathers seek their sons or send others to look for them, and find them. And the sons are as sad to be dragged away from that existence as if they were being taken to their deaths.] (3:63–65)

In summary, the introductory section (A) of *La ilustre fregona* is purposely deceptive. Everything contained therein is designed to give the reader the impression that this is going to be a picaresque tale—albeit an unusual one in which the main *pícaro* is in reality a spoiled rich kid. The real action begins when, returning for a brief visit to the manorial homestead after spending three years at the fisheries, the sly and persuasive Carriazo convinces his lifelong friend Tomás de Avendaño to embrace the picaresque lifestyle. The deceitful pair concoct a clever plan to persuade their parents to bankroll a year of "studies" at Salamanca, the funds for which they plan to use in their search for high adventure. At this point the reader might well expect a story modeled after *Rinconete y Cortadillo*, but that reader would be quite mistaken.

Transition I: Conversation overheard at the gates of Illescas

The second section of the story is really nothing more than a transitional interlude that takes place at the town of Illescas, where the two heroes overhear the conversation of two muleteers about the beautiful scullery maid at the Posada del Sevillano in Toledo. This is the spark that kindles in the boys—but especially in Avendaño—the desire to see this notable beauty, a decision that will alter the course of their wanderings, and indeed of their lives.

Ana María Barrenechea has commented on the unusual passive role Costanza plays in this novella. This is underscored by the manner in which the figure of the Illustrious Kitchen Maid is presented to the reader: through a series of oblique, indirect testimonials about her physical and moral qualities from people who have met her (e.g., the two young mule drivers, various guests at the inn, the innkeeper, the other employees of his establishment, etc.) combined with two direct descriptions of her angelic appearance and modest behavior, as they seem to the admiring eyes of Avendaño.[59] (More will be said about this in the next section; for the moment we need note that Costanza *does nothing*; she merely exists so that others may notice her and react to her.)

The transition scene reprises a narrative technique that Cervantes uti-

1 / Cervantes and the Crucible of Love

lized earlier during the battle of Don Quixote and the Biscayan in chapter 8 of the 1605 *Quixote:* when Cervantes's narrator suddenly interrupts his account to introduce a completely new and supplemental authorial figure, Moorish historian *(autor)* Cide Hamete Benengeli. In this novella, the narrator suddenly interrupts his account of the boys' escape to provide us instead with the full text of the explanatory letter they leave for Carriazo's majordomo as they make their break for freedom. When he resumes his account of the boys' adventures, the narrator declines to speculate about what the majordomo may have reported to the elder Carriazo upon returning to Burgos because the (unnamed) original author of this story has left no clue: "destas cosas no dice nada el autor de esta novela" (2:146). The action simply resumes, following this strategic ellipsis, at the gates of Illescas, where the protagonists come upon the two Andalusian mule drivers mentioned earlier.

(C) Bifurcated narrative:
  (C¹) Courtship of Costanza by Avendaño at the inn
  (C²) Adventures of Carriazo in town as a water seller

The third narrative block begins with the arrival of Carriazo and Avendaño at the Inn of the Sevillian in Toledo, and it is at this point that the narrative breaks into two distinct channels: (C¹) to trace Avendaño's courtship of Costanza; and (C²) to follow the misadventures of Carriazo as a water merchant in Toledo. For the duration of this rather extended section Cervantes will present alternating scenes dealing with the two leading male characters.

(C¹): Upon arriving in Toledo, the boys immediately search for the Posada del Sevillano. On this initial occasion only Avendaño actually enters the inn to meet the famous *fregona;* Carriazo chooses to remain outside. The complete details of Costanza's physical appearance are consciously withheld at this point; the narrator presents his subject here solely as she appears to Avendaño's eyes, which we are told focus only on the young girl's face. The result is a dreamlike, angelic vision, framed in soft candlelight, that leaves young Tomás stunned and speechless:[60]

> No puso Avendaño los ojos en el vestido y traje de la moza, sino en su rostro, que le parecía ver en él los que suelen pintar de los ángeles. Quedó suspenso y atónito de su hermosura, y no acertó a preguntarle nada, tal era su suspensión y embelesamiento. (2:149)

> [Avendaño was oblivious of the girl's dress but stared at her face, which to him looked like an angel's, just as in the paintings. He was

awestruck by her beauty and could not think of anything to say to her, so stunned and entranced was he.] (3:73)

The mysterious atmosphere surrounding the renowned beauty builds in a predawn scene when the boys are awakened by the sounds of the elaborately staged serenade in honor of Costanza by the corregidor's son. Although the legendary *fregona* never actually makes an appearance at this impromptu concert, we are told that the performance manages to stir feelings of jealousy in Avendaño's soul. It is only with Costanza's arrival at breakfast the next morning that the reader—along with Carriazo, let us note—finally receives an objective glimpse of the central character's physical attractiveness:

> Su vestido era una saya y corpiños de paño verde, con unos ribetes del mismo paño. Los corpiños eran bajos; pero la camisa, alta, plegado al cuello, con un cabezón labrado de seda negra, puesta una gargantilla de estrellas de azabache sobre un pedazo de una colu[m]na de alabastro, que no era menos blanca su garganta; ceñida con un cordón de San Francisco, y de otra cinta pendiente, al lado derecho, un gran manojo de llaves. No traía chinelas, sino zapatos de dos suelas, colorados, con unas calzas que no se le parecían sino cuanto por un perfil mostraban también ser coloradas. Traía tranzados los cabellos con unas cintas blancas de hiladillo; pero tan largo el tranzado, que por las espaldas le pasaba de la cintura; el color salía de castaño y tocaba en rubio; pero, al parecer, tan limpio, tan igual y tan peinado, que ninguno, aunque fuera de hebras de oro, se le pudiera comparar. Pendíanle de las orejas dos calabacillas de vidrio, que parecían perlas; los mismos cabellos de servían de garbín y de tocas. (2:155–56)

> [Her skirt and bodice were of green material, with a border of the same cloth. The bodice was low-cut but the chemise was high and pleated at the throat with a collar of embroidered black silk, a necklace of jet-black stars on an alabaster column, for her throat was no less white. She had a cord of St. Francis around her waist and a big bunch of keys hanging from a ribbon at her right side. She did not wear clogs but double-soled red shoes with stockings which could hardly be seen except from the sides and they were also red. She wore her hair in plaits which were tied with white gimp ribbons, but they were so long that they hung below her waist. Her hair was lighter than chestnut, verging on blonde, and seemed so neat, even and well-combed that none could compare with it, even though it were strands of gold. From her ears there hung two little glass pendants, gourd-shaped, which looked like pearls. Her hair served both as a coif and a head-dress.] (3:79)

Although special attention is placed here on Costanza's clothing and accessories, once again, as more than one critic has observed, the emphasis is clearly upon the frame of the young girl's face, neck, and hair.[61] Monique Joly observes that the inauthenticity of Costanza's servant-girl appearance is slyly alluded to in the fact that she wears "zapatos de dos suelas" ['double-soled red shoes'] instead of the usual *chinelas*, and that no reference at all is made to an apron, which should be an essential part of her livery.[62]

A third descriptive passage—this time of Costanza's behavior rather than just her physical appearance—is used to give testimony to the maiden's most outstanding virtues: her religiosity *(devoción)* and modesty *(recato)*. In one of his most effective pieces of characterization, Cervantes manages to capture the essence of her personality in a single paragraph describing her reaction upon discovering the two boys observing her devotional activities on the patio:

> Cuando salió de la sala se persignó y santiguó, y con mucha devoción y sosiego hizo una profunda reverencia a una imagen de Nuestra Señora que en una de las paredes del patio estaba colgada; y alzando los ojos, vio a los dos que mirándola estaban, y apenas los hubo visto, cuando se retiró y volvió a entrar en la sala, desde la cual dio voces a Argüello que se levantase. (2:156)

> [When she came out of the room she made the sign of the cross and in a composed, devout fashion she genuflected deeply before a statue of Our Lady which was hanging on one of the walls of the courtyard. Looking up she saw the pair staring at her and no sooner had she seen them than she went back into her room. From there she shouted to Argüello to get up.] (3:79)

There is yet another curious note about this encounter: we are told that Carriazo is much less captivated by Costanza's pulchritude than is his companion; unlike the smitten Tomás, Carriazo sees no reason to delay their departure for the tuna fisheries in Cádiz:

> a Carriazo le pareció tan bien como a su compañero, pero enamoróle mucho menos; y tan menos, que quisiera no anochecer en la posada, sino a partirse luego para sus almadrabas. (2:156)

> [she seemed as beautiful to Carriazo as to his companion, but . . . she aroused less passionate feelings in him. So much less that he did not want to spend another night at the inn but to set off for the tunny fisheries there and then.] (3:79)

Luckily for Avendaño, their sojourn at the inn is prolonged when the boys are able to secure jobs there, Tomás working indoors at the inn and Carriazo (under the name "Lope Asturiano") on the outside as a water merchant. At this point we are also introduced to Argüello and Gallega, a pair of ragged serving wenches who recall the lubricious Maritornes who plagued poor Don Quixote. This pair will provide a measure of comic relief via their unbridled romantic pursuit of "Lope" and Tomás, respectively.

For Thomas Hanrahan, erotic attraction in Cervantes's works is always a question of passion versus reason. Romantic antagonists like Argüello and Gallega—following in the footsteps of Juana Carducha in *La gitanilla* and the lustful Turks of *El amante liberal*—are those characters "whose passions and appetites are not completely under the control of reason, who satisfy these appetites choosing that which is morally reprehensible."[63] Cervantes places them in the story to serve as the comic antithesis of the moral perfection of Costanza.

(C²): "Lope"/Carriazo almost immediately finds himself in a violent encounter with a rival water vendor, an event that terminates with his being taken into custody when the other man is found near death from the wounds Carriazo has inflicted upon him. It is left to Avendaño to secure his release and smooth over all the hard feelings by paying for the lost mule and other damages to the tune of sixteen *ducados*. Once released from jail, Carriazo is reluctant to return to the inn because of the unwanted attentions of Argüello.

(C¹): Meanwhile, back at the inn, Avendaño continues to face mild competition for Costanza's attention from the son of the corregidor, a mediocre amateur poet who composes sonnets in honor of the beautiful scullery maid. To complicate matters even further, the offensive Argüello and Gallega are becoming more and more aggressive in their attentions to Carriazo and Avendaño. The situation takes a turn even less favorable for Tomás when the innkeeper and his wife discover some verses he has composed in Costanza's honor.

Tomás's first opportunity to speak with Costanza presents itself when she is suffering from a toothache and he offers to write for her a special prayer to relieve the pain. He hands her instead a love note in which he mentions his noble background, confesses his passion for her, and actually proposes marriage. Her reaction could not be more deflating or crushing to the delicate, shy spirit of Avendaño: she shreds his note, believing it to be some kind of cruel joke he is playing on her. His only consolation is that he still believes no one else is aware of his feelings for the young beauty.

(C²): Back in the real world, Carriazo—now called simply el Asturiano—is attempting to purchase a hearty beast of burden that will enable him to continue in the role of water carrier. Having invested some sixteen

ducados in a donkey and its trappings, the foolish young man immediately loses his entire investment in a shady card game. Somehow he manages to convince the other players to let him play one final hand using the ass's tail as his last bargaining chip. He stages a tremendous comeback and winds up not only regaining his lost animal but sweeping up all of his opponents' money as well. Having triumphed so magnificently, Carriazo then graciously distributes all his winnings among the other players—he's really an aristocrat, we must recall, so this should not be a surprising development—and walks away from the game with a well-deserved reputation among the water sellers for his skill as a gambler. To his dismay, however, the only part of the episode that anyone remembers is the fact that he gambled an ass's tail and won. Consequently, he will soon be haunted by jeers from the townspeople and their children such as "¡Daca la cola, Asturiano!" [Give us the tail, Asturiano!]. The combination of this new notoriety and the increasing attentions of the slovenly Argüello eventually compel poor Carriazo to seek lodging at another hostelry.

The physical separation of the two protagonists at this point is not absolutely essential to the telling of the story, but it does have the poetic effect of confirming and underscoring the previous splitting of the story line into two parallel and alternating narrative threads. This bifurcation has been viewed by several critics as a simply an artistic representation of a fundamental duality that permeates the story.

Casalduero was the first to observe that the contrast between the respective personalities of Carriazo and Avendaño is intended to symbolize a series of natural oppositions that Cervantes found to exist in human society: *pícaro* versus student; the carefree life versus a life with social responsibilities; the inn versus the convent, etc. The two polar extremes of erotic attraction, for example, are portrayed especially well in the lascivious figures of Argüello and Gallega, on one hand, and in the wholesome and virtuous Costanza, on the other.[64]

In the judgment of Ruth El Saffar, Carriazo and Avendaño are simply twin substitutes for the Andrés character in *La gitanilla;* Carriazo bears the athletic, physical, adventuresome attributes of the conventional male protagonist, while Avendaño represents the more passive, patient attributes of the obedient and hopeful suitor. La Argüello and La Gallega, conversely, can be said to duplicate the role of Juana Carducha; these characters, according to El Saffar, are evil, grotesque, and occasionally ridiculous blocking agents who foolishly attempt to force circumstances or other characters' wills.[65]

Ann Wiltrout has a slightly different configuration in mind: the female characters—Argüello and Gallega to some extent, but principally Costanza—serve as a point of reference for both the amorous and picaresque literary motifs, which are represented by the adventures of Avendaño and Carriazo, respectively.[66] B. W. Ife contends that the novella deals with the following contrasting opposites: order/disorder, stasis/movement, and the geographical opposition of Old Castle/Burgos and New Castile/Toledo.[67]

To Ana María Barrenechea's way of thinking, the parallel secondary intrigues reflect a number of Cervantine preoccupations, ranging from the purely literary (the *novela sentimental* in Avendaño's case versus the adventure story in Carriazo's) to the social (Costanza as the embodiment of chaste romantic attraction *[amor ideal]* versus the base, picaresque coupling sought by Argüello and Gallega). Barrenechea views Avendaño's series of adventures as noble and exemplary, while Carriazo's are considered purely comic in inspiration.[68] The alternating pattern of narration, then, indicates that Cervantes is employing a point/counterpoint method: each of Avendaño's "serious" romantic adventures at the inn is immediately followed by a comic parody of it in a parallel episode involving his friend Carriazo.

(D) Transition II: Six days without incident

The next narrative block is a very brief synopsis of the stagnation that soon afflicts both strands of narrative. For a period of six days Carriazo refuses to leave his new lodging in daylight for fear of encountering the army of tormentors who seem to await him on every street corner; at the same time Tomás Avendaño's pursuit of Costanza, because of the embarrassing episode of the love note, appears to have bogged down completely. This section has the strictly transitional function of terminating the section devoted to the boys' misadventures in Toledo and preparing us for the introduction of new characters and the startling revelations that will follow in the final two narrative sections.

(E) Arrival of the corregidor
(F) The innkeeper's story

As was the case also in *La gitanilla*, the climax of this story is reached with the sudden and unexpected appearance of a deus ex machina, the corregidor (and his wife). The royal official, his curiosity aroused by the copious ravings of various townspeople and his own smitten son, arrives at the inn to witness the celebrated beauty of the wondrous scullery maid for himself. The corregidor's many questions about Costanza and how she came to reside and work at the inn provoke the inn's proprietor to reveal the strange occurrences and odd coincidences that were responsible for bringing her to them. The innkeeper's account, narrated in a flashback sequence

(F), reveals only half the secret—the maternal circumstances, so to speak—of Costanza's mysterious birth at the inn fifteen years before to a middle-aged widow of very noble lineage. The corregidor is also shown the two keys that will unlock the mystery: a gold chain with six missing links and a parchment torn along a zigzag line to reveal alternating letters in a coded message.

(G) Arrival of the elder Carriazo and Avendaño; Denouement
(H) Don Diego's story

The final pieces of the puzzle are set in place the next day with the arrival of two distinguished-looking elderly gentlemen who turn out to be—ever so conveniently—the fathers of Carriazo and Avendaño. In addition to the anticipated pair of reconciliations between father and son, this section also features a surprising revelation regarding the paternal circumstances of Costanza's birth: her real father is the elder Diego de Carriazo, which provides a "natural" explanation for young Carriazo's initial and continuing resistance to her charms. Still another startling development awaits us in don Diego's summary of past events (H), where we learn that Costanza was conceived in an act of rape. Once again, Cervantes relies upon hereditary factors and bloodlines to explain the bizarre behavior of one of his characters. The elder Carriazo's youthful libertine misconduct also serves to provide us with a plausible explanation—at least in terms of seventeenth-century medical science—for his son's strange and persistent attraction to the roguish lifestyle of the *pícaros*.

Casalduero considers *Fregona* to be primarily about original sin (with Costanza in the mediating role of the Virgin Mary), which makes it a novella more appropriately termed picaresque than idealistic.[69] For Casalduero, a major theme, albeit one that is not introduced until very late in the story, is the transmission of a sinful, hedonistic nature from father to son. The elder Carriazo has passed his libertine disposition to his namesake, who relishes the unrestrained and immoral life he has found at the tuna fisheries of Cádiz. Ultimately, however, each is obliged to atone for his sins. The senior Carriazo is obliged to acknowledge publicly the illegitimate daughter his lust has brought into this world, then endow her in a proper marriage. Young Diego is made pay for his earlier misadventures with the pain he endures and the blood he sheds as part of his experiences as a water seller. Even as an adult, we are told in the story's final sentence, Carriazo is periodically haunted by fearful flashbacks of the taunt "¡Daca la cola, Asturiano!" whenever he comes across a water seller and his animal.

All of this notwithstanding, the denouement of *La ilustre fregona* is remarkably optimistic and upbeat. As a gesture of nobility, don Diego provides ample compensation to the innkeeper and his wife, who have generously raised the orphaned Costanza as their own daughter. At the same time a number of dynastically satisfying marriages are quickly arranged to resolve matters neatly and dispose of annoying loose ends. Costanza's union with young Tomás de Avendaño is the key, of course, but we must also admire the smoothness with which Cervantes, from the chaos that has reigned to this point, is able at the final moment to restore harmony on all fronts by weaving a tapestry of marital bonds that will produce firm and enduring political and economic alliances among three powerful families. We cannot ignore the strategic importance of the corregidor in the disposition and arrangement of these marriages; he provides two essential elements: a daughter to be wed to young Carriazo and a son to be united with Avendaño's daughter. It should not surprise us that the daughters of the corregidor and Avendaño remain unidentified by name. With good reason B. W. Ife has called this "one of the most outrageously daring and brilliantly executed denouements in Spanish Golden Age fiction."[70]

The most uplifting message of all is one that has to be read between the lines: that it is possible to break the chain in the transmission of sins from generation to generation. We learn on the final page that Carriazo and the corregidor's daughter produce three fine sons, none of whom have ever breathed a word about tuna fisheries and all of whom have taken after their uncle Tomás by becoming serious university students at Salamanca.[71]

Aside from the purely structural concerns that have been the focus of the previous discussion, I would like to mention one outstanding element of *La ilustre fregona* that merits special attention: Cervantes's insertion of witty dialogue at key points in the narrative for comic relief. This tale features some of the breeziest and snappiest repartee in all of his writings. In this respect it is reminiscent of *Rinconete y Cortadillo* as well as some of the more hilarious scenes from *Don Quixote* and the theatrical *entremeses* (one-act comedies).

I will begin by referring to an excerpt of street jargon reminiscent of Monipodio's underworld brotherhood *(cofradía)*, a comic exchange that Carriazo and Avendaño overhear in section B between two young muleteers—one coming from Seville, the other headed toward the Andalusian metropolis—who meet at the gates of Illescas:

> —Si no fueran mis amos adelante, todavía me detuviera algo más, a preguntarte mil cosas que deseo saber; porque me has maravillado mucho con lo que me has contado de que el Conde ha ahorcado a Alonso Genís y a Ribera, sin querer otorgarles la apelación.
> —¡Oh pecador de mí!—replicó el sevillano—. Armóles el Conde zancadilla, cogióles debajo de su jurisdic[c]ión, que eran soldados, y por contrabando se aprovechó dellos, sin que la Audiencia se los pudiese

quitar. Sábete, amigo, que tiene un Bercebú en el cuerpo este conde de Puñonrostro, que nos mete los dedos de su puño en el alma. Barrida está Sevilla y diez leguas a la redonda de jácaros; no para ladrón en sus contornos. Todos le temen como al fuego, aunque ya se suena que dejará presto el cargo de Asistente, porque no tiene condición para verse a cada paso en dimes ni diretes con los señores de la Audiencia.

—¡Vivan ellos mil años—dijo el que iba a Sevilla—, que son padres de los miserables y amparo de los desdichados! ¡Cuántos pobretes están mascando barro no más de por la cólera de un juez absoluto, de un corregidor, o mal informado, o bien apasionado! Más ven muchos ojos que dos: no se apodera tan presto el veneno de la injusticia de muchos corazones como se apodera de uno solo.

—Predicador te has vuelto—dijo el de Sevilla—, y según llevas la retahila, no acabarás tan presto, y yo no te puedo aguardar; y esta noche no vayas a posar donde sueles, sino en la posada del Sevillano, porque verás el ella la más hermosa fregona que se sabe; Marinilla la de la venta Tejada es asco en su comparación; no te digo más sino que hay fama que el hijo del Corregidor bebe los vientos por ella. Uno desos mis amos que allá van jura que al volver que vuelva al Andalucía se ha de estar dos meses en Toledo y en la misma posada, sólo por hartarse de mirarla. Ya le dejo yo en señal un pellizco, y me llevo en contracambio un gran tornisón. Es dura como un mármol, y zahareña como villana de Sayago, y áspera como una ortiga; pero tiene una cara de pascua y un rostro de buen año: en una mejilla tiene el sol, y en la otra, la luna; la una es hecha de rosas y la otra de claveles, y en entrambas hay también azucenas y jazmines. No te digo más sino que la veas, y verás que no te he dicho nada, según lo que te pudiera decir, acerca de su hermosura. En las dos mulas rucias que sabes que tengo mías la dotara de buena gana si me la quisieran dar por mujer; pero yo sé que no me la darán: que es joya para un arcipreste o para un conde. Y otra vez torno a decir que allá lo verás. Y adiós, que me mudo. (2:147–48)

["If my masters weren't so far ahead I'd stay here a bit longer to ask you a hundred and one things I'd like to know. For I'm staggered by what you said about the Count hanging Alonso Genís and Ribera, without granting them an appeal."

"Lord help us," replied the one coming from Seville. "The Count played a dirty trick on them, seizing them when they were under his jurisdiction, saying they were soldiers, and he craftily took advantage of them without the High Court being able to claim them from him. I tell you, my friend, this Count of Puñonrostro is the very devil, and he doesn't give us a moment's peace. Seville, and ten leagues round about, has been swept clean of villains. Not a single robber lingers round there. They all fear him like fire, though they say he'll soon leave the office of Asistente because he isn't a man to put up forever with squabbling with the gentlemen of the High Court."

"Long may they live!" said the other, "for they watch over and protect the wretched! How many poor devils are dead and buried because of the anger of a hardline judge acting alone or a corregidor who is ill-informed or biased! Many eyes see the truth clearer than two; the poison of injustice takes effect more quickly in one heart than in many."

"You've become a real preacher, you have," said the first man. "The way you're going on, you'll never stop, and I can't afford to wait for you. And tonight, don't stay where you usually do but in the Sevillano Inn, because there you'll see the most beautiful kitchen-maid ever. Mantilla, of the Tejada Inn, isn't a patch on her. I'll say no more except that it's rumoured that the Corregidor's son is besotted with her. One of my masters who's gone ahead swears that when he comes back to Andalusia he intends to stay two months in Toledo at the very same inn just so that he can feast his eyes on her. I gave her a pinch to remember me by and I got a cuff for my pains in return. She's as hard as marble, as unsociable as a peasant-girl from Sayago and her sting is sharp as a nettle's. But she's a fair lass, with a face like an angel. On one cheek the sun shines, on the other the moon gleams. One cheek is made of roses, the other of carnations, and on both there are lilies and jasmine besides. I'll say no more but you go see her for yourself, and you'll see that what I've told you about her beauty is as nothing compared with what I might have said. I'd make a dowry to her of those two grey mules of mine if they'd give me her as my wife. But I know they will not: she'll be the treasure of some archpriest or count. I tell you again you'll see all that. Goodbye now; I'm for the road."] (3:69–71)

The same might be said for the dialogue between innkeeper, who favors hiring Carriazo as a water carrier, and the chambermaids Argüello and Gallega, who are opposed to the idea:

La Argüello . . . oyendo decir a Avendaño que él se fiaba a su compañero, dijo:

—Dígame, gentilhombre, ¿y quién le ha de fiar a él? Que en verdad que me parece que más necesidad tiene de ser fiado que de ser fiador.

—Calla, Argüello—dijo el huésped—; no te metas donde no te llaman; yo los fío a entrambos, y por vida de vosotras que no tengáis dares ni tomares con los mozos de casa, que por vosotras se me van todos.

—Pues qué—dijo otra moza—, ¿ya se quedan en casa estos mancebos? Para mi santiguada que si yo fuera camino con ellos, que nunca las fiara la bota.

—Déjese de chocarrerías, señora Gallega—respondió el huésped—, y haga su hacienda, y no se entremeta con los mozos, que la moleré a palos.

—¡Por cierto sí!—replicó la Gallega—. ¡Mirad qué joyas para codiciallas! Pues en verdad que no me ha hallado el señor mi amo tan juguetona con los mozos de casa, ni de fuera, para tenerme en la mala

1 / CERVANTES AND THE CRUCIBLE OF LOVE 87

piñón que me tiene: ellos son bellacos, y se van cuando se les antoja, sin que nosotras les demos ocasión alguna. ¡Bonica gente es ella, por cierto, para tener necesidad de apetites que los inciten a dar un madrugón a sus amos cuando menos se percatan!
—Mucho habláis, Gallega hermana—respondió su amo—; punto en boca, y atended a lo que tenéis a vuestro cargo. (2:158)

[Argüello . . . on hearing Avendaño say he could guarantee his companion's trustworthiness, said:
"Tell me, good sir, who on earth would put their trust in *him?* Indeed, I'd say, someone ought to stand surety for him, not him for another."
"Hold your peace, Argüello," said the innkeeper. "Don't poke your nose in where you're not wanted. I'll be guarantor for both of them, and don't you dare squabble with my inn-lads. It's your doing that they all leave me."
"Well I never," said another girl, "so are these lad staying at the inn then? I'm blessed if I'd trust them with the wineskins if I were travelling with them."
"Enough of your lip, madame Gallega," retorted the innkeeper. "You get on with your work and don't you meddle with my lads or I'll give you a walloping."
"Oh yes indeed," answered Gallega. "What precious stones they are to take your fancy! When has my master seen me flirting with the boys, in the inn or outside it, to have such a low opinion of me, may I ask? They're rogues and they'll leave when it takes their fancy without any of us giving them an excuse. They're a fine lot, says I, to need inducements to desert their masters suddenly when they are off their guard."
"You talk too much, Gallega my sister," replied the innkeeper. "Hold your tongue and attend to the work you have to do."] (3:81–83)

For a reprise of the sometimes barbed and nonsensical dialogue that characterizes the discussions of Don Quixote and Sancho we need look no further than the absurd argument about the legendary beauty of the *ilustre fregona* between the skeptical Carriazo, who to this point has never seen Costanza, and the totally smitten Avendaño.

—¡Ta, ta!—replicó Carriazo—. A mí me maten, amigo, si no estáis vos con más deseo de quedaros en Toledo que de seguir nuestra comenzada romería.
—Así es la verdad—respondió Avendaño—; y aun tan imposible será apartarme de ver el rostro desta doncella como no es posible ir al cielo sin buenas obras.
—¡Gallardo encarecimiento—dijo Carriazo—y determinación digna de un tan generoso pecho como el vuestro! ¡Bien cuadra un don Tomás de Avendaño, hijo de Juan de Avendaño, caballero lo que es bueno, rico

lo que basta, mozo lo que alegra, discreto lo que admira, con enamorado y perdido por una fregona que sirve en el mesón del Sevillano!

—Lo mismo me parece a mí que es—respondió Avendaño—considerar un don Diego de Carriazo, hijo del mismo, caballero del hábito de Alcántara el padre, y el hijo a pique de heredarle con su mayorazgo, no menos gentil en el cuerpo que en el ánimo, y con todos estos generosos atributos, verle enamorado, ¿de quién, si pensáis? ¿De la reina Ginebra? No, por cierto, sino de la almadraba de Zahara, que es más fea, a lo que creo, que un miedo de santo Antón.

¡Pata es la traviesa, amigo!—respondió Carriazo—. Por los filos que te herí me has muerto; quédese aquí nuestra pendencia, y vámonos a dormir, y amanecerá Dios, y medraremos.

—Mira, Carriazo; hasta ahora no has visto a Costanza; en viéndola, te doy licencia para que me digas todas las injurias y reprehensiones que quisieres.

—Ya sé yo en qué ha de parar esto—dijo Carriazo.

—¿En qué?—replicó Avendaño.

—En que yo me iré con mi almadraba y tú te quedarás con tu fregona—dijo Carriazo.

—No seré yo tan venturoso—dijo Avendaño.

—Ni yo tan necio—respondió Carriazo—que por seguir tu mal gusto deje de conseguir el bueno mío. (2:152–53)

["I see, I see," said Carriazo. "I'll swear, my friend, you'd rather stay here in Toledo than continue the pilgrimage we've begun."

"That's a fact," answered Avendaño. "So much so that for me to give up seeing the face of that maid is as impossible as to go to heaven without good works."

"Praise indeed," said Carriazo, "and a decision worthy of a heart as generous as yours! How fitting it is for one Don Tomás de Avendaño, son of Don Juan de Avendaño, every bit a gentleman, well off, a merry young man, eminently sensible, to fall head over heels in love with a serving-girl at the Sevillano Inn!"

"In just the same way it seems to me," answered Avendaño, "we may consider one Don Diego Carriazo, son of a gentleman of the same name, the father a knight of the order of Alcántara, and the son as agreeable in body as in mind, on the point of inheriting his *mayorazgo*. With all these fine qualities, witness him in love, and with whom if you please? With Queen Guinevere? Certainly not, but with the tunny fisheries at Zahara, which are more repugnant, in my opinion, than the temptations of Saint Anthony."

"Touché, my friend!" responded Carriazo. "You've given me a dose of my own medicine. Let our quarrel rest there, and let's turn in now. With the new day our fortunes will look up."

"Look, Carriazo, you've not seen Costanza yet. When you do, I give you leave to revile me and scold me as much as you like."

"I know how all this is going to end up," said Carriazo.
"How?" asked Avendaño.
"I'll go off to my tunny fisheries and you'll stay here with your kitchen-maid," said Carriazo.
"I won't be so lucky," said Avendaño.
"Nor I so stupid," retorted Carriazo, "as to miss out on my good fortune by following your bad judgement."] (3:75)

Another comic dialogue results from the boys' ridiculous speculations as to how Costanza could have come to be called "la ilustre fregona" when no one has ever seen her touching, much less actually washing, a dish.

—Paso señor Tomás—replicó Lope [Carriazo]—; vámonos poquito a poquito en esto de las alabanzas de la señora fregona, si no quiere que, como le tengo por loco, le tenga por hereje.
—¿Fregona has llamado a Costanza, hermano Lope?—respondió Tomás—. Dios te lo perdone y te traiga a verdadero conocimiento de tu yerro.
—Pues, ¿no es fregona?—replicó el Asturiano [Carriazo].
—Hasta ahora le tengo por ver fregar el primer plato.
—No importa—dijo Lope—no haberle visto fregar el primer plato, si le has visto fregar el segundo, y aun el centísimo.
—Yo te digo, hermano—replicó Tomás—, que ella no friega ni entiende otra cosa que en su labor, y en ser guarda de la plata labrada que hay en casa, que es mucha.
—Pues ¿cómo la llaman por toda la ciudad—dijo Lope—la fregona ilustre, si es que no friega? Mas sin duda debe de ser que como friega plata, y no loza, la dan el nombre de ilustre. (2:163–64)

["Hold on, Tomás my friend," answered Lope; "go steady in praising your kitchen-maid unless you want me to take you for a heretic as well as a fool."
"Are you calling Costanza a kitchen-maid, brother Lope?" answered Tomás. "May God forgive you and bring you to a true understanding of your error."
"Well, isn't she a kitchen-maid?" retorted Asturiano.
"I've yet to see her wash her first dish."
"It doesn't matter," said Lope, "that you haven't seen her wash her first dish, if you have see her wash her second or even her hundredth."
"I tell you, brother," answered Tomás, "that she does not wash dishes nor is she concerned with anything but her needlework and with looking after the silverware at the inn, of which there is a great amount."
"Then why do they call her the illustrious kitchen-maid throughout the city, if she doesn't wash the dishes?" said Lope. "It must be because she shines silver, and not crockery, that they call her 'illustrious.'"] (3:87–89)

Some gently barbed remarks are exchanged again when the innkeeper and his wife—neither of whom is particularly qualified to make such a judgment—attempt to make sense out of the verses Tomás Avendaño has composed in honor of Costanza. We have here echoes of Sancho and Teresa Panza. And finally I would like to point to the rambling comic monologue delivered by La Gallega. In response to a simple inquiry as to the name of the beautiful kitchen worker, the foul-mouthed serving wench suddenly launches into a venomous, whining tirade against Costanza that only Fernando de Rojas's Celestina could have hoped to equal.

—La moza se llama Costanza; ni es parienta del huésped ni de la huéspeda, ni sé lo que es; sólo digo que la doy a la mala landre, que no sé qué tiene que no deja hacer baza a ninguna de las mozas que estamos en esta casa. ¡Pues en verdad que tenemos nuestras facciones como Dios nos las puso! No entra huésped que no pregunte luego quién es la hermosa, y que no diga: "Bonita es; bien parece; a fe que no es mala; mal año para las más pintadas; nunca peor me la depare la fortuna"; y a nosotras no hay quien nos diga: "¿Qué tenéis ahí, diablos, o mujeres, o lo que sois?" (2:192)

["The girl's name is Costanza. She is a relative of neither the innkeeper nor his wife, nor do I know what she is. All I can say is a pox on her, for I don't know what it is about her but she doesn't let any of us girls in this inn get a look in. Hasn't God given us good looks too? There's not a guest who comes in that doesn't ask who the beautiful girl is and that doesn't say: 'Isn't she pretty?'; 'She's gorgeous'; 'My, she isn't bad-looking'; 'You won't see any to beat her'; 'May my luck with women hold.' And as for us, they don't even say: 'What have we here, devils, women or what?'"] (3:125)

Conclusion

Although, as I have demonstrated graphically, *La gitanilla* and *La ilustre fregona* share the same basic narrative pattern, their correspondences go beyond that single point. Each story's denouement, for example, features a contrived recognition scene that manages to resolve neatly all the principal characters' conflicts. Thematically, both are structured around the classical model of a hero's descent into the underworld to rescue a damsel in distress. Theresa Ann Sears offers an unconventional interpretation of the "damsel in distress" device, particularly as it is portrayed in *La gitanilla*'s kidnap motif. In virtually all of Cervantes's novellas that culminate in the marriage of the protagonists, she asserts, the real issue is how a culture's morality regards property, marriageable females being "the most symbolically resonant property of all." Cervantes frequently sets the stage by having the beautiful heroine transported to a perilous situation or some morally inferior society as a result of a clearly inappropriate act like kidnapping, rape, or seduction; the hero's ensuing quest is to have the precious "property" restored to civilized society, where valuable objects are bought and paid for, not stolen. The moral of the story, by implication, is that in a "right" society valuable commodities like nubile daughters must not be kidnapped, raped, or auctioned off; they can be legitimately acquired only through the socially sanctioned institution of marriage.[72]

Of far greater significance and interest are the many fundamental points where *Gitanilla* and *Fregona* diverge. Both stories can be said to have competing romantic and picaresque intrigues, but in *Gitanilla* the romantic thread of narrative clearly dominates the action. In *Fregona* both themes are more equally balanced, and are often directly counterposed in alternating scenes. This is the "generic cross-breeding" *[hibridación genérica]* to which Jorge Checa refers in his analysis of the story.[73] The picaresque existence of Carriazo, characterized as it is by gratuitous reversals of fortune and dominated by elements of pure chance, contradicts the strict sense of order and causality that permeates the parallel universe where Avendaño courts the lovely Costanza (36).

As for plot movement and tone, we note that the pace of the highly symbolic Gypsy narrative tends to be slowed by its inherent thematic gravity, and, except for a couple of early scenes when Preciosa's sprightly personality *(desenvoltura)* is being showcased, the story is uncharacteristically lacking in the sharp verbal levity we have come to expect from Cervantes's wit. The story of the beautiful scullery maid, conversely, manages to combine both serious and comic scenes with the same enthusiasm and effectiveness that Cervantes demonstrates in his popular *entremeses*.

Although each narrative is named after a central female love interest, the two women involved could not be more dissimilar. The Gypsy Preciosa, in addition to being beautiful, shrewd, and clever, is prominently displayed as a talented dancer and singer who enjoys a somewhat "loose" reputation. The qualities of Costanza, the eponymous *fregona*, are limited to being simply beautiful and modest, but she is always portrayed as a paragon of those virtues.

The denouement of *Gitanilla* is, with regard to at least one of its major plot threads, unsatisfyingly open-ended (we never learn what happens to the fugitive Clemente, for example). This may explain the high esteem this story has generally enjoyed among modern critics and indeed all those who favor the novel over romance. *Fregona*, on the other hand, features a neat, totally satisfying resolution of all the major plot points, which probably made this romance-type novella more appealing to seventeenth-century readers than it has been to our own contemporaries.

In my view, these two novellas are like a perfect set of bookends crafted by Cervantes to bracket the first section of his *Novelas ejemplares*. They represent, respectively, the alpha and the omega of a series of eight rather "traditional" novellas. Primarily because of its rich symbolic content—the heroic descent/quest motif involving young men and women who undergo spiritual purification in the crucible of life—*La gitanilla* is the ideal lead-off story for the string of narratives to follow. However, the cycle reaches its zenith, both thematically and structurally, in *La ilustre fregona*.

As Casalduero, Ife, and Wiltrout have observed, the final four stories in Cervantes's *Novelas ejemplares* feature a lot of doubling and pairing of contrasts.[74] Therefore, because it relies so heavily upon dualities and oppositions, *Fregona* also serves as the ideal gateway to the closing set of four narratives. Following the parallel narrative pattern he established in the preceding case of Carriazo and Avendaño, Cervantes offers us in *Las dos doncellas* a carefully matched pair of antagonists, Teodosia and Leocadia, who will vie for the affections of Marco Antonio. Similarly, in *La señora Cornelia* we have not one but two heroes—a pair of Spaniards, Don Juan de Gamboa and Don Antonio de Isunza—who act in separate but complementary ways to bring together the marital union of the lady Cornelia and the Duke of Ferrara, who has fathered her illegitimate child. Still another tandem of protagonists, Ensign Campuzano and the Licenciate Peralta, combine to bring us the cautionary story of *El casamiento engañoso*, which in turn leads to the fascinating and instructive dialogue between two canine companions, Berganza and Cipión, that is presented in *El coloquio de los perros*.

Others may not agree with my view, but *La ilustre fregona*, from a purely artistic standpoint, appears to be a daring attempt by Cervantes to stretch the conventional narrative boundaries he observed earlier in *La gitanilla*. We see here, for example, the innovative concept of splitting the central plot line into a pair of parallel threads, one following the conventions of romance, the other in the picaresque tradition. This technique is not in evidence in Cervantes's earlier *novelas* and certainly is not the usual narrative pattern for seventeenth-century short fiction. Similarly, the dialogue in *Fregona* is far more colloquial than the rhetorical verbal exchanges characteristic of Preciosa's story. And finally, in keeping with the conventions of the prose romance, Cervantes manages to tie up neatly all the loose narrative threads and provide a satisfying denouement for both male protagonists in *Fregona*. From the standpoint of romance conventions, this is a marked improvement over the closing scene of *La gitanilla*, where we are informed that the luckless fugitive Clemente is hastening to the port of Cartagena, barely ahead of the relentlessly pursuing royal gendarmes, to board a ship that will carry him off to Italy and a most uncertain future.

In summary, then, *La ilustre fregona* should be viewed as an experimental combination of narrative techniques: a variation on the basic plot outline of *La gitanilla* with added touches borrowed from *Don Quixote*, Part Two. Although most literary analysts have made a strong case by concentrating on the thematic and formal similarities between these two Cervantine novellas, I believe that the many virtues of *La ilustre fregona* can best be brought to light by concentrating on the many ways it which this story playfully seeks to diverge from the rather serious-minded pattern established by the preceding *La gitanilla*.

2
Patterns of Symmetrical Design in *El amante liberal, La fuerza de la sangre,* and *La española inglesa*

When we think of Cervantes's *Novelas ejemplares*—of any of his short fiction, for that matter—structural balance and symmetry are *not* the narrative qualities that come immediately to mind. If anything, at first glance Cervantes's tales appear to be unique and amorphous in their structural design, each one developing at its own peculiar pace and in tune with some unique and very personal program. At the same time, most of the great Spanish writer's short works exhibit the same literary qualities found in his more widely read novels, such as finely wrought psychological portraits, minimal use of physical description and weighty decorative passages (and even then only when such details are absolutely essential to a keener understanding of the characters or to the advancement of the plot), and a generally realistic tone, even in tales that come perilously close to exceeding the limits of our suspended disbelief.

As opposed to other artists of the Spanish baroque period like Gracián or Calderón, Cervantes is not given to imposing heavy doses of symbolism, symmetrical design, or syllogistic ratiocination on his works. When, therefore, we come upon stories in the 1613 collection that abound in these elements, accounts that proceed according to a carefully balanced narrative scheme or whose characters lack psychological verisimilitude, our curiosity is aroused and our interest is heightened by their sharp deviation from the Cervantine norm. *El amante liberal, La fuerza de la sangre,* and *La española inglesa* are three prime examples of this phenomenon.

El amante liberal

In his *Sentido y forma de las "Novelas ejemplares"* (1962) Joaquín Casalduero suggested for the first time that the narrative structure of *El amante liberal* might be a key to understanding the work. He posits *four* narrative divisions for *Amante*:

1. Ricardo's account of his capture by the Turks and the storm that separated him from Leonisa.
2. The reunion of Ricardo and Leonisa; her recapitulation of what happened to her after the storm.
3. The naval battle that sets Ricardo and Leonisa free.
4. The return of the hero and heroine to Sicily.[1]

Casalduero was also the first to recognize the pivotal role that physical beauty plays throughout the story; this observation enables him to cite the thematic and structural importance of a brief scene that most commentators have ignored or passed over lightly: Ricardo's analeptic account of how a beautiful Moorish slave girl once dazzled the Emperor Charles V in his tent after the Spanish victory near Tunis (83). I will have more to say on this matter at a later point.

Amezúa y Mayo's analysis (1958), while more historical (i.e., source-oriented) than literary in its focus, nevertheless did manage to make certain valid observations with regard to the artistic merits of *Amante*. He dismissed the earlier criticisms of Savj-López and Menéndez y Pelayo as excessively harsh, adding that the story of Ricardo and Leonisa's travails in the Turkish theater are the work of "un escritor experto" [an expert writer] and bear a remarkable similarity to Heliodorus's story of Theagenes and Chariklea.[2] This judgment was later seconded by Karl-Ludwig Selig (1978), who declared *Amante* to be an "articulation in mini-form," and "an experimentation in the byzantine mode" by Cervantes, with "much emphasis on interruption and disjuncture."[3]

This trend toward a more favorable valuation of the story was continued by Ruth El Saffar in her 1974 study of Cervantes's novellas.[4] While acknowledging the complaints of earlier twentieth-century scholars regarding *Amante*'s flaws (weak character development, lack of psychological insight, unconvincing dialogues, affected style, and highly contrived coincidences that serve to diminish the work's verisimilitude), El Saffar argues that *Amante*, if judged by seventeenth-century precepts for verisimilitude, is "an intellectually satisfying adventure story" (139). In her view, the narrative pattern here is circular: Ricardo and Leonisa work their way back to their point of origin, but, because of all they have experienced in captivity, it is a new and very different beginning for them (149). In 1987 Gonzalo Díaz Migoyo offered an alternate version of El Saffar's circular design: he envisioned two distinct narrative entities forming a chain that circulated simultaneously in opposite directions.[5]

Julio Rodríguez-Luis's two-volume study of the *Novelas* (1980, 1984) provided an excellent analysis of *Amante*, particularly with regard to detailing the gradual changes in attitude that can be noted in Ricardo and Leonisa as the story progresses.[6] For Rodríguez-Luis, Leonisa plays the practical realist to Ricardo's hopeless romantic. The two lovers move in stages toward a comfortable middle ground and Rodríguez-Luis painstakingly leads us through each stage of the journey. The most controversial statement to be found here is Rodríguez-Luis's assertion that Ricardo's final speech (in which he renounces all claims to Leonisa's affection and offers her complete freedom in the selection of a husband) is a late insertion and a complete departure from the original ending (1:29). The critic goes on to compare this eleventh-hour revision to a similar prepublication alteration Cervantes made in the early Porras version of *El celoso extremeño* in order to give Leonora's essentially submissive character a healthy measure of backbone and psychological independence (1:30).

The combination of an almost interminable chain of stories told by a variety of characters, along with a series of intrigues that are hatched in the Turkish court, gives the plot of *Amante* a labyrinthine appearance, but this is deceptive. What Guillermo Díaz-Plaja finds to be a ridiculous and confused action is seen by Eleodoro J. Febres to have poetic order and a deliberate aesthetic goal.[7] This deceptiveness is also observed in the lack of physical motion in the characters. While in the first part of the story Ricardo and Mahamut seem to remain in one place while they converse, there is actually a great deal of commotion taking place under the surface.[8]

Thomas A. Pabon (1982) also makes reference to the labyrinthine motif, but his focus is on the labyrinth as a symbol of the world of political corruption and marital deceit into which the two protagonists are suddenly plunged when they are captured by the Turks. The point of the story is to contrast Christian virtue with Ottoman depravity; in the end Ricardo and Leonisa's nuptials are supposed to represent the triumph of the elevated spiritual ideals of Christian marriage over the wanton infidelity that characterized the matrimonial state among the infidels.[9]

Gonzalo Díaz Migoyo (1987) views Ricardo as the reincarnation of the chivalric figure of Richard Coeur-de-Leon.[10] Nina Cox Davis (1993) follows Díaz Migoyo in viewing *Amante* as a cross between the Byzantine and chivalric romance forms. More specifically, she sees a chivalric subtext that is obscured by the predominant Byzantine format.[11] By constructing *Amante* in this fashion Cervantes was attempting to create a new literary form by dressing up the old chivalric values (marriage = a feudal institution; a reflection of aristocratic class values like landholding and family bloodlines) in new bourgeois trappings (marriage = a capitalist venture, an agreement between equal partners; a reflection of new commercial values such as profit and exchange). In the end, Ricardo's "liberal" offer to Leonisa marks his return to the moral high ground of the Christian (i.e., feudal, aristocratic, noncapitalistic) community (120).

All of the above notwithstanding, no thorough analysis of *Amante* can fail to take into account the story that immediately precedes it in the collection: *La gitanilla*. As almost any reader will readily note, the first and second novellas in Cervantes's collection bear a remarkable similarity with regard to their principal theme: jealousy *(celos)*. The most obvious correspondences are found in the painful processes by which the male romantic leads must undergo a kind of Babylonian captivity in order to overcome their jealous nature. From a purely structural standpoint, however, *El amante liberal* is almost totally different from *La gitanilla*.

In *Amante* Ricardo follows the same sort of circular route to adulthood and marriage that was traced by Don Juan de Cárcamo, the rich man's son, in *La gitanilla*. In the earlier case, we recall, the descent stops somewhere short of the absolute bottom rung; young Juan falls merely to the level of becoming a Gypsy rogue (which, for a Spaniard, was not appreciably higher than slavery on the scale of social dignity), with a new name, Andrés Caballero, and a new social perspective. The young nobleman is restored to his wealth at the close of the action, but not before undergoing a series of painful experiences and undergoing some serious adjustments in his social attitude. His real reward, however, is the hand in marriage of the lovely Preciosa, who, it turns out, is not a Gypsy at all, but rather the long-lost daughter of aristocrats.

In *Amante* Ricardo is introduced as the same sort of spoiled aristocrat, the scion of a wealthy Italian noble who presumes entirely too much about his worthiness to woo and win the heart of the beautiful but relatively poor Leonisa. Before he can convince her to accept him as a husband, however, he must suffer the great indignity of being reduced to slavery. In effect, he is forced to descend to the absolute bottom rung of the social ladder where, symbolically, he is also required to change his name to Mario. From such an inglorious position he is impelled to rethink his priorities, reexamine his social values, and finally learn how to love a woman truly and selflessly. His wealth is restored to him at the end, but only after he has learned a much-needed lesson.

A second point of comparison between these two stories is the emotional change that each couple must undergo before they can be allowed to join hands in matrimony. The male partners, as is naturally to be expected in any Spanish Golden Age intrigue, have to learn to overcome their intense feelings of jealousy. Having learned to conquer their jealousy, Ricardo and Don Juan are deemed worthy to enter into matrimony with the respective objects of their affection.

The women in these stories, Preciosa and Leonisa, are also obliged to undergo a measure of emotional growth through adversity before being allowed to marry, but their individuation process is generally less radical and dramatic than the men's. Strong female characters like Preciosa and Leonisa (not to mention the universally celebrated Marcela and Dorotea from *Don Quixote*) are quite a common occurrence in Cervantes's fiction. Conversely, we find assertive, flexible, and well-adjusted bachelors to be in short supply, as Louis Combet has shown.[12] Don Juan and Ricardo are welcome exceptions, in spite of their obvious initial flaws.

The final and most important affinity I would like to point out is a structural one; it has to do with the manner in which certain secondary characters are presented in these two stories. Cervantes relies upon subordinate figures in some cases to provide an axis around which the romantic intrigue will revolve, in others to represent a rival or blocking agent necessary to maintain the proper amount of romantic tension in the narrative.

To illustrate the former situation, let us consider the role of Lotario as the go-between in the story *El curioso impertinente* or that of the *renegado* in the tale of the Capitán Cautivo, a character who is entrusted to take care of all the annoying but essential details of the escape plan while Ruy Pérez and Zoraida pursue their romantic interests. In both cases, without the contribution of these secondary characters to the plot, there simply would have been no story. The corresponding role in *La gitanilla* is played by the page-poet Clemente. His lyrical verses in praise of Preciosa, introduced early on in the story, continued at intervals throughout, and culminating in the famous *canto amebeo* at the Gypsy camp, are a major catalytic element in the maturation process that eventually enables Don Juan/Andrés to overcome his feelings of jealousy. The apostate Mahamut takes over that function in *El amante liberal*, serving as the catalyst for the romantic fireworks that eventually erupt between Ricardo and Leonisa.

With regard to the classic figure of the romantic rival in these two tales, Cervantes tends to deal with shadows rather than real impediments. We have seen how in *La gitanilla* the reader is falsely led to believe that the mysterious page-poet will seriously compete with Don Juan/Andrés for the heart and affection of Preciosa. But as soon as Clemente completes his poetic duel with Andrés in praise of the beautiful Gypsy maiden, Cervantes allows the page-poet to slip away forever into the night, his objective achieved. At this point Don Juan/Andrés has reaped the maximum educational benefit possible from Clemente's verses; similarly, he has come to realize that the poet's presence no longer represents—and probably never has represented— any real threat to his blossoming romantic relationship with Preciosa.

Cervantes changes his narrative strategy in *El amante liberal*, assigning the rival's role to a dandy named Cornelio, a minor character of little substance who serves principally as a convenient foil whose shortcomings will illustrate Ricardo's finer qualities by comparison. Here again, the apparent blocking agent is never really a serious rival for the hand of the female love interest, Leonisa.

In view of the various technical and thematic similarities that can be found between *La gitanilla*, a deservedly popular novella, and the less-esteemed *El amante liberal*, I believe critics would do well to reconsider some of the negative judgments that have circulated about *Amante* in our century and evaluate it anew in direct comparison with the more acclaimed *Gitanilla*.[13] The result, I feel, will be a new appreciation for the former and perhaps a clearer understanding of the meaning of the latter.

La gitanilla, it will be recalled, was recounted in two distinct stylistic parts, a slow-moving first half dedicated to novelistic character-building, then a second part marked by rapid plot movement and a host of peripeties associated with the romance genre. *Amante*, as Jennifer Lowe pointed out in 1971, "depends upon a conscious sense of balance for its construction and, consequently, for the full appreciation of its meaning."[14] The second story in the collection features a double-decked structure rather than two adjoining halves. On the main level we have a fast-paced series of scenes broken at regular intervals by a second tier of analeptic summaries. These three interrupting flashbacks allow the narrator to control his material and manipulate the reader by altering the passage of time while he pushes the story to its inevitable conclusion. As we can see in schema 18, the design of *Amante* consists of seven (versus Casalduero's four) distinct sections, arranged in a symmetrical pattern.

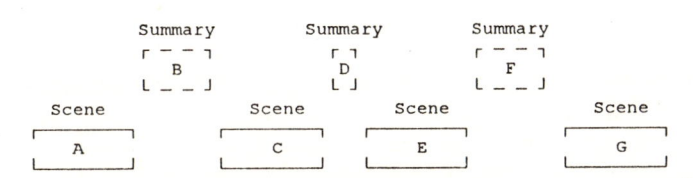

```
         Summary        Summary        Summary
         ┌ ─ ─ ┐        ┌   ┐          ┌ ─ ─ ┐
           B              D              F
         └ ─ ─ ┘        └   ┘          └ ─ ─ ┘
  Scene          Scene          Scene          Scene
 ┌─────┐        ┌─────┐        ┌─────┐        ┌─────┐
 │  A  │        │  C  │        │  E  │        │  G  │
 └─────┘        └─────┘        └─────┘        └─────┘
```

Schema 18. *El amante liberal*

(A) In medias res opening: Ricardo, now a slave of the Turks on Cyprus, bemoans his fate to his friend, Mahamut.
(B) Ricardo's account of his love for Leonisa back in Sicily and how they were captured, then separated, by Turkish pirates.
(C) Reunion of Ricardo and Leonisa at Nicosia; Mahamut begins to act as a go-between.

——————————————— structural midpoint ———————————————
(D) Poetic interlude: verses (*coplas*) composed by two Spaniards in praise of a Moorish beauty.

(E) Complications arise in the form of the Cadí and Halima, who have romantic designs on Leonisa and Ricardo, respectively.
(F) Leonisa's account of how she survived a shipwreck and came to Cyprus.
(G) Conclusion: Ricardo, Leonisa, Mahamut and Halima manage to escape from the Turks and are reunited with their families in Sicily; Ricardo and Leonisa agree to marry; Mahamut and Halima are reconciled with the Church.

In *El amante liberal* sections A, C, E, and G represent the thread of the main action that takes place on the island of Cyprus, on the high seas, and then finally back in Sicily. Sections B, D, and F are flashbacks of one kind or another: B and F are the accounts related by Ricardo and Leonisa, respectively, regarding how they came to find themselves in Moorish captivity; D is the timely anecdote about the Moorish beauty who inspired two Spaniards, working separately, to compose a set of *coplas* in her honor. As such, it represents a pivotal moment in Ricardo's life, the point at which he begins to develop a new outlook regarding Leonisa.

(A) Opening scene

The story begins in medias res with the protagonist, Ricardo, standing distraught before the ruins of Nicosia, newly captured from the Greek Christian defenders by the Turks, a historical reference which places the events of the story in the period shortly after 1570. In a very poetic opening soliloquy he compares his woeful condition as a slave and prisoner of war to that of the demoralized and downtrodden Cypriot capital. Also present is the renegade Mahamut, Ricardo's boyhood companion who later renounced his Christian faith to become a Muslim, but who now decries—and recounts in full detail for the reader—the rampant corruption within the Turkish political system and expresses a burning desire to return to the Church. The major part of the story will indeed be devoted to the bold and daring scheme concocted by these two men to escape from Cyprus and return to their families in Sicily, but first the reader must be apprised of the strange sequence of events that has served to bring these two old friends together again under such unusual circumstances.

(B) Partial analepsis #1

Ricardo's account of his most recent misadventures is the first and most extensive of a series of three flashback sequences that are used in this tale.

He recalls the rather presumptuous manner in which he once courted the lovely Leonisa. He confesses that he counted upon his family's wealth and superior social status to gain the favor of her poor but ambitious parents and eventually win her hand in marriage:

> Sabían sus deudos y sus padres mis deseos, y jamás dieron muestra de que les pesase, considerando que iban encaminados a fin honesto y virtuoso, y así muchas veces sé yo que se lo dijeron a Leonisa, para disponerle la voluntad a que por su esposo me recibiese. (1:142)[15]

> [Her relatives and her parents knew of my desires and never gave any indication that they displeased them, judging them to be directed toward a chaste and virtuous end, and I know that they said so many times to Leonisa in order to dispose her will to accept me as her husband.] (1:115–17)

The intended bride, however, seems to have eyes for only a certain Cornelio, who is described by the jealous Ricardo as a man of delicate features who is viewed as a somewhat effeminate dandy:[16]

> mancebo galán, atildado, de blandas manos y rizos cabellos, de voz meliflua, y, finalmente, todo hecho de ámbar y de alfeñique, guarnecido de telas y adornado de brocados.... (1:143)

> [an elegant, refined young man with soft hands and curled hair, a honeyed voice and loving words, and, in short, made all of ambergris and soft almond paste, attired in fine clothes and adorned with brocades....] (1:117)

The sight of Cornelio and Leonisa together one day in a garden is more than Ricardo can endure; in a jealous rage he attacks his rather diffident nemesis both verbally and with a drawn sword. His bullying actions result in seven or eight wounded bystanders, who are joined on the ground by the swooning Leonisa. The jealous suitor fails, however, to wreak his vengeance upon the fleeing Cornelio on account of the sudden intervention of Turkish pirates, who subdue the rampaging Ricardo and carry off both him and the unconscious Leonisa. During the very brief time that they are together the two captives exchange acts of Christian charity: he offers to fund her ransom so that her parents will not have to incur a debt beyond their limited means; she intervenes to convince the pirates not to execute Ricardo for having killed four Turks during the struggle. Fate eventually places the couple on separate ships, a situation that is worsened still by a storm that drives Ricardo's vessel to Tripoli and eventually Cyprus; There he pines for Leonisa, whom he believes to have perished in the storm.

(C) Reunion of Ricardo and Leonisa

In the third narrative section we return to the situation at Nicosia and the continuing action of the principal plot. Ricardo practically disappears from the story for a brief interlude while the reader's attention is focused on Leonisa's unexpected reappearance and Mahamut's attempts to effect a rapprochement between the displaced lovers.

One day an elegantly bejeweled Christian slave is brought before a gathering of Turkish officials for auction. To the amazement of Ricardo, it is Leonisa. Such is her dazzling beauty on that occasion that three of the Turkish dignitaries vie for the privilege of possessing her.

Eventually Mahamut is able to approach the new arrival and test her sentiments about Ricardo; he deliberately misinforms her that both Ricardo and Cornelio have been captured by Moorish pirates, that Cornelio has luckily been sold to a wealthy Turkish merchant from Rhodes, while the less fortunate Ricardo has perished. Her reaction is quite unexpected, especially the coolness and mordant sarcasm with which she receives the news about the foppish Cornelio: "sabe guardar muy bien la suya" (1:162); ['he is well used to safeguarding his own'] (1:139). On the other hand, Leonisa offers some surprisingly kind words for the memory of the other suitor: "más liberal es Ricardo, y más valiente y comedido" (1:163); ['Ricardo is infinitely more generous, infinitely more courageous and gallant'] (1:139).

(D) Partial analepsis #2

Leonisa's stunning appearance in the pasha's tent inspires the next narrative section. Ricardo recounts to Mahamut an anecdote that his father often told about some *coplas* that were composed in honor of a beautiful Moorish slave by a pair of Spanish soldiers who fought under Charles V at Tunis when the Goleta fortress was captured.[17] The two scenes are worthy of comparison.

In the pasha's tent Leonisa is referred to as a marvelous light ("maravillosa luz"). Her eyes are compared to the sun in their luminous brilliance and their capacity to bring joy to those who behold them; she has

> un rostro que así deslumbró los ojos y alegró los corazones de los circunstantes, como el sol que por entre cerradas nubes, después de mucha escuridad, se ofrece a los ojos de los que le desean: tal era la belleza de la cautiva cristiana, y tal su brío y gallardía. (1:157)

> [a face which dazzled the eyes and stirred the hearts of those present. Just as the sun, after a long period of darkness, peeps between thick clouds

and shows itself to those who wait anxiously to see it, such was the beauty, majesty and exquisiteness of this Christian slave.] (1:131)

In much the same way, the reflection of the sun's rays on the golden locks of a Moorish beauty in Ricardo's story are said to have inspired an Andalusian bard to forge a series of verses with a difficult and unusual rhyme scheme:

> Como cuando el sol asoma,
> por una montaña baja,
> y de súpito nos toma,
> y con su vista nos doma
> nuestra vista, y la relaja;
>
> (1:165)

> [Just like the sun as it peeps over
> a low hill and shows its face,
> taking us unawares and without cover,
> and with its rays, we discover,
> captivates and dazzles our gaze;]
>
> (1:143)

But when his poetic muse abandoned him, the verses were then continued and completed by a Catalan colleague.

> como la piedra balaja,
> que no consiente carcoma,
> tal es tu rostro, Aja,
> dura lanza de Mahoma,
> que las mis entrañas raja.
>
> (1:165)

> [just like the yellow chrysoprase,
> which resists time and weather,
> so is your countenance, Grace,
> a hard knife free of its leather
> tearing pitilessly at my entrails.]
>
> (1:143)

On the surface, the purpose of this material might appear to be merely decorative. In fact, however, these verses constitute the fulcrum upon which the two equal halves of the story are perfectly balanced. The point of the anecdote is to highlight the vast differences between Muslims and Christians in the way they respond to great physical beauty. Whereas the overpowering beauty of the Christian slave Leonisa has inspired only carnal desire among the lusting Turks who have beheld her, the Christian witnesses to the equally captivating charms of the Moorish girl were moved to react on a more spiritual plane by composing verses in praise of her.

As Ricardo recites these verses, Mahamut notices a change in his friend's attitude toward Leonisa, a more "dispassionate" (i.e., less obsessive) ardor:

> y mejor me suena y me parece que estés para decir versos, Ricardo, porque el decirlos o el hacerlos requieren ánimos de ánimos desapasionados. (1:165)

> [but more pleasing and better, it seems to me, is the fact that you feel up to reciting verses, Ricardo, for the reciting or composing of verses requires the same spirit as those who are guided by reason rather than by passion.] (1:143)

In El Saffar's view, the art of love is comparable to the artistic process: Ricardo is seen to have the passion necessary to begin a love quest/poem, but not the dispassionate distance required to carry his quest to conclusion in the face of all the difficulties that will be presented.[18] Ricardo's recitation of these verses, followed immediately by his contemplation of their meaning with regard to his feelings for Leonisa, marks the turning point in their relationship. From this point forward, Ricardo will demonstrate an increasing appreciation of Leonisa's spiritual qualities and a greater capacity for suppressing his previous possessive instincts.

(E) Complications arise

With the return to the main thread of narration in the fifth section, plot complications are introduced in the persons of the Cadí and his wife, Halima, a former Christian turned Muslim; they are a wanton pair who lust mightily after Leonisa and Ricardo (now called Mario), respectively. The most important occurrence here is the chance meeting of Ricardo and Leonisa at the home of the Cadí and Halima. We are told that when their eyes finally meet, Leonisa and Ricardo display their hidden emotions, but with very different results. Leonisa, having been apprised by Mahamut of Ricardo's supposed death at sea, cannot believe her eyes when she spies her former suitor. Such is her fear and shock that she retreats four or five steps up a flight of stairs, all the while feverishly kissing a small cross she had hidden in her bosom and repeatedly making the sign of the cross, as if she had just seen a ghost.

2 / Patterns of Symmetrical Design

Ricardo's reaction is less dramatic—he already knew Leonisa was alive and well in Cyprus, so the element of surprise plays no part—but equally significant. We are told that he is suddenly inundated by a wave of jumbled thoughts and mixed emotions that leave him feeling both saddened and overjoyed, fully aware of his status as a prisoner, but delighted to be one under such fortuitous conditions:

> En un instante, al enamorado Ricardo le sobrevinieron tantos pensamientos, que le suspendieron y alegraron, considerándose veinte pasos a su parecer, o poco más, desviado de su felicidad y contento; considerábase cautivo, y a su gloria en poder ajeno. Estas cosas revolviendo entre sí mismo, se movía poco a poco, y con temor y sobresalto, alegre y triste, temeroso y esforzado, se iba llegando al centro donde estaba el de su alegría. . . . (1:169)

> [In an instant, the love-struck Ricardo was overwhelmed by a multitude of thoughts which suspended his senses and raised his spirits, thinking himself to be twenty feet or so away from his happiness and his joy. He felt like a prisoner and yet in bliss in the power of another. Turning these things over in his mind, he moved slowly, and with fear and trepidation, happy yet sad, fearful yet bold, he advanced toward the centre of the room where sat the centre of his joy. . . .] (1:147)

It is at this point that the second half of Cervantes's narrative design gets underway. Ricardo, having reflected upon the story of the beautiful Moorish girl who inspired the chaste and dispassionate verses of her Spanish admirers, is now presented with an opportunity to reconsider his relationship with and feelings toward Leonisa. In light of the hopeless conditions under which they meet here, he can no longer look upon her as simply an object of his desire, a treasure to be seized, or a prize to be won in competition. A lowly slave among Turkish masters, Ricardo realizes that he can never hope to possess her in any way, but this does not prevent him from looking upon her as the center or source of all his earthly happiness. He has taken the first step in forging a deeper and more enduring relationship with the woman who will become his wife. Leonisa, in the conversation that follows, provides Ricardo (and the reader) with the remaining pieces of the prehistory.

(F) Complete analepsis

Leonisa recounts how she managed to survive the storm and eventual shipwreck that Ricardo, in his account earlier, imagined had taken her life. The two most important pieces of information provided here are (1) the revelation that Leonisa, despite the circumstances of her capture and enslavement, has succeeded in preserving her virginity; and (2) Leonisa's confession of having experienced real sorrow upon hearing the report of Ricardo's death:

> Aquí he sabido de tu fingida muerte, y séte decir, si lo quieres creer, que me pesó en el alma y que te tuve más envidia que lástima, y por no quererte mal, que ya que soy desamorada, no soy ingrata ni desconocida, sino porque habías acabado con la tragedia de tu vida. (1:172)

> [Here I learned of your feigned death and I can tell you, if you will believe it, that it grieved my soul and I envied rather than pitied you and not because I wished you ill, for although I am loveless I am neither ungrateful nor unappreciative, but because you had put an end to the tragedy of your life.] (1:151)

From these revealing words we learn that Leonisa has also undergone a meaningful reevaluation of her feelings toward Ricardo; although she may have seemed cool to his affections in earlier times, she insists now that she is neither ungrateful nor unappreciative of all Ricardo's previous attentions to her.

(G) Conclusion

With all of the necessary background information now in place, the story continues and concludes in the seventh and longest of the narrative sections. The star-crossed lovers must now concoct a plan that will free them from their captors and eventually return them to their homes in Sicily. But first a confession is in order. Leonisa is moved to reveal that her previous negative feelings about Ricardo are no longer operative:

> que siempre te tuve por desabrido y arrogante, y que presumías de ti algo más de lo que debías. Confieso también que me engañaba, y que podría ser que [al] hacer ahora la experiencia me pusiese la verdad delante de los ojos el desengaño, y estando desengañada, fuese con ser honesta más humana. (1:173–74)

> [I always considered that you were unpleasant and arrogant and that you valued yourself more than you ought. I confess too that I deceived myself and that perhaps, while meeting with you now, reality opened my eyes to the truth and, being enlightened, I was, though frank, more human.] (1:153)

The delicate weaving in the final section of several intricate plots and counterplots involving certain treacherous machinations on the part of the Cadí, Halima, and a number of other Moorish conspirators need not concern us here. Suffice it to say that Halima's role here is analogous the one played by Juana Carducha in *La gitanilla*, that of a blocking agent; in the end, however, Halima's selfish designs will be frustrated and the final result will be victory and freedom for the Christian captives. The focus of our attention should be the denouement, the long-awaited arrival of the escapees in Sicily, where Ricardo, following the example given earlier by Leonisa, will make an important discovery about himself and offer an expiatory confession.

One particularly puzzling aspect of the final scene is the manner in which Ricardo stages the captives' return to Trapani: he orders all of them to wear Turkish outfits as they sail into the port. The theatricality of this final scene has been ably explicated by Díaz Migoyo: by wearing Turkish garb Ricardo wishes to present for all to see a symbol of his former self, the self-centered, possessive Ricardo who was more like the Turks he served in Cyprus than a real Christian.[19] It is an image that he will soon publicly—and spectacularly—cast aside.

Once all the newcomers have been welcomed home by their friends and families, Ricardo undertakes the process of reconciliation. He begins by clasping the hand of his somewhat startled and trembling rival Cornelio in a gesture of sincere friendship. He then acknowledges his own boorish behavior on that notable occasion some months earlier, immediately prior to his capture by the Moorish pirates. With regard to his well-publicized offer to liquidate his entire estate to ransom the captured Leonisa, he dismisses it as a pitiful—and certainly not praiseworthy—attempt to assuage his own conscience for having been responsible for her capture in the first place. The true gesture of his generosity *(liberalidad)*, he says, is the one that he will make now. At which point he uncovers the face of the heretofore veiled Leonisa and presents her to Cornelio along with a sum in excess of thirty thousand escudos.

But then, after a moment or two of silence and an apparent epiphany, he suddenly reverses himself: he declares that neither he nor anyone else—save her parents—has the right to dispose of Leonisa's person. He reaffirms his offer to liquidate his estate on her behalf, but renounces any role in the selection of a mate for her. Subsequently, Leonisa asks for and receives her parents' permission to state her own choice. She immediately selects Ricardo, explaining that her previous attention to Cornelio was motivated principally by a desire to please her parents. If Ricardo has demonstrated his extreme *liberalidad*, she now wishes to show herself to be correspondingly grateful *(agradecida)*.

It should be noted that this final scene is open to more than one interpretation. While most readers would probably consider Ricardo and Leonisa to be passionate lovers at this point, Theresa Ann Sears considers Leonisa's final choice to be merely "a lukewarm offer," motivated more by gratitude than any amorous desire on her part.[20] A careful reading of the text reveals that Sears is absolutely correct: at no point in this scene does Leonisa confess to any romantic feelings for Ricardo. Cervantes has carefully allowed his narrator to cite Leonisa as a rare example of discretion, virtue, modesty, and beauty ("discreción, honestidad, recato y hermosura") (1:188), thereby inviting the reader to infer the presence of a totally appropriate reaction to these qualities that is not actually posited: love.[21]

Despite the ambiguity of Ricardo and Leonisa's relationship in the final pages, it cannot be denied that Ricardo's cathartic experiences as a hostage among the Muslims in *El amante liberal* are very reminiscent of the important lessons learned in *La gitanilla* by Don Juan/Andrés as a result of his submersion within the Gypsy culture. Such a thematic resemblance is no mere coincidence, I feel. Cervantes's writings abound in accounts of the trials of immature aristocrats who are obliged to undergo a rite of passage into manhood—the ordeal that I call the crucible concept—by submitting themselves to some sort of physical and emotional ordeal that will ultimately prepare them for adulthood in general and marriage in particular. Such a trial is designed to endow the young man with the deeper, more mature social values he will need in order to forge a successful marriage bond. Usually there is no difficulty in making the proper choice of a partner; the ideal woman is generally present from the start or is encountered a short time thereafter. The major task set before the young man is to make himself worthy of her and in the process convince her to accept him as her mate.

Structurally, however, *La gitanilla* and *El amante liberal* are poles apart. Because the Gypsy tale concentrates on the gradual emotional growth of Don Juan's character (a narrative technique with a distinctly modern appeal), it necessarily moves rather slowly, especially in the first half. In contrast, *El amante liberal*, which was designed to fit the pattern of the Greek romance, downplays character development in favor of unexpected plot complication, heavy intrigue, and exciting, fast-paced action (e.g., pirate raids, storms at sea, shipwrecks, naval battles) generally associated with Heliodorus's *Ethiopian History*. Vis-à-vis Bakhtin's chronotope for the "adventure novel of ordeal,"[22] *El amante liberal* generally conforms to the pattern of the Greek romances, with one notable exception: Cervantes's employment of geographical and historical specifics designed to enhance the exotic quality of the strange, new world into which the protagonists are suddenly hurled.[23]

The first half of *La gitanilla* plods steadily along in what seems to be a relatively uninspired and straightforward narrative plan. Because of the strong character development in these opening scenes, this novella has become a favorite of modern readers/critics who prefer firm characterization to the kind of ingenious plot intrigue that characterized the romance genre. *El amante liberal*, on the other hand, continually jerks its readers back and forth in time as various characters step forth to provide them with important background information about previous occurrences via a series of flashback narratives. The theme, however, remains the same: if Don Juan/Andrés in *La gitanilla* must learn to conquer and control his feelings of jealousy vis-à-vis the poet Clemente so that he may become worthy to call Preciosa his own, Ricardo must do the same in *El amante liberal* with regard to his foppish rival Cornelio before he will be permitted to claim the hand of Leonisa in marriage.

For some there may be a question as to which of these two narrative techniques is superior, but such readers are missing the point. In my view, Cervantes—or whoever decided the order of publication—deliberately placed these two tales, parallel treatments of the same theme that the author undoubtedly considered to be of equal merit, in the first and second positions in the *Novelas ejemplares* as a challenge to his readers to extract the same exemplary lesson from stories with very different narrative plans.

La fuerza de la sangre

There are only a couple of points on which the critics appear to reach unanimous agreement when discussing *La fuerza de la sangre*: (1) the remarkable amount of balance and symmetry Cervantes employs in the execution of a stylized narrative plan; and (2) the supremely important role played by the small silver crucifix that Leocadia has the presence of mind to remove from the scene of her sexual violation.

Regarding the first point, Casalduero prefers an allegorical (sin/redemption) reading of the text, which therefore enables him to see in *Fuerza* an expression of "el maravilloso equilibrio entre el pecado y su expiación y la purificación de la vida" [the marvelous balance between sin and its atonement and the purification of life].[24] Ruth El Saffar, who considers it a late composition, lists among the story's virtues its carefully wrought scenes and accomplished descriptions, features that she believes contribute to the work's "structural perfection."[25] Similar judgments in praise of Cervantes's use of structural and metaphorical symmetry have been issued by Robert V. Piluso (1964), Karl-Ludwig Selig (1972), Margarita Levisi (1973), and David M. Gitlitz (1981).[26]

A good example of the kind of balance Cervantes imposes throughout the story is Rodolfo's bedroom, which serves not only as the demonic place where Leocadia loses consciousness twice in the course of being raped, but also as the blessed locale in which little Luisico is twice given life. For El

Saffar, the entire point of *Fuerza* is to demonstrate the ultimate reconciliation of all things, even those which seem to be polar opposites: "[A] correspondence is established between supernatural and natural causes, neither one usurping or replacing the role of the other."[27]

Forcione goes El Saffar one better; he calls *Fuerza* a "secularized miracle."[28] Forcione was perhaps the first to note that the story is constructed around a central event—Luisico's near-fatal accident—rather than a central character, and that Cervantes's exacting eye for symmetry and balance allowed him to divide the story almost perfectly into two halves, one of darkness, the other of light (355–56). For Forcione, Cervantes was at the height of his creative powers when he orchestrated so many antitheses in *Fuerza*, a work he terms "a carefully designed, ingeniously narrated, and richly allusive short story" (378).

In most matters, Rodríguez-Luis's highly secular interpretation of *Fuerza* stands at the opposite pole from Forcione's, but he joins him in noting the story's perfect structure: the final happiness counterbalances the early misfortune, matrimony and healing ultimately cancel out the rape and its shame, and a perfect balance is achieved between the first night and the last.[29]

As for the telltale crucifix, Casalduero was among the first to cite the poetic character of that item as a witness to Rodolfo's crime.[30] The same allegorical interpretation is espoused by Piluso, who views the icon as both an implicit symbol of redemption and an instrument for achieving eventual justice.[31] Rodríguez-Luis deals with the crucifix in narrower literary terms by calling it Cervantes's way of deepening the story's intrigue and then of blessing the final solution.[32] For Ruth El Saffar, the silver cross serves symbolically as a sign of Leocadia's redemption and of the prospect of her reconciliation and union with Rodolfo.[33] Forcione manages to have it both ways; he sees Cervantes presenting the crucifix in a double perspective: (1) as a "neutral" instrument in Leocadia's plan to discover the identity of her assailant; and (2) as the wonder-working image of Christian miracles in general.[34]

Once we move past the rich religious symbolism and structural perfection of *Fuerza*, however, there remains the problem of the story's obvious weakness in the area of character development. In the eyes of some critics, not a single one of the characters introduced in the novella ever actually performs as a realistically drawn human personality. Leocadia, for example, is clearly cast in the rather stereotypical role of the saintly virgin and helpless female victim. The perpetrator of the assault against her virtue is the libidinous Rodolfo, and while it must be conceded that he undergoes a radical change of heart in the course of the story, the transformation is more miraculous than consistent with normal human behavior. And even though seven full years are said to elapse between the opening and closing scenes, we are never permitted even a glimpse of his conduct during that period; the narrator at no time provides the slightest clue as to the how and why of Rodolfo's sudden maturation and his decision to accept responsibility for the heinous act he committed earlier. In short, the entire plot appears to depend exclusively upon wild coincidence of a divine and miraculous design.

Ruth El Saffar accepts the accuracy of such judgments but then dismisses them as irrelevant, i.e., a misapplication of modern realistic or naturalistic standards that had no validity in Cervantes's time. The so-called idealistic tales, she says, were designed around concepts like honor and religion that the modern reader finds virtually impossible to understand.[35] Forcione takes a similar stance: he admits that *Fuerza* is often unintelligible and melodramatic, and that is steeped in sensationalism; he does not deny that it has inconsistencies in characters and flagrant violations of plausibility. In an effort to soften that criticism he also points out that, because it is a miracle narrative, *La fuerza de la sangre* is governed by a totally different literary logic from that of the modern novel.[36]

Rodríguez-Luis is more outspoken in his defense of this story and Rodolfo, whom he considers to be an excellent example of literary characterization. Cervantes's narrator, he observes, almost immediately begins to qualify Rodolfo's vile act with mitigating factors, most notably his immaturity and consequent inability to control his strong sexual instinct in the face of Leocadia's overpowering physical beauty.[37] Conversely, the feeble attempt by Cervantes's narrator to defend Rodolfo's criminal behavior is cited by Patricia E. Grieve (1991) as evidence of a lingering patriarchal mind-set in *Fuerza*. Grieve goes on to argue that Cervantes, especially in comparison with María de Zayas y Sotomayor, was not nearly so attuned to contemporary women's issues as some critics have supposed.[38]

In his defense of Rodolfo, Rodríguez-Luis underscores the fact that a repentant Rodolfo decides not to tell his friends the real truth about what he has done to Leocadia. The final, most outrageous defense of Rodolfo's "character" comes with Rodríguez-Luis's declaration that Rodolfo's dominant personality trait, his unbridled sexual aggressiveness, which was defended in the first part of the novella as an excess of youthful enthusiasm, is viewed in the second part first as a mere quality and then as a virtue, or at least as a positive aspect of his nature.[39] Rodolfo's view of physical beauty as a more important attribute for a wife than spiritual virtues like prudence (*discreción*), honorability (*honestidad*), and good upbringing (*buenas costumbres*) is apparently excused by Rodolfo's belief that he possesses enough nobility, wealth, and prudence for the two of them (1:64). In the eyes of Rodríguez-Luis, at least, Rodolfo represents a much more attractive male romantic lead than does the passive and teary-eyed Andrés of *La gitanilla* (1:64).

This issue of feminine pulchritude is the subject of several key passages in *Fuerza*. Throughout the narrative Leocadia is the absolute essence of *hermosura*; her beauty alone is what is said to have activated Rodolfo's libido to the point of inciting him to rape.

> Pero la mucha hermosura del rostro que había visto Rodolfo . . . comenzó de tal manera a imprimírsele en la memoria, que le llevó tras sí la voluntad y despertó en él un deseo de gozarla a pesar de todos los inconvenientes que sucederle pudiesen. (2:77-78)

> [But the great beauty of the face which Rodolfo had seen . . . so far began to print itself on his memory that it took over his will, and awakened in him the desire to enjoy her, despite all the consequences there might be.] (2:103)

As we noted earlier with the elder Diego Carriazo in *La ilustre fregona*, the crime of rape in Cervantes's fictional universe tends to be a spontaneous eruption, a totally unpremeditated occurrence.[40] In *Fuerza*, however, Leocadia'a striking beauty, if it is shown to be responsible in some small way for her dishonor, is also—albeit belatedly—portrayed as the efficient cause of her restoration to grace in society's eyes. Her stunning good looks capture Rodolfo's heart in the climactic recognition scene when he comes face-to-face with his victim for the second time. In keeping with the Neoplatonic tradition, Cervantes would have his reader believe that Leocadia's beauty is the only force that can persuade Rodolfo to accept her as his mate for life.

As Cervantes showed earlier in the tragic case of Marcela and Grisóstomo (*DQ* 1, chaps. 12–14), the problem of abundant physical beauty lies in the fact that it often arouses an excess of passion in its admirer. Beauty and passion are a volatile and potentially lethal combination, as we shall soon observe again in the case of Isabela and Arnesto in *La española inglesa* and as Calderón demonstrated so ably in the case of Segismundo and Rosaura in *La vida es sueño*. The Calderonian solution to the problem, as all Hispanists know, is the need to *reportarse*, i.e., to keep one's passions in check at all times. Although it is doubtful that Cervantes would disagree with his younger contemporary's insistence upon the need for greater self-control, such is not the solution offered in *Fuerza*. For Cervantes, moral rectitude eventually brings its own reward, either in this life or the next; man must have faith in God's plan. As Ruth El Saffar has argued, *Fuerza* was probably written toward the end of Cervantes's life, close to the time of the composition of the optimistic *Persiles*, in a period when the great writer was most confident about the existence of a benevolent Divine Plan that lies quietly behind our earthly trials and tribulations.[41]

This blatantly optimistic tone is naturally considered unrealistic and inverisimilar nowadays, but if *Fuerza* falls short with regard to its realism, it soars in its employment of symbolic elements, of which I shall mention only a few. The first appears in the opening pages of the story, as the innocent Leocadia and her pacific family approach their fateful encounter with Rodolfo and his predatory cohorts. The imminent encounter between good and evil is described as the clash of two mismatched opponents: one an army of sheep, the other of wolves. The sanguinary motif announced in the title is likewise given symbolic treatment: the blood shed by little Luisico upon being trampled by a racing steed is intended to evoke the earlier image of the ruptured hymen of his mother, Leocadia, on the occasion of the boy's violent conception in the opening scene. Both the crime and its eventual reparation are portrayed as having their origins in violence and bloodshed; the wrong will be righted, poetically, through *la fuerza de la sangre*.

The latter point is reinforced by the role played in the tale by the crucifix Leocadia has the presence of mind to remove from Rodolfo's bedroom after he has violated her. As many commentators have already pointed out, the crucifix, a universal symbol of violence, martyrdom, and consequent redemption, has a variety of other roles to play here. It is introduced as the sole witness to the despicable act that is perpetrated by Rodolfo on Leocadia's pure and saintly person, and it eventually comes to serve as the concrete and incontrovertible proof of Rodolfo's guilt in the matter.[42] But above all else, it is intended to be seen as God's instrument for restoring order in the universe by bringing together in matrimony the victim and her violator.

In my view, violence is an important motif in *Fuerza*, not simply because it is the catalytic force that both creates and resolves the problems presented in the narrative, but also because it is the element that best enables us to glimpse the symmetrical structure Cervantes designed for this tale.

The story opens in violence with the heinous abduction and rape of Leocadia by Rodolfo, an act that creates a very real honor problem for the guiltless victim. The resolution of this problem, i.e., the restoration of Leocadia's virtue, begins rather poetically at the linear midpoint of the text with a second senseless and unforeseen act of bloodshed: the trampling of the child Luisico beneath the hoofs of a bolting stallion. Consequently, there has been a temptation to see this novella as one composed of two equal parts, and R. P. Calcraft and Nina M. Scott have viewed it this way, although others have perceived an even more complex arrangement. David M. Gitlitz, for example, considers *Fuerza* to be divided into three sections, each consisting of three scenes; the first scene in each part occurs in the street, the second in Rodolfo's room, the third in a private residence. Dina de Rentiis describes the structure of this novella as "divided into four parts disposed geometrically around a center, with the first mirroring/opposing the fourth, and the second one mirroring/opposing the third."[43] I would like to elaborate on these various schemes and propose a slightly different configuration.

In my view, *La fuerza de la sangre* is essentially a balanced narrative told in two symmetrical—but not identical—halves, each of which is designed to be the mirror image of the other. Luisico's accident, which I designate section D (2:85–87) in my scheme, is intended to serve as the focal center of the story and the point of support against which are carefully offset all preceding and subsequent events.

The main line of narrative is made up principally of sections A and G, the lengthy first and final scenes that portray the creation and resolution, respectively, of Leocadia's honor problem. Minor components include sections C and E (Leocadia's situation in Toledo), plus section D, Luisico's accident. Separate from these narrative modules are sections B and F, which concern Rodolfo's period of self-imposed exile in Italy. In the interest of clarity, I have raised the linear representation of sections B and F above the main thread of action because, like the flashback sequences in *Amante*, these scenes are ancillary to and take place far away from the main action (schema 19).

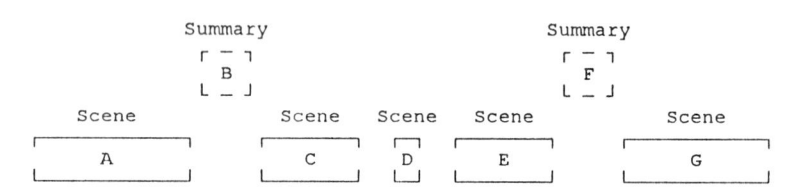

Schema 19. *La fuerza de la sangre*

(A) Toledo: Leocadia is raped by Rodolfo; she takes a small crucifix from his bedroom.
   (B) Action offstage: Rodolfo has escaped to Italy, where he remains for seven years.
(C) Leocadia's pregnancy and the birth of Luisico; seven years pass.
—————————Focal and structural midpoint—————————
(D) Luisico's near-fatal accident.

(E) Meeting of Leocadia and Doña Estefanía, Rodolfo's mother. Doña Estefanía sees the crucifix and realizes the truth about Luisico's birth.

(F) Action offstage: Doña Estefanía writes to Rodolfo in Italy and summons him home to meet his intended bride.
(G) Confrontation and reconciliation of violator and victim; marriage of Rodolfo and Leocadia.

To understand the originality of *La fuerza de la sangre* we need look no further than the opening, middle, and closing scenes. The extended narrative section that opens the story is concerned exclusively with Rodolfo's attack on Leocadia's body and provides a meticulous account of this violent episode. It is balanced at the other end by an equally long and detailed representation of Doña Estefanía's scheme for bringing about a final reconciliation between the violator and his victim. What catches our attention, however, is how totally different are the respective styles and narrative techniques employed in these two sections. A side-by-side comparison of these scenes could easily lead a person to believe that we are dealing with two entirely distinct narrative forms in the same work. To put it another way, if *La gitanilla* had hinted at some sort of Manichaean struggle between the conventions of the novel and the romance, those antagonists seem to wage an all-out war in *La fuerza de la sangre*.

Section A describes and comments on a single action: Rodolfo's criminal assault upon Leocadia's body. Marcia L. Welles has criticized Cervantes's treatment of the rape theme for "demythifying" the violence that is done to Leocadia's body in the course of Rodolfo's sexual assault.[44] The ferocity of male desire is projected away from the act of penetration and onto the earlier moment in which Rodolfo snatches Leocadia away from her parents and carries her off (242). In fact, the bloodshed mentioned in the title does not refer to Leocadia's ruptured hymen, but rather to Luisico's fractured skull (243).

In a similar vein, we have Patricia E. Grieve's claim that Cervantes "sublimates" (i.e., purifies or decriminalizes) the violence against Leocadia in *Fuerza* by transforming Leocadia into an object of devotion, similar to the crucifix that plays so prominent a role in the story. Her function, then, is simply to serve as the instrument—Grieve uses the term "vessel"—through which Rodolfo will be redeemed.[45] In this interpretation, the primary focus of Cervantes's attention is the lascivious Rodolfo, who thereby becomes the true protagonist of the novella. The story, then, is actually about this young man and his struggle to put his priorities in order through the mediating benevolence and love of his victim. In Grieve's words, "Cervantes merely inscribes patriarchal theology . . . into a social context" (96).

Such feminist criticisms seem valid enough on the surface, but fail to take into account the peculiar circumstances in which Cervantes wrote, not to mention the extreme political and public reaction he might have faced had he portrayed the rape of Leocadia in all its grisly detail. Given those realities, the description of the innocent Leocadia's rape that Cervantes has left us in *Fuerza* is wrought with as much sympathy and sensitivity as any modern critic has a right to expect.

Let us return to Cervantes's text. As we might expect, there are a number of preliminary paragraphs that deal with the events preceding the attack and a few others that treat Leocadia's confused mental state in the moments immediately following her ordeal. The focus, however, is on a single act and the pace is predictably slow and methodical: no important physical or psychological detail is overlooked by the narrator's keen eye. The seconds immediately preceding the assault are vividly portrayed in a graphic account of both the internal and external factors that come into play during an ominous encounter on a darkened Toledo street between Rodolfo's unruly band and Leocadia's unsuspecting family:

> Encontráronse los dos escuadrones, el de las ovejas con el de los lobos, y, con deshonesta desenvoltura, Rodolfo y sus camaradas, cubiertos los rostros, miraron los de la madre, y de la hija, y de la criada. Alborotóse el viejo y reprochóles y afeóles su atrevimiento. Ellos le respondieron con muecas y burla, y sin desmandarse a más, pasaron adelante. Pero la mucha hermosura del rostro que había visto Rodolfo, que era el de Leocadia, que así quieren que se llamase la hija del hidalgo, comenzó de tal manera a imprimírsele en la memoria, que le llevó tras sí la voluntad y despertó en él un deseo de gozarla a pesar de todos los inconvenientes que sucederle pudiesen. Y en un instante comunicó su pensamiento con sus camaradas y en otro instante se resolvieron de volver y robarla, por dar gusto a Rodolfo: que siempre los ricos que dan en liberales hallan quien canonice sus desafueros y califique por buenos sus malos gustos. Y así, el nacer el mal propósito, el comunicarle y el aprobarle y el determinarse de robar a Leocadia y el robarla, casi todo fue en un punto. (2:77–78)

> [The two squadrons, one of sheep and the other of wolves, met; and Rodolfo and his party, covering their faces, looked with lewd insolence into the faces of the mother, the daughter, and the maid-servant. The old gentleman was furious; he reproached the young men and upbraided them for their bad manners; they responded with grimaces and jeers and, without any further bad behaviour, went on. But the great beauty of the face which Rodolfo had seen, that of Leocadia (the name of the gentleman's daughter) so far began to print itself on his memory that it took over his will, and awakened in him the desire to enjoy her, despite all the consequences there might be; he at once communicated his thoughts to his friends, and in a moment they decided to go back and kidnap her, to please Rodolfo; for rich people who are inclined to generosity always find people who legitimize their crimes and praise their evil desires. And so, the birth of the evil idea, the sharing of it, agreeing to it, and the

2 / PATTERNS OF SYMMETRICAL DESIGN 117

decision to kidnap Leocadia and kidnapping her, all happened at almost the same moment.] (2:103)

Cervantes presents us here with a descriptive passage worthy of any nineteenth-century third-person omniscient narrator. We learn not only *what* occurred, but *why* and *how* each fateful decision was made. The same highly realistic technique is in evidence again when the narrator offers us a detailed summary of what Leocadia feels and observes when, following the assault, she awakens alone in a strange, dark room:

> Sintió Leocadia que quedaba sola y encerrada, y, levantándose del lecho anduvo todo el aposento, tentando las paredes con las manos, por ver si hallaba puerta por do irse o ventana por do arrojarse. Halló la puerta, pero bien cerrada, y topó una ventana que pudo abrir, por donde entró el resplandor de la luna, tan claro, que pudo distinguir Leocadia las colores de unos damascos que el aposento adornaban. Vio que era dorada la cama, y tan ricamente compuesta, que más parecía lecho de príncipe que de algún particular caballero. Contó las sillas y los escritorios; notó la parte donde la puerta estaba, y aunque vio pendientes de las paredes algunas tablas, no pudo alcanzar a ver las pinturas que contenían. La ventana era grande, guarnecida y guardada de una gruesa reja; la vista caía a un jardín que también se cerraba con paredes altas; dificultades que se opusieron a la intención que de arrojarse a la calle tenía. Todo lo que vio y notó de la capacidad y los ricos adornos de aquella estancia, le dio a entender que el dueño della debía de ser hombre principal y rico, y no como quiera, sino aventajadamente. En un escritorio, que estaba junto a la ventana, vio un crucifijo pequeño, todo de plata, el cual tomó y se le puso en la manga de la ropa, no por devoción ni por hurto, sino llevada de un discreto designio suyo. Hecho esto cerró la ventana como antes estaba y volvióse al lecho, esperando qué fin tendría el mal principio de su suceso. (2:81–82)

> [Leocadia realized that she was alone and locked in, and, getting up from the bed, went round the room, groping along the walls, to see if she could find a door to go out by, or a window to throw herself from. She found a door but it was firmly locked; and she came across a window which she was able to open, through which came the light of the moon, so clearly that she could see the colours of some tapestries which decorated the room. She saw that the bed was painted with gold leaf, and so richly adorned that it seemed more like the bed of a prince than of a private gentleman. She counted the chairs and the writing-tables; she noted the location of the door, and although she saw picture-frames hanging on the walls she could not make out the paintings in them. The window was large and ornate, covered by a stout grille; it looked out over a garden, also enclosed by high walls, obstacles which made her intention of throwing herself into the street impossible. All that she observed of the size and

rich decoration of the room made her realize that its owner must be a nobleman, and more than ordinarily wealthy. On a writing table near the window she saw a small silver crucifix, which she picked up and put in her sleeve, not for devotion, or as a theft, but inspired by a clever plan she had. Having done this, she closed the window, and went back to the bed, to await the conclusion of this incident, which had had so evil a beginning.] (2:109)

In a passage that could have come from the pen of Edgar Allan Poe or Sir Arthur Conan Doyle, Leocadia makes a full moonlight inventory of her well-appointed prison: the doors, windows, furniture, tapestries, and so forth, and a small silver crucifix that she will keep as a means of identifying her attacker. Cervantes's narrative technique here is totally novelistic; the aim is clearly that of mimetic representation, striving for a maximum degree of verisimilitude. In these early pages of *Fuerza* we find no evidence whatsoever of the narrative devices generally associated with the chivalric, pastoral, or Byzantine romance. The last section of the story is quite a different matter.

Section G takes place at Doña Estefanía's house and represents the final resolution of Leocadia's honor problem. Like the opening section, this sequence of events is long and detailed, but now the action is bathed in a soft, comforting light we associate with the literary romance. And furthermore, while the opening scene moved deliberately toward a careful, realistic depiction of the crime and its aftermath, the closing one seems to be composed of a rapid-fire series of incredibly fortuitous occurrences that are bound together only by their being part of Doña Estefanía's elaborate plan to unite Leocadia and Rodolfo in matrimony. The conclusion of *Fuerza* adheres to virtually all the conventions of the romance format: in a single scene all of the following events take place in quick succession:

1. Doña Estefanía begins by persuading two of Rodolfo's friends to confess to taking part in the rape of Leocadia.

2. She then presents Rodolfo with a small portrait of a rather plain girl she says she has selected to be his bride.

3. Rodolfo reacts to the picture by declaring that he prizes physical beauty above all other virtues in a wife.

4. Estefanía agrees to find him a more suitable bride, then summons Leocadia from an adjoining room. Leocadia's entrance is one of dazzling beauty.

5. When Rodolfo glimpses Leocadia's beauty for what he believes to be the first time—everyone else involved, including the reader, knows the real truth—he is moved to love, not lust, and refers to her as an "ángel humano" (2:92) [angel in human form].

2 / Patterns of Symmetrical Design 119

6. Overcome with emotion because of what had taken place years before and because of the proximity of her beloved Rodolfo at that moment, Leocadia faints.

7. Hearing a great commotion, Leocadia's parents, along with a parish priest, emerge from the room in which they had been hiding. They find not one but two *desmayados*: Rodolfo has fainted as well and has fallen on top of Leocadia.

8. When Rodolfo emerges from his swoon, his mother tells him that Leocadia (still unconscious) is the *real* bride she has selected for him. With great enthusiasm he leaps upon her prostrate figure and revives her with a passionate kiss.

9. Doña Estefanía orders the priest to unite the new lovers in matrimony on the spot, which the narrator informs us was an acceptable practice before the Council of Trent (1545-63), which is when this story is said to have taken place.

10. The industrious Doña Estefanía next reveals to the entire wedding party the violent circumstances of the first meeting, seven years earlier, of the new bride and groom.

11. To confirm the truth of these revelations, Leocadia produces the small silver crucifix she had taken that fateful night from Rodolfo's room.

12. The revelations having been concluded, all the participants settle down to a wedding banquet, at which time Rodolfo notices how much Luisico resembles him.

13. The meal concluded, everyone retires for the night, especially the newlyweds, who, we are informed, will go on to live happy and fruitful lives in Toledo, where their descendants still reside.

A few observations from the critics regarding the final scene are worth noting here. Nina M. Scott underscores the great theatricality of *Fuerza* in general, but especially in the final recognition scene where Cervantes painstakingly describes Leocadia's dramatic entrance.[46]

> Venía vestida, por ser invierno, de una saya entera de terciopelo negro llovida de botones de oro y perlas, cintura y collar de diamantes. Sus mismos cabellos, que eran luengos y no demasiado rubios, le servían de adorno y tocas, cuya invención de lazos y rizos y vislumbrantes de diamantes que con ellos se entretenían, turbaban la luz de los ojos que los miraban. Era Leocadia de gentil disposición y brío. Traía de mano a su hijo, y delante della venían dos doncellas alumbrándola con dos velas de cera en dos candeleros de plata. (2:92)
>
> [Since it was winter, she came in dressed in a long gown of black velvet, covered with buttons of gold and pearls, and a waistband and

neckband of diamonds; her own hair, which was long and not over-fair, served as a decorated head-dress, and its arrangement of loops and curls, with diamond ornaments woven in with them, dazzled the eyes of all who looked at her. She was of pleasing appearance and manner; she was holding her son by the hand, and two maids preceded her, lighting her way with candles in silver candlesticks.] (2:123)

With regard to the sudden change in Rodolfo's character in the final scene, Calcraft offers an exculpatory explanation: Rodolfo's seven-year sojourn in the cultural capital of the West must have had a decidedly beneficial effect on his moral compass.[47] But not all scholars have made such a positive assessment of Rodolfo's behavior. Dina de Rentiis has a contrary opinion: that Rodolfo's character has failed to evolve in any meaningful way during the seven years of his residence in Italy. And, she adds, this moral stagnation was no mere oversight on Cervantes's part. When Rodolfo acknowledges in the climactic scene the powerful effect that a woman's physical beauty has always had on him, he is echoing the Neoplatonic principles espoused by León Hebreo, but from a different perspective. De Rentiis claims that the fact that the young man's easily aroused passion remains undiminished in the final scene is Cervantes's way of demonstrating that the sexual desire that beauty inspires can be used as often for the commission of evil acts (e.g., rape) as for good ones (marriage), depending upon the circumstances under which that desire is aroused.[48]

The motives behind the efforts of Leocadia and Estefanía to bring Rodolfo to his senses have also been severely scrutinized. Adriana Slaniceanu's reading of the text results in a judgment against these two women as "calculating" individuals.[49] Edward H. Friedman believes that their aggressiveness in bringing Rodolfo to justice elevates them to the status of "metatheatrical figures."[50]

Sadly, the critics have not always been able to agree on Cervantes's ultimate purpose in writing *Fuerza*. David M. Gitlitz, for example, considers the ending of *Fuerza* to be filled with moral ambiguity. Rodolfo's final "conversion" or "reformation" is no more believable than was Fernando's sudden change of heart in agreeing to marry Dorotea in the *Quixote* (pt. 1, chap. 36). The symmetry of the story allows the reader to see how every element in the novella has changed, except Rodolfo. For Gitlitz, the ending of *Fuerza* is a human, therefore imperfect, one.[51] Marcia L. Welles has a very different interpretation. She convincingly argues that although the patriarchal family structure appears to be remain intact at the end of *Fuerza*, "the painstaking process by which it is 'pieced together' after Rodolfo's initial assertion of power calls into question the politics of a corrupt aristocracy and the prerogatives of male sexuality."[52] Edward H. Friedman offers yet another perspective; he asserts that Cervantes wants his reader to be actively engaged with his text, which is why he presents in *Fuerza* a superficially happy ending that masks an ironic breaking of literary and social norms. The sophisticated reader is expected to note that the heavy-handed rhetoric shows through on both levels to discredit the "official" moral of the story.[53] And finally there is the opinion of Catherine Davis Vinel, who, following Forcione's lead, offers an original and very convincing theory in this regard. She proposes that the great writer was experimenting with contrasting narrative formats in *Fuerza;* Cervantes fused within a single work two literary styles that were normally considered incompatible, the "dark" novel and the "light" romance.[54]

From the selections I have provided above, the reader can easily see how the gloomy opening of *Fuerza* possesses all the characteristics of the modern novel: slow meticulous descriptions of situations, scenes, and actions taken from real life and viewed from the base level of the common people; and painstaking characterization, particularly in the area of a stream-of-consciousness report of all the jumbled thoughts that can race through a character's mind during a stressful moment. The novel—and *Fuerza* in its opening pages—is an ironic genre that reflects the world in less-than-ideal terms, as a place where chaos frequently reigns supreme and where the Church and other revered structures and institutions of the patriarchal order prove to be either useless or corrupt.

Conversely, we see how the brightly lit final scene employs many of the conventions of romance: an idyllic, aristocratic view of life; a strong reliance upon sudden plot turns, but little evidence of psychological development in the characters, who seem to be mere stereotypes; the sudden resolution of all conflicts, often brought about by a most fortuitous turn of events or a contrived set of coincidences; the use of a wedding ceremony (and the implied commingling of noble bloodlines) as a popular means of confirming and certifying the final reconciliation; and frequent use of images of fertility and abundance, often in the form of progeny and elaborate feasts.

Once again, the pivot point upon which the narrative thread switches from the novel to the romance format is found in section D, which consists of two paragraphs, the first of which is as dark and gloomy as the opening scene.

> Sucedió, pues, que un día que el niño fue con un reca[u]do de su abuela a una parienta suya, acertó a pasar por una calle donde había carrera de caballeros. Púsose a mirar, y por mejorarse de puesto pasó de una parte a otra a tiempo que no pudo huir de ser atropellado de un caballo, a cuyo dueño no fue posible detenerle en la furia de su carrera. Pasó encima dél, y dejóle como muerto tendido en el suelo, derramando mucha sangre de la cabeza. Apenas esto hubo sucedido, cuando un caballero anciano

que estaba mirando la carrera, con no vista ligereza se arrojó de su caballo y fue donde estaba el niño, y quitándole de los brazos de uno que ya le tenía le puso en los suyos, sin tener cuenta con sus canas ni con su autoridad, que era mucho, a paso largo se fue a su casa, ordenando a sus criados que le dejasen y fuese a buscar un cirujano que al niño curase. Muchos caballeros le siguieron, lastimados de la desgracia de tan hermoso niño, porque luego salió la voz que el atropellado era Luisico, el sobrino de tal caballero, nombrando a su abuelo. Esta voz corrió de boca en boca hasta que llegó a los oídos de sus abuelos y de su encubierta madre, los cuales, certificados bien del caso, como desatinos y locos salieron a buscar a su querido. Y por ser tan conocido y tan principal el caballero que le había llevado, muchos de los que encontraron les dijeron su casa, a la cual llegaron a tiempo que ya estaba el niño en poder del cirujano. (2:85–86)

[It happened then, that one day, when the boy was sent with a message from his grandmother to a relation of hers, he happened to go along a street where some gentlemen were racing horses; he stopped to look, and, in order to find a better vantage point he crossed the street at a moment when he could not avoid being knocked down by a horse, whose rider could not hold him in the fury of his gallop. The horse went over him and left him as if dead, stretched out on the ground, with blood pouring from his head. Hardly had this occurred when an old gentleman, who was watching the race, leapt with extraordinary agility from his horse, rushed up to the boy and, taking him from the arms of a bystander who had picked him up, took him in his own arms, and without any regard for his advanced years and personal dignity, rushed off to his own house, ordering his servants to leave him and go to look for a surgeon to attend to the child. Many gentlemen followed him, distressed at the accident to such a beautiful child, because the news soon spread that the victim was little Luis, the nephew of such and such a gentleman (naming his grandfather). This news flew from mouth to mouth until it came to the ears of the grandparents, who, when the matter was confirmed, rushed madly out to seek their beloved child. So well-known and important was the gentleman who had taken him home that many people they met told them where the house was, and there they arrived when the boy was already being treated by the surgeon.] (2:115)

The second paragraph is as bright and life-affirming as the final scene:

El caballero y su mujer, dueños de la casa, pidieron a los que pensaron ser sus padres que no llorasen ni alzasen la voz a quejarse, porque no le sería al niño ningún provecho. El cirujano, que era famoso, habiéndole curado con grandísimo tiento y maestría, dijo que no era tan mortal la herida como él al principio había temido. En la mitad de la cura volvió Luis en su acuerdo, que hasta allí había estado sin él, y alegróse en ver a sus tíos, los cuales le preguntaron llorando cómo se sentía. Respondió

2 / PATTERNS OF SYMMETRICAL DESIGN

que bueno, sino que le dolía mucho el cuerpo y la cabeza. Mandó el médico que no hablasen con él, sino que le dejasen reposar. Hízose ansí, y su abuelo comenzó a agradecer al señor de la casa la gran caridad que con su sobrino había usado. A lo cual respondió el caballero que no tenía que agradecelle, porque le hacía saber que cuando vio al niño caído y atropellado, le pareció que había visto el rostro de un hijo suyo, a quien él quería tiernamente, y que esto le movió a tomarle en sus brazos y a traerle a su casa, donde estaría todo el tiempo que la cura durase, con el regalo que fuese posible y necesario. Su mujer, que era una noble señora, dijo lo mismo, y hizo aún más encarecidas promesas. (2:86)

[The gentleman and his wife, the owners of the house, asked them, thinking they were the child's parents, not to weep or raise their voices in lamentation, because it would be of no help to the boy. The surgeon attended to him with great care and skill, and announced that the wound was not as dangerous as he had at first feared. In the course of this treatment, Luis, who had been unconscious until then, came to, and was delighted to see his uncle and aunt, and they, in tears, asked him how he felt. He replied that he felt well, except that his head and body hurt a great deal. The surgeon ordered that nobody should talk to him and that he should be allowed to rest. This they did, and the grandfather began to thank the master of the house for the great kindness he had shown the boy. The gentleman replied that there was no need to thank him, and told him that, when he saw the boy knocked over, it had seemed to him that he was looking at the face of a son of his, whom he loved dearly, and that this had moved him to take the child in his arms and bring him to his house, where he could stay until he was quite cured, and they would provide every necessary comfort. His wife, who was a well-born lady, said the same, and made even more fervent promises.] (2:115)

These two paragraphs, which I and many others have already called the central episode of *Fuerza*, can now be seen to function also as a microcosmic representation of the general structure of the complete novella, divided neatly into two parts: novel and romance.

Leaving aside purely literary considerations and moving onto the moral plane, I believe that Cervantes has done for rape in *Fuerza* what Calderón would later do for wife murder in *El médico de su honra*: call attention to the horrific nature of some men's criminal abuse of women by treating the heinous acts in question with heavy doses of irony. By creating absurd literary scenarios in which the rape and murder of good women not only go unpunished at the end but are in fact rewarded, these two writers have focused the public's attention on a terrifying social problem more effectively than any strident essay in defense of women could ever have done.

In *La fuerza de la sangre* Cervantes accomplishes this goal by dividing his story neatly into two mirror-image halves that don't quite jibe. The first part is written in the new, realistic tradition of *La Celestina* and *Lazarillo de Tormes*, a style that would come to be called novelistic; the action here takes place in a gloomy world of violence and sin, of disharmony and darkness, of pain and despair. The more uplifting second half clearly follows the conventions of the prose romance and is characterized by images of radiant light and shimmering jewelry, a world of affirmation and redemption, of harmony and resolution.[55] The starkly ironic clash of these two antithetical literary attitudes—and competing worldviews—in the same novella is perfectly designed to produce a strong sense of dis-ease in the reader. If he were living in a well-ordered universe, a rapist like Rodolfo would not be rewarded for his misdeeds with a Church-sanctified marriage to his victim. Cervantes's deliberately unsatisfying denouement was intended to underscore the same fundamental incongruity he had attempted to signal in the first part of the *Quixote* (1605): to prescribe remedies based on age-old literary conventions as a solution for the serious social problems of contemporary Spanish society is sheer madness. The "happy" union of the predator and his victim at the end of *Fuerza* ought to be considered as grand a literary pipe dream as any of Don Quixote's ridiculous fantasies.

The irony of *Fuerza*'s contrived and superficial happy ending has been emphasized by Stacey L. Parker Aronson in a 1996 article. She points out that Rodolfo's easily provoked lust for Leocadia is as strong at the end when he agrees to marry her as it was in the opening scene, when he brutally assaulted her.[56] Parker Aronson points out that the ending of *Fuerza* can be considered either reasonable or ironic, depending upon the reader's selection of either a historical or a discursive level of interpretation. The critic herself takes the ironic view: "This supposed happiness could be interpreted as an ironic commentary on the salvation of a dishonored woman through marriage and her assessment as a reproductive tool" (86). Ultimately, neither the historical nor the discursive interpretation has very much to do with seventeenth-century Spanish reality, which is perhaps the point Cervantes was attempting to make.

Let us now compare the symmetrical design we have observed in *Amante* and *Fuerza* with the structure of yet another of Cervantes's novellas, one whose narrative plan few Cervantist critics would ordinarily select for such a direct comparison.

La española inglesa

The story of Isabela, the Spanish girl who becomes separated from her natural parents and is raised in Elizabethan England, is a rather long, rambling narrative that to some extent could be said to be a potpourri of favorite Cervantine themes. This tale features, for example, the kidnapping or imprisonment motif that Cervantes used first in the Capitán Cautivo's Story (*Don Quixote* 1, chaps. 39–41) and then in certain other novellas like *La gitanilla*, *El amante liberal*, and *La fuerza de la sangre*. Other popular literary themes present here are jealousy (cf. *Amante*, *Gitanilla*), the son who is destined to pay for the sins of his father *(Fregona),* and the potentially destructive power of physical beauty *(Fuerza)*.

Of all Cervantes's so-called trial novellas, *Española* also seems to be the one in which the writer exercises the greatest amount of authorial control, the one that features the most complicated plot structure, and the one that appears to toy to the maximum extent with the reader's emotions by offering false happy endings and near-disastrous occurrences that continually threaten the happiness of the young protagonists, Ricaredo and Isabela. Ruth El Saffar (1974) was the first to observe that, of all Cervantes's short narratives, this one seems to approximate most directly the intensely spiritual atmosphere as well as the narrative techniques and themes of the *Persiles*, which is why she considered it one of the last written of the *Novelas ejemplares*.[57]

El Saffar was also the first to notice that *Española* is the only one of Cervantes's *Novelas* to exhibit a real balance between the competing desires of men and women in the game of courtship. In their portrayal of the struggle between the male's desire for carnal possession and the female's search for a lasting marital union, stories like *Gitanilla*, *Amante,* and *Fregona* present overly arduous young men in pursuit of overly cautious young women; in the end both have to modify their respective positions in order to reach a workable compromise. This is what El Saffar calls the victory-over-self pattern. In *Fuerza*, *Doncellas,* and *Cornelia*, on the other hand, the required modification is made on the basis of victory over the other: the unbridled passions of the young man are eventually tamed by the solicitations of the woman he has dishonored; she must convince the seducer to right—by marriage—the wrong he has done to her. In *Española* neither Ricaredo nor Isabela needs to conquer or modify; each character achieves separately "the proper attitude toward the adversities and uncertainties that are basic to the human condition" (152).

Shortly following the publication of El Saffar's study, David Cluff (1976) furthered our understanding of this story by pointing out—correctly, it seems to me—the importance of the next-to-last paragraph of *Española* in providing the reader with a capsulized summary of all the major plot points of the story. Cluff noted that critics have tended to ignore the major subplot of the story, the lost-daughter motif, in favor of more attractive themes like the trials and tribulations of the lovers and Ricaredo's gradual spiritual development.[58] In the first half of the penultimate paragraph Cervantes, perhaps anticipating some inattention on the reader's part after having plowed through such a long and intricately woven text, offers a quick summary of the major events of the story:

> Por estos rodeos y por estas circunstancias los padres de Isabela cobraron su hija y restauraron su hacienda, y ella, favorecida del cielo y ayudada de sus muchas virtudes, a despecho de tantos inconvenientes, halló marido tan principal como Ricaredo.... (1:282–83)

> [By and through all these vicissitudes and circumstances Isabella's parents regained their daughter and their property, and she, favoured by heaven and sustained by her many virtues, despite so many obstacles, found a husband as noble as Ricaredo....] (2:57)

The very first thing Cervantes mentions here is how Isabela's parents, having endured many frustrations and unexpected turns of events, ultimately succeeded in recovering their long-lost daughter; secondly, he notes that her parents' financial losses were coincidentally restored in the process; and finally he reminds us that Isabela, with heaven's blessing and thanks to her many personal virtues, was able to overcome a great many obstacles and acquire a first-rate husband. Here, in a nutshell, Cervantes is laying out the three major actions of his story. This summary is quickly followed by additional remarks concerning certain economic transactions that took place immediately after Ricaredo and Isabela's marriage:

> en cuya compañía se piensa que aún vive en las casas que alquilaron frontero de Santa Paula, que después las compraron de los herederos de un hidalgo burgalés que se llamaba Hernando de Cifuentes. (1:283)

> [with whom, it is said, she lives to this day in the house they rented opposite Santa Paula, and which they afterwards bought from the heirs of a gentleman from Burgos, called Hernando de Cifuentes.] (2:57)

Critics who have studied *Española* in the wake of El Saffar and Cluff's important examinations have generally directed their efforts toward either fathoming the story's exemplary content or explicating Cervantes's technical genius in composing it. A combination of both methodologies can be found in the 1978 study of Thomas A. Pabon, who asserts that Cervantes uses the movement of the labyrinth to provide unity and baroque complexity to this novella.[59] If, as Pabon asserts, "in baroque fiction, just as everything seems on the point of being resolved, another complication arises to create new disorder, returning the characters to the winding complexity of the labyrinth" (60), *Española* would certainly be an excellent example of baroque literary technique. Pabon also proposes that in *Española* the labyrinthine structure symbolizes seventeenth-century man's role in Spanish society as he works toward his ultimate goal, salvation. The trials, separations (e.g., Ricaredo's pilgrimage), and acts of self-purification that the two lovers experience are simply representative of the labors that every person must perform to wash away the stain of original sin and prove him- or herself worthy before God (66).

There seems to be considerable disagreement among scholars as to whether *Española* leans more heavily toward plot intrigue or fine characterization to make its point. Julio Rodríguez-Luis (1980), following El Saffar's lead, declares that this story follows the example of Heliodorus's *Ethiopian History* and Cervantes's own *Persiles* in considering plot intrigue more important than characterization, social factors, intellectual content, etc.[60]

A contrary view is taken by Mercedes Alcázar Ortega (1995), for whom the major literary value of *Española* lies in the characterization of the two protagonists.[61] For this critic, Cervantes has created Isabela from the Neoplatonic poetic models of writers like Garcilaso de la Vega, but with a new twist: unlike Garcilaso's Isabel Freyre or Petrarch's Laura, Cervantes's Isabela has no identity of her own; she exists only as an axis upon which the author sets up shop (36). At first Isabela's principal role in the story is that of providing motivation ("la necesidad de amar" [the need to love]) for Ricaredo's heroic deeds: Isabela is not simply a poetic Renaissance *donna*, but also the prime reason for which Ricaredo feels obligated to go off to war (40). But in the second half she has a more purely literary function: Cervantes uses Isabela as a text-generating element, a voice that can be raised to prevent the obliteration of her story (45).

What I intend to show here is that the story of *La española inglesa* is perhaps the most deceptive unit in Cervantes's collection of novellas. Consequently, the interpretations of both Rodríguez-Luis and Alcázar Ortega eventually must be considered inadequate, because they wrongly assume that the love intrigue is Cervantes's principal focus in this story. In 1988 Carroll B. Johnson convincingly demonstrated that in *Española* the union of these two lovers is actually secondary in importance to the overriding economic issues that are presented in the second half.[62] I shall have more to say about this matter at a later point in my analysis.

Let us now summarize what the critics have had to say about the internal structure of *La española inglesa*. Joaquín Casalduero (1962) observed several intricate numerical patterns in *Española*, but he never quite envisioned the story as a work divided into two equal halves. He discerns four narrative sections, each representing a change of venue: London, on the high seas, back in London again, and the finale in Seville.[63] Within these four narrative units Casalduero observes certain paired elements. There are, for example, two major incidents that threaten the lovers' happiness, the first being the proof of valor demanded by the queen before acquiescing to Ricaredo's marriage to Isabela, the second consisting of the hero's rivalry with Arnesto (120). Then there are the paired physical illnesses: Ricaredo's love-sickness in the first half and Isabela's near-lethal bout with poison in the second (121). Another matched tandem are the heroic exploits of Ricaredo: his brief career as an English naval officer in part one; his pilgrimage to Rome and subsequent captivity in Algiers in the second part (121).

One wonders why Casalduero, having noted all these curious parallels and a certain "binary rhythm" (120, 121) and "binary accent" (128) in the narrative, failed to grasp the obvious: that *Española* itself is an overwhelmingly binary work, even to the point of being divided into two equal parts.

In 1968 Jennifer Lowe published an article on the structure of *Española* in which she sought to combine Casalduero's observations about the work's binary rhythm with those of Guillermo Díaz-Plaja (1948).[64] Lowe correctly notices that *Española* is divided into two main sections, if not exactly into two comparable halves; her proposed design for the work is as follows:[65]

Section I
   1. Opposition of Ricaredo's parents; their plan to marry him to Clisterna.
   2. Separation of the lovers during Ricaredo's mission.
   3. Appearance of Arnesto as a suitor for Isabela.
   4. Isabela's illness and loss of beauty.

Section II
   1. Renewal of the opposition of Ricaredo's parents; the arrival of Clisterna.
   2. Separation when Ricaredo leaves for Rome and Isabela for Spain.
   3. Numerous admirers for Isabela.
   4. News of Ricaredo's death.

Lowe observes that in each section the first obstacle affects Ricaredo in particular, the second is equally hard for both lovers, while the third (and most serious) is related specifically to Isabela. By the end, of course, each lover has overcome an equal number of obstacles and thereby proved to be worthy of the other. One very important observation made by Lowe here is that the first three adversities in section II are an intensification of those in section I, a pattern that provides the basic balance and harmony for *Española*. In summary, Prof. Lowe's principal contribution lies in her being the first to cite *La española inglesa* as evidence of Cervantes's realization that structure and content could and should complement each other in a work of fiction (290).

Some years later (1981) Guido Mancini proclaimed that *Española* was a work consisting of three main divisions, which he called "episodes." He refers to the first episode as an "idilio amoroso" [a romantic episode] that extends up to the queen's intervention; the second picks up the action with Ricaredo's naval adventures and ends with Arnesto's jealous opposition, at which point the third and concluding episode begins.[66]

The next major advance in understanding of Cervantes's narrative plan for *Española* was David Cluff's 1976 investigation of the interplay of structure and theme in that novella. Cluff begins his study by elaborating upon an observation made earlier by Díaz Plaja: the basic pattern of *Española* consists of the creation of suspense and rising expectations regarding the marriage of Ricaredo and Isabela, followed by the interruption of those expectations just as they are about to be fulfilled.[67] In support of this theory, Cluff signals the three principal turning points in the story: the queen's intervention, the poison administered by Arnesto's mother, and the announcement of Ricaredo's "death." Cluff also maintains that these episodes are arranged in an order of rising intensity; with each successive interruption the difficulties become greater and the rhythm of the narrative becomes more rapid and violent.[68]

According to Cluff, if the seemingly star-crossed courtship of Ricaredo and Isabela can be considered the main plot of *Española*, the relationship between Isabela and her parents must be viewed as the secondary thread of action or subplot. The function of the subplot is to reinforce the rhythm of the principal action and heighten the tension. Cluff shows how each of the three interruptions forces the characters involved in the main plot to deal with some new obstacle or difficulty. In the meantime, however, the subplot is being resolved in only two stages, the first falling between the first and second interruptions, the second resolution coming between the second and third interruptions (268) (see table 2.1):

Table 2.1

Principal Plot	Secondary Plot
Interruption #1: the queen Ricaredo proves himself worthy (physically).	Isabela is reunited with her parents
Interruption #2: the disfigurement Ricaredo proves his worth (spiritually).	Isabela and parents recover home and fortune; Isabela recovers beauty.
Interruption #3: Ricaredo's "death" Ricaredo returns from the dead.	

Cluff also attempts to deal with a major inconsistency in Cervantes's plot construction: the sudden and sharp shift in the attitude of Ricaredo's parents toward Isabela from approval to disapproval, solely because of the young girl's unfortunate disfigurement. Such a mercenary change of heart in characters who previously have been motivated by elevated Christian principles seems psychologically out of tune. Cluff's explanation for this is that Cervantes apparently was willing to sacrifice consistency to the momentary needs of the plot (269), a view with which I agree.

My own analysis of the structure of this story borrows key elements from the previous observations and interpretations of Professors Casalduero, Lowe, and Cluff. In the linear design of *Española* that I provide in schema 20 it can be seen that this story conforms to the same structural pattern we observed earlier in *Amante* and *Fuerza*, i.e., symmetrical halves, each of which offers complexities that I consider especially thought-provoking and unusual (schema 20).

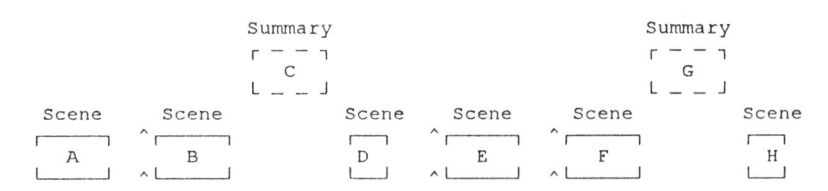

Schema 20. *La española inglesa*

(A) Problem #1 established: separation of Isabela from her natural parents.
(B) First set of complications introduced:
 • Ricaredo falls in love with Isabela despite a previous agreement to marry a Scottish girl;
 • the English queen demands that Ricaredo prove his worthiness to marry Isabela;
 • politico-religious dilemma: how can a Catholic soldier serve a Protestant queen against a Catholic enemy?

 (C) ANALEPSIS: Isabela's father's story; final element put in place to resolve the original problem.

(D) Solution #1 achieved: reunion of Isabela and her parents in England.

[structural midpoint]

(E) Second set of complications introduced:
 • Arnesto's jealousy; his mother's attempt to murder Isabela;
 • Isabela's sudden ugliness as a result of poison administered by Arnesto's mother;

- Ricaredo's parents' decision to renew his engagement to Clisterna.
(F) Problem #2 established: separation of Isabela and Ricaredo.

> (G) ANALEPSIS: Ricaredo's account of his two-year odyssey: how he survived 1) Arnesto's murder attempt and 2) his subsequent captivity in Algiers.

(H) Solution #2 achieved: reunion and marriage of Isabela and Ricaredo in Seville.

As we note in the summary given above, the only real structural difference between the two halves of *La española inglesa* lies in the fact that the second part features an accumulation of complications prior to the delayed introduction of the major problem, the physical separation of the lovers. In the first part the main problem is introduced in the very first paragraph, when Isabela is abducted; all attendant complications follow from that initial event. Leaving aside this one difference, the narrative formula is essentially the same for each half of the story:

1. to present a problem and an attendant series of complications;
2. to propose a course of action that may resolve the problem;
3. to delay the final resolution while one of the characters offers an explanatory or informational exposition (at the same time that the final element is put in place for the ultimate solution); and then
4. to arrive at a successful resolution with a culminating recognition scene and a joyful denouement.

Although this story plan includes two analeptic pauses, one in each half, the narrative does *not* begin, as one might expect, in medias res. The first flashback seems natural enough, but the second instance has the appearance of being contrived and unnecessary. The events related in the second analepsis could easily have been recounted as part of the main narrative thread, but the narrator clearly opts to hold this section in reserve for a concluding flashback that will counterbalance the first one.

The how and why of Cervantes's preference for symmetry and balance here may be explained by noting how different this tale is from the majority of the stories in the 1613 collection. In most of the other novellas there is only a single obstacle to surmount. *La española inglesa*, in contrast, presents two sets of problems, the first simple, the second complex, each with its own set of vexing complications. The obstacles to the happiness of Ricaredo and Isabela are many and diverse, for as soon as one thorny issue is resolved, another is immediately injected to replace it.

In the first half there are two interruptions (not one, as Cluff has proposed): the kidnapping of young Isabela, separating her from her natural parents; and the queen's demand for a demonstration of Ricaredo's valor before allowing him to marry Isabela. By the end of the first half these obstacles have been neatly resolved. At the midpoint of *Española* we find Isabela restored to and reunited with her parents and certain of the queen's approval of her marriage to Ricaredo.

In the second half we find two additional interruptions, but these are much more complex, therefore more difficult to resolve than was the first set of obstacles: Isabela's disfigurement and the subsequent opposition of Ricaredo's parents to the marriage; and the (false) report of Ricaredo's demise. The first of these interruptions serves simply to bring about another forced separation of the young lovers, thereby setting in motion a new plot intrigue for the second half. The final interruption indeed conforms to Cluff's theory of progressively heightened tension.[69] It comes at a time when all the previous obstacles to Isabela's happiness appear to have been cleared away: Isabela has been allowed to return to her native Spain, her physical beauty has been completely restored, and her parents' future economic prosperity is assured. It is then that Isabela receives word that her betrothed has been vilely slain by his rival, Arnesto. Cluff's analysis of the second part of *Española* is completely on the mark; where he goes wrong is in not noticing that the second half is merely a replication and intensification of the first.

Let us now examine each of these narrative sections more closely.

(A) Problem #1 established: Separation of Isabela from her natural parents

While *Española* cannot be said to begin in medias res, it does commence with a startling event, the kidnapping of young (seven-year-old) Isabela by an English captain named Clotaldo during a late-sixteenth-century sack of Cadiz by the English navy. Critics have spent an extraordinary amount of time and energy attempting to determine the historical basis of Cervantes's story, i.e., which of several such English raids Cervantes may have had in mind for the historical setting of his story. While the majority of those others who have studied the issue (e.g., Casalduero, Schevill and Bonilla) have preferred to root the story in the English invasion of 1596, Georges Hainesworth (1933) and Mack Singleton (1947) have suggested an earlier attack on that port city in 1587.[70] Francisco Rodríguez Marín (1901) had proposed an entirely different historical event as Cervantes's inspiration: the 1585 attack on Cartagena.[71]

Amezúa y Mayo (1958) accused Cervantes of muddying the historical waters by referring to the leader of the raid as "el conde de Leste," which is to say Leicester, instead of using the name of the actual English commander in 1596, the count of Essex.[72] As Singleton notes, Leicester was also not personally involved in the 1587 attack, which was carried out under Sir Francis Drake's command.[73] Leicester's name was familiar to Spaniards principally because of his sterling performance as commander-in-chief of the English forces that defeated the Spanish Armada in 1588, the very same year he died.[74] Critical efforts to establish some precise historical basis for Cervantes's novella have continued to the present. In 1989, for example, one scholar even ventured to suggest the name of Hugh Tipton, an English merchant who was stationed in Seville during the 1560s, as a likely primary source regarding much of the historical and commercial material Cervantes later infused into this story.[75]

My personal feeling is that all the aforesaid efforts have been wasted on a wild-goose chase, a quest for a nonexistent prize. Whatever historical or pseudohistorical information Cervantes has included in the telling of *Española* is merely so much window dressing, I fear. One of the salient characteristics of Cervantes's narrative style has always been his studied *im*precision. *La española inglesa* simply happens to be one of the Spanish writer's more remarkable feats of legerdemain: Cervantes skillfully lays a veneer of pseudohistorical facts atop a totally imaginative moral tale. No date is ever given for any particular event in this story; even the internal time references between events in the story are inconsistent and often contradictory. In short, there is absolutely no historical or chronological peg upon which to hang our critical hats. The only historical figure mentioned is the count of Leicester ("Leste"). Elizabeth I of England is never mentioned. Critics have reasonably assumed the English monarch mentioned in the story to be the daughter of Henry VIII, but a careful examination of the text will reveal that her baptismal name is never given. All references to her are limited to terms such as "la reina," "Vuestra Majestad," and "Su Majestad." Given the historico-political realities of Cervantes's time, readers would be safe in assuming that the English queen presented here is Elizabeth, the last ruler of the Tudor dynasty, but the author never states that as a fact. For centuries critics have been distracted by the bait that Cervantes left dangling before their hungry eyes and gone running off in all directions in search of a factual "truth" that never was.

Amezúa and Singleton, for example, object to the chronological inconsistencies that a 1596 starting point would create: Isabela's eventual return to Spain with her parents doesn't take place for another fifteen years, which would leave Elizabeth on the English throne until 1611, a full eight years after her actual death. El Saffar was among the first to underline the relative insignificance of the historical footnotes when she observed that "[t]he conflict highlighted in *La española inglesa* is not one between the English and the Spanish. Elizabeth and Leicester, popularly conceived of as villains in the Spanish imagination, are neutral, if not even slightly admirable characters in this novela." For El Saffar, the social or political concerns are less important that the moral ambiguities of characters like Clotaldo, whom El Saffar considers pusillanimous.[76]

A totally different spin is placed on the historical facts surrounding this novella by Carroll B. Johnson (1988). For Johnson, *Española* is actually a literary representation of—and a subtle, searing comment on—the political and commercial rivalry between the Spanish port cities of Cadiz and Seville in Cervantes's time. The author's "historical" inspiration, according to Johnson, was the nefarious role played by the duke of Medina-Sidonia, who had links to the powerful mercantile families of Seville, in delaying his counterattack on the English after their sack of Cadiz in 1596, thereby allowing the raiders to wreak considerable economic havoc on the merchants of the Atlantic port.[77]

If Johnson is correct—and I believe he is—his theory may explain Cervantes's deliberate obfuscation as to the exact date of the English raid mentioned in the opening sentence. The Spanish writer perhaps preferred the safer political course of making only an oblique reference to the 1596 sack of Cadiz and Medina-Sidonia's cowardly—or calculated, if one is inclined to suspect secret economic motives—response to it. In any case, *La española inglesa* clearly bears all the characteristics of pseudohistorical romance. Originally conceived as a purely imaginative story, it is artfully narrated in a deceptively "historical" style that secretly cloaks a very mordant piece of political and social criticism.

Cervantes wastes no time in establishing the first of Isabela's many problems when he informs us that a seven-year-old Spanish girl has been forcibly separated from her natural parents and will be raised in a hostile foreign culture. The initial goal, then, will be to reunite Isabela with her natural Spanish parents. The resolution of this problem is delayed for several years (seven, to be exact), but Providence ultimately resolves the matter, as we shall see, with the same inscrutability employed in creating it. Curiously enough, the two issues that any knowledgeable reader might reasonably expect to become major difficulties for the kidnapped girl are never allowed to develop beyond the stage of a minor inconvenience. These are the dangers connected with practicing her Catholic faith in a hostile Protestant land and the difficulty of preserving her native Castilian tongue and values in a foreign culture. But we are immediately informed that Clotaldo and his entire family are secret and practicing Catholics who keep their adopted daughter bilingual with furtive Spanish lessons taught by itinerant, underground Spaniards who are smuggled into their home on a regular basis. From the outset it is apparent that Cervantes is not at all concerned about the social, religious, and political problems such an un-

2 / PATTERNS OF SYMMETRICAL DESIGN 135

usual case would present. As we shall see, he has more profound and complex questions with which he prefers to deal.

(B) First set of complications introduced

The first additional complication to the problem arises seven years later when Clotaldo's son, Ricaredo (twenty years of age), realizes that he is in love with the fourteen-year-old Spanish girl who has been raised in his home. Unfortunately, his parents have already contracted to have him marry a Scottish girl named Clisterna (also a secret Catholic), who will bring with her a considerable dowry. Secondarily, there is the matter of obtaining the queen's permission. The first part of the dilemma proves relatively easy to dispose of: Ricaredo's parents agree to sacrifice the substantial economic gain they would have realized from the original marital arrangement and terminate the agreement with Clisterna's parents. Dealing with the queen is quite another matter entirely. The monarch, presumably Elizabeth I, insists that Ricaredo earn the right to Isabela's hand by valorous military service.

Although it appears that time itself will in due course provide a simple solution to this prickly complication, the queen's proposal actually creates still another dilemma for the perplexed Ricaredo: how can a clandestine Papist serve in the armed forces of a Protestant nation without raising his sword against a fellow Catholic? Faced with a real and very personal church-state conflict, the young Englishman nonetheless chances upon the perfect solution for his multiple difficulties. Shortly after assuming command of a pair of English warships, Ricaredo lucks upon two Turkish pirate ships that have captured a large Spanish cargo ship laden with spices, pearls, diamonds, and gold from Portuguese India.[78]

Ricaredo attacks the Turks, killing most of the corsairs and liberating a large number of Spanish prisoners in the process. At this point he wisely rejects the crueler course of action (mass execution) proposed by some underlings and decides instead to offer freedom to the handful of surviving Turks and all the Spaniards aboard. By this remarkable act of generosity Ricaredo achieves a viable solution to his personal church-state conflict. In addition, the problem of his having to earn the right to wed Isabela can be resolved by presenting the luxurious contents of the seized Portuguese merchant vessel to the queen. As a reward for this valorous service to the crown he expects to be granted permission to marry Isabela.

C. Partial analepsis #1: Isabela's father's story

As fate would have it, among the Spaniards aboard the Turkish frigate are Isabela's parents, who recount to Ricaredo their sad tale and ask to be taken to England, where they hope to find their long-lost daughter. The young Englishman immediately suspects their true identity and wisely seizes the opportunity to make amends for his father's earlier transgression against the Spanish family.

D. Solution #1 achieved: Reunion of Isabela and her parents:

In a single stroke Cervantes provides his lovers with a timely solution not only for the principal obstacle to their happiness but also for all the subordinate complications introduced in part 1. Ricaredo's arrival back in London with Isabel's parents at his side offers an immediate resolution to the primary problem of reuniting Isabela with her natural parents. The boatload of oriental treasures he brings in tow will also provides a quick and happy conclusion to the secondary obstacle that the queen has imposed to the couple's happiness.

At this point the reader is treated to the kind of emotional recognition scene that traditionally takes place at the very end of a prose romance: a dark mole behind Isabela's right earlobe quickly confirms the Spanish woman's suspicions about Isabela's true identity. As at least one other critic before me has noted, the use of the lost-daughter motif here involves a radical departure from the way Cervantes employs it in *Gitanilla* and *Fregona*. In these other cases, the recognition scene is the key to bringing two aristocratic lovers together in matrimony; it legitimizes an otherwise socially unacceptable marital union.[79] This does not apply in *Española*; here there are more complex issues to be resolved.

The insertion of an anagnorisis at the midpoint rather than at the end of *Española* is a clear indication that Cervantes's design for the novella was bipartite from the outset. Cervantes was holding in reserve a formidable arsenal of knotty problems and sticky complications that he would soon unleash. And so, at what appears to be the happy conclusion of Ricaredo and Isabela's journey to the altar, the narrator presents us with a totally new stumbling block and a new set of intricate complications that will carry us along in suspense for yet a second perilous voyage. What is most interesting about this new adventure is that the narrative pattern of the first section will be reprised in the second half, but now with a more complex weave.

E. Second set of complications introduced

In contrast to the immediacy with which the first problem was introduced in the opening paragraph of *La española inglesa*, the second dilemma—which we eventually learn will be that of reuniting the star-crossed lovers Isabela and Ricaredo—is introduced slowly and somewhat obliquely through the figure of the haughty and extremely jealous would-be suitor, Count Arnesto. The English nobleman is consumed by a wild passion for Isabela and refuses to acknowledge or accept her choice of Ricaredo over him as her intended husband. This character is described at the outset by Cervantes as arrogant, haughty, and overbearing; and his actions soon confirm every one of those descriptors. Even so, it soon appears that Arnesto's thirst for vengeance will come to naught when the choleric count is quickly jailed by the queen for challenging the innocent Ricaredo to a duel.

At this point a second contributing factor is introduced in the person of Arnesto's unscrupulously ambitious mother, who remains free to put into effect her own wicked plan for driving a permanent wedge between the would-be lovers. The older woman serves as the queen's personal handmaid (*camarera*) and manages to administer a powerful potion to the unsuspecting maiden, a poison that is intended to kill her but that merely throws the unlucky Isabela into a temporary but life-threatening coma. The most horrible effect of all, however, is that the vile mixture eventually causes the young girl's beautiful features to become hideously disfigured.[80]

Ruth El Saffar has observed that, contrary to the pattern we observe in *Gitanilla* and *Fregona*, whose main characters display a great deal of egotistical conduct, in *Española* all the selfish characters are secondary ones.[81] Count Arnesto's only role, El Saffar maintains, is to incarnate the very passions that Ricaredo must subdue in his own character before he can take possession of Isabela in marriage (160). Rodríguez-Luis prefers to draw a comparison between Arnesto and the figure of Ricardo as he appears in the opening scene of *Amante*.[82] A better comparison, I feel, would be to draw a parallel between Arnesto's obsessive passion and that of the various Turkish figures who lust after Leonisa in *Amante*.

F. Problem #2 established: Separation of Isabela and Ricaredo

While all the aforesaid nastiness is taking place at the palace, Cervantes injects still another complication. The extreme ugliness that suddenly afflicts Isabela eventually undermines her suitability as a daughter-in-law in the eyes of Ricaredo's parents. Clotaldo and his wife work to convince the queen to send the now-hideous Isabela back to Spain with her parents so that they can be free to reinstitute their earlier plan to marry their son to Clisterna, who suddenly reappears on the scene.

The name of Ricaredo's Scottish fiancée and her function in *Española* are subjects worthy of comment here. It seems odd that such a strictly tangential character—she is never actually present in the story, although her specter is invoked on two separate occasions to represent a formidable obstacle to the marriage of Ricaredo and Isabela—should be given a name,

Clisterna, while more significant characters like Isabela's parents go unnamed throughout the story. Mercedes Alcázar Ortega calls her a character pulled straight out of a chivalric romance ("personaje . . . extraído de la novela de caballerías"), i.e., she has a purely poetic function.[83] Ricaredo's parents hope Clisterna's attractiveness will soon erase the image of Isabela's beauty that Ricaredo says is stamped on his soul. This reference recalls a similar conceit forged by Garcilaso de la Vega in his Sonnet V.

Using her name as a starting point, Carroll B. Johnson offers a different and rather malicious interpretation of the Scottish girl's function in *Española*. "Clisterna" is derived from the noun *clíster* (Fr. *clystère*, enema), which Johnson translates in purely materialistic terms, i.e., as an economic remedy rather than a medical treatment.[84] The daughter of wealthy Scots, Clisterna represents the notion of a financial influx, a sudden infusion of capital by way of marriage, that the struggling Clotaldo sorely needs. Catherine Davis Vinel echoes these sentiments, charging Clisterna with being the symbol and embodiment of the medieval custom among the aristocracy of contracting marriage for principally economic reasons.[85]

Realizing that it would be fruitless to resist openly the machinations of his parents and the queen, Ricaredo opts for a delaying action. The first part of his plan is to persuade Isabela to acquiesce to the scheme to banish her and her family. The reluctant bridegroom will then circumvent his elders' wedding plans by insisting upon making a prenuptial pilgrimage to Rome, supposedly for the purpose of assuaging his troubled conscience. Ricaredo promises that, having bought some time with such a ploy, he will secretly make his way to Spain, where he will rejoin Isabela and her family in either Cadiz or Seville within the next two years.

There are two observations to be made here. First, note how skillfully Cervantes manages to postpone until such a late point the introduction of the key moral issue of *Española:* Ricaredo's constancy as a lover. Even though the young Englishman has been firm and unswerving in his devotion to Isabela following her terrible physical disfigurement, his faithfulness will be even more severely tested by their forced physical separation. If the primary objective of the first part was to bring about the reunion of Isabela with her natural parents, the principal project of the second half will be to reunite the separated lovers Ricaredo and Isabela after they have been pulled apart by the combined machinations of Arnesto, his overly-zealous mother, Ricaredo's upwardly mobile parents, and the queen. From a structural standpoint, the resolution of this second dilemma mirrors that of the first part insofar as it will again require Ricaredo to embark upon a long and potentially perilous journey.

Second, note how slyly Cervantes introduces here a totally new but supremely important element that many critics have either ignored or glossed

2 / PATTERNS OF SYMMETRICAL DESIGN 139

over in their analysis of *Española:* the finely detailed description of international banking and credit procedures. This becomes essential because the relocation of Isabela and her family in Seville will require them to engage in a great deal of financial manipulation involving certificates and letters of credit to be exchanged among bankers and merchants in England, France, and Spain. The Spanish family receives a certificate *(cédula)* for their ten thousand gold escudos, payable in Seville. The entire procedure is very complicated and will require the money to pass first through Paris—direct payment between England and Spain apparently being impossible in Elizabethan times—and will necessitate the eventual submission of an undated letter of notice *(letra de aviso)* with a secret password *(contraseñas)* for payment. Similarly, Ricaredo's voyage to the Eternal City and his ransom from the Moors in Algiers will involve him in a comparable arrangement with some Florentine merchants.[86]

Only a handful of commentators on the *Novelas ejemplares* have attempted to wrestle with Cervantes's surprising decision here to inject a large dose of commercial and banking terminology into what has been an exotic love story. Casalduero considers the preoccupation in *Española* with these monetary concerns and financial activities to be nothing more than an expression of "lo pintoreso" [picturesque elements] a element more likely to be found in a realistic/naturalistic novel or drama of the nineteenth century than in a baroque composition. He finds the presence of such blatantly material values in a seventeenth-century work like *Española* to cause a profound imbalance in the work's composition, the kind of contrast (material versus spiritual values) that baroque literature and other artistic forms sought to harmonize.[87]

Stanislav Zimic (1987), who considers *Española* to be primarily a chivalric narrative, offers a different view. He believes that Cervantes inserted these commercial details primarily for aesthetic reasons, namely, to develop personal and social problems that would appeal to seventeenth-century readers.[88] The experimental infusion of elements like business trips and international banking transactions lends a refreshing air of verisimilitude to an otherwise highly poetic work; the resulting imbalance contributes to the harmonizing of contrasts that baroque writers like Cervantes were searching to achieve (481). Reasoning in a similar manner, María Caterina Ruta (1987) defends the injection of these prosaic, materialistic details as a welcome dose of realism that is justified by what she calls "the general economy of the narration."[89] Whatever may have been the author's intention in this matter, there can be no doubt at all that the insertion of so many commercial and financial details was a deliberate act on Cervantes's part. I tend to believe, along with Carroll B. Johnson, that Cervantes introduced these elements not for any artistic purpose but as a biting commentary on certain political and economic issues that he and his fellow countrymen were obliged to confront in the early 1600s.

In recent years critics have begun to comment on the very strong link that Cervantes forges in this story between Isabela's physical and emotional well-being and her family's economic prosperity. As her father informs us in his flashback account to Ricaredo in section C, following the loss of his daughter in the English raid he was seized with feelings of total despair, which soon led to the ruination of his formerly prosperous business enterprise in Cadiz. An estate valued at more than fifty thousand *ducados* was eventually liquidated, and the Spanish merchant has no doubt whatsoever as to the cause of his bankruptcy: "Todo lo perdí, y no hubiera perdido nada como no hubiera perdido a mi hija" (1:257) ['I lost it all, but it would have been nothing if I had not lost my daughter'] (2:21).

But once the family has been reunited and settled in Seville, everyone's destiny seems to take a turn for the better: the miraculous recovery of Isabela's health and physical attractiveness closely parallels the revival of her family's economic prosperity and her father's burgeoning stature in the Sevillian mercantile community. Adam Gai, David Cluff, and Carroll B. Johnson have signaled the poetic correspondence between the fortunes of Isabela and her father, as has Harry Sieber in the introductory essay to his edition of the *Novelas ejemplares*.[90] Sieber also underscores the significant role played in the story by the French merchants whose intervention facilitates the final solution.

It is Johnson, however, who, by uncovering a tight weave of financial and mercantile symbols in *La española inglesa*, has produced the most extensive commentary on the economic aspects of this story. Johnson expands Casalduero's earlier concept of Clotaldo as a "lukewarm Catholic"[91] into the commercial sphere; the English captain who plundered Cadiz and abducted Isabela is now viewed simply as a Catholic manqué, the victim of an outdated economic ideology that deprives him of an essential part of his Catholicism and causes him to commit unspeakable acts. In this antiquated use-value system, the only wealth worth having is the kind over which one has immediate possession and use; and the only means of acquiring valuable property is to take it away from someone else (= Isabela) or to marry it (= Clisterna).

Counterposed to Clotaldo in Johnson's scheme is Isabela's father, who belongs to the modern exchange-value system based on the investment of capital and the exchange of letters of credit. In this ideology, capital that exists only on paper can nonetheless be invested in commercial enterprises that will generate profits. This is precisely what Isabela's father does with the ten thousand escudos they receive from the English queen. The fact that Cervantes describes in such great detail the manner in which Isabela's new capital is transferred to Spain is a strong indication that seventeenth-century economic practice is one of the principal themes of *Española*. The letters of credit that slowly make their way from London to Seville are, in a sense, a kind of Protestant innovation being used to generate a new dimension of prosperity within the old Catholic economic order.[92]

In the first half of the story in London, when it appeared that Ricaredo and Isabela would easily gain the queen's approval to wed, any moments of happiness and tranquility the lovers enjoy are always short-lived. Similarly, in the midst of Isabela's physical recovery and the family's renewed prosperity in their homeland, there soon arise unexpected complications that make it seemingly impossible for Ricaredo to be reunited with her in Spain. After eighteen months of waiting in Seville, Isabela receives news from Ricaredo's parents that their son has been brutally murdered by Arnesto somewhere in France. Calmly accepting the cruel blow that fate appears to have dealt her, the lovely Spanish maiden plans to take a nun's habit at the conclusion of the agreed-upon two-year period. On the day of her scheduled entrance into the convent, however, Ricaredo suddenly appears on the street dressed in the habit of a recently ransomed prisoner of war from the North African camps. He intercepts her outside the convent gate and offers to fulfill his earlier promise of marriage.

G. Partial analepsis #2: Ricardo's account of his two-year odyssey

With a happy ending assured, the narrator now suddenly pauses to provide us with a brief flashback narrative of the events that nearly caused Ricaredo to miss the deadline and lose Isabela to the nunnery. The young Englishman recounts a series of exciting adventures and narrow escapes from a variety of physical dangers. Most importantly, he tells how he was almost murdered by the villainous Arnesto, an event that required him to spend a full two months recovering from the four bullet wounds he received in the attack. After barely escaping death on that occasion, Ricaredo was immediately thrust into a new life-threatening situation when his ship, bound for Spain from Genoa, was intercepted by two Turkish galleys, leaving him a prisoner of war in Algiers. Ricaredo finishes by recounting—in considerably greater detail than the average reader would normally expect—the manner in which the Trinitarian friars eventually ransomed him in time for him to meet his deadline in Seville.

H. Solution #2 achieved: Reunion of Isabela and Ricaredo

Reunited at long last with Isabela and having concluded the amazing account of his recent adventures, Ricaredo next moves to put his financial house in order: he cashes in a bond/certificate he has been carrying in the amount of sixteen hundred ducats, reimburses the Trinitarians for their expenses in ransoming him (adding a bonus of five hundred *ducados*, as he had promised to do earlier), and begins to make arrangements for his wedding to Isabela the following week. The story closes with a brief epilogue followed by a moral coda that extols the strange power of moral virtue and physical beauty to overcome life's adversities, not to mention the Divine Plan that somehow enables us to turn life's most severe trials into profitable experiences.

At this point it would be useful to revisit a selection from *Española* that I cited earlier. As David Cluff observed in 1976, the penultimate paragraph of *Española* serves as an accurate summary of the major themes of that novella.

> Por estos rodeos y por estas circunstancias los padres de Isabela cobraron su hija y restauraron su hacienda, y ella, favorecida del cielo y ayudada de sus muchas virtudes, a despecho de tantos inconvenientes, halló marido tan principal como Ricaredo, en cuya compañía se piensa que aún vive en las casas que alquilaron frontero de Santa Paula, que después las compraron de los herederos de un hidalgo burgalés que se llamaba Hernando de Cifuentes. (1:282–83)

> [By and through all these vicissitudes and circumstances Isabella's parents regained their daughter and their property, and she, favoured by heaven and sustained by her many virtues, despite so many obstacles, found a husband as noble as Ricaredo, with whom, it is said, she lives to this day in the house they rented opposite Santa Paula, and which they afterwards bought from the heirs of a gentleman from Burgos, called Hernando de Cifuentes.] (2:57)

The information Cervantes provides here helps us focus on the fact that *Española*, much like *La gitanilla*, manages to interweave two entirely different narrative threads within a single story. The initial intrigue deals with a father's loss and recovery, first of his daughter, then of his wealth and social reputation. The second story, seamlessly blended with the first, is the history of two lovers, Ricaredo and Isabela, who struggle to overcome a series of disruptive obstacles on their romantic journey to matrimony. In and around the first and second narrative threads of *Española* Cervantes also adds a third element that was not present in *La gitanilla*: the mechanics of capitalism.

Running beneath the surface of the two principal narrative units is an incongruous and seemingly tangential series of references that focus on the complex financial transactions that are required to bring about the economic recovery of Isabela's father, then Ricaredo's release from his Alge-

2 / PATTERNS OF SYMMETRICAL DESIGN 143

rian captivity. That this third factor—the entrepreneurial element, so to speak—is no mere afterthought on the part of Cervantes is demonstrated by the fact that it continues to function in a major way in the narrative even after the first two intrigues have reached their conclusion. At the very end the readers are informed, for no apparent reason having to do with the story, that the newlyweds currently reside in the same house, opposite the Convent of St. Paula, that they initially rented, then purchased from the heirs of a wealthy Burgos hidalgo.

There is yet another point to consider: as was the case in *Gitanilla*, the final word of *Española* can be said to summarize and signal the primary moral lesson of the story. The opening novella ends, we recall, on a celebratory note when the authorities opt to forgo vengeance in favor of clemency. In a similar fashion the concluding phrase of *Española* is designed to remind the reader of that story's main socioeconomic theme: how heaven can turn our greatest adversities into our greatest blessings ("cómo sabe el cielo sacar de las mayores adversidades nuestras, nuestros mayores provechos") (1:283).

The notion that the final scenes of *Española* may contain a hidden economic message that can only be decoded by reading between the lines has been touched upon by several critics over the years. Marsha S. Collins takes special note of the circuitous route Isabela's money takes; Collins points out that the funds illegally cross a number of national borders before being finally being transfigured into an instrument of Christian charity in ransoming Ricaredo from the Moors and Isabela from the convent.[93] A rather different interpretation is given by Julio Rodríguez-Luis, who was among the first to call attention to the fact that Isabela's marriage is a symbol of her family's resurgent social mobility as she ascends by marriage to a social rank higher than that of her merchant father.[94] Carroll B. Johnson seizes that very narrow and particular observation and expands it to encompass an even more wide-ranging historical conclusion: in *Española* Cervantes is indicating that the traditional (Old Christian) aristocracy, whose origins date back to feudal times, must now prepare to yield center stage—in both history and fiction—to the more vigorous (New Christian) bourgeoisie, to the more able merchant class whose overwhelming economic clout can no longer be ignored or denied.[95] In other words, Cervantes's fictional world attempts to confront the primitive economic system, the ultranationalistic political program, and the ultraracist social and religious institutions that Lope de Vega repeatedly celebrated in his *comedias*. In Johnson's view,

> Cervantes's text affirms that the bourgeoisie need not attempt to assimilate into the aristocracy, that the bourgeoisie qua bourgeoisie can come forward with honor as a protagonist of history, that there is no dishonor

attaching to the profession of merchant capitalist, that the wedding of a bourgeois family is a public event as worthy to be chronicled as the aristocratic festivities in Vallodolid, and finally that these *converso* business types with their international connections are among the best Catholics. In short, Cervantes's text is a direct refutation of the official rhetoric. (412)

Further proof of Cervantes's socioeconomic focus here is offered by Johnson in the fact that Isabela's family resettles in bourgeois Seville, not aristocratic Cadiz, and that their *converso* (i.e., originally Jewish, now New Christian) family name is conveniently glossed over while that of a marginal Old Christian from Burgos is loudly trumpeted (415). We should also note that the epilogue of *Española* breaks sharply from the pattern established in the two stories that most resemble it in Cervantes's collection, *Amante* and *Fuerza*. In both of those stories the final sentences include clear references to the abundant progeny ("los muchos hijos" in both cases) produced by the union of the protagonists. The closing words of *Española*, as we noted above, are quite explicit regarding a certain real-estate purchase the newlyweds made, but there is no mention whatsoever of offspring (414).[96]

Leaving aside for a moment these mundane issues, we need to say a few words about *La española inglesa* as a work of art. Adam Gai points to Cervantes's novella as a unique historical model that reflects the clash between the fluid and imprecise narrative techniques of the ancient Greek romance in the treatment of time and place, on the one hand, and, on the other, the more empirical notions of chronological and historical accuracy that were beginning to make their presence felt in modern, i.e., seventeenth-century, European literature.[97] What had previously been an atemporal and universal literary world was now being merged with a universe of measurable time and particularized, often familiar geographical references (71).

A rather different view is held by Stanislav Zimic, who sees in *Española* the subordination of the traditional Byzantine elements to a concept and structure more characteristic of the *novela de caballerías*.[98] For Zimic, *Española* represents nothing less than the new, modern chivalric romance, modeled on *Amadís de Gaula* (483). In this critic's interpretation, Ricaredo and Isabela are simply reincarnations of Amadís and Oriana, while Arnesto and his mother replace Arcalaus and Dardán as blocking agents; the witch's brew that nearly destroys Isabela is just a modern version of the old black magic that worked similarly grotesque transformations in the medieval original; and Ricaredo's pilgrimage to Rome is meant to parallel Amadís's self-imposed penance at Peña Pobre (472–76).

I find Gai's argument more convincing. Despite some distinctly chivalric overtones, *Española* clearly appears to imitate the structure of the Greek romance. Of even greater importance, however, are the key areas in which *Española* deviates from the traditional Byzantine formula:

1. *Lack of Initial Suspense:* because the narrator eschews the traditional in medias res beginning, there is never any mystery as to Isabela's origins; the element of suspense is derived instead from subsequent events that lead to a pair of anticipated reunions for Isabela, first with her parents, later with her fiancé Ricaredo.

2. *False Alarms:* the narrator introduces characters or events that seem to be problematic but eventually turn out to be innocuous or uneventful.

3. *Hidden Clues:* the narrator introduces what seem to be tangential elements (e.g., details about certain banking transactions) that ultimately play a very significant role in the story.[99]

I shall have more to say in a moment about the narrator's penchant for slipperiness and deception; for the present I will simply point out that this caginess on the narrator's part tends to confirm Riley's thesis about Cervantes's ambivalence toward "romance" conventions.[100] The peculiar mixture of romance and novelistic elements that we find in so many of the tales that deal with courtship—but especially in *Española*—is a clear indication that the great Spanish writer may have had more than a single reading audience in mind when he penned them. Catherine Davis Vinel believes, for example, that Cervantes constructed each of his novellas to appeal simultaneously to two distinct reading publics: traditionalists who wished to maintain the Old Christian (i.e., aristocratic) set of tastes and values, and the more skeptical and discerning readers among the emergent bourgeois merchant class who were more revisionist in their social and political attitudes.[101]

As Collins has pointed out, from a structural standpoint *Española* is a classic example of narrative gemination, a popular feature of the romance genre.[102] This judgment is confirmed by the large number of paired episodes and events that we find in the first and second parts of the story. Each half of the story features, for example, a long voyage that Ricaredo must undertake in order to resolve some problem he faces. Similarly, in each part the reader is treated to a detailed description of a certain elegant outfit of Isabela's: in the first part she selects her finest gown for her appearance before the queen; in the second she opts for the same luxurious garment on the occasion of her formal entrance into the convent.

Even the illnesses suffered by the lovers are offsetting: Ricaredo's lovesickness in part 1 is counterbalanced by Isabela's poison-induced coma and disfigurement in part 2. Other matched elements include a pair of tearful separation scenes and a tandem of elaborate processions (the first in London, the second in Seville). The ultimate parallelism, of course, is the structural one: each half features a recognition scene and a brief recapitulating flashback immediately before the end.

Regarding the subject matter, I would concur with those who have cited the virtue of constancy as the principal theme. For Ruth El Saffar the exemplarity of this particular novella lies in the constancy and devotion to eternal principles that we see exhibited in Ricaredo and Isabela.[103] The key to understanding constancy as the principal theme of *Española* is found in the story's most heinous episode, Isabela's tragic disfigurement from a potion administered by the queen's handmaid.

From a psychological standpoint Isabela's physical deterioration exerts no influence at all on the development of Ricaredo's character. Cervantes does not specify at which point Ricaredo's desire for Isabela changes from the carnal to the spiritual kind, but it must have occurred at a point prior to her being poisoned. The heroine's illness functions in two distinct ways: dramatically, as a pretext for advancing the action in the second half of the story, as David Cluff has argued;[104] and thematically, as an effective device for demonstrating Ricaredo's moral exemplarity and worthiness to be Isabela's husband.

Worthy of comment are the various chronological and/or factual errors, logical inconsistencies and seemingly irrelevant episodes we find sprinkled throughout the text. The most obvious cases are well documented. El Saffar and Cluff have noted, for example, how both the English queen and Ricaredo have widely fluctuating abilities to handle spoken Spanish. At one moment we are told that they are virtually fluent in the language, while at others they require the assistance of a translator.[105]

Adam Gai has signaled a number of temporal incongruities in *Española*, particularly in the computation of the main characters' ages. At the time of her abduction Isabela is said to be a child of some seven or eight years of age, while Ricaredo is reported to be a twelve-year-old (1:242–43). At a later point in the story their ages are recorded as fourteen and twenty, respectively (1:246). But when the twenty-year-old Ricaredo comes across Isabela's father, the old man declares that his daughter's abduction took place some *fifteen* years before (1:257), which is more than double the amount of time the narrator had accounted for to that point. In a similar fashion, we are told that Ricaredo's naval expedition consists of a six-day outgoing trip, a brief skirmish with some Turkish ships near Gibraltar, and a return trip to London that lasts nine days. Upon their return, however, the narrator informs us that the crew had been away from port a full *thirty* days. The explanation Gai offers for Cervantes's peculiar treatment of these chronological data is that he seeks to create a unique kind of chronology that values *symmetry* and the *effect* of precision over any actual chronological accuracy.[106]

Under the rubric of "irrelevant episode" we would include the cheerful scene that takes place in the English palace between Ricaredo, clad in a full set of armor, and some of the ladies of the court. Two of these women in particular—one called "Lady Tansy," the other referred to simply as "a tender-aged damsel"—stop to admire Ricardo's dashing figure and engage in a bit of lively banter with the young hero. I am unaware of any critical attempt to explicate the why and the wherefore of Cervantes's decision to include this scene in *Española*.

Of greater import than mere cases of inconsistent logic or factual error are the instances in which Cervantes appears to be actively manipulating the text to deceive the reader. One of the most intriguing aspects of *Española* is the manner in which that story's narrator consciously strives to mislead and/or deceive the reader all along the way. In this novella the reader is continually led to expect certain factors and issues to play an important role in the development of the plot, only to discover in the end that these factors have been no more than minor inconveniences with little or no real influence on the outcome of events.

A good example of this kind of deception is the noxious potion that the jealous stewardess administers to Isabela in the second half of the story. The near-lethal effects of the poison turn poor Isabela into a hideous creature, a turn of events that seems poised to sabotage the young girl's marriage to Ricaredo. But here again the promise remains unfulfilled. In a matter of months, Isabela recovers all her former beauty, her family is allowed to relocate in Seville, and her father's new commercial enterprise begins to flourish. In the total scope of the story, the significance of the evil philter is short-lived and relatively small.

A similar bit of narrative legerdemain is displayed in the case of Ricaredo's pilgrimage to Rome. The reader is aware from the outset that this journey is simply a pretext to permit Ricaredo to leave England and eventually be reunited with his lover in Spain, but the destination seems an ideal locale for some kind of religious experience. Unfortunately, as we learn in from Ricaredo's own flashback account of his travels (section G), the Eternal City is merely the first stop in his odyssey, and nothing of any importance occurs there. The intrigue begins to intensify only after he sets out on the road to Genoa, where at a roadside inn he sustains four serious bullet wounds when Arnesto attempts to assassinate him. Later, following a two-month recuperation period, Ricaredo resumes his journey and sets sail for Spain, only to be captured by Turkish pirates and held for ransom in Algiers. What had been presented originally as an uplifting spiritual voyage turns out to be a harrowing physical and psychological ordeal.

The most substantial deception of all is the pseudoissue of religious conflict between Catholics and Protestants in Elizabethan England. Isabela's status as a Spanish child being raised by kidnappers in England seems perfectly constructed to present sharp religious and linguistic conflicts in her life. The linguistic issues are easily dealt with: Clotaldo regularly manages to smuggle Spaniards into his home for the purpose of maintaining the girl's fluency in Spanish. On the theological front, it turns out that Clotaldo and his entire family are clandestine Catholics who continue to practice their faith in a Protestant land, so young Isabela's doctrinal needs are always fully attended to. In the end, as Cluff observed, the Catholic-Protestant rivalry never actually becomes a functional element in the story.[107]

Manuel da Costa Fontes, while proposing to explicate the important role played by love in *Española*, also touches upon the issue of religion and its curious function in that story.[108] His theory goes something like this: being of the merchant class, Isabela's parents were probably New Christians, a second-class group whose status in Spain was very much akin to that of Catholics living in Protestant England. When Isabela is transported from Spain to England, therefore, her status as a member of an "outsider" community isn't really altered, it is simply transferred to a different political and social sphere. Consequently, the Catholic-Protestant friction in England portrayed in *Española* is merely a kind of allegorical representation of the very real Old Christian–*converso* conflict Cervantes observed daily in his own country. In the words of Costa Fontes,

> The situation parallels very closely that of the Spanish converts who continued to practice Judaism in secret; with the difference that, to Cervantes's contemporaries, those who remained faithful to Catholicism in England deserved praise. One wonders whether a seventeenth century Spaniard was aware of the irony of the situation when reading Cervantes's "novela." (744)

Along with this critic, I would argue that it was Cervantes's unmistakable intention to underscore the ironic parallel. *Española* clearly appears to be arguing for greater tolerance on all sides.

Let us consider, in the light of Costa Fontes's thesis, the essence of the plot in this novella: a young English noble falls in love with and marries the daughter of a Spanish merchant. Social (i.e., class) and national barriers are scaled here, but not religious ones, since faith is never an issue. As Costa Fontes points out, a Spanish noble of Cervantes's time would have had to think twice before agreeing to such a marriage, given the stigma that would be attached to his family's name for centuries to come (746). But when Cervantes's English noble marries into a *converso* family, no stigma is attached and the reader notices nothing but the triumph of true love. Such a story could never have been told in a straightforward fashion, i.e., in strictly Spanish terms. In order to examine this uniquely Spanish social problem in a neutral, objective way, Cervantes was forced to transfer the scene to England, where the Catholic minority could be made to represent the New Christian element in Spain. Such a transfer required him to resort to an array of narrative tricks, some of which now seem deceitful, others merely pointless.

Costa Fontes uses the *converso* issue to explicate still another ironic aspect of *Española*: the fact that the English queen and the Spanish girl have the same name. In a sense, he notes, these women are both religious converts in their respective countries. In England, those who renounced their former faith to embrace a new one were honored for their conversion; in Spain, those whose ancestors had done the same thing were ostracized (746).

Albert A. Sicroff follows the same line of reasoning; he states that the perseverance of clandestine Catholics in Protestant England was given prominence in this story by Cervantes "to remind the Spanish reader of his country's own two-century old preoccupation with *conversos* suspected of clandestine judaizing."[109] Joseph V. Ricapito goes even further in making the same essential point. He declares: "Elizabeth I could be replaced symbolically by Philip II and/or Philip III; Clotaldo and his family, by false Christians paying lip service to the demands of the dominant culture. This perusal of history in England shows to what an extent the perils of being Catholic in England so greatly resembled those of being a *converso* in Spain."[110] Ricapito states bluntly that Cervantes's *novela* includes "a set of masquerading symbols: Roman Catholics versus English Protestants for *conversos* versus traditional Catholics in seventeenth-century Spain" (68).

In the final analysis, *Española* is not about English-Spanish political confrontations, nor is it about the Catholic-Protestant rivalry; and it is certainly not about lukewarm Catholics like Clotaldo, as Casalduero has suggested.[111] The constant deception Cervantes employs in his text makes the dominant theme very difficult to discern. Cluff goes so far as to say that the story has no particular theme at all, that it's simply an exercise in the marvelous, a case of technique overriding theme.[112] I would not go that far. To find the real subject of Cervantes's message we need to focus again on the little deceptions the author employs to tell his tale. We must ignore the many obvious red herrings Cervantes uses to cover his tracks and concentrate instead on the seemingly minute and inconsequential details that surprise us in the end by paying big dividends: the bonds *(cédulas)* and passwords *(contraseñas)*, the security measures *(recaudos)* and letters of credit *(cartas)* that were becoming the everyday instruments of international business and finance.

Ultimately, I agree with Carroll B. Johnson that *La española inglesa* is about the economic ups and downs of Spaniards like Isabela's parents; it's about the rivalry between Cadiz and Sevilla and how nobles like the duke of Medina-Sidonia were attempting to sabotage the prosperity of bourgeois *conversos* in the mercantile community; it's about improving the flow of commercial documents between Spain and her European neighbors; it's about how newly married couples need to establish their financial security before raising a brood of children; it's about the possibility and feasibility of intermarriage between Old and New Christians, between the nobility and mercantile class; it's about the necessity and inevitability of change and the passing of property from impoverished Old Christian families like Hernando de Cifuentes's to the new, hybrid aristocracy represented by the noble Ricaredo and the bourgeois Isabela.

A few words are now in order with regard to what Cervantes is specifically advocating in *Española*. I believe Catherine Davis Vinel has summarized these points very effectively; she views this story is an appeal for

• A new philosophy or form of government based on trust between rulers and their subjects; society needs to provide more freedom for the individual.
• Free trade to replace the old monopolies that controlled Spanish ports such as Seville.
• An exchange value system to replace the outmoded use-value concept.
• An egalitarian concept of marriage; a more even distribution of rights and benefits between husbands and wives.
• A new, hybrid aristocracy whose "nobility" would be determined on the basis of personal virtue and conduct rather than on lineage and purity of one's bloodlines.[113]

CONCLUSION

As we have seen here, many of Cervantes's *Novelas ejemplares* begin with some kind of attention-grabbing device. They may commence in medias res, as we saw in *El amante liberal* with Ricardo's tearful lament before the ruins of Nicosia; or open with the commission of some terrible crime, like the rape of Leocadia in *La fuerza de la sangre;* or the kidnapping of a seven-year-old child in *La española inglesa*. The three stories I have examined in this chapter also show that, with regard to thematic choice, romantic love is a strong Cervantine favorite, and that he often prefers to celebrate the magical qualities of eros by foregrounding it against the somber backdrop of some other powerful passion like jealousy, hatred, or obsessive desire.

A recurrent design can also be discerned in the unusual narrative structure Cervantes gives to these three stories, the common denominator being symmetry. Cervantes's imaginative plan for *Amante* and *Fuerza* calls for the suspension of two mirror-image halves over a fulcrumlike central episode. With *Española*, however, he offers a slightly different arrangement that allows him to alter the pattern slightly without abandoning the general symmetrical design. *Española* has no key episode or turning point on which to balance the narrative scaffolding. Instead, Cervantes simply divides the story into two equal halves, each of which follows a similar narrative pattern.

Actually, some sort of artful strategy for grabbing the reader's immediate attention is employed in more than half of Cervantes's *Novelas*. As we shall see, similar gambits are to be found in *Las dos doncellas, La señora Cornelia, El casamiento engañoso,* and *El coloquio de los perros.*

We have also seen that all three of these stories contain deeper and more complex thematic material than can be appreciated in a cursory or superficial reading. In all three cases, Cervantes appears to be reaching out to more than a single reading audience.

Because of the author's well-documented casual—some have even called it careless—attitude regarding the use of certain details, Cervantes's fiction has always been considered effortless and free-flowing rather than precise and well designed. In light of the structural precision and thematic complexity we have seen displayed in these three stories, perhaps the time has come to alter that judgment and reexamine the evidence.

3
Porras's Manuscript and the Curious Configuration of *Rinconete y Cortadillo*, *El celoso extremeño*, and *El licenciado Vidriera*

THE PORRAS MANUSCRIPT

Long, long ago, in what now seems to have been a former lifetime, I proclaimed my personal doubts about Cervantes's assumed authorship of two of his published works.[1] My thesis at the time was that the unattributed versions of *Rinconete y Cortadillo (R/C)* and *El [z]eloso extremeño (ZE)* contained in the now-lost Porras MS were originally penned by one or more anonymous Sevillian writers, and that Cervantes later "borrowed" and refashioned them for publication in his 1613 volume *Novelas ejemplares*. I have recently reaffirmed my beliefs in a 1994 review article.[2]

My reasons for denying Cervantes's authorship of the Porras versions are the following:

1. The testimony of Isidoro Bosarte, who actually handled the Porras document before it was lost in 1823, certifies that the texts of *R/C* and *ZE* were written in distinctly different hands in the Porras MS.[3]

2. Manuel Criado de Val's very thorough study of these texts in *Análisis verbal* (1953) reveals a sharp disparity in style between the Porras and Cervantes versions of these two tales, especially regarding the selection of *-ra* versus *-se* forms of the imperfect subjunctive. The evidence clearly points to the existence of more than one author (31–35).

3. Other changes in verb tense, form or mood in the two versions of these tales indicate that they were penned by different writers (35–36, 47–48, 63–65).

4. Consistent and significant differences of style regarding the authors' selection of proclitic and inclitic object pronouns emerge in a side-by-side comparison of the two versions of the same story (41–43)

5. The Porras versions employ a more latinized spelling of certain unstable vocabulary items (e.g., *sancta*), in contrast to the more modern spellings found in Cervantes's text (*santa*) (43, 62).

6. The alteration and/or expurgation of various sexual innuendoes and vulgar expressions become apparent as we move from the Porras to the 1613 version (55–57).

7. A multitude of serious scribal errors and inconsistencies render completely untenable the theory that one or the other version of *R/C* or *ZE* could have been copied from the other by the same author; Cervantes simply could not have misread his own handwriting so many times (65–66).

8. There exists prima facie evidence to show that it was Cervantes who was copying from the Porras text, not the other way around (67–68).

In support of this final contention I offer a comparison of the same section of *ZE* as it appears in the two versions. The more detailed Porras text reads as follows:

Cada parroquia o barrio tiene su título diferente, como las academias de Italia, y en una de ellas a los viejos ancianos y hombres maduros, que toman de asiento las sillas y se las clavan al cuerpo por no dexallas desde en acabando de comer hasta la noche, llaman *mantones*; a los recién casados, que aún tienen en los labios las condiciones y costumbres de los mozos solteros, llámanlos *socarrones*, porque, como digo, participan de la sagacidad de los antiguos casados y de la libertad de los mozos; a los mozos solteros llaman también *birotes*, porque ansí como los birotes se disparan a muchas partes, éstos no tienen asiento ninguno en ninguna, y andan vagando de barrio en barrio, como se ha dicho. Los de otra collación se llaman los *perfectos*; de otra los del *portalejo*; pero todos son unos en el trato, costumbre y conversación.

Uno, pues, de éstos, que era birote, acertó a mirar la casa de Carrizales. ... (Schevill and Bonilla 2:173)[4]

[Each parish or district has its own peculiar social terminology, very much like the Italian academies, and in one of these they use the term *mantones* (cloaks) to refer to the oldtimers and more sedentary younger males, which is to say, those who finish their midday meal and then come outside to spend the rest of the day seated in their comfortable chairs as if they were nailed into them, and they stay there until nightfall. The term *socarrones* (wisecrackers) is applied to the newly married men who still speak in the customary manner of single young men, for, as I say, they enjoy both the wisdom of old married men and the freedom of adolescents. The young bachelors are called *virotes* (darts), because, like darts or arrows, they tend to go off in all directions; they have no roots, no place to call home, and they roam from district to district, as I have indicated. Bachelors from another district are called *perfectos* (perfect ones); in still another area they are called "porch boys." But they're all the same in their conversation, their customs, and the way they treat other people.

And so, one of these fellows, a *virote*, stumbled upon Carrizales's house. . . .]

Cervantes's subsequent version is significantly different: he deletes the long paragraph describing the various kinds of men in the lower classes of Sevillian society and attempts to summarize the material with a single succinct statement:

Uno destos galanes, pues, que entre ellos es llamado *virote*—mozo soltero, que a los recién casados llaman *mantones*—asestó a mirar la casa del recatado Carrizales. . . . (Sieber 2:107)[5]

[One of these young blades, then, a bachelor, belonging to the type called *virotes* (the newly married ones are called *mantones*), chanced to notice the secretive Carrizales's house. . . .] (3:17)

It should be obvious to even the casual reader that the writer of the Porras version demonstrates much more detailed knowledge about the hierarchy of Sevillian social classes than does Cervantes, who calls newlyweds *mantones* instead of *socarrones*, the proper term. Cervantes clearly miscopies from the Porras version: he misses a semicolon after the word *mantones*, which causes him then to get all the subsequent terminology wrong in describing the Sevillian *gente de barrio*.

The reader should note that my attack on Cervantes's paternity is in no way a denial or denigration of the considerable artistic value of the Cervantine versions of these tales. Within the corpus of Cervantes's works, these two stories represent some of his most unusual and intriguing literary achievements. For reasons that will soon become apparent, I would now like to add the enigmatic history of *El licenciado Vidriera (LV)* to the list of *novelas* in the 1613 collection that deserve separate and special consideration because there are serious questions about Cervantes's paternity.

We begin by noting some of the special features that clearly set these three tales apart from the other tales in *Novelas ejemplares*. The first distinction we observe is that the narrative techniques used in *R/C, ZE,* and *LV* are noticeably different from those Cervantes employed elsewhere, especially in their avoidance of the flashback technique (analepsis) or any other narrative device designed to break the principal thread of narration. In effect, these three tales move steadfastly from beginning to end, always narrating events in their actual chronological sequence; there is no deviation whatsoever from the main story line. In contrast, virtually all of the other *novelas* employ one or more flashback narratives at some point in order to recapitulate certain events.[6] By avoiding such temporal disjunctions, the three tales under discussion here exhibit a structural simplicity that contrasts sharply with the multiple narrative divisions that characterize the rest of the collection.

It is also significant that *R/C*, *ZE,* and *LV* stand out from the other stories in *Novelas ejemplares* in their failure to conform to the taste of seventeenth-century readers for neat, "happily ever after" endings. Instead, these tales feature what modern readers cherish as "novelistic" conclusions: untidy, "loose," or not completely satisfying denouements. Their common lack of a comfortable resolution may explain why these stories went largely unappreciated until more recent (i.e., postromantic) times.

The generally jovial *R/C*, for example, doesn't have a formal denouement at all; the action at Monipodio's house simply comes to a halt, leaving the reader clinging to nothing more than the vague promise of a future sequel. Those expecting a neat wrap-up to the boys' adventures in the Sevillian underworld are bound to be disappointed.

Conversely, in the Porras version of *ZE*, Carrizales's belated discovery of Isabela's adulterous liaison with Loaysa and the young bride's tearful confession at the end supply a credible finale for what was from the beginning a dreadful and doomed marriage. This highly verisimilar and morally satisfying conclusion disappears in Cervantes's "exemplary" version when he adds peripeteia to the original anagnorisis by having the bride, now called Leonora, refuse to go through with the adulterous act. For many critics, this highly improbable turn of events serves only to diminish the story's credibility. Aside from the issue of verisimilitude, the denouement Cervantes imposes upon *ZE* is also disturbing because it neglects to provide a convincing explanation of the innocent Leonora's refusal or failure to defend herself against a false charge of adultery. At no time does she attempt to tell what really happened—or, rather, what didn't happen—while Carrizales was dozing away in a drug-induced stupor.[7]

Cervantes's attempt to add a new and unexpected twist to an otherwise predictable story is certainly praiseworthy, but some critics consider his concluding paragraph weak and simply inadequate to explain the young woman's strange silence in the face of such a serious accusation: "la turbación le ató la lengua, y la priesa que se dio a morir su marido no dio lugar a su disculpa" (Sieber 2:135) ['bewilderment made her tongue-tied, and the speed with which her husband died gave her no chance to absolve herself from guilt'] (3:55). As it turns out, this "turbación" extends to many readers as well.

The story of *El licenciado Vidriera* also manages to avoid a felicitous wrap-up, for the narrator caps his account of the final period of Tomás Ruedas's unusual life with an ironic coda:

se fue a Flandes, donde la vida que había comenzado a eternizar por las letras la acabó de eternizar por las armas, en compañía de su buen amigo el capitán Valdivia, dejando fama en su muerte de prudente y valentísimo soldado. (Sieber 2:74)

[Tomás went off to Flanders, where, in the company of his good friend Captain Valdivia, the life he had begun to make famous by learning he ended by fame in arms, leaving behind him, when he died, the reputation of having been a wise and most valiant soldier.] (2:97)

But here the disquieting note is generally conceded to be perfectly synchronized with the tone and events of the preceding narrative, not a careless or ill-advised late insertion or addition.

Perhaps the strongest reason of all for discussing these three tales as a unit has to do with their suspicious origins. As I have already pointed out, notably different versions of both R/C and ZE are already known to have existed within the Porras MS. As we shall presently see, there is also reason to believe that LV, never linked heretofore in any way with R/C and ZE, may, in fact, have been derived from the same Porras source. Let us examine the structure of each of these tales more closely.

RINCONETE Y CORTADILLO

At first glance, this story of two ruffians who aspire to become professional thieves appears to belong to the picaresque genre established by *Lazarillo de Tormes* and later given concrete form by *Guzmán de Alfarache*. In recent years, however, critics have had second thoughts about such a facile classification. For Casalduero (1962), for example, the element that separates R/C from the rest of the picaresque catalog is its optimistic attitude—more specifically, the heroic idealism with which Cervantes manages to illuminate his memorable urchins. The authors of the more common picaresque entries, on the other hand, contemplate with deep despair the sight of their contemporaries pulling farther and farther away from God's will.[8]

Eliodoro Febres (1972), while claiming to side with Menéndez y Pelayo, Predmore, Casalduero, and Pfandl in rejecting the picaresque classification for R/C, actually goes them one better by refusing to consider it even as an example of literary realism.[9] Instead, Febres views Cervantes's story as a uniquely baroque invention, "a large frame into which he places small baroque pictures arranged in linear perspective."[10]

Flowing from Casalduero's idealistic interpretation is the concept of Thomas R. Hart (1981), who finds the story of Rinconete and Cortadillo's adventures in Monipodio's Sevillian demimonde to be something quite unique, a "sojourn in the picaresque variant of the pastoral oasis."[11] A similar view is offered by Ronald G. Keightley (1982), who finds a number of reasons—e.g., the slow pace, the third-person narrative format, the intercalation of contrasting first-person narratives throughout *R/C*—to believe that the author's literary models were pastoral, rather than picaresque or chivalric.[12] Dian Fox echoes these sentiments in a 1983 article, then adds a touch of burlesque when she notes that "nearly every standard pastoral motif appears, slightly askew, in the patio of the Casa de Monipodio. The plot pattern and sense of distance are the entreé into a burlesque of the pastoral's ideal landscape."[13] In short, for some critics everything about Monipodio's lair is intended to be the antithesis of the traditional pastoral *locus amoenus*.

For Carroll B. Johnson (1991), *R/C* can be fully appreciated only if it is read against the picaresque prototype, Mateo Alemán's *Guzmán de Alfarache*.[14] In Johnson's view, Rinconete and Cortadillo are designed to be the polar opposites of Alemán's protagonist and their adventures have to be read in terms of *Guzmán*, but also against the grain of that model:

Both texts deal with the same social and economic problems, from the same general perspective, but in a different spirit. Alemán's hero wants to identify with the old order; Cervantes's characters want to leave it behind. Both projects are doomed to failure. (87)

Casalduero's analysis of *R/C* presents that story as exemplary in the obverse, i.e., it is a clever story about two very wise and sensible youths who confront the institutionalized hypocrisy of the Sevillian underworld. The moral content resides in its faithful representation of human nature, particularly the ridiculously false sense of security about their eternal salvation that the various criminals manage to create in their own minds, even as they go about committing despicable acts against their fellow citizens.[15]

Johnson's analysis is much more penetrating and complex. He has proposed that *R/C*, particularly the portion dedicated to Monipodio's confraternity of thieves, is partially an attack upon Roman Catholic orthodoxy, especially upon the entrenched economic powers that governed Seville in Cervantes's time. In Johnson's view,

... Monipodio's operation reflects the official, feudo-monarchical organization of society, with Monipodio in the role of king, and simultaneously the contemporary idealization of that social order in reactionary literary genres such as the *comedia*, the *libros de caballerías* and the *romancero*.
... Monipodio and his group represent the feudo-monarchical social order enshrined in the majoritarian literary genres noted above; Rinconete

and Cortadillo seem instead to have something to do with bourgeois capitalism and the picaresque.[16]

It should be obvious to any knowledgeable reader that religious terminology and practice play a major role in this story. Johnson avers that the pseudoecclesiastical ambience at Monipodio's residence reflects the reactionary rules of worship imposed in Spain and other Catholic countries to combat Protestant heresy following the Council of Trent (1545–63). In other words, Monipodio's society portrays the new Tridentine orthodoxy carried to an extreme. The principal Tridentine doctrines, according to Johnson, were the following:

> • Renewed emphasis on outward, public displays of religious fervor (versus the more subjective interior forms of worship preferred by the Protestants—and Erasmists).
> • The importance of good works (i.e., charity), as opposed to the Protestant emphasis on faith and predestination.
> • The mystery of transubstantiation in the Mass (belief that the bread and wine really and truly are transformed into the body and blood of Christ) versus the Calvinist or Zwinglian tenet that the bread and wine were merely symbolic of Christ's corporeal presence, or the Lutheran dogma of consubstantiation (that wherever Christ was spiritually present, he could also be corporeally present at the same moment).
> • The veneration of saints and belief in the efficacy of their intervention (a view rejected by Protestant and Erasmist reformers).
> • The veneration of images and the efficacy of elaborate ceremonies (both roundly rejected by the reform movement).
> • The dignity of the clergy and the sanctity of the monastic state (both de-emphasized by Erasmus, Luther, Calvin, et al. with the intention of allowing more freedom for the individual Christian to interpret for himself the teachings of Christ as revealed in the Bible). (93)

In *R/C*, Johnson reminds us, members of the *cofradía* reserve a portion of their "earnings" to purchase lamp oil for a popular devotional icon displayed somewhere in the city; and Pipota regularly lights devotional candles to "Our Lady of the Waters" and the "Holy Crucifix of St. Augustine." We learn a few pages later that Ganancia lights devotional candles to St. Michael and St. Blaise, her personal heavenly protectors. And Escalanta does the same for certain other saints to whom she has special devotion. Monipodio's society is indeed organized along the lines of a religious order, including a probationary novitiate year, which is subsequently waived for Rinconete and Cortadillo.[17]

On the whole, *R/C* might easily be taken for an Erasmian satire on the post-Tridentine Church and its glitzy ceremonial excesses. The scene at

Monipodio's house is, in Johnson's words, "a caricaturesque exaggeration that throws the salient features of [Roman Catholic orthodoxy and feudomonarchism] into prominence and invites our critical meditation on them."[18] Similar observations about the subtle religious undertone of R/C are rendered by Pierce, Fox, and Keightley.[19] One point that all these insightful critics have missed is that this type of direct satirical assault upon specific Catholic dogmas is a totally unique phenomenon, one not to be found in any other of Cervantes's published writings. From a thematic standpoint, then, it is not illogical to hypothesize that the great Spanish novelist was not the original author, but simply the one who edited, polished, and prepared for publication—cf. Fernando de Rojas with *La Celestina*—a received manuscript that happened to reflect his own strong views on a number of salient social and religious questions.

With regard to the economic issues presented in R/C, Johnson[20] echoes Rodríguez-Luis's earlier judgment that Monipodio's criminal enterprise operates along the same lines as a medieval guild: closed membership, rules for apprenticeship, and a monopolistic claim on certain activities within the city.[21] Monipodio's crime syndicate also reflects the same kind of commercial monopoly (cf. "monopolio" and "Monipodio") that Seville exercised in all matters of commerce involving the American colonies. It doesn't require a great stretch of the imagination, therefore, to view the Casa de Monipodio as merely a poetic rendering of the powerful Casa de Contratación in Seville.[22] Taking the analogy one step further, Johnson then goes on to identify the historical figure represented in R/C as Monipodio, the man who controlled virtually every commercial enterprise in Seville: the duke of Medina-Sidonia (99).

In Johnson's scheme, both Monipodio and Medina-Sidonia represent the prevailing economic mind-set of the period: monopolistic control. The two newcomers, on the other hand, can be seen to symbolize entrepreneurial capitalism, which is to say, the independent individual whose initiative runs up against the interests of the powers-that-be. What we have here is the opposition of the old, safe, limited premercantilist economic system versus modern entrepreneurship. In R/C, thief = businessman. Monipodio/Medina-Sidonia and company stand in defense of a rigidly controlled monopoly, based upon the medieval guild mentality, still dominated by the postfeudal nobility; the two youngsters represent the challenge being posed by the free enterprise system championed by the burgeoning bourgeoisie. The text is clearly designed to alienate the reader from Monipodio and the old order while forging an identification with the two boys and the new mercantile middle class (100–103).

It should be noted that there is absolutely nothing in Johnson's brilliant and convincing thesis that would exclude the possibility of a different original author for *R/C*. I propose that the original draft was written by someone who had an intimate knowledge of the Sevillian mercantile community and all the political and legal corruption involved therein. At some subsequent point I believe Miguel de Cervantes came upon the Porras codex and, finding in that document what he considered to be a virtual treasure trove of material in the story of Rinconete and Cortadillo, developed and polished it until it became the literary masterpiece we know today.

Aside from the questions of genre and theme, the other major topic of critical debate regarding *R/C* has to do with its narrative structure (schema 21).

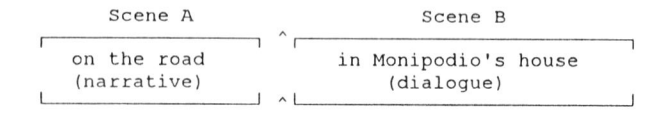

```
         Scene A                    Scene B
   ┌──────────────────┐  ^  ┌──────────────────────┐
   │   on the road    │     │  in Monipodio's house│
   │   (narrative)    │     │     (dialogue)       │
   └──────────────────┘  ^  └──────────────────────┘
```

Schema 21. *Rinconete y Cortadillo*

The story opens with a heavily descriptive account (A) of the adventures of the two lovable urchins as they go about fleecing the patrons of a roadside inn just outside Seville. But the format changes radically once the boys arrive in the bustling metropolis on the Guadalquivir and the protagonists are invited to undergo initiation into the brotherhood of thieves at the house of Monipodio, kingpin of the Sevillian underworld. What has begun as a heavily controlled narration (A) now becomes an exercise in comic dialogue (B), not unlike the format of the one-act *entremés*, a dramatic form of which Cervantes was a justly renowned practitioner in his own time.

The concept of *R/C* as a story that exhibits some noticeably theatrical techniques was first presented in 1966 by Domingo Yndurain Múñoz. Casalduero's 1962 study of Cervantes's *Novelas* had discerned a totally different structural arrangement for *R/C:* (1) the outdoor scenes that served as a frame for (2) the major action that takes place within the confines of Monipodio's home, followed by (3) a brief epilogue.[23] The lengthy scene in Monipodio's residence is itself divided into four smaller units, which are conveniently separated by three noisy interruptions.[24] Yndurain's new approach to the story entailed a comparison of the two versions of *R/C* and called attention to a number of purely narrative fragments in the Porras text that were recast in a more dramatic format in Cervantes's 1613 published version.[25]

Utilizing slightly different terminology, Eleodoro Febres (1972) also viewed the story of these two would-be *pícaros* in terms of narrative versus dialogic "moments." The first of these, the *momento picaresco*, is primarily narrative, embraces a two-day time frame, contains few significant secondary characters, and is completely dominated by the actions of Rincón and Cortado. The portrait of Seville's underworld society that follows contains much more dialogue, lasts only a few hours, and focuses on the interaction taking place between Monipodio and his very colorful band of underlings. In Febres's view, during the first part the two major characters are sketched primarily by the narrator's description, later by their own conversation; in the second half the image of Monipodio is created from a dialogue in which he himself does not participate, then by a summarizing narrative passage.[26] Karl-Ludwig Selig (1978–79) divides *R/C* along the same general lines, but he places more emphasis on the widely divergent roles the two protagonists play in the respective halves, first as initiators of the action, later as passive observers of events enacted by others.[27]

The more recent studies by Julio Rodríguez-Luis (1980) and Francisco J. Sánchez (1989) have continued to stress the notably theatrical character of the second part of *R/C*. Sánchez flatly states that in *R/C* "we have a narrative which incorporates many of the elements of an *entremés*."[28] This echoes a similar judgment by Rodríguez-Luis, who compared the rapid entrances and exits of the many characters we meet at Monipodio's place to theatrical stagecraft: "The abundance of characters, its lively movement and especially the preference for dialogue over narration are what make *Rinconete y Cortadillo* a unique case among the *Novelas* by virtue of its approximation of theatrical devices, an area in which Cervantes was also a master."[29] In 1970 José Pascual Buxó built upon the foundation laid by Casalduero and Ynduráin's theories and offered an outline of the events that take place at Monipodio's den as if the text were a Golden Age *comedia*.[30]

It should be noted that Ronald G. Keightley also discusses the narrative structure of *R/C*, but only with regard to the portion of the text that takes place at Monipodio's home. Keightley discerns three equal divisions: (1) the induction of the two protagonists into the society and the conferring upon them of their new names; (2) the tempestuous confrontation of Juliana la Cariharta and her lover Repolido; and (3) the "business meeting" that concludes the festivities.[31]

A very different two-part division was posited by Ruth El Saffar in *Novel to Romance* (1974). In this work El Saffar's distinctions are drawn along the lines of what she calls the temporal and spatial planes. The former deals with the development and transformations of the two protagonists, the second with a description of Sevillian society as viewed from the perspective of Monipodio's confraternity of thieves. The two narrative entities are so unintegrated that they appear to be almost independent of one another.[32] These two incompatible elements explain, says El Saffar, Cervantes's decision to eliminate the subtitle, *Casa de Monipodio, padre de los ladrones de Sevilla*, that introduced the action at Monipodio's house in the Porras text: "The omission of the subtitle in the published manuscript suggests that in his later view of the work Cervantes was more interested in Rinconete and Cortadillo's developing role in the story than in depicting the life of the underworld in Seville" (37).

Although it did not occur to her to posit a different author for the Porras text, El Saffar has, nonetheless, come upon here the key to understanding the changes made by Cervantes for the 1613 publication of *R/C*: a completely new authorial focus. The original author wrote a clever, tongue-in-cheek satire about the political and economic corruption that was rampant in early-seventeenth-century Seville, as seen from the unusual perspective of the underworld characters who benefited from it. To this satirical core Cervantes added new elements designed to enhance the work's literary qualities: shades and subtleties of characterization that were presented principally in the dialogue.

One major area in which the Porras and 1613 versions of *R/C* diverge sharply is in the final paragraph, where the Porras text is much darker and more mordant than Cervantes's. As we can see from the following excerpt, in the Porras version the fates of Rinconete, Cortadillo, and Monipodio are clearly portended and the narrator's bitterness and clearly satirical intentions are exposed in his final words about Rinconete:

> Sacábalo de su juicio lo que en el libro de caxa había leído, y los exercicios en que todos se ocupaban, y sobreexageraba quan poca o ninguna justicia había en aquella ciudad, pues quasi públicamente vivía en ella y se conservaba gente de tan contrario trato a la naturaleza humana; y propuso en sí de aconsejar a su compañero no durase mucho en aquella vida tan perdida, peligrosa y disoluta. Mas, con todo, llevado de su poca experiencia y años, y del vicio y ocio de la edad y tierra, quiso pasar más adelante, por ver si descubría en aquel trato cosa de más gusto de lo que imaginaba. Y así, pasó en él los tres meses del noviciado, en los cuales le pasaron cosas que piden más larga historia y así, se contará en otra parte la vida, muerte y milagros de ambos, con la de su maestro Monipodio, con otros sucesos de algunos de la infame junta e academia, que todas son cosas dignas de consideración, y que pueden servir de ejemplo y aviso a los que las leyeren, para huir y abominar una vida tan detestable y que tanto se usa en una ciudad que había de ser espejo de verdad y de justicia en todo el mundo, como lo es de grandeza. (Schevill and Bonilla 1:327)

> [He gradually changed his original judgment because of what he had read in the book of accounts and the duties that they were all engaged in. And

this tended to underscore the fact that there was little or no justice to be had in that city because in it were living, even prospering, people who almost brazenly comported themselves in a manner quite contrary to human nature. And he promised himself that he would advise his companion not to continue much longer in a way of life that was so godforsaken, dangerous, and corrupt. Nonetheless, despite the fact that he was not very old and still wet behind the ears, and because of the general vice and idleness of the place and times, he intended to spend a bit more time with Monipodio's bunch to see if he could find something more pleasurable than what he imagined. And so he endured the three-month probationary period, during which time he witnessed things that would require yet another story to recount, and these will be told in another chapter that will deal with the life, death, and wondrous doings of both boys, along with those of their master, Monipodio, and of what happened to those other members of the academy of vice. All such stories will be of great moment and will provide to all who read them an example and warning to flee from and denounce such a detestable way of life in a city that should be a mirror of truth and justice for the whole world, just as it is for grandeur.]

We are told here that a sufficient number of interesting events are supposed to have happened during the three-month probationary period to warrant a separate continuation, which is forthcoming and will deal, as if it were hagiographic literature, with the boys' lives and deaths, as well as the miracles attributed to them. We are promised more regarding Monipodio as well, including, presumably, his death, although it is uncertain from the article employed ("la") whether the narrator is referring to the Sevillian godfather's life or his death.

Unmistakable, however, is the bitter tone of the narrator's final words here. These future adventures—and, one assumes, the present ones—are intended to serve as a warning ("ejemplo y aviso") to all who read them to avoid and shun what is a detestable way of life ("aquella vida tan perdida, peligrosa y disoluta") in a city that, because it is steeped in such grandeur, was supposed to serve as a shining example of truth and justice. The harsh tone of these words would seem to betray the frustration of a Sevillian citizen—probably a native son—who is absolutely revolted by the moral and ethical decline of his cherished city.

As Rodríguez-Luis points out, Cervantes's epilogue has a totally different and less condemnatory tone than the Porras ending.[33] Although the focus once again is on Rinconete, the reader does not perceive the same kind of moral outrage that we observe in the earlier version:

Consideraba lo que había leído en su libro de memoria y los ejercicios en que todos se ocupaban. Finalmente, exageraba cuán descuidada justicia había en aquella tan famosa ciudad de Sevilla, pues casi al descubierto vivía en ella gente tan perniciosa y tan contraria a la misma naturaleza, y propuso en sí de aconsejar a su compañero no durasen mucho en aquella vida tan perdida y tan mala, tan inquieta, y tan libre y disoluta. Pero, con todo esto, llevado de sus pocos años y de su poca experiencia, pasó con ella adelante algunos meses, en los cuales se sucedieron cosas que piden más luenga escritura, y así se deja para otra ocasión contar su vida y milagros, con los de su maestro Monipodio, y otros sucesos de aquéllos de la infame academia, que todos serán de grande consideración y que podrán servir de ejemplo y aviso a los que las leyeren. (Sieber 1:240)

[Rinconete thought about what he had read in Monipodio's note-book, and the duties that they were all engaged in. Finally, in his mind, he made a great deal of the fact that what justice there was in that celebrated city of Seville, was so lax that people who were so obnoxious and whose behaviour so contradicted the laws of nature could live in it virtually unchecked. He made up his mind that he would advise his companion that they should not stay long living that God-forsaken way of life, which was so evil, so precarious, so libertine and so corrupt. Nonetheless, despite all this, since he was not very old and still wet behind the ears, he went on to spend several months living like that. Things happened to him during that time which deserve to be written about at greater length, thus we will leave for another occasion an account of his life and wondrous doings together with those of his master, Monipodio, and of what happened to those other members of the academy of vice. All such stories will be of great moment and will provide an example and warning to all who'll read them.] (1:229]

Life among the criminal element in Seville is still portrayed in negative terms, but with a diminished sense of fear and intimidation. The three blunt and harsh qualifiers used to describe the lifestyle of the *hampa* in Porras ("perdida, peligrosa y disoluta") [so godforsaken, dangerous, and corrupt] is softened and extended in 1613 to "tan perdida y tan mala, tan inquieta, y tan libre y disoluta" ['so evil, so precarious, so libertine and so corrupt']. The element of lurking danger ("peligrosa") is eliminated entirely, now replaced by the less threatening "tan mala, tan inquieta" ['so evil, so precarious'] and while the terms "perdida" and "disoluta" are repeated in the published version, their original damning effect is muted by the adverbial "tan" ['so'] that precedes them.[34] The same process is at work when Cervantes in 1613 consciously pulls back from the ominous note on which the Porras version ended; there is no mention at all here of death, either for the protagonists or for their demonic mentor.

In my view, once the text moves firmly into the dramatic mode at Monipodio's headquarters, we begin to glimpse an outstanding feature of the original Porras text that caught Cervantes's attention and inspired him to rework and publish it under his own name: the use of the theatrical device of verbal self-portrait *(autorretrato)* to flesh out the characters in a prose narrative. It is my contention that Cervantes borrowed the clever Porras original for an experiment in characterization-through-dialogue.

As I have shown in detail in *Pioneer and Plagiarist*, the seeds of Cervantes's *autorretrato* technique were already present in the Porras text. We begin to note the use of colorful self-portrait in the rambling account of the bibulous Celestinesque hag, Pipota (Sieber 1:76–77); it continues in the verbal exchange between Monipodio and the long-suffering prostitute Juliana la Cariharta, who alternately denounces and begs forgiveness for her bullying boyfriend, Repolido (Sieber 1:78–79). In both cases, the Porras version is almost as effective as Cervantes's.

Perhaps the most memorable example of this technique can be found toward the end of the story in the utterances of the dim-witted goon, Chiquiznaque, whose frequent verbal infelicities and limited reasoning capacity remind us of Sancho Panza, but without the latter's redeeming wit. Let us compare the two versions of Chiquiznaque's feeble explanation as to why he was unable to carry out the instructions that Monipodio had given him to slash the face of a certain merchant:

Porras:
—Pues lo que pasa en eso es, dixo Chiquiznaque, que yo le aguardé anoche a la puerta de su casa, y él vino antes de la hora un poco, y lleguéme a él y tanteéle y marquéle el rostro con la vista, y vi que le tenía tan pequeño, que era imposible cabelle en él cuchillada de a catorce puntos; y hallándome imposibilitado de hacer lo prometido y cumplir lo que llevaba en la destruición que el señor Monipodio me dio . . .
—*Instrucción* querrá decir vmd., dixo el caballero.
—Esa debo de querer decir, dixo Chiquiznaque. Digo que, viendo la pequeñez y estrechura del rostro del mercader, y hallándome atajado, por no haber ido en valde, le di una cuchillada a un lacayo del dicho mercader, que yo aseguro que si hubiera pregmática en las cuchilladas, que hubiera de ser penada por mayor de marca. (Schevill and Bonilla 1:307)

["Well, the situation with this one," replied Chiquiznaque, "is that last night I waited at his doorway, and he came a little before the hour; I closed up on him, glanced at his face, and saw that it would be quite impossible to fit a gash of fourteen stitches on it as it was so wizened. Seeing that it was going to be exceedingly problematic to accomplish the mission and to carry out the destruction Sir Monipodio gave me . . ."

"You mean 'instruction' rather than 'destruction,' don't you?" interrupted the gentleman who had ordered the slashing.

"That's what I must have meant," replied Chiquiznaque. "What I'm saying is that seeing the small, narrow face of the merchant, and feeling unable to complete my plan, I did not want my journey to be wasted so I inflicted the slashing on one of the merchant's lackeys; and I assure you that if there were published guidelines regarding slashes, this one would have been found punishable for going beyond the limit.]

Cervantes:

—Pues lo que en eso pasa—respondió Chiquiznaque—es que yo le aguardé anoche a la puerta de su casa, y él vino antes de la oración; lleguéme cerca dél, marquéle el rostro con la vista, y vi que le tenía tan pequeño, que era imposible de toda imposibilidad caber en él cuchillada de catorce puntos; y hallándome imposibilitado de poder cumplir lo prometido y de hacer lo que llevaba en mi destruición . . .

—*Instrucción* querrá decir vuesa merced—dixo el caballero—que no *destruición*.

—Eso quise decir—respondió Chiquiznaque—. Digo que viendo que en la estrecheza y poca cantidad de aquel rostro no cabían los puntos propuestos, por que no fuese mi ida en balde, di la cuchillada a un lacayo suyo, que a buen seguro que la pueden poner por mayor de marca. (Sieber 1:233)

["Well, the situation with this one," replied Chiquiznaque, "is that last night I waited at his doorway, and he came before the hour for prayer; I closed up on him, glanced at his face, and saw that it would be quite impossible to fit a gash of fourteen stitches on it as it was so wizened. Seeing that it was going to be exceedingly problematic to accomplish the mission and to carry out my destruction . . ."

"You mean 'instruction' rather than 'destruction,' don't you?" interrupted the gent.

"That's what I meant," replied Chiquiznaque. "What I'm saying is that when I saw that long, narrow face, far too thin to take the intended number of lacerations, I did not want my journey to be wasted so I inflicted them on one of his lackeys, for there was no problem with the target this time as it was much larger."] (1:219–21)

Aside from the fact that the Porras author uses the *-ra* form of the imperfect subjunctive where Cervantes's preference is for the *-se* form, the content and tone of the Porras material might easily be mistaken for a Cervantine text.

This and numerous other passages of dialogue from *R/C* are clear and certain evidence of Cervantes's innovative experimentation with verbal self-portrait through the use of popular colloquialisms and specialized underworld argot (e.g., *finibusterrae*, gallows; *gurapas*, service on a galley ship; *abispones*, bird dogs). Letting the characters in a work of fiction—as opposed to the narrator—take on the task of sketching their own psychological profiles was a truly novel idea in the seventeenth century. Consequently,

Cervantes's reworking of the Porras text in his version of *Rinconete* ought to be considered one of the major technical accomplishments of Spanish Golden Age literature.

The fact that the story of Rinconete and Cortadillo has come down to us in two very distinct versions has provided Cervantists with a great deal of grist for their critical mills in regard to certain passages that appear in one or the other text. Some notable examples would be the issue of the boys' respective weapons, the mortifying slap *(bofetón)* that Rinconete receives in only one of the versions, and finally the nickname "el Bueno" [the Good], which is applied first to one youth, then to the other.[35]

The episode of the *bofetón* is linked directly to the issue of the weapons insofar as the sudden blow provokes both boys into drawing their respective blades in anger. The Porras version, generally considered the earlier of the two, reads as follows:

> Y haciendo [Monipodio] del ojo a uno de los bravos, se llegó uno de ellos a Rinconete y, cogiéndolo descuidado, le dio un gran bofetón enmedio del rostro; y no lo hubo bien dado quando, echando mano al de cachas y Cortadillo a su espada media o terciado, arremetieron al bravo con tal denuedo, que si el otro no se metiera de por medio, lo mataran. (Schevill and Bonilla 1:263)
>
> [And when Monipodio gave the signal to one of his ruffians, another of his thugs came up to the unsuspecting Rinconete and gave him a big slap across the face; Rinconete's immediate response was to reach for his slaughterhouse knife while Cortadillo pulled out his broken half-sword. They both charged the attacker with such courage that if the other thug hadn't stepped between them, they'd have killed him.]

Rodríguez-Luis takes great pains to cite the disappearance of this violent episode in the 1613 published version as a demonstration of Cervantes's literary good taste in revising his own earlier manuscript. Here are some of his comments:

> Perhaps the comparison with the military orders seemed excessively crude to the novelist when he revised his work.... Even so, Cervantes, preferring to have his protagonists function on a secondary plane, probably considered it sufficient to have them reject Monipodio's brotherhood categorically at the end in order to demonstrate their superiority.... [36]

The critic also makes much of the fact that here Cortado is reported to be armed with a broken half-sword ("espada media o terciado") that earlier—in both versions, says the critic—had been wielded by Rinconete.

In the first version Cervantes places the half-sword in the possession of Cortado in this scene ... a weapon which previously, in both versions, belonged to Rincón, since it specifically states that the slaughterhouse knife was Cortado's. ... The confusion regarding the short sword ... shows, in my opinion, Cervantes's desire, in both versions, to make the two boys equals, as well as a certain vacillation on his part regarding the need to choose one of them to serve as spokesman for the pair. (1:180)

Unfortunately, Rodríguez-Luis has misread the two texts in question, a slip that seriously damages his argument.[37] In the opening paragraph of the Porras text the two boys are described as two shepherd boys, one fifteen years of age, the other seventeen ("dos muchachos zagalejos, el uno de edad de quince años y el otro de diez y siete" [Schevill and Bonilla 1:209]). It is clearly established here that the first boy described is the fifteen-year-old, while the older boy is always treated in second place. From this point on the narrator keeps referring to the youths strictly in terms of "el uno" and "el otro," even in the final sentence when the narrator describes their respective weapons:

el uno tenía media espada puesta en un puño de palo, y el otro un cuchillo jifero de cachas amarillas. (Schevill and Bonilla 1:211)

[One had the broken half of a sword with a wooden haft; the other a yellow-hafted knife, of the kind used in a slaughterhouse.]

At a later point (Schevill and Bonilla 1:215) the older boy gives his name as Pedro Rincón, which clearly makes him the one carrying the yellow-handled slaughterhouse knife ("cuchillo de cachas amarillas"), while the younger Cortado is armed with the *media espada*. There is absolutely no confusion or inconsistency about the weapons in the Porras text.

As for the definitive Cervantine version, the opening paragraphs are more nebulous than was Porras in the presentation of the protagonists, who are merely described as

dos muchachos de hasta edad de catorce a quince años; el uno ni el otro no pasaban de diez y siete; (Sieber 1:191).

[two lads maybe fourteen or fifteen years old, neither more than sixteen or seventeen.] (1:175)

It must be noted that neither boy is referred to as either the older or taller one. As a consequence of this vagueness, when Cervantes's narrator eventually refers to "el uno" having the *media espada* and "el otro" bearing a *cuchillo de cachas amarillas*, the reader is still unable to tell which is which. In succeeding paragraphs Cervantes's narrator begins to make a distinction between the two youths in terms of their size and age, using such terms as "el que parecía de más edad" [the one who seemed older], "el mayor" [the elder one], and "el grande" [the bigger one] to describe the one who will be called Rincón, and "el más pequeño" [the smaller one], "el mediano" [the medium-sized one], "el menor" [the younger one], etc. to refer to Cortado. And because there is no violent slap *(bofetón)* in this version, we never get to witness the boys drawing their weapons.

I would respectfully maintain that the 1613 excisions regarding the slap and the weapons demonstrate that Cervantes was editing another writer's work and decided to remove a particularly violent passage that he correctly perceived to be inappropriate for and extraneous to the generally jocose tone of *R/C*. The fact that in the 1613 version the protagonists have no occasion whatsoever to draw their weapons is a strong indication that Cervantes chose to infuse a more comic or pastoral tone to this story than did the original author, who chose to include at least one episode of gratuitous violence.

In the matter of the epithet "el Bueno," suffice it to say that our critical interest stems from the fact that it is applied originally to Cortadillo, then almost twenty pages later to Rinconete. For a discussion of this issue we need look no farther than Cervantes's definitive version, for there is no mention of the term in the Porras text, as Casalduero has noted.[38] Rodríguez-Luis believes the term is used with careful intent by Cervantes, first to raise the level of Cortadillo's esteem to that of his companion, then to confer preeminence once again to the older boy.[39] Aden W. Hayes offers a similar theory: that there is no inconsistency here because Monipodio, being illiterate, uses language—more specifically, the spoken word—to compliment and/or censure his underlings, i.e., as a means of manipulating them.[40] A slightly different interpretation of this incident is Gonzalo Díaz Migoyo's assertion that the illiterate Monipodio is simply using the sobriquet as a way of demonstrating his fantastic memory.[41]

All of these suggestions pale in comparison, I believe, to the theory advanced by Carroll B. Johnson. The key, says Johnson, lies in the historical reference Cervantes adds to the text in 1613:

> y Cortadillo se quedó confirmado con el renombre de *Bueno*, bien como si fuera don Alonso Pérez de Guzmán *el Bueno*, que arrojó el cuchillo por los muros de Tarifa para degollar a su único hijo. (Sieber 1:218)

> [and Cortadillo basked in the enjoyment of his new nickname, the Good, exactly as if his name was Don Alonso Pérez de Guzmán the Good, the one who threw down the knife from the walls of Tarifa, so that the throat of his one and only son could be cut with it.] (1:203)

Citing historical sources,[42] Johnson makes the point that it is the epithet itself, not the person on whom it is momentarily conferred, which carries the real meaning here. The Pérez de Guzmán who sacrificed his only son rather than surrender the city of Tarifa in 1294 was an ancestor of the duke of Medina-Sidonia, the scheming aristocrat whose figure cast such a long shadow in Sevillian politics and whose symbolic appearance throughout *R/C* has already been discussed here. Johnson believes that the reference to the duke's heroic ancestor is simply one more clever device used by Cervantes to link the duke, represented here by Monipodio, with his musty feudal roots.[43]

※

Although the evidence is admittedly circumstantial, a comparison of the Porras and 1613 texts provides us with sufficient data to support the theory that *R/C* may have originally been composed by someone other than Cervantes, someone who was extremely knowledgeable about the workings of Sevillian society, particularly within the mercantile community, and was intimately aware of the political and legal corruption that abounded in that city. I believe we have been graced with this very enlightening portrait of the Sevillian underworld because Miguel de Cervantes stumbled upon this virtual treasure trove of undeveloped sociopolitical satire, probably in the now-lost Porras MS, and decided to rework it in accordance with his own superior literary precepts. The rest is history.

El celoso extremeño

My interest in the artistic design of the *ZE* was sparked by Casalduero's *Sentido y forma de las "Novelas ejemplares"* (1962), which was the first critical study to comment meaningfully on the special arrangement of narrative elements in that work. Casalduero noted, for example, that the Porras text had more "social depth" than the 1613 version (171); he also observed that the second part of the story is divided into five different units, each of these corresponding to one of five distinct dialogues that take place within it (173–74). Casalduero used the term "Gothic verticality" to characterize the Porras codex, while referring to the "Escorial-like horizontality" of Cervantes's published account (176). While Casalduero clearly recognized a number of significant artistic differences between the two known versions of *ZE*, he never entertained the notion that these competing texts might actually represent the work of two different writers.

Of far greater interest to Casalduero was a comparison of elements to be found in both Cervantes's 1613 *Celoso extremeño* and the story of *El curioso impertinente*, an intercalated narrative within *Don Quixote*, Part One. Casalduero's comparisons between the two stories (183–84) are shown in table 3.1.

Table 3.1

ZE	*Curioso*
Carrizales contributes only *indirectly* to his demise; he can't help himself.	Anselmo provokes his own downfall *directly*.
Carrizales dies with some dignity because he refuses to take vengeance on Leonora.	Anselmo dies ignominiously, an end he richly deserves.
Loaysa is only an instrument of Carrizales's downfall; he does not deserve the vile death he suffers in the Porras text, so Cervantes allows him at the end to become a new Carrizales who will go off to the Indies. There he will repeat all of the experiences of Carrizales, which is punishment enough.	Lotario is a tragic figure, a good friend who succumbs to Anselmo's temptation. He is permitted, consequently, a heroic battlefield death.
Leonora exercises her free will and wisely opts *not* to sin (except in thought). She is allowed to live out her life in service to God and have an honorable death.	Camila misuses her free will; she actively participates in the plot to deceive Anselmo, which effectively brings her a well-deserved death shortly thereafter.
All three principal characters suffer a fate different from what most seventeenth century readers would have expected. The ironic denouement is a major part of the moral lesson of the story.	The three protagonists suffer predictable fates that would have been both expected and demanded by the reading public of that era.

The key to understanding *ZE* lies in noting the changes Cervantes makes in the Porras original—and *why* he makes them. Cervantes recognized that the Porras version conformed very much to the traditional Boccaccian formula he had used previously in the *Curioso*, i.e., it mechanically provides the austere sort of moralistic denouement readers had come to expect in stories about adultery. What Cervantes gives us in his 1613 version moves beyond the norms of stock characterization and predictable moralizing to offer his readers something new and different, a moral lesson that is quite special and out of the ordinary.

A similar comparison of characters in ZE and the *Curioso* was made in 1986 by Clorinda Donato.[44] Her study focuses on the psychological makeup of Leonora and Camila, Donato's thesis being that Cervantes was experimenting in these two works with the creation of strong female characters who make important choices about their life. Donato points out (13–14) the fact that all three of the *Curioso*'s characters have basic limitations, which reflects the same kind of narrow presentation I alluded to in referring to the a priori characterization we find in ZE with Carrizales's prehistory.

Donato recognizes important changes that Cervantes has wrought in the 1613 version: he allows the reader to perceive a growth process taking place in the young bride; Leonora—unlike her Porras counterpart, Isabela—eventually develops the qualities of circumspection and thoughtfulness; and finally, there are levels of deliberation and introspection in ZE that go beyond the mere fulfillment of conventional expectations we observe in the more rhetorical *Curioso*, where the language tends to be overly eloquent as the three protagonists take turns quoting external sources of social morality in the form of parables, proverbs, snippets of poetry, and passages from Scripture (16–17).

In Cervantes's ZE the three major characters are anything but stock figures; each emerges from a different background and brings a different set of life experiences to the story (18–19). In Donato's view, Leonora's refusal to succumb to Loaysa's demonic charms represents a sharp break with the standard pattern of behavior for female characters like Camila. The passive Isabela is changed into the active Leonora, who takes control of her own life in Cervantes's story, as we see when she insists that Loaysa take an oath (20–21). In a sense, then, Leonora's actions represent the triumph of free will, but there are consequences that the young bride is not quite prepared to handle (22–23).

The value of Donato's study is that it enables us to appreciate the magnitude of Cervantes's evolution as a writer by comparing his conventional early effort in the *Curioso* with the daring experiment in narrative technique he later made in reworking the Porras text. Although she never specifically mentions Boccaccio or any Italian writer as Cervantes's model, Donato's argument can be said to point to the various ways in which the *Curioso* conforms to the traditional Italianate model for the short story.

As I see it, Cervantes inserted the story of Anselmo's foolish curiosity—a highly moralistic tale in the Boccaccian tradition—into the *Quixote* for the specific purpose of providing a direct and contrasting commentary on Cardenio's previous account of his foolishness in courting Luscinda. One case quite naturally reflects upon the other; Cardenio's excessive timidity in the main story is counterposed to Anselmo's unbridled temerity in the inserted *Curioso*, with both stories ending in disaster. The heavy-handed moralism generally associated with Boccaccio's technique is quite effective and appropriate when employed in this manner.

In adapting ZE as a freestanding entity, however, Cervantes apparently felt the need to temper with a more nuanced treatment the predictable outcome and ponderous moralizing he found in the Porras original. The personalities we find in Cervantes's published version have considerably more psychological independence than had their Porras counterparts or the three characters of the *Curioso:* here we find a young wife who somehow summons up the strength of character to resist a would-be seducer's considerable charm; the stock figure of the pathetic old cuckold is elevated and transformed by Cervantes's able hand into a far more rounded and sympathetically drawn character.

For Alban K. Forcione, there is no question as to the classical pedigree of ZE. In *Cervantes and the Humanist Vision* (1982), Forcione points to the story of Loaysa's attempt to seduce Carrizales's teenage bride as the most traditional of all the Cervantine novellas: "Of all the tales in the collection none is more directly indebted in form and content to the central tradition of the European short story, which found its classical expression in the *Decameron*, and none reveals more clearly Cervantes's mastery of the narrative techniques which Boccaccio perfected and left as the classical standard for future short story writers."[45]

Adhering closely to Erich Auerbach's interpretation, Forcione notes that in the Boccaccian model a sharply pointed plotline is emphasized over character drawing or setting; furthermore, the action of the story is designed to hasten quickly toward a single climactic moment, which is fully anticipated because it follows logically from the premises presented in the initial situation. In the Porras ZE, for example, we find the climactic infidelity of the young bride to be the logical outcome of the excessively jealous behavior of her foolish old husband. Forcione observes that the Boccaccian model only rarely does anything to disorient the reader or disrupt his anticipation of what will happen at the climactic moment; unity and concentration, then, are the key elements of Boccaccio's storytelling technique (32–33).

In Forcione's view, Cervantes's ZE is actually a concentrated Boccaccian narrative that has been infused with a fascinating variety of demonic symbols (34–41). First among the recurring elements that Forcione says point to an evil or fiendish presence is the sinister nocturnal atmosphere that dominates the action of the second half of the story. Next we have the "demonically beautiful intruder," Loaysa, and the candles that are used to illuminate his handsome figure; we also note recurrent leaps of jubilation by Loaysa, Leonora and the servant girls at various moments of triumph in the story, the seductive music played by the "wondrous musician" Loaysa in order to win entry into Carrizales's fortress/house, and the reference to the "wicked sound of the saraband," a dance that was considered a lascivious display of unbridled sensuality in Cervantes's time. Forcione sums up the power of Loaysa's music and the orgiastic dancing it inspires in the following words: "The dance climaxes in a riotous scene of disorder and confusion, as the group scatters in fear and the terrified Negro eunuch maniacally continues to strum his untuned guitar, a conclusion that underscores the destructive nature of the passions that the music represents" (40).

And finally there are the instances of diabolical kissing. On two occasions the scheming Loaysa kisses his disciple and accomplice, Luis, a black eunuch who guards Carrizales's kingdom; later the unscrupulous intruder kisses the cross, in order to convince the unwitting servants of "good intentions" in entering the forbidden territory. At another point we observe the conspiring duenna, Marialonso, pressing her lips to Leonora's ear as she passes her the soporific ointment with which to drug her hapless husband.

Cervantes's desire to infuse diabolical imagery into the story of Loaysa's attempt to seduce the wife of a jealous Extremaduran is also cited by Forcione to explain why the lengthy description of Sevillian society from the Porras version—the reference to *mantones* and other low social types—is sharply abridged in the 1613 Cervantine version. In addition to his desire to provide greater narrative concision and concentration, Cervantes also realized that the real theme of the story should be the presence of pure evil in the world, which was a far more serious topic than mere social satire (48).

The 1613 version of ZE clearly contains a great deal more satanic imagery than does the Porras text; consequently, Forcione proceeds to enumerate the various additions Cervantes made to heighten the demonic character of the "world of instinct" he wished to portray in the final version:

> While he eliminated Loaysa's lengthy social characterization, he added the powerful message in which the Negro illuminates him with a candle as he first appears before his dazzled audience. The description of Loaysa's somersaults following his initial entry and his discussion of the virtues of wine with the Negro are similar additions, and it is probable that Cervantes wished to exploit the traditional associations of wine as an instrument of demonic activity and celebration. In the second version Cervantes places additional emphasis on the cacophony in the *dueña*'s ecstatic song, and he adds a detail suggesting violence in the orgiastic dance that it pro-

vokes ("se comenzaron a hacer pedazos bailando"—literally: "they began to tear themselves apart dancing"). (57)

Forcione also points out the increased importance of the duenna's role in the final version: she assumes a central role in the conspiracy from the outset, which was not the case in the Porras text. And what had been her *falsa risa de mono* (phony monkey's laugh) in Porras is turned by Cervantes into a *risa falsa de demonio* (demon's phony laugh). For Forcione, even the Porras version of this story is about the corruption of innocence, not a celebration of primal human instinct. Isabela's seduction is carefully removed from the foreground, where it is traditionally found in the Italian novella (and where Cervantes himself placed it in his *Entremés del viejo celoso*); the inevitable scene of sexual union between the lovers (and the consequent humiliation of the old husband) is replaced in the foreground by a concluding remark about how the young bride's fall from grace was a misfortune brought about by her old husband's folly in placing his trust in evil duennas (64).

At some point, says Forcione, Cervantes saw "enormous unexploited potential" in the original character of Isabela (in Porras). He perceived in the early ZE more than a simple tale of sexual repression and human weakness; he sensed the potential for "grander themes of human freedom, moral growth and self-affirmation" (68). In order to draw a more positive portrait of the innocent young wife, Cervantes was obliged to make several significant alterations in the text for his 1613 published version. First and foremost was his decision to excise the part where the newly corrupted Isabela gleefully kisses the container of ointment that would be used to immobilize her husband during Loaysa's awaited nocturnal visit. Referring to this act of desecration on the part of the young bride, Forcione remarks: "In his revised version Cervantes eliminates it and removes her from a powerful pattern of negation" (69).

A second major change has to do with a certain "demonic kiss" that takes place between the young bride and the evil duenna. Cervantes's decision to minimize Leonora's culpability required him to reduce her role in the kissing scene from that of an instigator to that of a passive recipient, and is explained in the following words:

> In [the] first version he describes her lying on the floor, "her lips pressed to the ear of the *dueña*." The gesture recalls the demonic kisses of Loaysa and underscores her active participation in the evil plot. In the revised version Cervantes emphasizes the victimization of the maiden by her companions, and it is not surprising that he should alter this disturbing description by having the serpentine *dueña* place "her mouth to the ear of her mistress," in the traditional pose of the demonic tempter. (69)

The third change—to introduce the evil duenna as Leonora's governess *(aya),* thereby reinforcing the bride's role as a guiltless and passive disciple being molded by a perverse and demonic teacher—was likewise intended to enhance the theme of spiritual growth that would be stressed in the revised version (69).

As Forcione so ably points out, Leonora's inner world is much more complex in the 1613 version. The original Isabela's anguish and compassion seem unmotivated and melodramatic in Porras, but Leonora's similar reaction in the 1613 version comes off as quite plausible because Cervantes has so convincingly laid the foundation for her sudden awakening to the hidden dangers of instinct and sin and to the question of innocence versus guilt (70). Cervantes's additions and changes tend to increase the moral complexity of the situation in which Leonora finds herself embroiled: she's caught between the antithetical extremes of unnatural restraint and unnatural license. In Forcione's view, then, Leonora is a heroic figure who ultimately reveals "remarkable moral courage" (71).

I would simply point out here that Forcione's observations about the 1613 *ZE* do not depend upon any assumption that Cervantes must have been revising an early draft of one of his own creations for publication. The same critical judgments apply even if we posit the contrary scenario of Cervantes refurbishing a conventional piece of social satire originally penned by some other author, transforming it into a narrative masterpiece.

Forcione's main point is that although *ZE* appears to be Cervantes's most conventional novella, the simple classical facade is merely an illusion, because toward the end the narrative turns unpredictable and confusing—"elliptical and elusive" are Forcione's terms (91). Readers familiar with my earlier analysis of *ZE* in *Cervantes: Pioneer and Plagiarist* will recall that this sort of authorial legerdemain is precisely what I was hinting at in 1982. I professed on that occasion that Cervantes probably discovered a "classical" Boccaccian novella in the Porras codex and found a way to turn it into a totally Cervantine text (i.e., one unpredictable and confusing to the casual reader) by simply making a series of significant alterations— some obvious, others more subtle—in the original.

The superiority of the new-and-improved 1613 version of *ZE* stems from the irony Cervantes injects into the story in its final pages. In the Porras text both husband and wife come to a full knowledge of each other's moral transgressions: Carrizales comes to the realization that his insane jealousy has driven Isabela to commit adultery; for her part, Isabela is aware that she has violated her wedding vows and that old Carrizales has irrefutable proof of her errant behavior. In the conversation that follows Carrizales's discovery there is absolutely no deception or misunderstanding between the spouses. But then the old man defies both literary and social convention by accepting the blame for the entire matter and offering Isabela his forgiveness. The Porras story ends with a good, albeit unconventional, denouement, but Cervantes seems to have sensed that the original text still fails to fulfill its great artistic and moral potential.

To remedy that shortcoming Cervantes introduces a handful of noteworthy alterations that provide a strong dose of dramatic irony, thereby sharpening both the artistic merit and the moral exemplarity of the story without sacrificing the effective dramatic impact of the original Porras confrontation scene. In the revised version Carrizales still offers forgiveness from his deathbed, but now his pardon is totally unnecessary. In Cervantes's version the reader knows what Carrizales does not: that, all appearances to the contrary, Leonora has freely chosen *not* to commit adultery with Loaysa and is therefore guiltless. By allowing Leonora to remain free from sin Cervantes manages to enhance the moral character of both protagonists while still maintaining the powerful effect of Carrizales's final comeuppance.

In the final analysis, *ZE* is more about forgiveness than it is about divine retribution, which explains why Cervantes frustrates his reader's expectations by allowing Leonora's last-minute exculpatory explanation to fall on deaf ears. Had Carrizales been able to hear her entire account, he might have believed her, in which case no final act of forgiveness would have been required on his part. The whole purpose of Carrizales's death is that he must pass from this life believing he has been cuckolded, yet forgiving the transgression. In order for this to happen in the original story, Isabela was required to commit adultery, then repent. Cervantes found a way to retain the full pathos of Carrizales's death while at the same time rehabilitating the wife's moral reputation. It was a stroke of genius, but heretofore few critics have taken the time to fathom precisely how and why Cervantes achieved it.

Ruth El Saffar's analysis of *ZE* in *Novel to Romance* (1974) concentrates on the story's characterization rather than on the plot. Of particular interest to El Saffar are Carrizales's solipsism, his passivity, and his "scant ability to communicate."[46] However, her insistence upon giving the story a psychoanalytical reading ("Carrizales is simultaneously Leonora and Loaysa: he is passive and self-absorbed and at the same time aggressive and abusive" [43]) causes El Saffar to overlook or undervalue certain simple structural parallels. For example, while she observes that "Loaysa embodies the youthful Carrizales" (43) and that "Carrizales, equally selfish and possessive, suggests Loaysa's destiny, just as Loaysa reveals Carrizales's past" (50), El Saffar never quite manages to state the obvious corollary that a number of critics have since pointed out: in the final pages of the 1613 version Cervantes clearly intends to portray Loaysa as a virtual reincarnation of the profligate Carrizales, now deceased.

In the Porras version, we should remember, Loaysa's fate was quite different: the narrator informs us that he enlisted in the army and perished when his own weapon exploded in his hands. Cervantes obviously saw greater artistic and ironic possibilities in Loaysa's fate than did the Porras author: by having Loaysa sail off to a "new" life in the Indies, Cervantes is able to highlight the undeniable parallels that can be noted in the lives of the young seducer and the old man whom he had attempted to victimize.

The emergence of Loaysa as a newborn Carrizales at the end of the 1613 version is cited as an important development by A. F. Lambert (1980), Juan Bautista Avalle-Arce (1984), and Maurice Molho (1990). Lambert praises this subtle conversion as Cervantes's way of having the punishment better fit the crime; the added irony serves only to intensify the final moral lesson of the story.[47] In Avalle-Arce's view, Cervantes ultimately saw the need to do away with the closed ending of the earlier draft of ZE because it did not accurately reflect reality. The 1613 version, then, offers a new perspective, an open ending that artistically represents the circularity of life; he accomplishes this, says Avalle-Arce, by having Loaysa become a second Carrizales.[48]

Maurice Molho views the story of Loaysa and Carrizales as a modern re-creation of the Oedipus myth, with a special twist at the end that transforms the combined figure of Carrizales/Loaysa into "un edipo doble y reversible."[49] In the primitive Porras account, says Molho, Loaysa's untimely death without issue makes it impossible for us to view him as Carrizales's double or spiritual heir. At the end Carrizales is seen to be a Phoenix-like figure, condemned to die on a flaming pyre of his own making, but without resurrection (because Loaysa will also die) from the ashes.[50]

In Molho's eyes, then, Cervantes improves an already good story by giving it circularity, which he achieves by having Loaysa escape to the Indies to relive Carrizales's tragic oedipal life. A notable dissenting voice in this matter is that of Edwin Williamson (1990), for whom Loaysa actually represents the *antithesis* of old Carrizales.[51] As for the influence of Cervantes's ZE on the Spanish *comedia*, Manuel García Martín notes that Antonio Coello later authored a dramatic work that borrowed the title, *El celoso extremeño*, but little else of significance from Cervantes's novella. The rakish Loaysa figure is transformed in the *comedia* into Don Juan, Carrizales's nephew, who manages to sweep Leonora off her feet shortly before her intended nuptials with the old gentleman. Carrizales eventually takes the more mature Marialonso as his bride.[52]

Cervantes's 1613 denouement is infinitely more satisfying than its Porras counterpart because he infuses the story with a double dose of irony. Both versions allow us to glimpse the circular pattern of Carrizales's life; in light of his early profligacy, the old man's final punishment is richly deserved and most appropriate. But only in the revised 1613 version does Loaysa suffer an equally ironic fate. The vivid account of his dissolute lifestyle and brazen attempt to debauch the innocent Leonora is topped off with the announcement that Loaysa will soon be heading off to the New World, where (we may safely assume) he will retrace the footsteps of his spiritual father, Carrizales. And so, precisely as the old scoundrel's life draws to a pathetic close, his younger adversary and spiritual heir is portrayed setting out on the same profligate journey through this world, destined to share the same moral destiny as his predecessor. None of this ultimate and final irony can be inferred from the Porras text; the artistic triumph here is Cervantes's alone.

Another significant point that appears to have eluded El Saffar's otherwise prodigious grasp has to do with the outcome of the final confrontation between Carrizales and Leonora about her supposed adultery. Their discussion ultimately settles nothing because each of them is working under a totally erroneous assumption about the nature of the wife's guilt. For some reason El Saffar does not find this total failure to communicate to be of any significance; she simply states "the misunderstanding between them does not matter."[53] I would strongly disagree. In my view, the ironic misunderstanding between them and their frustrating inability to reach a rapprochement in the final pages are the foundation upon which Cervantes's reconstituted story is built. And the sharply ironic tone of the 1613 text is what sets Cervantes's *ZE* far above the Porras original.

El Saffar correctly notes that when she enters his room, Leonora doesn't suspect that Carrizales has witnessed her fall from grace with Loaysa. The old man's misery and illness awaken in Leonora a concern for her husband and inspire her to offer him her caresses, which in turn cause him to experience an ambiguous kind of happiness. El Saffar, by seeking a psychologically viable explanation for the behavior of Carrizales and Leonora (46), has completely overlooked an even more valid artistic point that Cervantes was making in the final pages.

In order to appreciate the ironic twist that Cervantes was attempting to achieve in this scene we must compare his version against the earlier Porras text. As I mentioned earlier, in the original story both Carrizales and Isabela know the entire truth about what has taken place between the young bride and Loaysa; furthermore, each partner is cognizant of the other's full knowledge of the facts. There is absolutely no deception or misunderstanding between husband and wife during their final confrontation. Conversely, in Cervantes's final version each partner begins the conversation with an erroneous understanding of the other's point of view: Carrizales mistakenly believes that Leonora has cuckolded him; Leonora, still unaware that her husband has seen her in the arms of another man, experiences remorse only to the extent that she has erroneously concluded that her husband's physical collapse has been brought on by the somniferous unguent she administered to him. Each partner, therefore, has a completely different interpretation of the apologetic words that issue from Leonora's lips during this scene. As Edwin Williamson has so ably noted, the upshot of the final confrontation between the spouses is that Leonora ultimately learns that Carrizales's pain and suffering were not brought on by the demonic ointment, but rather by his overpowering suspicions of adultery on her part; Carrizales, on the other hand, dies without disabusement, believing to the end that Leonora has been unfaithful to him.[54]

A slightly different interpretation of Cervantes's altered denouement is offered by A. F. Lambert, who notes that the young bride's attempt at adultery, which had been the climactic moment (followed by an epilogue) in the Porras text, becomes in 1613 the turning point of the story. Leonora's decision not to sleep with Loaysa, in Lambert's view, "enables us to discover a new Carrizales, a character capable of real suffering."[55] Similarly, whereas the Porras version had accented Isabela's physical beauty, Cervantes's account lays emphasis on her moral strength (229). In Lambert's view the 1613 version of the story is superior to the Porras text because it contains elements of pathos and poignancy that were completely lacking in the earlier draft (230).

The final failure of Carrizales and Leonora to establish essential lines of communication between them is what makes Cervantes's version of the spouses' climactic confrontation so special. The Porras version of *ZE* is about punishment and vengeance; the denouement of the 1613 version, however, is imbued with tragic overtones that are totally absent in the earlier account. What must not be overlooked is the fact that all these new tragic implications are derived entirely from the ironic twist Cervantes adds in the final paragraphs of the story: Carrizales is first brought down by— and then learns to forgive—a moral transgression that has taken place only in his mind. This brilliant new note of tragic irony at the end is precisely what elevates Cervantes's 1613 version over the original *ZE* in the estimation of most modern critics.

In El Saffar's view, Leonora's choice to reject Loaysa's advances is an act of *self-definition* and *liberation*. Although this new ending is commonly viewed as considerably less verisimilar (in the classical sense), the final result is deeper characterization as each spouse is allowed "to discover the other as real."[56] Such a view presupposes Leonora to be the major character, the one whose moral development is of principal interest to Cervantes (49). Such an assumption, however, is tenuous at best. When it comes to determining the central character of *ZE*, a strong case can be made for either spouse. It seems to me that Cervantes's interest was divided equally between them, which may explain why he chose to end his story on an ironic note, i.e., the final misunderstanding assures that neither partner will emerge entirely vindicated or condemned. In Cervantes's version—but certainly not in Porras's—it can even be argued that each spouse learns to be a better person as a result of Loaysa's unwanted intrusion into their lives. Carrizales, having learned the moral impropriety of his insane jealousy, ultimately finds it in his heart to forgive Leonora's marital indiscretion (which the reader knows to be far less serious than the husband imagines). For her part, Leonora learns to take pity on the silly old man who has served more as her jailer than as her husband.

I must reiterate my judgment that Cervantes's *ZE*—but clearly not Porras's—is primarily about forgiveness. In support of my opinion I cite Thomas R. Hart's observation (1993) that both Leonora's decision to enter a convent and Carrizales's final act of forgiveness surprise us because nothing in the text suggests that either is capable of such a wise or charitable decision. And with regard to Leonora's curious silence regarding her innocence, I can only echo Thomas R. Hart's words: "To allow Leonora to attempt to justify her actions . . . would turn the reader away from Carrizales' exemplary act of forgiveness. The story is his, not hers, as the title makes clear."[57]

In the end, Carrizales's dying act of absolution proves to be at least as important to the outcome of *ZE* as is Leonora's decision not to sin. When Cervantes altered the original ending of *ZE* he was not principally concerned with the "liberation" of Leonora, but rather with applying a new, ironic twist to an old, traditional motif. Hart hits the nail squarely on the head when he posits two explicit morals for *ZE*. The first, that in matters of home security a man should not put too much trust in mechanical devices or servants, especially old duennas ("no se fíen de torno ni criadas, si se han de fiar de dueñas de tocas largas"), is provided directly by the Porras narrator in the penultimate sentence of the earlier text; the other, that offering forgiveness is always a better choice than taking vengeance, is never stated but rather must be inferred from the final actions of Carrizales in Cervantes's version.[58]

In the final analysis, the dominant motifs of Cervantes's *ZE* are a conscious deviation from the traditional Boccaccian principles of revenge and retribution; Cervantes offers in their stead the more Christian elements of compassion and forgiveness. And the impression left by that forgiveness on the reader's consciousness is greatly intensified by the unmistakably ironic and pathetic circumstances under which it is given.

The question of irony in Cervantes's *ZE* has been thoroughly examined by Gwynne Edwards (1973).[59] While Lambert (1980) generally agrees with Edwards's view, he says Edwards underestimates the complexity imparted by the "calculated pathos" and poignancy of the revised story.[60] A slightly different view is expressed by Charlotte Stern (1983), who finds irony in the fact that the wife's greater freedom in Cervantes's 1613 version leads Leonora to embrace fidelity, not adultery. As a consequence, Stern considers the denouement of ZE to be a clever inversion of the customary ending of the medieval fabliaux; the deception of old Carrizales, she avers, turns him into a tragic figure, not a ridiculous one.[61]

At the opposite end of the critical spectrum are the bitterly feminist (i.e., totally anti-Carrizales) interpretations of ZE's denouement offered by Alison Weber (1984) and Myriam Y. Jehenson (1995). While Weber's psychoanalytical approach does allow that, as we move from the Porras version of ZE to Cervantes's, there is a "shift from the affective distance of comedy to the pathetic involvement of tragedy,"[62] she completely fails to appreciate any of the abundant allegorical and/or symbolic elements in the story, nor does she note the overpowering irony of Carrizales's final gesture of forgiveness at the end. Jehenson, for her part, insists that Carrizales's final act of forgiveness is simply "a vengeful and effective wielding of power."[63] It would be difficult, in my opinion, to devise more wrongheaded interpretations of Cervantes's ZE than either Weber's or Jehenson's.

Among the first critics to study the special narrative structure of ZE was Eleodoro J. Febres, whose 1976 article generally follows Casalduero's reasoning with regard to the various baroque influences (e.g., use of chiaroscuro and contrasting elements) on Cervantes's work.[64] Febres joins Amezúa and Casalduero in dividing the work into three distinct narrative sections, but his lines of separation fall at slightly different points. Earlier, Amezúa had divided the work into sections he labels "exposition," "incidents," and "denouement," without citing any specific points of division.[65] Casalduero later marked the separation of the first and second parts at the introduction of the Loaysa character with "Hay en Sevilla un género de gente" [There is in Seville a class of people]. The same critic posits the beginning of a third and final section at the point when the narrator suddenly addresses the reader: "Bueno fuera en esta sazón preguntar a Carrizales" [One might well have asked Carrizales at this juncture].[66] In his analysis, Febres views ZE as consisting of (1) a preamble (which carries up to Carrizales's decision *not* to marry), (2) a central part (from the introduction of Leonora's character to Carrizales's awakening from his slumber) and (3) an epilogue.[67]

Febres posits a clear symmetrical design for ZE, but the symmetry he notes is more poetic (suggestions, comparisons, antitheses) than one rooted in any rigid analytical or mathematical formula (11). Furthermore, the "new" ending Cervantes pens for the final version of ZE provides for a complete change of perspective for each of the main characters: before dying,

Carrizales comes to realize the error of his insane jealousy; Loaysa moves from *engaño* to total *desengaño*; and Leonora, who from the beginning is totally in the dark regarding romantic or conjugal love, ultimately achieves full understanding of what a loving relationship entails (21). I would propose a somewhat different design for *ZE*.

As I pointed out in *Cervantes: Pioneer and Plagiarist*, the history of Felipo de Carrizales's unhappy marriage features a peculiar combination of two totally different—some might even say contradictory—narrative techniques. The story begins with a stylized a priori portrait of the rich old merchant Carrizales (A), including a brief synopsis of his prodigal lifestyle as a young man in Spain and the New World. Given the narrator's forced presentation of Carrizales's character, especially his emphasis on the Extremaduran's excessively jealous nature, the range of possibilities to be deduced about how Carrizales might behave when faced with a romantic rival is quite narrow. Frankly speaking, the image created here of a psychologically warped *indiano* is more caricature than characterization, a technique closely associated with the farcical *entremés*, but not with Cervantes's more realistic prose fiction.

Having completed this brief prehistory, the omniscient narrator suddenly abandons the obsessive Carrizales to focus now on the figure of Loaysa, a streetwise young rake who hatches a scheme to breach the carefully constructed security system employed at Carrizales's mansion and seduce the old man's lovely teenage bride. This section of the story (B), which encompasses almost 80 percent of the text, slows the action down and utilizes a more realistic approach, which I call the a posteriori or empirical method. Little is indicated ahead of time about Loaysa's character; the reader is left to draw his own conclusions from Loaysa's words and actions regarding the young man's intelligence, cunning, considerable physical charm, and dogged determination to penetrate the ingenious defenses Carrizales has erected around his supposedly impregnable fortress.

Schematically, the design of *ZE* is very similar to the format we noted earlier for *R/C*. In both cases, because of the absence of analeptic flashbacks, the narrative and chronological ordering of events is the same (schema 22).

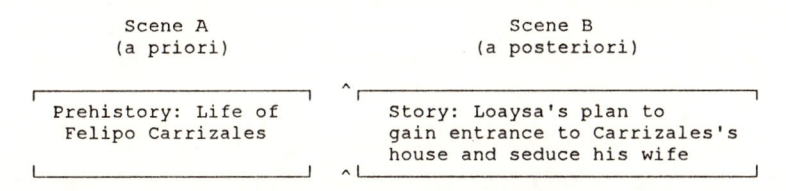

```
        Scene A                      Scene B
       (a priori)                 (a posteriori)
┌──────────────────────┐   ┌──────────────────────────────┐
│ Prehistory: Life of  │   │ Story: Loaysa's plan to      │
│ Felipo Carrizales    │   │ gain entrance to Carrizales's│
│                      │   │ house and seduce his wife    │
└──────────────────────┘   └──────────────────────────────┘
```

Schema 22. *El celoso extremeño*

A comparison of the Porras and 1613 versions of this remarkable narrative reveals a number of interesting changes wrought by Cervantes prior to publication. Noteworthy among these are the alteration and suppression of certain details that, according to Castro, might have betrayed the secret and subversive theme of the original Porras version: an unflattering political allegory commenting on the union of Philip II and his third wife, Isabel de Valois.[68] The historical Isabel married the austere Spanish monarch when she was only fourteen; she was later rumored to have had an affair with Philip's son Don Carlos shortly before both she and the prince came to separate but equally mysterious ends in 1568. The suspicious circumstances of Isabel de Valois's unexpected demise at the age of twenty-two provoked a great deal of titillating speculation in court circles. This would explain, I stated in 1982, Cervantes's otherwise unaccountable decision to change the female lead's name to the harmless "Leonora" from the dangerous Porras original, "Isabela."[69]

Another noteworthy alteration carried out by Cervantes is his augmentation of certain symbolic elements found in the early Porras text. The initial description of Carrizales's strange house is as follows:

Porras:
Compró una [casa] en doce mill ducados en un barrio principal de la ciudad, que tenía agua de pie, y jardín con muchos naranjos, con las ventanas que salían a la calle, y dióles vista al cielo, y lo mesmo hizo a todas las otras de la casa. En el portal de ella, que en Sevilla llaman casapuerta, hizo una caballeriza para una mula, y encima de ella acomodó un pajar, y un apartamiento para un negro que curase la mula. Hizo ansimesmo su torno, que salía al patio, y levantó las paredes de las azoteas, de tal manera, que los que entraban en la casa, si no era el cielo abierto, otra ninguna cosa podían ver. (Schevill and Bonilla 2:161)

[He bought a house costing twelve thousand ducats in one of the best parts of town and had running water and a garden full of orange trees; it had windows that faced the street, which he then had turned skywards, as he did with all the other windows in the house. In the main doorway (which, in Seville, is called the *casapuerta*), he built a stable for a mule, and above that, a hayloft and quarters for a Negro who would look after the mule. He also had a revolving door made that led to the patio, and he raised the walls so high above the roof that anybody coming into the house could see nothing but the open sky.]

Cervantes's presentation is essentially the same, but he adds certain details (italicized below) that serve to increase the symbolic, as opposed to the merely realistic, content of the passage:

3 / PORRAS'S MANUSCRIPT 185

Cervantes:
compró una en doce mil ducados en un barrio principal de la ciudad, que tenía agua de pie y jardín con muchos naranjos; *cerró todas las ventanas que miraban a la calle*, y dióles vista al cielo, y lo mismo hizo de todas las otras de casa. En el portal de la calle, que en Sevilla llaman casapuerta, hizo una caballeriza para una mula, y encima della un pajar y apartamiento, donde estuviese el que había de curar della, que fue un negro *viejo y eunuco*; levantó las paredes de las azuteas de tal manera que el que entraba en la casa, *había de mirar al cielo por línea recta, sin que pudiesen* [sic] *ver otra cosa*; hizo torno que de la casapuerta respondía al patio. (Sieber 2:103–4)

[he bought a house costing twelve thousand ducats which was in one of the best parts of town and had running water and a garden full of orange trees; *he blocked off all the street-facing windows* and turned them skywards, as he did with all the other windows in the house. In the main doorway (which, in Seville, is called the *casapuerta*), he built a stable for a mule, and above that, a hay-loft and quarters for the man who was to look after it, an *old* negro *eunuch*. He raised the walls so high above the roof that anybody coming into the house *had to look directly up at the sky and could see nothing else*. He had a revolving door made which led from the *casapuerta* to the patio.] (3:13)

The addition here of "viejo y eunuco" ['old ... eunuch'] to the description of the African slave more than doubles the image of sexlessness connoted by Carrizales's house. (In the Porras version, the only symbol of neutered sexuality was the mule in the stable.) The added specifics about closing the windows facing the street and forcing visitors to look directly skyward when they enter the house are intended to reinforce the moral and spiritual focus of the ridiculous restrictions Carrizales has imposed within his domain.[70]

Even so, the alteration that has most frequently occupied the thoughts of literary scholars was Cervantes's decision to graft onto *ZE* an ironic new ending that, despite some objections about the work's diminished verisimilitude, transforms this familiar tale into a genuine masterpiece of characterization. Recent critics, most notably Ruth El Saffar, have applauded Cervantes's bold decision here to create a strong female character and endow her with enough moral fortitude to resist the handsome intruder's charms.[71] I shall have more to say on this issue at a later point.

In summary, then, there is much to praise about Cervantes's rendition of *ZE*. First of all, we should appreciate the bold blending of conflicting a priori and a posteriori narrative styles he found in the initial version. With regard to the allegorical references to Philip II, Cervantes manages to tone down the more obvious parallels while otherwise maintaining the integrity of the plot. At the same time he adds to and actually intensifies the occasional symbolic elements presented in the Porras original. Most notably, however, he created still another of his characteristically strong and independent female personalities (cf. Marcela, Dorotea, Claudia Jerónima, Ana Félix) who dare to rebel against traditional behavior patterns while working out their own destiny.

We should also consider the various ways in which Cervantes managed not only to forge a highly intellectual and artistic variation on a very popular theme, but also to give sharper psychological definition to the three stock characters he found in the primitive text of ZE.

Loaysa's transgression, while serious, certainly did not merit the sudden and horrible death he received in the original version. Instead, Cervantes fashioned for the hedonistic young rake a long-term punishment that was more poetically just and as well as perfectly tailored to his sin: he is allowed to sail off to the New World, not to be rewarded with fame and fortune, but rather condemned to repeat all of Carrizales's unfortunate experiences. As Francisco J. Sánchez so aptly puts it, the elderly Carrizales is what Loaysa will eventually become; the hedonistic Loaysa is what Carrizales used to be.[72] We may suppose that in his final years an infirm Loaysa will be set adrift in an empty, loveless marriage that may very well find him wearing his own set of cuckold's horns. The implied circularity of Loaysa's fate in the 1613 version is as ingenious as it is novel.

As for the teenage bride, Cervantes infuses Leonora with a great deal more moral backbone and character autonomy than was ever displayed by Isabela, her Porras counterpart. Cervantes's admirable heroine is endowed with a true free will *(libre albedrío):* although she teeters on the edge of sin for a while, in the end she finds a way to triumph over a powerful temptation. At whatever point Cervantes would have come upon the story of the jealous Extremaduran, he must have recognized in it a magnificent opportunity for literary experimentation. In ZE he was presented with a very traditional and popular folktale that he could stand on its head for both artistic and moral ends. By making a handful of significant alterations at certain strategic points in the narrative, Cervantes could fashion a totally unique literary character, an unfulfilled young bride who, although trapped in a marriage to a self-centered old man, somehow manages to summon up the moral fortitude to resist temptation and opt for something other than the conventional adulterous conduct of her literary predecessors.

It is, however, in the figure of the "new" Carrizales that Cervantes achieves his most significant success. In the Porras version we find Carrizales portrayed as a grotesque, one-dimensional figure who never displays any redeeming personal qualities and goes to a most ignominious death without ever actually forgiving his wife's infidelity. It should be remembered that on his deathbed the Porras Carrizales says he blames the world rather than Isabela for her transgression and then requests that she marry her young lover once she is free. This is, I maintain, a far cry from acknowledging and forgiving her sin (even if the transgression is only imagined), which is what Cervantes allows him do in the 1613 version.

The ridiculous cardboard figure of Carrizales we find sketched in the Porras text becomes a sympathetic and tragic character in Cervantes's story. The "new" Carrizales is allowed to acquire a measure of dignity and sympathy in his final hours. He is ultimately redeemed in the reader's eyes—and, presumably, in God's—because he finds it in his heart to forgive Leonora. And for even more poignancy Cervantes adds a final ironic note: Carrizales's forgiveness is doubly redeeming because it is entirely unnecessary. The reader knows, as Carrizales does not, that Leonora has not been unfaithful to him.

This "forgiveness" theme is also present in the Porras version, but there it is almost completely obscured by the more dominant motif of retribution/poetic justice that is imposed upon Carrizales in the end. Cervantes found a way to play down the issue of retribution while bringing the moral virtue of Christian forgiveness to the forefront. He accomplishes this by injecting an ironic note into the proceedings. At the last moment Leonora opts *not* to commit adultery, but Carrizales nonetheless goes to his death believing that she has cuckolded him.

The ironic circumstances of Cervantes's version also underscore the new generosity of spirit that the old man achieves in his final hour. The reader realizes in the closing paragraphs that he or she knows more about the truth of what happened between Leonora and Loaysa than does the protagonist, which was certainly not the case in Porras. Consequently, the reader's attention is drawn more forcefully to Carrizales's magnanimity in the 1613 text than it would have in the earlier version.

As Thomas R. Hart has noted, the *real* protagonist of ZE is Felipe Carrizales, for whom the story is named.[73] In recent years critics have too easily been distracted by the remarkable moral fortitude exhibited by the teenage bride in the Cervantine version. As a consequence, some scholars have tended to overvalue Leonora's role and treat her as the main character of the story. This does Cervantes a great disservice, I believe, in that it ignores the clever way in which the great writer has restructured ZE so as to reflect a real and significant moral epiphany for Carrizales, whom Cervantes clearly intended to be the primary character in the story.

These critics have carefully noted the alterations Cervantes makes in Leonora's conduct during the climactic bedroom scene, but they have not fully appreciated the full range of consequences—most of them having to do with Carrizales's mental state—that result from that simple reversal:

1. Carrizales, confronted with what he mistakenly considers irrefutable proof of Leonora's adultery, plans to take revenge but, upon returning to his room in search of a dagger with which to kill the pair of lovers, topples onto his bed in a swoon.

2. The next morning Leonora mistakes her husband's unconsciousness for the prolonged effects of the soporific ointment she had administered to him. At this point she is consumed with guilt, but only because she fears she has damaged her elderly husband's health. Her remorse has nothing to do with Loaysa or his unsuccessful attempt to seduce her, but Carrizales fails to realize that.

3. The tears that flow from Leonora's eyes are out of genuine concern for Carrizales's well-being, but the old man believes—again, wrongly—that they are crocodile tears.

4. At a later point, as Carrizales finally reveals the true cause of his emotional distress and physical deterioration in the presence of Leonora and her parents, Leonora manages to declare that she has offended him only in thought, but her apology is cut short when she passes out from the emotional distress of the situation.

5. Despite his highly imperfect understanding of his wife's conduct, Carrizales finds it in his heart to offer Leonora his forgiveness, an act of generosity that rehabilitates his character and earns him a measure of redemption in the reader's eyes.

The irony that Cervantes injects into the final pages of the story is designed to draw the reader's attention to the fact that Carrizales dies a reformed and repentant sinner. His final display of a Christian forgiveness is an element that went virtually unnoticed in the Porras version.

Although many critics do not share my belief that Cervantes was not the original author of *ZE*, I believe we all stand firmly together in acknowledging Cervantes's artistic genius in turning what had originally been a very conventional story about a disastrously adulterous May-December marriage into a tender tale that points to the need for mutual compassion and forgiveness between spouses.

EL LICENCIADO VIDRIERA

The question of genre has been a constant item of discussion among critics who have examined *LV* in recent years. Luis Rosales (1956) views Cervantes's pseudobiographical piece of fiction as the most archaic of the tales in the *Novelas ejemplares*, a curious fusion of Oriental novelistic techniques (his term for the series of apothegms attributed to Vidriera) and the picaresque novel.[74] A slightly different connection with the picaresque is made by E. Michael Gerli (1979), who considers Cervantes's novella to be the noted writer's critical response to the picaresque model presented in 1599 by Mateo Alemán in *Guzmán de Alfarache*. Gerli asserts that Cervantes employs certain picaresque elements in *LV* solely for the purpose of subverting and repudiating them in the final analysis; this is particularly true with regard to the noxious kind of determinism implied in Guzmán's perverse concept of bloodlines and lineage.[75] Still another picaresque interpretation is offered by Julio Rodríguez-Luis (1980), who notes the sharp social criticism contained in Vidriera's perceptive comments and calls *LV* a skeletal outline of a potential picaresque novel, minus the action ("el esqueleto, por decirlo así, de una novela picaresca despojada de la acción").[76]

Edward H. Friedman (1974), on the other hand, prefers to cast Tomás Rodaja/Rueda in the role of a tragic hero, i.e., a serious thinker who is guilty only of being incompatible with the society that surrounds him and who consequently receives a punishment (rejection, followed by death) that supersedes whatever offense his prickly nature may have given.[77] Moreover, Friedman maintains that the extended portion of *LV*'s text devoted to cataloguing examples of the mad scholar's mordant wit is not, as some have supposed, the key element of the story. Friedman considers the period of Tomás's amusing madness to represent a transitional stage in the life of Tomás Rodaja/Rueda; these witty *agudezas* form a diversionary parenthesis that is framed by a pair of more telling narrative sections portraying Tomás's mental, emotional, and physical development in the periods immediately before and after his bout with insanity. The collection of apothegmatic utterances are intended to provide an entertaining change of pace, says Friedman, adding that the interdependence of these witty remarks and the surrounding biographical text are what gives *LV* "a sense of both interior and exterior proportion."[78]

Joseph V. Ricapito offers a very similar interpretation of *LV*'s structure: he views the work as a triptych consisting of two flanking sides (Tomás's life) and a center panel (the apothegms), but all three parts are of equal importance. In analyzing Tomás's story, Ricapito notes that "For certain narrative purposes, the time he spent as Vidriera stands out above the other two phases of his life. It is usually the stage of disillusioned licentiate that has captured the imagination of the reading public (then and now) for obvious reasons, but in terms of the total narrative message, the flanking parts are as important as the altar centerpiece."[79]

Rodríguez-Luis, who as we noted earlier considers *LV* to be essentially picaresque, rejects the characterization of Tomás Rodaja/Rueda as a tragic figure on the grounds that Tomás does nothing to merit the punishment he receives.[80]

A slightly different interpretation of *LV* is offered by E. C. Riley (1976) and Alban K. Forcione (1982), who view Cervantes's pseudobiography as a satirical work presented in a nonpicaresque framework. According to Riley, the dour licenciado is the modern literary incarnation of a classical stereotype: the melancholy cynic whose uncharitable comments about a variety of social types echo the vituperative backbiting *(murmuración)* that Cipión so strongly deplores in the *Coloquio de los perros*. Riley concludes that Cervantes composed both the *Coloquio* and *LV* in a mood of disillusionment.[81]

A similar judgment is made by Forcione, who sees Tomás Rodaja/Rueda as a seriously flawed character who ultimately receives a well-deserved comeuppance. Forcione concurs with Riley's thesis and cites Diogenes in particular and the Cynics in general as the models for Vidriera's anger.[82] Forcione notes that at the last moment Cervantes redeems what the critic calls "his failed satirist," but I wonder if—combining the judgments of Riley and Forcione—we might not classify Tomás Rodaja/Rueda more accurately as simply a "failed Cynic."

The unusual narrative structure of *LV* is another subject that has fascinated and perplexed critics for centuries. Casalduero and Casa find four natural divisions within the tale: (A) Tomás Rodaja's studies at Salamanca; (B) his travels on the continent; (C) his return to Spain and subsequent madness; and (D) the ironic conclusion (see schema 23).

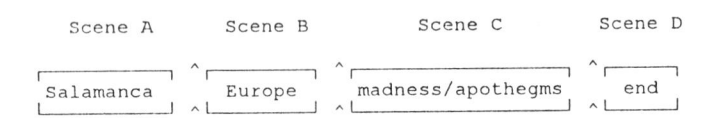

Scene A	Scene B	Scene C	Scene D
Salamanca	Europe	madness/apothegms	end

Schema 23. *El licenciado Vidriera*

Several other critics (Avalle-Arce, Francisco García Lorca, Febres, Forcione, Friedman, Lizama-Améstica, Ricapito and Russell), discern only three stages, one for each of the three names the protagonist employs in the course of the story: (A) the formative years (studies + travels) of Tomás Rodaja; (B) his two years as the celebrated madman Vidriera, the itinerant sage who believes himself to be made of glass; and (C) the last stage of his life which encompasses his return to sanity, his consequent disillusionment with a fickle public that now ignores him, and finally his heroic death in Flanders as the courageous infantryman Tomás Rueda (schema 24).

Finally, there are other scholars, most notably Edwards, Glannon, Heiple, Riley, and Singer, who consider *LV* to consist of only two essential

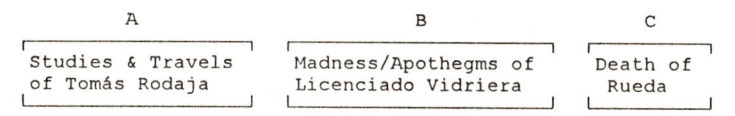

```
        A                    B                      C
┌───────────────┐    ┌────────────────────┐    ┌──────────┐
│Studies & Travels│   │Madness/Apothegms of│    │ Death of │
│of Tomás Rodaja │   │Licenciado Vidriera │    │  Rueda   │
└───────────────┘    └────────────────────┘    └──────────┘
```

Schema 24. *El licenciado Vidriera*

narrative parts, although they do not always agree as to what these entities represent or where the dividing line between them can be drawn. My own interpretation is most similar to those who take a binary view, insofar as I divide the story of Tomás Rodaja/Rueda into complementary sections of direct and indirect social criticism. The direct commentary is found at the core of the narrative, in the curious compilation of maxims, witticisms, puns, and satirical comments *(sentencias, agudezas, equívocos, toques satíricos)* that issue from the lips of the mad Vidriera in the central section of the text. This hard-hitting cavalcade of brickbats and clever put-downs is encircled by the crafty, implied criticism of Spanish society presented in the opening and closing segments that recount the rise-and-fall biography of Tomás Rodaja/Rueda (schema 25).

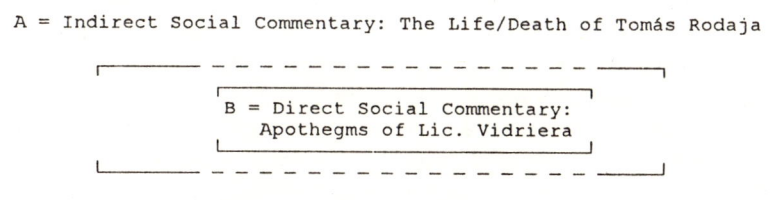

```
A = Indirect Social Commentary: The Life/Death of Tomás Rodaja
┌─────── ─ ─ ─ ─ ─ ─ ─ ─ ─ ─ ─ ─ ─ ─ ───────┐
         ┌──────────────────────────┐
         │B = Direct Social Commentary:│
         │   Apothegms of Lic. Vidriera│
         └──────────────────────────┘
└─────── ─ ─ ─ ─ ─ ─ ─ ─ ─ ─ ─ ─ ─ ─ ───────┘
```

Schema 25. *El licenciado Vidriera*

Even among those who propose a binary structure for *LV* there is not always agreement as to what the two divisions represent. Gwynne Edwards (1973) was among the first to examine *LV* from such a standpoint. Edwards views it as a work made up of contrasting sections of text, each of which sets forth a different theme or tone: past versus present; idealism versus realism; narrative versus commentary.[83] Ultimately, Edwards reduces the story to a question of freedom from outside pressures, as represented by the old arms-versus-letters debate (562). In the beginning Tomás appears to be attracted in equal measure to each of these fields. In the end, however, the mature Rueda concludes that *armas* is the only path to glory, that only the soldier is free to perform notable deeds on the basis of his own initiative and merits. University graduates *(letrados)* are forced to depend upon the favor and reception of others, who in many cases turn out to be corrupt individuals or simply fools (567). Edwards's final judgment is that *LV* represents a sad and ironic moment in Cervantes's career, a point at which the great writer can be seen to have come full circle, back to the ideals of his youth (568).

In *Novel to Romance* (1974), Ruth El Saffar disagrees; she sees instead the case of Tomás Rodaja/Rueda as a contest between the attractions of *fame*, not arms, against those of a career in letters.[84] In the opinion of this critic, Tomás's madness is simply an innovative technique, an attempt by Cervantes to distinguish between his main character and the narrator in the work. El Saffar ultimately pronounces the experiment a failure because it results in a fragmented production whose parts never fuse into a convincing whole (55–56). Eleodoro Febres (1982) also refuses to accept the traditional arms-versus-letters dichotomy as the main theme of *LV;* he views it more as a question of deception and disabusement *(engaño/desengaño)*. Febres argues convincingly that Cervantes never intended to resolve the paradox of arms and letters here, but merely employed that popular theme in an imaginative piece of fiction to expose what he considered an enigmatic and contradictory world.[85]

Walter Glannon discerns a very different kind of bipartite arrangement for the story of Tomás Rodaja/Rueda: a confrontation between aesthetic and ethical principles for control of his life.[86] This critic defines the former as a tendency toward intellectual introspection, the contemplative life, the study of abstract principles; the latter are seen to embrace an active, social lifestyle rooted more in practical experience than in intellectual pursuits (88). Tomás's life is divided by Glannon into two distinct stages: (1) the young Rodaja's neurotic obsession with aesthetics (i.e., intellectual development to the exclusion of all else) in his formative years; and (2) the final period of his life when the mature Rueda finally manages to break out of the abstract circle of academic letters that holds him prisoner, a liberating move to a state of *desengaño* with the realization that he will never be able to make a living off aesthetic pursuits (90). Consequently, Glannon does not consider Tomás's career as the eccentric Licenciado Vidriera to be a link in a linear chain of events, but rather a brief parenthesis that happens to separate two contrasting aspects of the same static mode (91). In the final analysis, Glannon declares *LV* to be simply a vehicle for conveying the following Cervantine thesis: "[T]he ethical has primacy over the aesthetic, for the latter cannot be sustained without the social framework implied by the former" (96).

Still another kind of dualism is proposed by Anthony J. Cascardi (1983): mind versus body.[87] In one sense, Vidriera's mania is the obverse of Don Quixote's: if Cervantes's most famous literary character can be said to be a man with virtually no mind at all, the licentiate is presented as pure intellect. Cascardi views Rodaja/Rueda as an acute skeptic (cf. René Descartes) who longs to become a brilliant mind totally unencumbered by his own corporeal nature (23–24). As Cascardi interprets it, Cervantes's purpose in composing *LV* was to portray the disastrous consequences of a Cartesian wish to transcend the body in search of knowledge. Ironically, Vidriera's knowledge serves only to separate him from the world; his example is intended to be a caustic comment on what Cascardi calls the "latent arrogance" of those who harbor such a desire (26). Even when he finally regains his sanity, self-understanding, and possession of his body, Tomás remains at odds with the world (29).

Despite the cogency of so many of these critics' arguments in support of other thematic interpretations, I feel that the key to understanding *LV* is found in the issue of *armas y letras*. My reading of Cervantes's text always comes back to the arms-versus-letters debate as the essential conflict in the life of Tomás Rodaja/Rueda, although the author certainly manages to touch upon a number of other contrasting elements in his text. The entire story— but especially the eight years of study at Salamanca and three years of travel on the continent prior to his unfortunate bout with insanity—portrays the struggle of these two antithetical forces for control of a bright and ambitious young man's destiny.

At first it seems that a distinguished legal career may be in the young man's future, but Tomás suddenly abandons the study of law/letters in favor of an extended sabbatical in the military. Tomás's commitment, however, to the life of a soldier is less than total; he attaches himself to the company of Captain Diego de Valdivia with the specific proviso that he not be obliged to carry arms or take part in any violent action:

> pero había de ser condición que no se había de sentar debajo de bandera, ni poner en lista de soldado, por no obligarse a seguir su bandera. Y aunque el capitán le dijo que no importaba ponerse en lista, que ansí gozaría de los socorros y pagas que a la compañía se diesen, porque él le daría licencia todas las veces que se la pidiese.
> —Eso sería—dijo Tomás—ir contra mi conciencia y contra la del señor capitán; y así, más quiero ir suelto que obligado. (Sieber 2:46)

> [but only on condition that he would not have to enlist or go on the muster-list, so as not to be obliged to serve with the colours; and although the captain told him that going on the muster-list did not matter (if he did, he would receive all the allowances and pay the company received) because he would give him leave whenever he asked for it, Tomás said: "That would be to go against my conscience and yours, captain, and so I would prefer to go as a free man rather than under obligation."] (2:65)

Tomás wishes to experience only the pleasures of the soldier's life, without any hardship or risk of personal injury. Although his travels take him to Italy and Flanders, he is never in any actual physical danger during his sabbatical, for he always manages to remain safely behind the lines. Having tired of the life of a camp follower, he decides to return to Salamanca to resume his university studies. His deep commitment to nonviolence is again underscored by the narrator's specific mention of the fact that Rodaja decided to return to Spain via France, but did so without going through Paris because it was in a state of war ("y por Francia volvió a España, sin haber visto a París, por estar puesta en armas") (Sieber 2:51).[88]

Upon his return to Salamanca and the successful completion of his law degree, Rodaja is suddenly rendered insane by a powerful potion administered by a scorned lover. He spends the next two years of his life in the role of the highly ingenious but slightly insane Man of Glass, the Licenciado Vidriera. More than half of the text of this story is devoted to recounting his more celebrated witticisms and mordant comments about a variety of notable social conditions and personality types he comes across in Salamanca and Valladolid, the Spanish capital of the time.[89] Not everyone he meets is the target of a barb; some categories of people receive abundant praise from his lips, e.g., good poets, theater managers, bailiffs and scribes who assist in law enforcement, members of religious orders, actors, and soldiers. Most, however, feel the sting of his wit.

The final stage, the cure and ultimate disillusionment of Tomás Rueda, is succinctly recounted. Cervantes brings the story to a rapid and ironic conclusion with the protagonist's heroic demise on the fields of Flanders. Here we begin to glimpse the main theme of this tale: society's foolish inability to appreciate a sane and functional Vidriera/Rueda. Once the colorful madman has been restored to his sanity, the public turns away from him. The ultimate lesson he learns is that the wit and intelligence of his sarcastic comments are esteemed only because they have been packaged for the entertainment of the masses. His remarks are tolerated only because they are delivered in the relatively "safe" and amusing form of a lunatic or fool's pithy utterances. By themselves, Vidriera's innate wisdom and mordant criticism of social evils are of no value to the general public.

Having learned this bitter lesson, Rueda reluctantly decides to abandon his legal practice in favor of the more lucrative military profession, which is precisely the calling he eschewed years earlier when he quit Valdivia's service. The subtle social commentary of Cervantes's ironic denouement cannot be overlooked: Tomás Rueda's life concludes at a point precisely 180 degrees away from his original destination. Having finally recovered the corporeal portion of his essence, he then opts to put that fragile existence at risk by embarking upon a military career, exchanging *letras* for *armas*, the security of Salamanca for the perils of Flanders. The renown and glory he had hoped to achieve by dint of his *ingenio* ultimately could only be achieved through the use of his strong right arm, a reversal of the strange twist of fate that transformed Miguel de Cervantes from a would-be war hero to the greatest name in Spanish letters. Such ironic twists of fate are the stuff of great novels.

How, then, are we to supposed to classify *LV* as a literary work? Otis H. Green (1964) was among the first to discern a singular artistic purpose in this work. Whereas Armand Singer[90] had panned *LV* for its lack of unity, Green saw the work as much more than simply a loose collection of apothegms.[91] The witty comments of Vidriera are seen by Green as Cervantes's attempt to modernize a centuries-old folkloric tradition in many nations (217). The unifying element both in *LV* and in *Don Quixote*, according to Green, are the medical and psychological theories published in 1575 by the physician Juan Huarte de San Juan in his *Examen de ingenios para las ciencias*.

Still another interpretation is offered by E. Michael Gerli, who considers *LV* as Cervantes's critical and artistic repudiation of the picaresque genre, particularly Mateo Alemán's *Guzmán de Alfarache*, and its pessimistic determinism. In search of greater verisimilitude and objectivity, Cervantes provides a third-person treatment of the life of Tomás Rodaja/Rueda, a work that Gerli sees as "un astuto e irónico experimento literario, donde se busca una alternativa novelística a la picaresca" [an astute and ironic literary experiment where a novelistic alternative to the picaresque is sought].[92] A similar judgment is made by Daniel L. Heiple, who, while focusing primarily on the section of Cervantes's story that deals with Tomás Rodaja's travels in Europe, calls *LV* an experiment in narrative form that is comprehensible if not entirely successful.[93] In my view, *all* of the tales in Cervantes's *Novelas ejemplares* are literary experiments of one sort or another; *LV* is simply the most obvious one because of the radical change in form and tone that takes place during the protagonist's career as the eccentric Licenciado Vidriera.

What kind of experiment, then, is Cervantes undertaking in *LV*? Following the lead of Otis H. Green and Alban K. Forcione, I would like to propose that Cervantes was attempting a bold literary innovation here: a purely verbal experiment with the *emblema*, that very peculiar Renaissance literary form which offered biting social commentary through a combination of drawings and popular aphorisms, i.e., a mixture of direct and indirect modes of satirical discourse. Green has demonstrated that these *emblemas* were a popular literary form in Cervantes's day, not to mention a well-established tradition in the folklore of many European countries in that era.[94] Forcione traces the origins of apothegmatic literature back to the sixteenth century and the followers of Erasmus who made the emblematic format extremely fashionable in Spain and other European nations.[95]

In the case of *LV*, Cervantes was responding to the mordant, heavy-handed satire of the popular picaresque genre by devising a less-vicious form of social satire: a pseudobiography fashioned around a core of witty observations and clever apothegms with which the protagonist manages to prick the egos of certain disagreeable social types while avoiding the cynical backbiting *(murmuración)* that Cervantes seemed to detest.

The indirect satire in Cervantes's literary *emblema* is found in the frame tale of Tomás Rueda's life story and the subtle irony of his demise. The core of the puzzle, the direct form of satire, takes the form of a catalog of the Glass Man's pungent remarks, which I suspect Cervantes took from an as yet unidentified collection of apothegms, puns, and witticisms he came across in his travels.

As for the apothegms themselves, Armand Singer has cataloged more than seventy different items, which he divides into categories of puns, humorous remarks, eulogies, didactic and philosophical remarks, and caustic/cynical comments.[96] Here are some of Vidriera's more celebrated utterances (all references are to the Sieber edition):

A comment on a group of prostitutes gathered outside a brothel:

> y dijo que eran bagajes del ejército de Satanás que estaban alojados en el mesón del Infierno. (2:55)

> [he . . . said that they were the baggage-train of Satan's army, billeted in the inn of Hell. (2:75)

His friendly advice to a husband whose wife has run off with another man:

> Dile que dé gracias a Dios por haber permitido le llevasen de casa a su enemigo. (2:55)

> [Tell him to thank God for having allowed an enemy to be removed from his house.] (2:75)

He then comments as to why it would be a bad idea for such a husband to go out in search of an unfaithful wife:

> porque sería el hallarla un perpetuo y verdadero testigo de su deshonra. (2:56)

[because finding her would be finding a permanent and accurate witness to his dishonour.] (2:75)

Regarding the rearing of children, the licenciado has his own version of the spare-the-rod theory:

> que los azotes que los padres dan a los hijos honran y los del verdugo afrentan. (2:56)

> [the blows that fathers give to sons are honourable—it's the lashes of the public executioner that are dishonourable.] (2:75)

On courtly sycophants:

> que yo no soy bueno para palacio, porque tengo vergüenza y no sé lisonjear. (2:56)

> [I am no good for the life of the Royal Court and capital, for I have a sense of shame and do not know how to flatter.] (2:77)

On the rigors of travel:

> Ningún camino hay malo como se acabe, si no es el que va a la horca. (2:57)

> [No journey is bad which comes to an end—except the journey to the scaffold.] (2:77)

Concerning the plethora of bad poets that society produces:

> ¿Qué se ha de decir sino que son la idiotez y la arrogancia del mundo? (2:59)

> [What can you say, except that they are the epitome of idiocy and arrogance?] (2:79)

Painters fare no better at his hands:

> dijo que los buenos pintores imitaban a naturaleza; pero que los malos la vomitaban. (2:60)

> [he said that good painters imitated nature, but that bad painters vomited it.] (2:81)

The insidious practices of publishers and book vendors—a favorite target of Cervantes's satire—are also exposed:

> Los melindres que hacen cuando compran un privilegio de un libro, y de la burla que hacen a su autor si acaso le imprime a su costa, pues en lugar de mil y quinientos, imprimen tres mil libros, y cuando el autor piensa que se venden los suyos, se despachan los ajenos. (2:60)

> [The petty difficulties booksellers put up when they buy the author's rights to a book, and the trick they play on the author, if they print at his cost, for, instead of fifteen hundred, they print three thousand copies, and when the author thinks his copies are being sold, the bookseller's are, instead.] (2:81)

Vidriera comments on the widespread use of carriages for the secret rendezvous of streetwalkers and their clients; he pretends to misunderstand the meaning of the term "alcagüete" [go-between] when he hears it:

> Si dijeras que sacaban a azotar a un alcagüete, entendiera que sacaban a azotar un coche. (2:60)

> [If you said they were going to bring out a procurer for flogging, I would think they were going to bring out a coach.] (2:81)

Similarly, his comment on the risk of contracting a social disease from one of the well-mannered ladies of the royal court includes an ingenious play on words with *cortesana* (*cortés,* courteous + *sana,* healthy):

> De las damas que llaman *cortesanas* decía que todas, o las más, tenían más de corteses que de sanas. (2:71)

> [Of the ladies people call courtesans, he said that they all, or the majority, were more courteous than healthy.] (2:93)

He skewers apothecaries for their poor judgment in substituting one medicine for another, frequently with disastrous results for the unsuspecting patient, and for their clandestine substitution of lamp oil for medicinal ingredients when mixing their potions:

> porque en faltando cualquiera aceite la suple la del candil que está más a mano. (2:62)

> [because, if you find you are short of any sort of oil, you make it up from the nearest oil-lamp.] (2:83)

On the subject of physicians, his condemnation is unequivocal:

> no hay gente más dañosa a la república que ellos.... Sólo los médicos nos pueden matar y nos matan sin temor y a pie quedo, sin desenvainar otra espada que la de un *récipe*. (2:62–63)
>
> [there are no people more dangerous to the state than them {*sic*}.... Only doctors can and do kill us without fear and without effort, without unsheathing a sword other than a prescription.] (2:85)

Of special interest are the various occasions when Vidriera finds a way to comment on some social phenomenon through the apt application of a phrase in Latin or some other foreign language. To comment on the Jewish ancestry (i.e., by referring to the daughters of Jerusalem) of a woman in the Salamancan garment district, he quotes St. Luke:

> Filiae Hierusalem, plorate super vos et super filios vestros. (2:55)
>
> [Daughters of Jerusalem, do not weep for me; weep rather for yourselves and for your children.] (2:75)

Regarding the few poets of high quality to be found, he cites Ovid:

> *At sacri vates, et Divum cura vocamus.* (2:59)
>
> [Yes, we bards are called sacred and the care of the gods.] (2:79)

When they ask him who has been the most fortunate man in the world, Vidriera answers with series of puns using the Latin pronoun *Nemo* (No one) derived from several different Latin sources (footnoted in the Sieber edition, 2:67):

From St. Matthew:

> *Nemo novit patrem.*
>
> [No one knows his Father.]

From Simonides:

> *Nemo sine crimine vivit.*
>
> [No one lives without crime.]

From Horace:

> *Nemo sua sorte contentus.*
>
> [No one is pleased with his lot.]

From St. John:

> *Nemo ascendit in coelum*
>
> [No one ascends to heaven]

Perhaps Vidriera's cleverest linguistic play on words is rendered in Portuguese. It occurs one day when the licenciado comes upon an old Lusitanian sporting a beard that has obviously been tinted; the old man is heard to say to another:

> —*Por istas barbas que teño no rostro* . . .
>
> [By this beard I have on my face!]

Vidriera cleverly suggests that the elderly gentleman replace his original verb, *teño* (I have), with a different but nearly homonymous Portuguese predicate *tiño* (I dye), whose meaning would be much more apt:

> —*Ollay, home, naon digáis teño, sino tiño.* (2:68)
>
> [Now man, don't say you have it, say you've dyed it!] (2:89)

One of the problems with this kind of intensive, heavy punning in classical and foreign tongues is that it is completely alien to Cervantes's known style. To be sure, there are numerous citations from Latin and Italian sources in the *Don Quixote* and other Cervantine works, but such quotes are almost always from popular sources and injected for strictly parodic purposes. In *LV* the device is used in a more a sophisticated manner, which hints at an author who possessed a stronger background in classical authors than is generally attributed to Cervantes, an author whose contemporaries referred to him as an *ingenio lego*, a self-educated man lacking the benefits of a formal university education. Cervantes's grasp of Latin and other European languages was more superficial and colloquial than solid or profound, and his use here of so many Latin quotations and expressions—nine different quotes, by my count—in his long catalog of the Vidriera's witty remarks has caused several critics to look to other authors as potential original sources of Vidriera's material.

The work most frequently cited by critics as a possible source of Vidriera's collected wit and wisdom is Juan Rufo's *Las seyscientas apotegmas y otras obras en verso*, published in 1596. In 1901 (and again in 1916) Francisco A. de Icaza cited Rufo's collection as the best example of apothegmatic literature in Cervantes's time; Narciso Alonso Cortés also mentioned Rufo's example in the prologue of his 1916 edition of *LV*. A few years later both Casalduero and Singer proposed Rufo's clever remarks as probable Vidriera prototypes. Citing Rufo's *Apotegmas* as the most likely literary source for the witticisms of Cervantes's Glass Man has continued to be a popular practice; as recently as 1990 Anthony Close echoed the nomination.[97]

It should be noted that Rufo's candidacy does not go unchallenged; other potential models have also been nominated. Referring to Narciso Alonso Cortés's prologue, Singer's 1951 article lists the names of several other possible sources of inspiration for Cervantes, among them a certain story about a madman from Valladolid that is found among the *Cuentos que notó Don Juan de Arguijo*. Singer also places in nomination the collected apothegms of Plutarch and Erasmus, both of which the critic declares were available in Spanish translations during Cervantes's lifetime; still other possible literary models he cites include the *Galateo español* of Lucas Gracián (1593) and Gaspar Lucas Hidalgo's 1605 publication, *Diálogos de apacible entretenimiento*.[98]

In addition to the names subsequently repeated by Casalduero, Singer, Riley, and others, Narciso Alonso Cortés's excellent 1916 prologue to his edition of *LV* offers for consideration several more possible literary sources of inspiration for the witty utterances Cervantes places into the mouth of Vidriera. Among this scholar's nominees are a trio of celebrated wits who are referred to as Garci Sánchez de Badajoz, el doctor Villalobos, and el duque de Nájera; D. Luisa de Zapata, whose *Miscelánea* contained a large collection of anecdotes and apothegms; Juan de Timoneda's anthology, *Sobremesa y alivio de caminantes*, which was taken largely from Italian sources; Luis de Pinedo's curious volume with a ponderous Latin title, *Liber facetiarum et similitudinem Ludovici di Pinedo et amicorum*, but whose text is written entirely in Castilian; the glosses to the *Sermón de Aljubarrota*, attributed without foundation to Diego Hurtado de Mendoza; the *Cuentos de Garibay* and Melchor de Santa Cruz's *Floresta Española*; and the "chocarrerías" and "bufonadas" of Pedro Gonela, jester of Duke Borso of Ferrara, remarks that were copied and published by Ludovico Domenichi. Cortés presents this long list of titles and authors, not to establish any one of them as Cervantes's personal model, but simply to demonstrate that such collections of popular wit and wisdom were a very popular literary genre in Spain during the early 1600s.[99]

In 1958 Agustín G. de Amezúa y Mayo uncovered a number of additional titles of aphoristic works published in Cervantes's time, publications from which the great novelist might have taken inspiration for *LV*. Among these are *Flor de sentencias de sabios glosadas en verso castellano por Francisco de Guzmán* (Antwerp, 1557), later revised and published under the title *Decreto de sabios* (Alcalá, 1553); *Sentencias y dichos de diversos sabios y antiguos auctores, así griegos como latinos, recogidos por M. Nicolás Liburnio y traducidas por Alonso de Ulloa* (Venice, 1553); and the anonymous tome, *Primera parte de las sentencias que para edificación de buenos [sic] costumbres están por diversos autores escritas* (Coimbra, 1555).[100]

Further suggestions as to who might have served as Cervantes's inspiration for *LV* were offered by E. C. Riley in 1976. He cites a possible classical model in the aphoristic, anecdotal biography of the celebrated Cynic Diogenes of Sinope that was included in Diogenes Laërtius's *Lives of the Philosophers*. This ancient work had been preserved in manuscript form during the Middle Ages and was available in the sixteenth century in Latin and Greek and vernacular translations. A fifteenth-century Castilian translation of Diogenes Laërtius's opus served as a basis for Hernando Díaz's popular *Vida y excelentes dichos delos mas sabios filosofos que uvo en este mundo*, which enjoyed six different printings between 1520 and 1545. An even more popular work of that era was also derived, at least in part, from Diogenes Laërtius: Pedro Mexía's *Silva de varia lección*, in which chapter 27 of part 1 treats of the "extraña condición y vida" [strange personality and life] of the famous Cynic philosopher, Diogenes of Sinope.[101]

The list of potential satirical and apothegmatic models for *LV* grows with the 1982 publication of Forcione's watershed study of the *Novelas ejemplares*. In addition to citing the aforementioned works of Diogenes Laërtius and Erasmus, Forcione also nominates Lucian's colloquies, medieval forms of satire like the dance of death and the ship of fools, Argensola's *Demócrito,* and Mondragón's *Censura de la locura humana y alabanzas de las excelencias de ella* (1598) as works Cervantes might have had in mind when composing *LV*. Daniel L. Heiple also cites Mondragón's work as a likely Cervantine model.[102]

Without wishing to denigrate the opinions of any of the aforementioned scholars, I must point out that none of them has been able to trace any of Vidriera's utterances back to any of these alleged sources. Similarities in tone and manner of expression abound, but no formal link to any written source has ever been established. For some reason these critics have overlooked a very strong candidate whose existence and reputation as a noted humorist and commentator of the time has been documented, a man who may indeed have served as the model for Cervantes's Vidriera: the Sevillian Juan Farfán.

3 / PORRAS'S MANUSCRIPT

In *Cervantes: Pioneer and Plagiarist* I listed the table of contents of the Porras collection, including several items that could easily have served as the source for all, many, or most of Vidriera's mordant remarks and witticisms. The entries in question are the following:

- Item #2: a biographical sketch on the life of a celebrated Sevillian wit of the times, an Augustinian friar named Juan Farfán;
- Item #3: a collection of stories, witty comments and brilliant remarks ("cuentos, agudezas y genialidades") authored by the same Farfán;
- Item #5: still another compilation of jokes, humorous observations, and witty remarks ("Floresta de chistes, prontitudes y ocurrencias") attributed to a number of Sevillians.[103]

Given the irrefutable links already established between two of Cervantes's other *novelas* and the Porras manuscript, would it be far-fetched to suggest that a similar connection might be made in the case of *LV* as well? I think not. Is Farfán any less likely a source of the Glass Man's clever remarks than Rufo or Mondragón? Hardly, although it would certainly be useful to have some prima facie evidence of his celebrated wit upon which to make a comparison. Scholars continue to unearth long-lost literary treasures; it is my hope, therefore, that we shall one day recover a sample of Farfán's satirical genius and perhaps put an end to all the speculation.

In any case, *LV* clearly has all the earmarks of a Cervantine experiment, a fusion of literary forms that had never been attempted before. The evolution of such a hybrid work in Cervantes's time is entirely plausible in view of what Green, Forcione, and others have documented about the literary traditions of seventeenth-century Europe. Given the popularity of *emblemas* and other published anthologies of witty comments at the end of the sixteenth and beginning of the seventeenth century, it seems quite reasonable to suggest that the recorded utterances and jottings of Juan Farfán may have served as source material for most or all of the aphorisms and puns found in *LV*.[104]

Time and taste have ultimately declared Cervantes's experiment with the *emblema* a failure. As we know, the writer himself never utilized this format again, there are no known imitations by other authors, and modern readers tend to treat this story as a curious anomaly rather than as an example of the Spanish writer's finest work. Even so, *LV* has captured the imagination of Cervantine scholars over the years and should continue to do so in the future as we contemplate the possibility that Francisco Porras de la Cámara's curious *Compilación*, tragically lost since 1823, may in fact have been the source document for as many as three of the tales Cervantes published as his own in the *Novelas ejemplares*.

Conclusion

The celebrated triad of Cervantine *novelas* that treat the big-city escapades of two young *pícaros* named Pedro del Rincón and Diego Cortado, the marital misadventures of the jealous old *indiano* Felipe Carrizales, and the bizarre career of the would-be intellectual Tomás Rueda have much more to bind them together than the mere fact that they all seem to derive from material Cervantes found in a curious miscellany known to have circulated among Sevillian literary buffs during the early 1600s. As I mentioned in the opening section of this chapter, the three stories in question also share the same fundamental narrative structure: a strict chronological ordering of events that makes no use whatsoever of the analeptic flashback technique that Cervantes employs so artfully in the rest of his collection.

Despite what appears to be a most unimaginative narrative plan, these three units are clearly highly experimental in nature; in each of these stories the audacious Cervantes strives to combine into a single artistic whole what most literary theorists of his time would have considered to be two distinct and seemingly incompatible forms of literary discourse. In *R/C* he attempts to fuse the picaresque novel with the theatrical *entremés*; in *ZE* Cervantes employs what most would consider to be diametrically opposite narrative techniques, the a priori and the a posteriori methods of presentation; and in *LV* we find a curious combination of the classical biography and the baroque *emblema*.

A third common element that binds *R/C*, *ZE*, and *LV* is the strong and unmistakable ironic tone that characterizes these works. In the first of these stories young Rincón and Cortado seek complete freedom from everyday social restrictions in the Sevillian underworld, only to find in the end that life among the denizens of Monipodio's realm is every bit as structured and confining as it is in "normal" Spanish society. In the second story, the hubris of Carrizales's futile and ill-advised attempt to insure his precious honor by locking his teenage bride away from the world is justly punished with a double dose of irony: not only does the jealous old man live to see his worst nightmare realized (he discovers Leonora asleep—innocently, as it turns out—in the arms of another man), but he is then required to forgive an act of adultery that has not actually taken place. And finally we have the story of Tomás Rodaja, a young man who spends the greater part of his life in scholarly pursuits, consciously avoiding any and all forms of violence and bloodshed. In the end he realizes that in his case the fates have determined that the only avenue to renown will be a military calling and a heroic death on the battlefields of Flanders.

In view of the significant literary characteristics they share (e.g., the experimental nature of their design, their curious bipartite structure, and their profoundly ironic tone), I firmly believe that *R/C*, *ZE,* and *LV* ought to be studied as three complementary units, each derived in some way from a common literary source: the Porras Manuscript.

4

Las dos doncellas and *La señora Cornelia:* Dramatic Echoes of *Don Quixote,* Part One

Among the first eight stories in Cervantes's collection of *Novelas ejemplares* (1613), the preponderant theme is that of romantic trial and redemption. For a demonstration of this fact we need look no further than the first two entries in the anthology, *La gitanilla* and *El amante liberal*, which, in essence, tell the same story. The only factors that can be said to distinguish these otherwise twin tales from one another are the radically different settings (Gypsy versus Moorish) in which their respective events take place and the clearly distinct sequencing patterns Cervantes employs in narrating them. As I have demonstrated in previous chapters of this book, *La gitanilla* is narrated in a straightforward, almost wholly chronological fashion, advancing steadily from opening to closing scene; there are only two brief breaks in the action when a pair of clarifying flashbacks are suddenly injected at strategic moments toward the close of the action. *El amante liberal*, on the other hand, is constructed in the classic Greek romance mould; the narration begins in medias res and advances fitfully thereafter, alternating sections of the main action with a series of expository flashbacks offered by various primary and secondary characters.

In each story we are presented with the case of a callow young nobleman whose immature behavior and shallow attempts at courtship are quickly spurned by the object of his desire; he subsequently descends—in one case voluntarily, in the other by force—into a hostile environment, an earthly netherworld where he experiences a kind of captivity and overcomes perils that confer upon him the maturity he had previously lacked and prepare him, at long last, to enter adulthood and the married state.

The fourth and sixth entries, *La española inglesa* and *La fuerza de la sangre*, return again to the theme of redemptive romantic trials: each tale features an attractive pair of marriageable adolescents who are forced to overcome seemingly insurmountable obstacles—including kidnapping, poisoning, attempted murder, and even rape—before finally being brought together in matrimony. The narrative intrigue is heightened in these stories by the fact that the female partners participate more fully in the travails and physical dangers than was the case in the opening pair of tales. The story of *La ilustre fregona*, which is found in the eighth position, completes the cycle by effectively reprising the thematic material of *La gitanilla*, but now in a comic motif, which is to say, in a nonhostile environment.

To alleviate the tedium and mitigate this thematic redundancy, Cervantes breaks the pattern in the third, fifth, and seventh positions by inserting the stories of *Rinconete y Cortadillo*, *El licenciado Vidriera* and *El celoso extremeño*, narratives that depart notably from the trial-and-redemption motif. The first of these tales is a comic picaresque narrative whose protagonists face no romantic involvement whatsoever. The second is a uniquely structured fictional biography of a celebrated pacifist/intellectual whose life, prior to an ironically heroic death as a soldier in Flanders, was almost completely devoid of romance. (His only romantic experience almost costs him his life, so he carefully avoids women thereafter.) The final story deals exclusively with protagonist Felipo de Carrizales's insane jealousy, an aberration that causes him to take increasingly ridiculous and extreme measures to guard against imagined threats to his honor. His feelings of love toward his young bride, if indeed he ever had any, are never delineated. In one sense, Carrizales can be said to undergo a severe test here, but there is no consequent redemption, merely a belated epiphany that comes much too late to benefit him in this life.[1]

As we reach the ninth and tenth entries in Cervantes's anthology, *Las dos doncellas* and *La señora Cornelia*, we note a distinct move away from the trial-and-redemption motif that has dominated the first two-thirds of the collection. These two tales resurrect the omnipresent themes of jealousy and passion (i.e., as vices easily aroused by great physical beauty), but the popular issue of family honor replaces the trial motif as the chief motivating force. Furthermore, here Cervantes introduces a brand-new theme: the plight of the virgin who has been seduced and abandoned by an unscrupulous suitor who has reneged on a promise of marriage in return for her sexual favors. But while this topic may be something of a novelty in the *Novelas*, those familiar with *Don Quixote* will recognize it as the central issue of Dorotea's pursuit of the inconstant Fernando and the troubled courtship of Cardenio and Luscinda in Part One of Cervantes's masterpiece.

The relationship between *Las dos doncellas* and *La señora Cornelia* is almost identical to the one we observed earlier between *La gitanilla* and *El amante liberal*. They are two variations on the same theme, two different approaches to the same basic story idea. *Las dos doncellas* takes the direct approach and features a much more tightly controlled plot, with little or no extraneous complication to distract the reader as the tale moves toward a swift resolution of the principal problem: restoring the lost honor of Teodosia and Leocadia, both of whom have been deceived by Marco Antonio.

For readers who prefer their intrigues in the baroque tradition, i.e., with a great deal of extraneous complication to tantalize the reader while the eventual resolution of the lady's problem is worked out, there is *La señora Cornelia*. Even though the characters in *Cornelia* have only half as many dilemmas to resolve, they require much more time and effort to accomplish the task than do the characters in the previous tale.

These two stories, which follow the popular Italianate models of Cervantes's time, have received far less critical attention over the years than their literary brethren. This disregard may stem from their peculiar narrative structure, or perhaps be attributable to their unconventional (i.e., relatively bloodless) treatment of the popular honor theme. When held up against the stark realism of *El coloquio de los perros*, the hilarious dialogues of *Rinconete y Cortadillo*, the action-packed intrigues of *El amante liberal* or *La española inglesa*, and the religious symbolism of *La fuerza de la sangre*, these two relatively lightweight comic tales understandably come off as relatively innocuous and unimportant.

The first thing we note about these stories is that they are more theatrical than novelistic in nature. Each account opens with a highly dramatic situation and strives to keep the reader in suspense as long as possible. In each case the action is fast-paced and the narrator is very punctilious about providing all the information necessary for the reader to understand and follow the various twists in the plot. Of the two, *Cornelia* clearly has the more complex design; *Doncellas* draws more deeply for inspiration from some of Cervantes's earlier works. What is undeniable is that each of these stories has its own special appeal, and there is much to be said about the careful manner in which they are constructed.

LAS DOS DONCELLAS

From the title itself we can surmise that *Doncellas* is going to involve a measure of structural parallelism as well as some kind of doubling effect in the narration. Predictably enough, over the years critical response to these factors has included both approbation and censure. In the commentary of their 1925 edition of the *Novelas ejemplares*, Schevill and Bonilla find the doubling of heroines to be totally unnecessary, noting that everything appears to be duplicated in the story.[2] On the other hand, Casalduero

(1962) praises the overall balance and simplicity of structure of the story and is somewhat more sanguine about the duplications, which he says render the thematic variations necessary to provide movement to the plot.[3]

The judgment of Amezúa y Mayo (1958) lies somewhere between the two. While noting that *Doncellas* appears to be nothing more than a *novella de relleno* used to round out the collection of *novelas* to an even dozen, Amezúa, following Casalduero's lead, also notes certain pleasant similarities that *Doncellas* shares with other works of Cervantes, ranging from the early *Galatea* to the stories of Cardenio and Dorotea in the 1605 *Quixote*. On the down side, Amezúa considers the story of Teodosia and Leocadia to be an uncomfortable mix of a fundamentally inverisimilar romantic point of view with a series of extremely realistic physical descriptions of places and events like roadside inns and a fierce skirmish that takes place in Barcelona's harbor.[4]

With regard to the subject of verisimilitude, Rachel Frank (1945) has studied the use of deceitful disguises by both of Cervantes's damsels and concludes that the device of a woman assuming a masculine disguise is employed to preserve and accentuate the virtue of Teodosia and Leocadia. In other words, Frank believes that Cervantes used this common dramatic ploy to achieve verisimilitude, not to violate it.[5]

Perhaps the most eloquent and effective defense of Cervantes's artistic purpose in presenting a pair of almost identical heroines in *Doncellas* is the 1963 study by Jennifer Thompson.[6] Prof. Thompson's thesis is that Cervantes has forged this curiously parallel structure so as to confuse and even deceive the casual reader by giving him or her a set of hollow expectations and a false trail to follow (147). While it is true that Cervantes creates a pair of attractive protagonists whose respective predicaments are remarkably similar—which is the point that seems to have captured the attention of Schevill and Bonilla, Casalduero, and Amezúa to the exclusion of all other matters—the key to understanding *Doncellas* is found in the subtle distinctions, both legal and moral, that separate the otherwise similar claims of Teodosia and Leocadia. These differences represent the real issues at stake and constitute the exemplary core of Cervantes's *novela*. We must credit Thompson with being the first to make this important observation.

According to Thompson, Cervantes's artistic purpose in writing *Doncellas* was to present for his reader's serious consideration a series of *cuestiones de amor:* (1) which of the two young ladies is the more unhappy? (2) which of them has the greater legal and/or moral claim to be the wife of the skittish Marco Antonio? and (3) which woman has the greater cause for jealousy (145–47)? The importance of Thompson's study has not diminished over the years, although recent criticism has tended to focus on other, more specialized aspects of this *novela*.

Julio Rodríguez-Luis (1980) signals the highly theatrical nature of certain scenes of *Doncellas* vis-à-vis the long, descriptive passages that otherwise tend to dominate the narrative; he makes particular mention of the opening scene and the epilogue, about the latter of which I shall have more to say at a later point.[7] Geoffrey Stagg's 1984 article deals with the possible influence of *Doncellas* on certain parts of the 1615 *Quixote*. It is Stagg's contention that, subsequent to the appearance in 1614 of Avellaneda's spurious Second Part of the Cervantine masterpiece, Cervantes felt obliged, at or about chapter 59, to transfer the bulk of the action of his own Second Part from Aragon to Catalonia. This sudden change of plan presented Cervantes with a series of narrative problems and required him to revert to the romantic mode for solutions. Consequently, the episodes of Claudia Jerónima (chap. 60) and Ana Félix (chap. 63), both of whom appear in the novel attired in distinctively male garb, would seem to have been inspired, at least in part, by the example of Teodosia and Leocadia in Cervantes's *novela*.[8]

In 1989 Caroline Schmauser offered a totally new approach to reading the *Novelas ejemplares* with an examination of the structural complexity of *Doncellas* and the author's organization of space within the narrative.[9] Schmauser discusses Cervantes's use of enclosed and open spaces in that story as symbolic representations of restricted/regulated social systems and the dynamism of life, respectively (177). Schmauser makes special note of the name of the town in which Leocadia recounts her story: Igualada, a small population center outside Barcelona that is completely unremarkable except for the fact that its name perfectly describes the equal footing on which the two young women now find themselves in their pursuit of Marco Antonio (185). The critic also observes that the story unfolds in alternating indoor and outdoor scenes (village, inn, room, copse, inn, balcony, room), and that the spatial divisions become increasingly complex once the action moves to Barcelona (183). In Schmauser's view, the unusual structure of *Doncellas* is intended to demonstrate the systolic and diastolic movements of life: the alternation of dynamic, risk-taking episodes with static phases designed for reflection and consolidation (200).

With regard to the formal design of *Doncellas*, we should note that the story can be divided into three distinct narrative sections or acts, each one concerned with events taking place in a different locale (schema 26).

One of the most notable characteristics of this story is that on various occasions the characters reflect and echo—almost verbatim, as we shall presently note—the sentiments and utterances of the two frustrated lovers Don Quixote meets in the Sierra Morena, Cardenio and Dorotea. This is no accident; there are also many other incidents in this story, e.g., the hubbub in the harbor that welcomes the travelers to Barcelona, the final joust between

4 / *Las dos doncellas* and *La señora Cornelia* 211

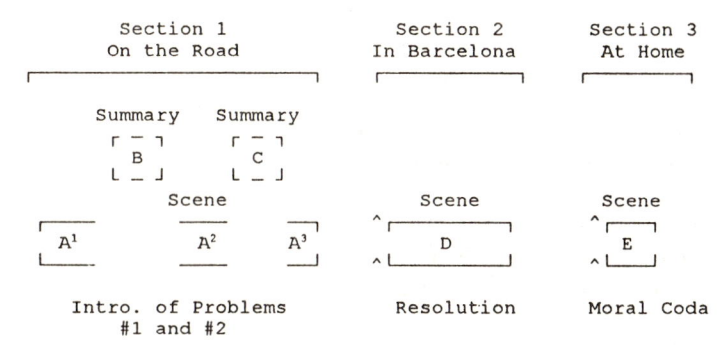

```
        Section 1                Section 2              Section 3
        On the Road              In Barcelona           At Home
    ┌──────────────────┐       ┌───────────┐          ┌───────┐

         Summary   Summary
          ┌ ─ ┐     ┌ ─ ┐
            B         C
          └ ─ ┘     └ ─ ┘
             Scene              Scene                  Scene
    ┌──────────────────┐     ┌───────────┐          ┌───────┐
     A¹      A²     A³             D                    E
    └──────────────────┘     └───────────┘          └───────┘

     Intro. of Problems        Resolution            Moral Coda
        #1 and #2
```

Schema 26. *Las dos doncellas*

the fathers of Rafael and Marco Antonio, etc., that bring to mind several memorable episodes from the *Quixote*—and even from the *Galatea*.[10]

Section 1: On the road

The opening act of this story deals with the journey of Teodosia, Rafael (her brother), and Leocadia from a point just outside Seville to the port of Barcelona, where they hope to intercept the fleeing Marco Antonio. The narration of events that take place on the road (A¹, A², A³) is interrupted at two points for the flashback accounts of first Teodosia (B) and then Leocadia (C) describing each girl's whirlwind romance with the elusive Marco Antonio. This gentleman has tendered a promise of marriage to each of the damsels—on separate occasions, naturally, and without a hint to either of the ladies of his double-dealing nature.

The story opens dramatically with the arrival of a mysterious *caminante* at a roadside inn, where "he" (it turns out to be Teodosia dressed as a man) pays for two beds to guarantee solitude during the night. Circumstances make it necessary nonetheless for her to share the room that night with a second traveler, her brother Rafael, whose true identity she will learn only at daybreak. Rafael's suspicions and curiosity are predictably aroused during the night when he notices his unidentified companion sighing repeatedly and bemoaning her cruel fate with words like:

> ¡Oh fementido Marco Antonio! ¿Cómo es posible que en las dulces palabras que me decías viniese mezclada la hiel de tus descortesías y desdenes? ¿Adónde estás, ingrato; adónde te fuiste, desconocido? Respóndeme, que te hablo; espérame, que te sigo; susténtame, que te descaezco; págame lo que me debes; socórreme, pues por tantas vías te tengo obligado. (*DD* 2:205)[11]

[Oh perfidious Marco Antonio! How can it be that mingled with the soft words you spoke to me, was the bitterness of your ill-treatment and disdain? Where are you, ingrate? Where did you flee to, stranger? Answer me, for I am speaking to you; wait for me, for I am following you; support me, for I am ready to fall; pay me what you owe; help me, since you are obliged to me in so many ways.] (3:147)

This is more than merely a little reminiscent of the words employed by Cardenio in a similar situation (*DQ* 1, chap. 23) to attract the attention and sympathy of his listener, Don Quixote:

¡Ah, fementido Fernando! ¡Aquí, aquí me pagarás la sinrazón que me heciste: estas manos te sacarán el corazón, donde albergan y tienen manida todas las maldades juntas, principalmente la fraude y el engaño! (*DQ* 1:223)[12]

[Ah, perfidious Fernando! Now, now you shall pay for the wrong you have done me! These hands will tear out your heart, abode and nesting place of every sort of evil, but especially of fraud and deceit!]

The parallel between Teodosia's case and Cardenio's is further reinforced by the unusual and highly dramatic precondition she imposes upon the listener before beginning her story:

habéisme de prometer . . . que por cosas que de mi oyáis en lo que os dijere no os habéis de mover de vuestro lecho ni venir al mío, ni preguntarme más de aquello que yo quisiere deciros; porque si al contrario de este hiciéredes, en el punto que os sienta mover, con una espada que a la cabecera tengo me pasaré el pecho. (*DD* 2:206)

[you must promise me . . . that as a result of what you hear about me in the story I tell you, you must not move from your bed nor come near mine, nor ask me anything other than what I decide to tell you. If you fail to do what I have asked, the moment I sense you move, I shall run myself through with a sword which I have here at the head of the bed.] (3:149)

Her threat, although of a much more dramatic nature, is not unlike the sort of precondition that Cardenio demanded prior to telling his tale:

habéisme de prometer de que con ninguna pregunta, ni otra cosa, no interromperéis el hilo de mi triste historia; porque en el punto que lo hagáis, en ése se quedará lo que fuere contando. (*DQ* 1:226)

[you must promise me that you will not interrupt with any question, or in any other manner, the thread of my mournful tale, for the moment you do so it will come to an end.]

Teodosia's story contains echoes of still other characters and episodes from the *Quixote*. For example, when she announces that her romantic involvement with Marco Antonio began with an exchange of glances through the open windows of their neighboring houses it reminds us of Doña Clara's nearly identical account of the beginnings of her romance with young Luis (*DQ* 1, chap. 43). And secondly, Teodosia's foolish error in judgment whereby she surrendered her virginity to Marco Antonio in return for his promise of marriage is clearly a duplication of Dorotea's mistake with the unfaithful Fernando. This is, however, virtually the only trait she shares with the daring damsel of the *Quixote*; it will be left to her rival, Leocadia, to assume most of that memorable character's attractive assertiveness. Teodosia seems to be designed to reprise instead the role of the timid Cardenio in this romantic intrigue, just as Marco Antonio will revive memories of the double-dealing Fernando.

The account of how Teodosia has been seduced and abandoned by her fickle suitor introduces the first of the two principal problems with which this story is concerned: how to compel the would-be bridegroom to fulfill his promise of matrimony. In conformity with the conventions of the Spanish Golden Age *comedia*, Teodosia's declared goal is either to achieve the sacramental remedy of marriage or to take bloody revenge.

Once Rafael and Teodosia have discovered each other's true identity in the morning light, the fraternal pair (with Teodosia still dressed as a man and calling herself Teodoro) set out for Barcelona, where they believe Marco Antonio's ship will dock before sailing for Italy. In a wooded area just outside that city they come upon a group of unlucky travelers who have just been robbed by a band of Catalan *bandoleros;* among these is a young girl named Leocadia who is, as per the popular literary convention, disguised as a man. Leocadia initially attempts to pass herself off with a series of clever fabrications as the son of a well-known gentleman and neighbor of Teodosia and Rafael (not unlike Dorotea's imaginative immersion in the role of Princess Micomicona), but Rafael and "Teodoro" quickly see through her facade.

The story enters a pivotal stage when Leocadia finally agrees to tell the real reason for her disguise, for what she narrates has as much importance for her listeners as it does for her. In the course of her narration (C), Leocadia informs her audience that she has been given a promise of matrimony—in a written document, she claims—by a certain Marco Antonio Adorno, the same unprincipled gigolo who stole Teodosia's maidenhood under a similar false pretext. As both the reader and Teodosia learn simultaneously, Leocadia is also in pursuit of the effusive but elusive Marco Antonio for the same purpose of obliging him to fulfill his ill-given promise of matrimony.

Leocadia's story is pivotal for several reasons. First of all, it introduces the second of the major problems to be solved. Although at first glance it may seem that Leocadia's dilemma is identical to Teodosia's, such is not the case. Teodosia's honor has been destroyed through the loss of her virginity; Leocadia's has not, which makes her predicament significantly less grave and morally compelling. Secondly, Leocadia's story uncovers the presence of a moral dilemma: a scenario in which two legitimate grievances are irreversibly locked on a collision course, from which only one of the aggrieved women will ultimately be able to emerge with a measure of satisfaction from Marco Antonio; the other will be left with absolutely nothing.

With regard to the romantic and legal showdown toward which the two desperate damsels are headed, Jennifer Thompson signals (145–46) a large number of important distinctions that separate Teodosia and Leocadia and their respective causes, differences that the critical reader must bear in mind:

1. Leocadia, like Dorotea before her in the *Quixote*, is clearly the bolder, more aggressive plaintiff; Teodosia, in comparison with her more intrepid counterpart, is relatively passive, almost submissive. While Marco Antonio plays the customary male pursuer in his courtship of the shy Teodosia, we learn that it was Leocadia who exercised the initiative in courting Marco Antonio. Leocadia also insisted that her would-be lover sign a formal marital agreement *(cédula)* beforehand. The naive Teodosia unwisely surrendered to her fiancé's ardor without taking any advance legal precautions.

2. When she sets out in pursuit of her faithless lover, Teodosia is totally unaware of the existence of a rival for Marco Antonio's affections. Leocadia, on the other hand, suspects from the start that Marco Antonio has run off with a woman named Teodosia, upon whom she has sworn to take vengeance. Following the exchange of their life histories, Cervantes presents us with a dramatic and highly suspenseful situation in which both the would-be assailant and her intended victim are suddenly thrown together in a common cause. Fortunately, only the passive Teodosia fully understands the situation; she now realizes that her traveling companion is both a rival for Marco Antonio's affections and a serious threat to her life. The vengeful Leocadia, mercifully, continues to remain in the dark as to the true identity of her recent acquaintance. The reader is now presented with a very interesting moral dilemma. At the conclusion of the two women's histories, we realize that Leocadia's basic motive is far less praiseworthy than is her rival's. While the submissive Teodosia's declared intention is simply to oblige her fickle fiancé to make good on his promise of marriage, Leocadia's main goal is to eliminate her rival; the consummation of her marriage with Marco Antonio remains a purely secondary consideration.

3. While Teodosia stakes her claim to Marco Antonio solely on the basis of a ring she has in her possession bearing the inscription "Marco Antonio is the husband of Teodosia," Leocadia is able to present a signed legal document to support her claim: the *cédula* in which Marco Antonio offered marriage in exchange for carnal knowledge of her. From a purely legal standpoint, Leocadia would initially seem to have the more valid claim, but the playing field is soon leveled when Leocadia loses her *cédula* during their journey to Barcelona.

4. Teodosia was the first to surrender to Marco Antonio's charming ways. Following an exchange of vows with her suitor, Teodosia willingly sacrificed her virginity to him. Marco Antonio's affair with Leocadia had a totally different outcome: despite Leocadia's aggressive pursuit of Marco Antonio and the written promise of marriage that she has extracted from him, they have not physically consummated their relationship. In the eyes of the Catholic Church, therefore, the shy, passive Teodosia has the stronger case.

Symbolically, *Doncellas* might be what Thomas Pabon in 1977 called Cervantes's attempt "to illustrate on a doctrinal level the teachings of the Council of Trent on the subject of Christian marriage."[13] It certainly has all the earmarks of a casuistic exploration of the conflict between the secular and religious definitions of marriage in Cervantes's time.

From a purely literary standpoint, however, the most fascinating aspect of Leocadia's woeful tale is the reaction it elicits from Teodosia when she hears mentioned the name of Marco Antonio; her behavior is very reminiscent of Cardenio's in chapter 28 of the 1605 *Quixote* when Dorotea pronounces the name of his rival, Fernando.

> No hubo bien nombrado a don Fernando la que el cuento contaba, cuando a Cardenio se le mudó la color del rostro, y comenzó a trasudar, con tan grande alteración, que el cura y el barbero, que miraron en ello, temieron que le venía aquel accidente de locura que habían oído decir que de cuando en cuando le venía. Mas Cardenio no hizo otra cosa que trasudar y estarse quedo, mirando de hito en hito a la labradora, imaginando quién era ella; la cual, sin advertir en los movimientos de Cardenio, prosiguió su historia, diciendo. (*DQ* 1:280)

> [The moment he heard Fernando's name mentioned, Cardenio turned pale and began to perspire profusely, displaying such signs of deep emotion as to lead the priest and the barber, who were watching him, to fear he was about to have one of those fits that they had been told would come over him from time to time. But he did nothing but sweat and sit there quietly, staring hard at the peasant girl, for by now he suspected who she

was. And she, without paying any attention to him, continued with her story.]

The words used to describe Teodosia's reaction in a similar situation may be different, but the emotions portrayed are the same. In my view, the passage from *Las dos doncellas* represents a more sophisticated and highly developed stage in Cervantes's narrative technique insofar as it is even more graphic than the earlier passage in its depiction of Teodosia/Teodoro's anxiety and near loss of self control. Cervantes describes the smoldering emotional turmoil that lies just beneath the deceptively calm exterior of the listener in the following terms:

> Hasta este punto había estado callando Teodoro, teniendo pendiente el alma de las palabras de Leocadia, que con cada una dellas le traspasaba el alma, especialmente cuando oyó el nombre de Marco Antonio y vio la peregrina hermosura de Leocadia, y consideró la grandeza de su valor con la de su rara discreción, que bien lo mostraba en el modo de contar su historia. Mas cuando llegó a decir: "Llegó la noche por mí deseada," estuvo por perder la paciencia y, sin poder hacer otra cosa, le salteó la razón, diciendo:
> —Y bien, así como llegó esa felicísima noche, ¿qué hizo? ¿Entró por dicha? ¿Gozástesle? ¿Confirmó de nuevo la cédula? ¿Quedó contento en haber alcanzado de vos lo que decís que era suyo? ¿Súpolo vuestro padre o en qué pararon tan honestos y sabios principios? (*DD* 2:218)

> [Up to this point Teodoro had not spoken, his spirit hanging on Leocadia's words, for with each one of them she pierced his soul, especially when he heard the name of Marco Antonio and saw the extraordinary beauty of Leocadia, and considered her great worth, and her unusual discretion, which was clearly shown in her manner of recounting her story. But when she came to say, "the night I had longed for arrived," his patience came to an end, and without being able to help it, he lost his self-control and said:
> "I see, and so when this happiest of nights arrived, what did he do? Did he by any chance arrive? Did you enjoy him? Did he confirm the document's validity once again? Was he happy to have got from you what you say was his? Did your father find out, or how did such wise and chaste beginnings come to an end?"] (3:165)

Instead of merely sitting and suffering in silence as Cardenio had done, the marvelously human Teodosia allows her morbid curiosity to overpower the cool self-restraint that has been in evidence up to this point. Her eager, rapid-fire questions in pursuit of whether Leocadia did or did not succumb fully to Marco Antonio's persuasive charm is a masterpiece of characterization. And when she learns that no consummation of the alleged marriage has yet taken place, the sensation of great relief that she feels—not to mention certain pangs of jealousy at the same time—is signaled in this memorable passage:

> Respiró con estas razones Teodosia, y detuvo los espíritus, que poco a poco la iban dejando, estimulados y apretados de la rabiosa pestilencia de los celos, que a más andar se le iban entrando por los huesos y médulas, para tomar entera posesión de su paciencia; mas no la dejó tan libre que no volviese a escuchar con sobresalto lo que Leocadia prosiguió diciendo. (*DD* 2:218)
>
> [At these words Teodosia breathed again, and she recovered her spirits, which were gradually draining from her, stirred up and troubled by the furious plague of jealousy, which, had it continued, would have begun to enter her bones to the very marrow, and take complete possession of her composure; still it did not leave her so untouched that she was able to listen calmly to what Leocadia went on to say.] (3:165)

At the close of section 1, just before the three principal characters enter the city of Barcelona, Cervantes summarizes for the reader the strange set of contradictory emotions that beset Rafael and Teodosia at that critical point. Leocadia's stunning beauty has ignited the flames of romantic desire in Rafael, while at the same time engendering in Teodosia only rabid jealousy. Rafael is no longer motivated so much by a desire to resolve the problem of his sister's stained honor as by a need to prevent Marco Antonio from consummating his marriage vow to the highly desirable Leocadia. Even the prospect of Marco Antonio's death—which, after all, would offer no real solution for Teodosia's dilemma—is not displeasing to Rafael, because such a result would keep alive his hope of winning Leocadia's heart. As the trio of travelers prepare to enter Barcelona, Teodosia wishes her rival for Marco Antonio were dead; at the same time Rafael is beset by conflicting feelings of loyalty toward his sister and the nascent signs of physical desire he has begun to feel toward their beautiful companion. The narrator summarizes their feelings in the following words:

> No se podrá contar buenamente los pensamientos que los dos hermanos llevaban, ni con cuán diferentes ánimos los dos iban mirando a Leocadia, deseándola Teodosia la muerte, y don Rafael la vida, entrambos celosos y apasionados. Teodosia buscando tachas que ponerla, por no desmayar en su esperanza; don Rafael hallándole perfecciones, que de punto en punto le obligaron a más amarla. (*DD* 2:222)
>
> [It will not be possible to describe adequately the thoughts which the brother and sister entertained, nor with what differing notions they would

look at Leocadia, Teodosia desiring her death and Don Rafael her life, both of them jealous and passionate. Teodosia looked for blemishes in her, so as not to despair of her hopes; Don Rafael found perfections, which increased his love for her little by little.] (3:171)

The simultaneous entertainment of both jealous and romantically passionate feelings extends as well to Leocadia, who has already declared, without knowing the true identity of her companion "Teodoro," her desire to kill her putative rival, Teodosia.

Section 2: In Barcelona

The events that take place in Barcelona (D) in the second part/act of the story serve to reinforce the author's original intention to contrast the timid, Cardenio-like nature of Teodosia with the assertive disposition of Leocadia, modeled after the agreeably aggressive Dorotea. When Marco Antonio is finally discovered, it is in the middle of a pitched battle in the harbor. He is immediately felled by a blow to the head and topples into the surf. Both Teodosia and Leocadia rush to his aid, but only the latter is able to maintain the strength to climb aboard the skiff that has come to carry the unconscious victim back to his ship; Teodosia is left behind on the shore, despairing. Even later, when Marco Antonio is brought ashore to recuperate at the home of Don Sancho de Cardona, Leocadia wastes no time in getting his attention and pressing her claim; she quickly steps forward to hold his hand and plead her case, very much to the dismay of the shy Teodosia, who can do no more than look on while her rival advances on her goal:

> Atentísima estaba a todo este coloquio Teodosia, y cada palabra que Leocadia decía era una aguda saeta que le atravesaba el corazón, y aun el alma de don Rafael, que asimismo la escuchaba. (*DD* 2:227)

> [Teodosia did not miss a word of all this conversation, and each one spoken by Leocadia was a sharp arrow which pierced her heart, and Don Rafael's soul even, for he too was listening to her.] (3:177)

Unfortunately for Leocadia, in Cervantes's romantic universe the race is not always to the swift nor the prize to the most aggressive. It is the retiring Teodosia whom Marco Antonio finally selects as his bride. From a purely moral standpoint, this is the only acceptable solution. Marco Antonio's oral promise to wed Teodosia antedates the written pact with her rival, and they have, after all, consummated the agreement; proper civil and divine restitution can be achieved only through the sacrament of matrimony. Leocadia, conversely, remains a virgin and is still technically able to contract an honorable and valid marriage. As I pointed out earlier, with the *cédula* in her possession, Leocadia has the stronger legal claim against Marco Antonio; without it, Teodosia's stronger moral case also becomes the more powerful legal argument as well.

A few words are in order here regarding the relationship between Teodosia and Leocadia. In her 1974 study of the *Novelas ejemplares*, Ruth El Saffar declared them to be essentially two halves of the same personality, as we note from the following excerpts:[14]

> Leocadia is Teodosia's dark shadow, exaggerating the dangers of her situation, the baseness of her motives, and the extent of her complicity in the destruction of her honor. . . . Leocadia is the image of Teodosia's self-doubts, having no real claim to a separate identity. (114)

> Leocadia has no independent meaning in the story, being representative of Teodosia's repressed active self. (116)

> Leocadia must be considered an unworthy image of Teodosia—unnatural both in her aggressiveness and in the weakness of her claims on Marco Antonio. . . . (116)

For El Saffar, Leocadia's importance in the story stems solely from her mediating role between Marco Antonio and Teodosia. This is a prime example of how a strictly psychoanalytical approach can sometimes blind a critic to other, more plausible explanations for what an author presents in his/her work. By fusing the similar but hardly identical personalities of Teodosia and Leocadia into a single psyche, El Saffar makes it virtually impossible to interpret the story of *Las dos doncellas* in any symbolic way, e.g., as an artistic representation of some of the legal and moral problems that are connected with the social institutions of courtship and marriage.

In a 1988 article Linda Britt took issue with El Saffar's rather narrow interpretation of the two *doncellas*.[15] Britt lays emphasis upon the well-rounded but very distinct personalities Cervantes bestows upon his two damsels, and she effectively argues for greater character autonomy in the cases of Teodosia and Leocadia than El Saffar was willing to allow. As Britt sees it, Cervantes considered Teodosia and Leocadia to be a single *subject,* but not a single character. Although their stories are inextricably linked, Leocadia and Teodosia at all times maintain completely separate identities (44–45). Clearly, Leocadia is less favorably drawn than Teodosia; she is somewhat mercenary, and perhaps even unworthy of Rafael. Britt echoes the earlier judgment of Thompson in noting that Leocadia's presence serves in part as a contrast to Teodosia, but also as a diversionary ruse to mislead the reader and to provide an element of suspense (45). Britt declares Teodosia—not Dorotea, as some might have supposed—to be Cervantes's ideal heroine (46).

As section 2 draws to a close, we are surprised to see the submissive Teodosia's honor problem neatly resolved, while the more assertive Leocadia is left without a husband. Leocadia's reputation appears destined to remain in a kind of limbo—for a few brief moments at least, i.e., until Teodosia's brother can rush out with his own proposal of marriage. As Britt has noted (46), Leocadia, because she is the less sympathetically drawn of the two protagonists, must settle for her second choice, Rafael.

Very much like the figure of Blanca in the *Galatea*, Rafael's character functions here almost invisibly on the periphery of the story until such time—at the end of section 2—as he is needed to provide a convenient and worthy marital partner for the luckless loser in the original romantic triangle. In the case of Rafael, however, Cervantes manages to present an independent character with his own psychological needs and desires, which was certainly not the case with Blanca.

Several critics have commented on the role of Rafael in *Doncellas*. Rodríguez-Luis asserts that even though the revelation of Rafael's true function in the narrative (i.e., to turn a romantic triangle into a quadrangle) is delayed until very late point in the story, from the beginning the narrator has prepared the reader for this final twist.[16] Like so many Cervantine *galanes* before him, Rafael's romantic ardor is kindled with his first glimpse of Leocadia's physical beauty when he and Teodosia discover her tied to a tree in the woods:

> Y no la [noche] pasó con más descanso don Rafael, su hermano, porque así como oyó quién era Leocadia, así se le abrasó el corazón en sus amores, como si de mucho antes para el mismo efeto la hubiera comunicado; que esta fuerza tiene la hermosura. . . . (*DD* 2:221)

> [And Don Rafael, her brother, spent it [the night] no less restively, because as soon as he heard who Leocadia was, his heart was inflamed with love for her, as if he had been expressing these amorous intentions to her for a long time; for beauty has this power. . . .] (3:169)

The view expressed by L. A. Murillo (1988) is slightly different: Rafael's ultimate triumph in winning the heart and hand in marriage of the beautiful and still-virginal Leocadia is his just reward for his exemplary behavior in the opening scene when, having learned that his sister had given herself to Marco Antonio outside of marriage, he refused to avenge his family's honor by killing her and opted instead to help her track down her faithless lover.[17] Ultimately, I am inclined to agree with Thompson that Cervantes's primary goal in penning *Doncellas* was to portray in concrete terms a complicated moral issue and then provide what he considered a viable Christian solution to one of the problems of courtship and marriage in seventeenth-century Spain.

Section 3: At home

With the twin *desposorios* that conclude section 2 of *Doncellas* all the important social and romantic issues appear to have been neatly resolved: Teodosia's quest for Marco Antonio's hand in marriage has ended on a high note, and the seemingly luckless Leocadia has found in the smitten Rafael a reasonable solution to her honor problem, albeit not the one she had originally sought. At this point, however, Cervantes has decided to append a rather lengthy epilogue (E) in which he brings the two couples back home to Andalusia (by way of a pilgrimage to Santiago de Compostela in Galicia), where he can conclude the action with a final episode designed specifically to underscore the moral message of the tale. The consciously religious implications of the final section are evident from the outset: Marco Antonio promises to make a pilgrimage to Santiago de Compostela if God will return him to good health. Upon his full recovery, he sets out to fulfill his vow in the company of his fiancée and the other happy couple. Their journey begins with a three-day visit to the celebrated Catalan shrine at Montserrat. Nothing is said about the particulars of their stay at either holy place; the reader is expected merely to note that they perform their Christian duty in the proper fashion. The core of the final section of narrative is concerned instead with the events the four friends witness upon their return home.

As they descend into the valley in which their neighboring villages lie, they notice below them a tableau that could easily have been lifted from the *Quixote* itself: three gentlemen on horseback are seen squaring off for what looks to be an old-fashioned joust; two of them actually begin to charge and pummel each other with heavy lances while the third looks on.[18] Rafael and Marco Antonio race down to restore peace, at which point they discover that the combatants are their respective fathers; the onlooker is Don Enrique, Leocadia's father, who is simply awaiting his turn to do battle. They learn that Marco Antonio's shameful and cowardly behavior with the two women has caused a great deal of ill-feeling between the respective families, and even between the residents of the two neighboring villages. Squadrons of peasants from the two towns soon enter, and they are armed to the teeth in anticipation of defending the cause of their respective hometown representative. Fortunately, cooler heads prevail; peace is soon restored and preparations are made to celebrate the weddings of the two couples at the home of Marco Antonio's father. The tale closes with the usual testimony as to the subsequent long and happy marriage of each couple, not to mention the strange effects that romantic passion can have on the behavior of young lovers:

> y si no se nombran [los dos lugares donde viven ahora] es por guardar el decoro a las dos doncellas, a quien quizá las lenguas maldicientes o neciamente escrupulosas les eran cargo de la ligereza de sus deseos y el súbito mudar de trajes; a los cuales ruego que no arrojen a vituperar semejantes libertades hasta que miren en sí si alguna vez han sido tocados destas que llaman flechas de Cupido, que en efeto es una fuerza, si así se puede llamar incontrastable, que hace el apetito a la razón. (*DD* 2:236–37)

> [And if we refrain from giving their names it is out of respect for the reputation of the two damsels. For malevolent and foolishly scrupulous tongues will perhaps accuse them of fickle desires and of sudden changes of dress. I beg them not to condemn such liberties too rapidly until they examine themselves to see if they have ever been pierced by those so-called arrows of Cupid, for this is indeed an irresistible force (if it can be described thus), which appetite exerts over reason.] (3:189)

With regard to any final message Cervantes may have wished to leave with his reader, let us consider the last sentence of the story, a statement in which the author makes it clear that young women can be both sexually aggressive and chaste at the same time:

> y los poetas de aquel tiempo tuvieron ocasión donde emplear sus plumas exagerando la hermosura y los sucesos de las dos tan atrevidas cuanto hermosas doncellas, sujeto principal deste extraño suceso. (*DD* 2:237)

> [And the poets of that time took the opportunity to exercise their pens extolling the beauty and the exploits of these two intrepid but virtuous damsels, who are the main subject of this extraordinary story.] (3:189)

The ultimate significance of Cervantes's epilogue is a matter of serious debate among critics. Most of them do not even refer to it as an epilogue, but rather simply as the final scene. In Casalduero's view, the journey home to Andalusia presents a radical change in the perspective of the narration. The formerly active quartet of protagonists suddenly become purely passive observers in the concluding scene. The narrator cleverly changes his presentation here so that the reader may have an understanding of human errors and thereby avert their tragic consequences.[19] Murillo prefers to interpret the final scene from a thematic standpoint: he considers the epilogue to be a final reinforcement of the general theme of the story, a demonstration of "how personal freedom and sentiment require the social sanction of family and tradition to attain permanence."[20] Schmauser would seem to agree with Murillo, but the reasons she gives have more to do with structure than with theme. She calls the journey home "a necessary complement without which the text would not be the dynamic and complex narrative of great structural unity that it is," adding that the final pilgrimage "concentrates on the metaphysical and spiritual factor; the final fight in the valley leads to their social integration."[21]

Rodríguez-Luis is one of the few critics to call the final section of *Doncellas* an epilogue.[22] In his view, it is both a confirmation of the essentially theatrical structure of the work and a "valoración del aspecto moral de la historia, en un tono especialmente amable y liberal" (1:86) [an assessment of the moral aspect of the story, in an especially agreeable and generous tone]. He views *Doncellas* as a dramatic representation consisting of three scenes or *cuadros:* (1) the chance encounter of Teodosia and Rafael at the inn; (2) the subsequent meeting of these two characters with Leocadia in the forest; and (3) the battle in the harbor at Barcelona where they all come upon Marco Antonio. Each of these scenes provides an important dialogue or series of dialogues that serve to move the action forward to the story's preordained conclusion (2:85–86). For this critic, each of the four protagonists has something for which he or she needs to make amends before the action is brought to a close. An epilogue is therefore provided

> para paliar la falta de recato de las doncellas, los engaños de Marco Antonio . . . y hasta el relativo deshonor de Rafael, todo ello narrado rápidamente en un párrafo. Mayor elaboración despliega la escena final, o el doble duelo entre los padres de Leocadia y de Teodosia con el de Marco Antonio, interrumpido por la llegada de las dos parejas. (2:85)

> [to mitigate the lack of modesty in the young girls, the deceitfulness of Marco Antonio . . . and even the relative dishonor of Rafael, all of it quickly summed up in a single paragraph. The final scene provides even greater elaboration, which is to say the double duel between the fathers of Leocadia and Teodosia and Marco Antonio's father, which is interrupted by the sudden arrival of the newlyweds.]

As Rodríguez-Luis would have it, the two couples' pilgrimage to Santiago de Compostela and the startling events they witness upon their return home to Andalusia are intended to provide some visible sign of repentance on their part for their previous moral misconduct. In my view, the potentially fatal duel between the fathers of Teodosia and Marco Antonio that caps the narration also offers a final moral lesson for the consideration of the four lovers. It obliges them to ponder the possible consequences of their actions, to consider the irreparable physical and emotional damage that their impulsive actions could have brought to their families.

Let us consider the epilogue from another angle. If, as Rodríguez-Luis has done, we look upon *Doncellas* principally as a dramatic presentation, it could be said that Cervantes offers us two endings instead of one. At the close of section 2 we are presented with the standard Cervantine—which is to say, sacramental—solution to the respective honor problems of his characters: marriage. The story might easily have ended at this point. I suggest that the seemingly superfluous duel between the fathers of Teodosia and Marco Antonio that we witness in the epilogue represents a parodic extension of the action to simulate one of the *capa y espada* plays popularized by Lope de Vega. Joseph V. Ricapito has provided the proper interpretation of the unusual epilogue to *Doncellas:*

> The coincidence of the two fathers doing their part to avenge the respective dishonors of their daughters seems like a last ditch effort by Cervantes to revive in the minds of his readers that old conventional bloody resolution. In a true tragic case of an *honra* violation, he might have had one or both of the fathers killed, not knowing that all infractions of their daughter's honor have been amended (a solution somewhat closer to Italianate stories).... The last gesture is exhausted—and in a happy way—leaving the readers with a nonconventional resolution of lost *honra* lingering in their minds and the belief of "All's well that ends well" as the author's final say on the matter.[23]

In other words, Cervantes serves up a surprising yet bloodless solution, then follows it with a parody of the kind of violent confrontation scene the public had come to expect regarding questions of family honor in the Spanish *comedia*. I believe Cervantes would have expected the discerning reader to grasp and appreciate the significance of the subtle distinction he was making.

In summary, I would like to return to a point I made at the beginning of my discussion: *Doncellas* is in many ways a reelaboration of the story of Dorotea in *Don Quixote*, Part One. Instead of one damsel in distress, however, Cervantes provides us here with two heroines who struggle with similar but hardly identical *cuestiones de amor*. Teodosia's honor problem indeed more closely approximates that of the original model; conversely, Leocadia's situation, especially in view of her still-intact virginity, more closely resembles the case of another female character from the 1605 *Quixote*: the impulsive Leandra, whose sad history is recounted in chapters 51–52 of

Cervantes's masterpiece. It might even be suggested that in composing *Doncellas* Cervantes was recreating the story of Leandra with a new and happier ending.[24]

LA SEÑORA CORNELIA

In the introduction to *La señora Cornelia* in his Cátedra edition of the *Novelas ejemplares*, Harry Sieber underscores the dramatic quality of this comic work. He calls it "a cape-and-sword play in prose," studded with exaggerations, an abundance of comic descriptions, a labyrinthine plot, and a generally jocose tone that tends to render all the rites, gestures, and customs of the Bolognese court the target of Cervantes's peculiar irony and satire.[25] Sieber is, of course, absolutely correct. As a good piece of stagecraft should, *Cornelia* abounds in fast action and attention-riveting intrigue; it features a strong and suspenseful opening scene plus a series of unexpected twists in the plot guaranteed to hold the reader's interest. I count four distinct "flashback" narratives, which raises it above even the highly complicated *Amante liberal* for honors in that category. Furthermore, Cervantes is very careful here to provide the reader with copious detail in his descriptive passages and full explanations at every point—and there are many—at which the action darts off in a new direction.

On the debit side of the ledger, there is little or no characterization to boast of; the actors in this comedy are more like puppets than real people. Additionally, the plot depends rather heavily upon coincidence, which tends to strain the reader's suspension of disbelief beyond a reasonable limit. If the dramatic beginning is encouragingly strong, the protracted denouement is disappointingly weak; the near-miss comings and goings of the major figures along the highways between Bologna and Ferrara in the second half soon grow tiresome and tedious. Most of all, the story suffers toward the end from a loose narrative focus that bounces annoyingly from one locale to another, thereby dissipating the tension and suspense generated earlier.

This is not to say that the narrative technique here is totally without merit. The marvelous air of mystery and intrigue with which the story opens is doubly effective insofar as it allows the narrator to deceive the reader with regard to who the real protagonists are in this tale. In the opening paragraphs Don Juan and Don Antonio appear to be the central characters, but it eventually becomes obvious that the role played by these two Spanish/Basque gentlemen is merely that of twin mediators among a trio of Italian protagonists: the honor-bound Don Lorenzo; his sister, the seduced and abandoned Lady Cornelia; and her hesitant and vacillating suitor (who is also the father of her newborn child), the duke of Ferrara. As we shall presently see, the critics have not always been of one accord in their evaluation of the merits of Cervantes's tenth exemplary novel.

Joaquín Casalduero (1962) perceives *Cornelia* as consisting of four basic narrative divisions. each of which contains multiple internal subdivisions.[26] The structural design this critic offers for *Cornelia* is very confusing and doesn't really give a clear picture of Cervantes's narrative scheme for the story or how he carries out that design. Thematically, Casalduero contrasts *Cornelia*'s superficial bourgeois social ambience with the more serious religious atmosphere of *Fuerza*, which means that he ends up dismissing *Cornelia* as a simple portrait of bourgeois social life (236).

Amezúa y Mayo follows Casalduero's lead and praises Cervantes's suspense-building technique in *Cornelia* as the author attempts to "divert the denouement with a few jokes and tricks that, when later revealed, will make the reader's satisfaction even greater."[27] Emphasizing the polished dramatic technique Cervantes exhibits in this story, Amezúa adds that nowadays, even in its original 1613 form, *La señora Cornelia* would be considered an excellent film script (2:372).

The interpretation of Ruth El Saffar, while acknowledging the influence of the Greek novel and the *comedia* on *Cornelia*,[28] places greater emphasis on the mediating role Cervantes has designed for his two Spanish/Basque heroes, Don Juan de Gamboa and Don Antonio de Isunza. She notes that one of the main functions of the two Spanish intermediaries is to maintain the required distance between the author of *Cornelia* and his characters (121). But they also mediate the thorny relationships that develop among the other characters in the story. Initially, the very active Don Juan and the more passive Don Antonio are successful in guiding the three main characters toward what appears to be a happy resolution of their problem, for they know more about the confusing situation than their friends do and are able to manipulate the others to some extent (123). But circumstances eventually work to strip them of that control late in the story, at which point the real or "absolute" narrator steps in to impose his control and bring the story to a new and satisfying conclusion (124–25). In El Saffar's view, the two Basque gentlemen can be said to serve four consecutive roles: (1) as characters within the story (even as apparent protagonists); (2) as mediators among the other characters; (3) as functional nonentities after they lose their control of Cornelia; and (4) as characters once again, when they gather with their friends for the felicitous finale (126).

In Rodríguez-Luis's *Novedad y ejemplo* (1980) we find a totally different interpretation; he calls *Cornelia* the best example of the Italianate novella in Cervantes's anthology, while at the same time calling attention to the work's strong theatrical technique.[29] What causes *Cornelia* to stand out among the novels of romantic intrigue, says this critic, is the nonstop action and the almost unending string of plot complications that characterize the narration from the first to the last scene. Conversely, Rodríguez-Luis notes an almost total absence of scenes of personal conflict that we observe in so many of the other romantic stories. He attributes this lack of internal conflict to the fact that, as opposed to the complications Ricaredo and Isabela face in *La española inglesa,* in *Cornelia* there are no genuine social obstacles to the marriage of Cornelia and the Duke (1:88).

The same critic also observes that *Cornelia* lacks the rhetorical brilliance of some of the "speeches and harangues of dramatic beauty" that characterize *Doncellas* (1:89). He asserts that *Doncellas* features a very simple story that abounds in psychological detail, while *Cornelia* sacrifices psychological depth in favor of fast-paced action (1:93). These judgments are in perfect accord with my own basic premise in studying these two novellas: although *Doncellas* and *Cornelia* share essentially the same basic narrative structure, the former strives mightily to develop the handful of personalities who appear in its pages, while *Cornelia*, with considerably more characters to choose from, eschews strong characterization in favor of a highly complicated plot intrigue.

At another point Rodríguez-Luis makes special mention of Cervantes's ability to slow the pace of the main action by infusing his work with refreshing comic interludes—very much in the tradition of the popular one-act *entremés* of the Spanish Golden Age theater. The critic notes a series of farcical scenes that take place toward the close of the action and that place the reader at the narrator's level, watching his characters' expectations being undermined by phony appearances. The first is the Italian housekeeper's lengthy and amusing counsel to Cornelia, in which she urges her mistress to flee before her brother returns to kill her for having dishonored their family. The hilarious harangue features a disdainful but justifiable reaction to the arrogance of many Spaniards who traveled to Italy in those times; the housekeeper simply represents the viewpoint of many Italian citizens who had come into contact with the frequently supercilious attitude of Spanish soldiers, students, and official emissaries (1:98–100).

The second delaying action occurs in a case of mistaken identity when the two Spaniards and their Italian friends discover that Don Juan's page has sequestered in his room a certain "Cornelia" who is believed to be the high-born Cornelia Bentibolli they are all seeking. The dramatic confusion that results from this mix-up—characters dashing up and down stairs, breaking into rooms, a half-naked woman being terrified by her intruders, etc.—is again highly reminiscent of the classic Spanish *entremés* (1:100–101).

The final delaying action Rodríguez-Luis cites is the prank that the Duke plays on his friends as they all gather at the house where Lady Cornelia has sought refuge. When he announces that he has decided to marry a local peasant woman instead of the mother of his child, the result is what the critic calls a "triple play with the characters' hopes," which is similar to the confusion that takes place at the end of *La gitanilla*. The succession of surprises and the repeated appearances of Cornelia and her child in the final scene are deemed "marcadamente teatral, sirviendo pues para subrayar la teatralidad de la novela toda" (1:103) [markedly theatrical, serving to underscore the theatricality of the entire novella].

Rodríguez-Luis closes by noting that *Cornelia* features a variety of parallelisms, confusions, and obstacles whose frequency of use is surpassed in the collection only in *Española* and *Amante*. Their employment in *Cornelia*, however, is notably superficial. In the final analysis, all the rapidly changing circumstances and situations that the characters confront in this story have little or no effect on their attitudes or their personal virtues (1:104).

The highly theatrical quality of *Cornelia* is underscored again by Joseph V. Ricapito (1996), who views this story as a parody of the popular honor theme.[30] While recognizing that the development of Cervantes's swashbuckling *novela* "comes very close to a Lopean play" (106), Ricapito also observes, quite accurately, that "[t]he potentially explosive situation never materializes; it is a tempest in a teapot" (108). Ricapito effectively summarizes the fundamental difference between Cervantes's nonviolent approach to the question of *honra* and the more sanguinary treatment of that theme in the Spanish Golden Age *comedia*:

> Cervantes takes the conventional *comedia*, re-frames it as prose, and deflates its means and intentions in favor of humane, rational, and Christian resolutions. This he does by contriving to metamorphose the original tragic situation to a semicomical, almost farcical one. Clearly, Cervantes's rejection of "bloody *honra*" must be read as a form of antihonor in "La señora Cornelia." (111)

Gail Bradbury (1984) posits an even tighter relationship between the works of Cervantes and Lope; she points out some very distinct parallels between Cervantes's *Cornelia* and Lope's drama, *El mayordomo de la Duquesa de Amalfi* (ca. 1606).[31] On the basis of the use of certain common themes such as nobility, honor, unequal marriage, and marriage for love, Bradbury declares that Lope's play may in fact have been the inspiration for Cervantes's *Cornelia* (15). To be sure, there are many points on which these two artistic works part company, and Bradbury is quick to acknowledge them. Notable among these is the portrayal of conventional aristocratic values. In this area Cervantes's work is more ambivalent than is Lope's, as we readily observe in the conduct of Lorenzo Bentibolli. Faced with the apparent dishonor of his sister by the socially superior duke of Ferrara, Lorenzo is seen to grow progressively less rigid on the honor question as a result of his contact with the two moderate Spanish gentlemen (16). One of the principal differences Bradbury finds between the two works is that Lope's play tends toward an uncompromising, didactic treatment of the honor theme while Cervantes's novella takes a more reflective, flexible approach (17).

Lest we become distracted by the strong technical resemblance of *Cornelia* to a Spanish *comedia,* it should be pointed out that the structure of Cervantes's story is still predominantly narrative, not dramatic. Characters move in and out of the story line, scenes shift often and with great rapidity, but very little action actually takes place in full view of the reader. Most of what passes for "action' in this story is received in a secondhand fashion from the mouth of one of the characters. Leaving aside the four major analeptic summaries delivered by Don Antonio, Lady Cornelia, Don Lorenzo, and the Duke at a variety of points in the story (see schema 28), there are more than a dozen other instances in which the reader receives important information from an account being given by one character to another.[32] In a dramatic work this would constitute an abuse of the principle of exposition; in a work of narrative fiction this technique is perfectly acceptable.

The first serious attempt to analyze the narrative technique of *La señora Cornelia* was made in 1976 by Esther Lacadena y Calero.[33] Because her approach depends heavily upon the cause-and-effect relationship (in both time and space) of certain pivotal scenes in the narrative, Lacadena's study necessarily falls short of a complete analysis of *Cornelia*, but she does offer some valuable insights into Cervantes's general design for the story. Lacadena observes a great deal of balance and harmony among the various narrative sections, all of which are held firmly together by a construction and dialectical kind of development that takes place in four stages, which she terms "Exposition," "Knotting," "Expectation" and "Denouement" (204). The structure of *Cornelia*, according to Lacadena, is "syntagmatic" in the sense that "the episodes or actions of each of the narrative sequences are connected to each other by causal, temporal and spatial relationships, and their characters are bound together by causal as well as affective bonds" (206).

Lacadena views *Cornelia* as a series of separations and reunions—she calls them "divergencias y convergencias"—that ultimately produce a resolution of all conflicts. The initial separation of Don Juan and Don Antonio (D^1—Exposition) effectively causes each of these gentlemen to witness or experience a completely different aspect of the romantic intrigue involving Lady Cornelia and the duke of Ferrara. When the two Spaniards are reunited

(C^1—Knotting) they bring together all the narrative strands of the story and four of the five major participants (only the Duke is not present at this point).

The second parting (D^2—Expectation) occurs when Cornelia's brother Lorenzo sets off with the two Spaniards in search of the Duke, an event that provokes Cornelia herself to flee for a second time. This second divergence is balanced by the eventual convergence of all the principals when the Duke arrives at the home of a friendly priest who coincidentally has given refuge to Cornelia (C^2—Denouement). The scene that immediately follows the joyful reunion of Cornelia and the Duke (D^3—Epilogue) offers yet another separation: as the bride and groom depart for Ferrara, the Spaniards opt to return to their homeland. In Lacadena's schematic representation of *Cornelia* (schema 27), the narrative plan is made up of opening and closing narrative blocks that are separated by a central section designed to maintain the narrative tension and raise the reader's expectations (207–8).

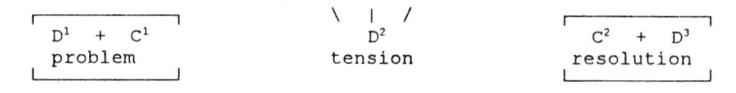

```
┌─────────────┐      \  |  /       ┌─────────────┐
│ D¹  +  C¹   │         D²         │  C²  +  D³  │
│  problem    │      tension       │  resolution │
└─────────────┘                    └─────────────┘
```

Schema 27. *La señora Cornelia*

While acknowledging the general validity of Lacadena's schematic representation of *Cornelia*'s plot, I find it insufficient for my purposes here, principally because it fails to provide an explanation for several ancillary scenes that contribute in an important way to the development of Cervantes's story line. Like Lacadena, I would divide *Cornelia* into three parts, but with a slightly different configuration. In accordance with the sound observations of Bradbury, Ricapito, and Rodríguez-Luis, I would divide the story into sections that more closely resemble the three acts of a Spanish Golden Age *comedia*.

Section 1, the longest of the three at fifteen pages of text (pp. 241–55 of the Sieber edition), opens dramatically with the birth, out of wedlock, of Cornelia's baby and her subsequent separation from the infant. The remainder of this section is dedicated to reuniting mother and child. A second thorny issue, that of uniting in matrimony the still unmarried parents of the infant, dominates the action of the second and third "acts" of the presentation.

The middle part (section 2), consisting of some eleven pages of narrative (pp. 255–66), serves to untie the Gordian knot of misunderstanding that has precipitated the separation of the lovers. But the resolution will take place only on an intellectual or emotional plane in this section. The formidable task of uniting the estranged lovers in matrimony is reserved for section 3, which is also eleven pages in length (pp. 266–77). This final act is where the intensity of the narration breaks down to some degree; the action begins to swing loosely back and forth between the cities of Bologna and Ferrara. The schematic design that I prefer for *Cornelia* is shown in schema 28.

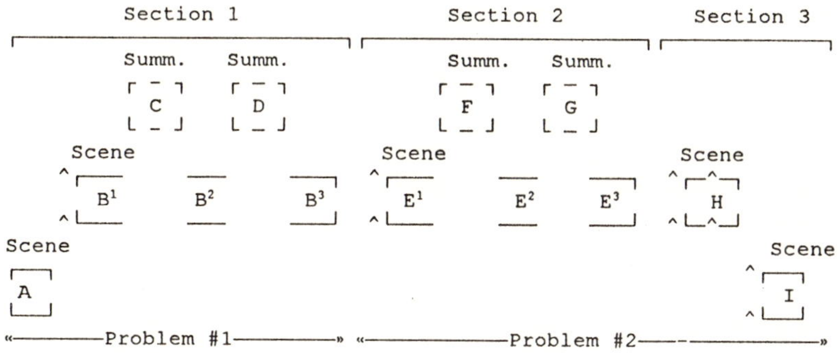

```
              Section 1                    Section 2              Section 3
       ┌─────────────────────┐      ┌─────────────────────┐    ┌──────────┐
            Summ.     Summ.              Summ.     Summ.
            ┌ ─ ┐     ┌ ─ ┐              ┌ ─ ┐     ┌ ─ ┐
              C         D                  F         G
            └ ─ ┘     └ ─ ┘              └ ─ ┘     └ ─ ┘
            Scene                        Scene                     Scene
          ^┌───────────────────┐       ^┌───────────────────┐    ^┌─^─┐
            B¹      B²      B³           E¹      E²      E³        H
          ^└──     ──     ──┘          ^└──    ──     ──┘        ^└─^─┘
    Scene                                                                Scene
    ┌──┐                                                                ^┌──┐
     A                                                                    I
    └──┘                                                                ^└──┘
    «─────Problem #1─────»   «─────────Problem #2──────────»
```

Schema 28. *La señora Cornelia*

A = Introduction.
B, E = Continually interrupted thread of narrative through sections 1 and 2, respectively.
C, D = Flashback narratives provided by Antonio and Cornelia, respectively, in section 1.
F, G = Flashback narratives provided by Lorenzo and the Duke, respectively, in section 2.
H = Thread of narrative in section 3, broken only by a single ellipsis.
I = Epilogue.

Section 1

The story begins with a brief, almost parenthetical, introduction (A) that presents four of the five major characters. These are the following: the high-principled Spanish students of Basque lineage, Don Juan de Gamboa and Don Antonio de Isunza; Lady Cornelia Bentibolli, daughter of a distinguished Bolognese family; and finally, her honor-bound and somewhat volatile brother Lorenzo Bentibolli. Juan Bautista de Avalle-Arce has recently (1995) offered a convincing argument as to why Cervantes chose two Basques to serve as the principal agents of salvation and redemption in this exemplary story.[34] Virtually all of the introductory material centers on the restless young men's delicate relationship with their strong-willed fathers. We are told that they have abandoned their studies at Salamanca in favor of a military adventure in the Low Countries. In Antwerp they are greeted with an unexpected outburst of peace (depriving them of any hoped-for military exploits) and the arrival of letters from their disapproving fathers; these angry missives reproach them for their immature folly and summon them home. The patriarchs are eventually persuaded to finance their sons' continued studies at the University of Bologna, but only with the proviso that they comport themselves in a properly aristocratic manner:

de modo que mostrasen en su tratamiento quién [sic] eran y qué padres tenían. (SC 2:242)

[so that their sons might show in their dealings with others who they were and the kind of fathers they had.] (4:7)

The full significance of the details Cervantes provides in the opening paragraphs will not be revealed until the final pages of the story; consequently, I will have more to say in the matter when I discuss the story's epilogue (I).

The main narrative thread of *Cornelia* (B^1, B^2, B^3) begins with the account of Don Juan's strange nocturnal encounter on the streets of Bologna, at which time a newborn baby is abruptly and mysteriously thrust into his hands. A short time later—after he has placed the infant in the care of his housekeeper—Don Juan returns to the streets and immediately stumbles upon an attempted murder; he proves his valor by coming to the rescue of an unidentified gentleman who has been set upon by a group of attackers.

A short time later Don Antonio has a strange story of his own to recount: an equally mysterious meeting he has he had on the streets of the city with a weak and woozy Cornelia. This account (flashback C) is the first of four retrospective narratives to be found in the opening two sections of the story. The second such recapitulation (D) is Lady Cornelia's explanation of the strange events that have caused her that very night to give birth out of wedlock to a child fathered by the duke of Ferrara. In a matter of moments Don Juan and Don Antonio are able to see the link between their respective adventures and arrange for the happy reunion of mother and child, which marks the end of the first problem.

Lacadena draws sharp distinctions between the respective narrative styles of accounts given by Don Antonio and Lady Cornelia in this section and their artistic function within the story. Only Cornelia's story can truly be called retrospective, since it recounts the history of her long courtship by the duke of Ferrara. Don Antonio, on the other hand, simply provides the reader with a summary of certain events he witnessed and in which he took part at the very moment when Don Juan's hands were receiving Lady Cornelia's baby from her servant on a dark street in Bologna. Consequently, while Antonio narrates with all the objectivity of a third-person omniscient author, Cornelia's story is strongly subjective by virtue of its narrow perspective and first-person narrative.[35]

Section 2

The principal narrative thread for the middle section of the story (E^1, E^2, E^3) begins the next day with the unexpected appearance of Cornelia's brother Lorenzo at Don Juan's lodging. The Italian gentleman, after introducing himself, informs the Spanish students (flashback F) about the secret courtship of his sister by the duke of Ferrara; he then begs Don Juan to accompany him to Ferrara to confront the man who has defiled his family's honor. Don Juan and Don Antonio immediately devise a plan to bring about the reunion of the lovers and a peaceful and happy solution (through marriage) to problem #2, salvaging Don Lorenzo's honor. The final piece of the puzzle as to how and why Cornelia came to be left seduced and abandoned is provided a short while later when Juan and Lorenzo accidentally come upon the elusive Duke himself on the road to Ferrara. The Duke explains (flashback G) the unusual family circumstances that made it difficult, if not impossible, for him to take Cornelia as his bride. He assures them that the final obstacle to his marrying Cornelia is about to be removed by the imminent death of his strong-willed mother, who had insisted for years that her son marry another woman. The final scene of section 2 is the reunion of the two Spaniards with Lorenzo and the Duke, at which point the entire intrigue is sorted out and clarified. At the conclusion of this meeting they all head back to Bologna.

At this point problem #2 appears to be on the brink of resolution; all that is required is to bring the Duke face-to-face with Cornelia and his newborn son. Up to this point the story is very much reminiscent of one recounted in Part One of *Don Quixote* about the difficult and problem-laden courtship of Cardenio and Luscinda. Even the narrative technique is similar: the reader enters the story in medias res and is gradually brought to full knowledge of previous occurrences by means of a series of flashback narratives, each one delivered by a different participant in the drama and each with a slightly different perspective on the events narrated. But Cervantes now injects one final and totally unexpected complication that will delay the anticipated reunion a while longer and cause the tale to be extended for still another eleven pages.

Section 3

The third and final section of the story—a long and somewhat tedious narration (H) that carries the reader from Bologna to a small village outside of Ferrara, then to the Duke's palace in that city—is devoted exclusively to creating and resolving a new and final set of misunderstandings that work to keep the lovers apart. It begins back in Bologna, where Cornelia, fearing that her life is in danger, abandons the quarters where Don Juan and Don Antonio have had her sequestered. By the time the four gentlemen arrive for what they expect to be a happy reunion, the mother and baby are nowhere to be found. Matters are further complicated by the discovery of a second "Cornelia" on the premises, the "other Cornelia" being a servant girl who has agreed to a sexual liaison with one of Don Juan's servants in an upstairs bedroom. Peter N. Dunn (1973) has accurately noted that this ironic episode is designed to parallel the subsequent revelation of the true Cornelia a few pages later.[36] The discovery of this peasant Cornelia wrapped in bedsheets is a comic masterpiece that rivals the hilarious encounter of Don Quixote and Maritornes at the inn, but the Duke and Don Lorenzo are not amused in the slightest. They storm out without saying a word, leaving the two Spaniards confused and highly embarrassed about their sudden lack of credibility.

Following a brief ellipsis, the action resumes at the residence of a local priest in a small village on the outskirts of Ferrara, where a disconsolate Duke comes, as is his wont in times of trouble, to ponder the recent events that have brought him so much sorrow. As fate would have it, Cornelia and the baby have preceded him to that spot. The curate, a playful character in the mold of the corregidor from *La gitanilla*, orchestrates a dramatic reunion in which the Duke comes to recognize his own child by the trinkets pinned to the infant's clothes. With the Duke reunited at last with his (soon-to-be) wife and baby, the narration moves to the final scene, which takes place three days later at the ducal palace in Ferrara following the arrival of Don Juan, Don Antonio, and Don Lorenzo. In accordance with the example set by Doña Estefanía with Rodolfo in *La fuerza de la sangre*, the Duke devilishly decides to toy a while here with the emotions of his friends before finally revealing his secret. He announces his decision to marry a certain peasant girl instead of Cornelia, a piece of information that nearly launches the two Spaniards and Don Lorenzo into an apoplectic fit. In a scene highly reminiscent of the denouement of *Fuerza*, the lovely and stunningly outfitted woman the Duke introduces as his future bride turns out to be none other than Lady Cornelia, a turn of events that produces great sighs of relief from those who witness her entrance.

The main thread of action closes with the customary betrothal ceremony *(desposorio)*, which is followed by a brief but important epilogue (I) in which the reader in informed that Cornelia becomes the Duke's wife after the death of his mother and that she eventually bears him two daughters. As for the Spaniards, we are told that they respectfully decline the Duke's offer of marriage to two of his cousins and some years later return to their Basque homeland to marry women selected for them by their parents. As Avalle-Arce points out, these final details are anything but gratuitous.[37] They are intended to underscore the proud Basque heritage of the two Spanish heroes, as symbolized, says Avalle-Arce, by the special chapel set aside in Seville's Church of San Francisco by the Brotherhood of Basque Pilots. Entry into this sanctuary is restricted to Basque pilots/navigators and their families (8). The fact that Don Juan and Don Antonio would dare to reject the generous offer of the duke of Ferrara to forge a political alliance between their families and his is itself an unmistakable comment on the high self-esteem of the Basque nobility in Cervantes's time. Albert A. Sicroff (1988) deems this final development a significant piece of social criticism and an oblique, sarcastic reference to what the writer considered an unsavory Old Christian trait among some of his compatriots: "Basque pride in considering themselves the most noble and pure Old Christians—without 'taint' of Jewish or Moorish ancestry—in all of the Iberian peninsula."[38]

The moral implications of the events portrayed in section 3 have provoked a considerable amount of critical commentary over the years. Thomas Pabon (1977) declares the episode of the *pícara* Cornelia to be "little more than a comic interlude."[39] In his opinion, the *señora* Cornelia's sexual conduct must be judged as superior to her plebeian counterpart's because "she [enjoys earthly pleasures] always within the context of a permanent marriage" (113). I find his argument far from convincing. To judge one woman morally superior to the other solely on the basis of some vague hope she may have had of eventually marrying the man with whom she was having sexual relations is pure sophistry.

Far preferable is Gail Bradbury's analysis of this episode.[40] She states that *Cornelia* contains "implied criticism of aristocratic concern with outward appearances and the suggestion that personal virtue is not commensurate with social status" (16). This notion is reinforced with the appearance of the second Cornelia, who, Bradbury notes, "shares the name of the heroine and imitates—albeit in a more brazen manner—her earlier behavior with the Duke" (16). In the final analysis, Cervantes's story offers a clear demonstration of the fact that "the idealized 'private marriage' of the nobles is but a step away from the undignified liaison usually associated with the commoner" (16). Bradbury believes that in *Cornelia* Cervantes is providing an important contrast to the "brutal pessimism" of the denouement of Lope's *El mayordomo de la Duquesa de Amalfi* (18). In fact, the great novelist might be said to be challenging the entire viewpoint expounded in Lope's play by proposing that "[t]he proper reward of 'true love'—even between partners of unequal status—is the blessing of the Church and the freedom to run its marital and parental course" (18–19).

Catherine Davis Vinel borrows Bradbury's thesis and uses it to construct a most interesting and unorthodox interpretation of Cervantes's story—and its relationship to *Las dos doncellas*.[41] In Vinel's judgment, Cervantes uses *Doncellas* to show how two ostensibly similar women are really very different in their conduct. *Cornelia*, on the other hand, demonstrates how two women from totally different social classes can be more similar, both in name and in sexual comportment, than anyone realizes. Although these two stories are quite similar in theme and structure, *Cornelia* employs a more complex literary technique and its exemplary message is consequently more difficult to fathom. The reader's ultimate interpretation of *Cornelia*, says Vinel, will depend upon whether he or she reads it as a novel or as a romance (205).

If the reader accepts the narrator as a disinterested and objective reporter, he or she will perforce interpret *Cornelia* according to the conventions of the classic romance in prose—conventions that are, in many cases, also the norms of the Spanish *comedia*. In such an interpretation the story will be viewed as an uplifting tale about the loss and recovery of a good woman's honor. The traditional romance pattern of employing a linear plot design, using stock characters, and providing a closed, poetically just ending (problems neatly solved, social equilibrium restored) will prevail.

To read *Cornelia* as a novel, on the other hand, will require us to take a skeptical approach to the narrator and his presentation. If we filter out the inherent bias of the narrator's presentation, we will be able to view the story as a nonlinear narrative, with characters that are ambiguously drawn, culminating in an open, ironic conclusion (206). This simultaneous use of two genres in the telling of a single story is precisely what we saw Cervantes do in *La gitanilla*. Vinel shows that a similar technique was used in Renaissance fine arts, most notably in Archimboldo's painting, *The Vegetable Gardener* (ca. 1581), a work she describes as follows:

> [W]hen viewed at one angle [it] appears to be a green bowl overflowing with root vegetables, but when turned upside-down suddenly reveals the head of the gardener, with the bowl serving as a hat. The exact same composition can be perceived as either a still-life or as a portrait, depending on the viewer's angle of vision. This is the same technique Cervantes employs—but now in literary form—in *La señora Cornelia*. (209–10)

Vinel's conclusion is that *Cornelia*, when read as a romance, is a story that revolves around the popular honor theme; if viewed from a novelistic perspective, however, it becomes a story about social injustice (210).

In section 3 we find a noteworthy scene that effectively illustrates Vinel's point: the two Spaniards' encounter with the "other" Cornelia in the bedroom of Don Juan's page. In a conventional romance interpretation this scene would have the appearance of being simply a superfluous digression, an ancillary adventure that Cervantes added to prolong the action.[42] But when this episode is viewed within a novelistic framework it emerges as a criticism of certain aspects of the main action that it interrupts.

The episode of the false Cornelia, in Vinel's interpretation, is actually a subtle commentary on the social consequences that result when single women freely consent to enter into sexual relationships with men outside the matrimonial covenant. In this story two women, both named Cornelia, are confronted with the unpleasant consequences of their promiscuous sexual conduct. The only real difference between them is that of social class, but that distinction makes all the difference in the world with regard to the social consequences of their actions and the way each of them is perceived in turn by society.[43] The *pícara* Cornelia is treated like a pariah, while her high-born counterpart is ultimately rewarded with marriage to the duke of Ferrara. Vinel notes that virtually the same kind of judgment is made on the extratextual level by the reader, who, on the basis of prior expectations, will decide to grant or withhold respectability in each case. These prior expectations, in turn, will be determined by the reading code the reader brings to the experience (214).

Vinel's final comment effectively summarizes her theory of double discourse as it relates to *La señora Cornelia:*

> For the unquestioning audience who are accustomed to Lope's romance-like *comedia*, [Cervantes] writes a charming story of honor restored, a theme designed to reinforce their belief in the validity of the social hierarchy that prevailed and to help them believe in a Divine Order above and beyond this imperfect world we live in. For the *discretos*, however, he includes "novelistic" elements which underline the ironic nature of our human existence. He tries to show that, under the skin, we are all just fallible and flawed human beings, differentiated only by the superficial trappings of wealth and social position. This is the fundamental human reality that, in Cervantes's eyes, fictional romances and the conservative Spanish *comedia* always failed to take into account. (221)

Conclusion

What sets *Doncellas* and *Cornelia* apart from most of the preceding "idealistic" novellas is the fact that there is no quasi-mythical quest or ordeal involved. No suitor is required to win the affections of his intended mate or "earn" the right to claim the heroine as his bride by undergoing some sort of test or trial, as was the case in *La gitanilla, El amante liberal,* and other tales. *Cornelia* and *Doncellas* are concerned instead with the important social question of family honor. There are various obstacles that need to be overcome, knotty problems that must be resolved, and annoying complications that require smoothing out, but the bottom line is that family honor must be restored through the sacrament of matrimony. Here the selection of a mate—which is always the central problem in the preceding "trial" novellas—has either already been made prior to the opening of the story (Marco Antonio and Teodosia; the duke of Ferrara and Cornelia) or the matter is in the process of being resolved from above by the fates (Rafael and Leocadia).

Ruth El Saffar has argued that both of these narratives would appear to be late compositions by virtue of the similarities to the posthumously published *Persiles* they exhibit.[44] Given the undeniably favorable light in which the unassertive female character role is projected and positive moral atmosphere that pervades both of these works, I heartily agree with her assessment. I would add only that we should not overlook the many echoes of the Cardenio-Luscinda-Fernando-Dorotea affair that appear in these tales. *Cornelia* is perhaps only vaguely reminiscent of Cardenio's timid and halfhearted courtship of Luscinda in the *Quixote*. On the other hand, *Doncellas* seems to be a deliberate and clever reworking of Cardenio and Dorotea's romantic dilemmas, with Teodosia assuming the reluctant-suitor role of Cardenio, Leocadia reprising the aggressive behavior of the determined Dorotea, and Marco Antonio recreating the duplicitous romantic dealings of Fernando.

The parallelism between the cases of Dorotea and Leocadia is only partial, as El Saffar points out (117–18). Dorotea's low birth is a special complicating factor with which only she is required to deal. Her humble origins require Dorotea to prove that she is worthy to marry into a distinguished family like Fernando's; hence the fuller development of her character in the *Quixote*. Leocadia's bloodlines, on the other hand, are assumed from the outset to be of the proper aristocratic stripe, so her characterization is more economically wrought.

These two similar stories diverge on a number of other points as well. Consider the case of the two male protagonists whose reprehensible behavior is responsible for the dilemmas faced by the ladies in question. Fernando, with the egocentrism so characteristic of the romantic leads in Cervantes's early stories, never quite grasps the fact that he is merely playing a role in a larger dramatic opus, even after he has confessed his guilt and offered to make an honest woman of the fair Dorotea. At the close of the action he seems to be no more cognizant of the moral and social implications of his actions than he was when he first decided to toy with the affections of an innocent and trusting maiden. Marco Antonio, on the other hand, actually does appear to have undergone a measure of moral and spiritual growth; he ultimately comes to recognize that his wants and needs are but a small part of a larger and more complicated scheme.

The basis for the complicated plot action of both stories, of course, is the issue of courtship and marriage. The presentation in the Fernando-Dorotea story is relatively simple (i.e., marriage is treated merely as a social convention, albeit a very important one). In *Las dos doncellas* we note unmistakable references to the restitutive powers of the sacrament of matrimony, a theme that doesn't begin to assert itself with force in Cervantes's works until after 1605. As might be expected, special sacramental blessings are not a factor in the case of Dorotea and Fernando, but they are clearly implied for both sets of lovers in *Las dos doncellas*.

We must also take into consideration the special formal relationship that exists between *Doncellas* and *Cornelia*. Just as Cervantes began the *Novelas ejemplares* with two totally different approaches to the "trial and redemption" novella (*La gitanilla* versus *El amante liberal*), he repeats the exercise here with the problem of honor. *Doncellas* presents a relatively simple, tightly wound narrative intrigue that moves briskly and effectively toward resolution with little or no wasted action. The literary models that come immediately to mind for Teodosia and Leocadia are the figures of Dorotea and Leandra in the *Quixote*, Part One. In *Cornelia* Cervantes presents the same theme immersed in a much more complex structure, an intricate weave of complications that extend the story beyond its normal limits and artificially delay the reader's gratification. This *novela* in many ways replicates the star-crossed courtship of Luscinda and Cardenio that the same author served up for our entertainment in the 1605 *Quixote*.

Because *Doncellas* and *Cornelia* are so very similar in theme and design, some might say that Cervantes's decision to place them in adjoining positions was itself an experimental gesture. I have demonstrated here that in these two *novelas* Cervantes is essentially repeating the same story, first within a relatively simple narrative structure, then a second time using a much more complicated (and openly dramatic) format.

For some, *Cornelia* seems to run a bit long and wander excessively from place to place, while *Doncellas* appears to be a model of narrative efficiency. Others, however, prefer the elaborate fuguelike structure of the baroque *Cornelia* over the simpler design of *Doncellas*. It is left to each reader to render the final judgment, for in matters of taste, as Cervantes would have been the first to assert, *De gustibus non disputandum est*.

5
The Enigmatic Layered Structure of *El casamiento engañoso* and *El coloquio de los perros*

CLASSICAL MODELS: APULEIUS, LUCIAN, AND THE CYNICS

Any thorough examination of Cervantes's *Coloquio* should begin with a few words about the work's peculiar format and its classical origins. Over the years many critics have noted certain similarities—particularly a common sense of irony—between Cervantes's unusual canine conversation and the satirical dialogues of the second-century Greek writer, Lucian of Samosata. Michael Zappala notes that some Hispanists thought it probable that Cervantes had become familiar with Lucian's writings through the works of a Renaissance intermediary like Erasmus of Rotterdam.[1]

In 1953 Antonio Oliver commented on a number of possible classical influences on Cervantes.[2] He points to a clear parallel between what happens to Cervantes's dogs and the protagonist of Apuleius's *Golden Ass*. There is a clever inversion of the model, however, in that in the classical model Lucius loses, rather than gains, the power of speech when he is transformed into an ass, while Berganza and Cipión move in the opposite direction (296). At a later point Oliver goes on to discuss certain stylistic similarities between Lucian of Samosata and Cervantes, bolstering his argument by noting that the Cynic's translated writings enjoyed considerable popularity in Europe during the sixteenth century (301).

The same critic offers what he considers to be clear examples of Cynical satire in Cervantes's *Coloquio*, a characteristic most observable in the very specific kinds of social vermin that are targeted for criticism in that work. Oliver flatly declares Berganza and Cipión to be inverted symbols of the ancient Cynics: if the followers of Diogenes were formerly said to bark like dogs, in Cervantes's topsy-turvy literary rendition the philosophizing dogs are suddenly endowed with human speech (306). The key to under-

240

standing this symbolism, says Oliver, is the lantern the two dogs are reported to carry every night when they accompany the good Christian Mahudes on his charitable rounds; the lantern is designed to be an unmistakable reminder of the Cynic Diogenes' search for an honest man (307). Agustín G. Amezúa y Mayo (1956) also noted the apparent influence of Lucian on Cervantes's prose dialogue, but he rejects the notion of any direct Cervantine knowledge of the Greek's work.[3]

The first stylistic comparison of the writings of Lucian and Cervantes was made by Michael Zappala in 1979. In Zappala's study these two literary figures are shown to share a number of characteristics. The first of these is a concern for the elusive nature of truth, which ultimately impels them to portray situations from more than a single perspective (68). The subsequent ironic distance that Lucian and Cervantes manufacture in their works serves principally to separate the author from his characters and his reader, thereby generating the all-important illusion of fictional autonomy and the characters' "freedom to function as coagents of creation."[4]

Zappala signals another point of convergence between these two writers in their sly use of lexical legerdemain. Both Lucian and Cervantes are masterful manipulators of insignificant information. They carefully feed the reader an abundance of small details designed to distract the reader from the basic implausibility of their fictional creation. Zappala cites Cervantes's Cave of Montesinos episode from *Don Quixote*, Part Two, as a prime example of what he calls the "triumph of detail over premise" (73). A third area of commonality between Lucian and Cervantes is their penchant for literary parody. In his masterpiece Cervantes parodies the novels of chivalry in the same way that Lucian earlier had burlesqued the excesses of the Greek romance and subjective (i.e., totally unreliable) historiography (73). Yet another possible source of inspiration—and a much more contemporary one—for Cervantes could have been Erasmus of Rotterdam. In Zappala's view, Lucian and Erasmus seem to be authors in search of a genre. Their writings contain the raw materials needed for the creation of the narrative apparatus that would become the modern novel, but they never discovered the proper literary format for its development. It was left to Cervantes to elaborate and incorporate these elements—the appreciation of the direct style, the deft handling of irony, the awareness of the relationship between character, author, and reader—into a viable new artistic form that would endure for centuries (76-77).

A slightly different observation regarding the influence of the Cynics on Cervantes's thought is found in E. C. Riley's 1976 article on the *Coloquio* and *El licenciado Vidriera*.[5] While both of these Cervantine novellas are judged to be steeped in Cynical pessimism, Riley prefers the "light and ironical" musings of the two dogs to the more bitter judgments of the disillusioned

Vidriera (195). Berganza and Cipión are fully aware of the dangers of malicious gossip *(murmuración)* and the fact that such backbiting is frequently passed off as high-minded philosophy. It is worth noting that this was precisely the charge their critics leveled most often at the Cynics. In Riley's view, the vice of *murmuración* was precisely what Cervantes found objectionable about Mateo Alemán's *Guzmañ de Alfarache* and its vituperative progeny (196). To *murmurar* was to act like the vindictive and pessimistic Alemán; Cervantes believed writers such as himself who had been attacked by bitter rivals needed to resist "[t]he temptation to lambaste others in kind" (198). The result is the more measured social satire of the *Coloquio*.

THE *CASAMIENTO* AND THE *COLOQUIO:*
SINGLE OR DOUBLE ENTRIES?

While many critics have observed the very strong thematic and formal ties that bind the two final entries in Cervantes's collection of novellas, Joaquín Casalduero was perhaps the first to declare openly (1962) that the *Casamiento* and the *Coloquio* were in fact one *novela*, not two.[6] It was also Casalduero who first pointed out what he called a Baroque "movimiento de fuga" in the *Coloquio* (242). This is the same "fugal structure" that Alban K. Forcione later posits as an essential element of both the *Coloquio* and the *Persiles*: "It enunciates a dominant theme and restates it continually in innumerable episodic variations, all of which are held together by a recurrent narrative rhythm and a carefully patterned repetition of symbolic imagery."[7]

Following Casalduero's bold declaration, other critics have taken up the gauntlet and continued to debate whether these two stories were conceived from the start as a single entity or were separate compositions belatedly fused into an a single artistic unit. Several noted Hispanists have supported Casalduero's assertion of thematic and formal unity for the *Casamiento/Coloquio*. Carlos Blanco Aguinaga (1957) considered Cervantes's two novellas to be a single work and wondered if they might not in fact be a parody of the picaresque genre.[8] He takes special note of the stylistic differences between Cervantes's a posteriori presentation in the *Coloquio* and the a priori technique Alemán used in his *Guzmán de Alfarache* (316-28). Pamela Waley (1957) considers the combined stories, taken together, to constitute "the most overtly didactic of all Cervantes' works."[9] She believes that while the *Casamiento* is seen to demonstrate amorality in an individual, the trailing *Coloquio* shows the same vice contaminating the entire social fabric (204).

In 1959 L. J. Woodward offered the view that the curious combination of these two stories was perhaps some sort of literary experiment. He observed that the *Casamiento*, taken by itself, was actually quite banal, but that it served quite well as an *inductio* to the following *Coloquio*.[10] Several years later (1973) Karl-Ludwig Selig supported the notion that the account of Campuzano's disastrous marriage is merely a frame story for the more important canine colloquy.[11] Selig noted that certain key expressions in the first story serve as a guide to the perspectivism we find in the main dialogue (395). The story of the ensign's bizarre *Casamiento engañoso* and all the double-dealing that takes place within it are designed, says Selig, to prepare the reader to face an even more implausible story in Campuzano's manuscript (399).

In *Cervantes and the Mystery of Lawlessness* (1984), Alban K. Forcione bolstered Woodward's experimentation theory and placed the *Coloquio*, in terms of its innovative technique, near the top of Cervantes's impressive list of literary achievements:

> In its assimilation and refashioning of traditional genres—including the picaresque novel, the Lucianic satire, the philosophical dialogue, the miracle narrative, the devotional and consolatory treatise, the sermon, the fable, the aphorism and the anecdote—[the *Coloquio*] goes beyond any of Cervantes' other works except the *Quixote*....[12]

Noting the hybrid nature of the combined stories ("[a] picaresque novel and ... Lucianic satire within the containing frame of a Christian miracle"), Forcione goes on to term the finished product "a striking case of the imaginative adaptation of conventional narrative forms and the innovative experimentalism that characterize Cervantes' fiction in general" (141). With regard to the question of whether Cervantes actually intended the story of Campuzano's hasty marriage to serve as a "containing frame" for the canine dialogue that follows, Forcione observes that the *Casamiento*'s structure mirrors the total design of the *Colloquy*, as well as that of the episodic units that continually repeat it: "It moves downward toward a climactic experience of disorder at its center, a moment in which supernatural powers are discernible behind the events of the narrative and a sudden illumination rewards the hero and compels him to reflect on events of profound significance" (138).

The most recent study in support of the frame-tale theory comes from E. C. Riley. In a recent article linking Cervantes and Sigmund Freud (1993), Riley notes the striking parallel between Berganza and Cipión's therapeutic discourse and the techniques of modern psychoanalysis; he calls the *Coloquio* "just one part of a narrative complex or metafiction."[13]

A completely different view of these two stories was presented by Amezúa y Mayo in 1958. Amezúa advanced the notion that Cervantes's original plan consisted solely of the transcript of Berganza and Cipión's unusual conversation, and that he later composed and appended the *Casamiento* to serve as a much-needed prologue for the strictly dialogic *Coloquio*. A few years later (1961) L. A. Murillo, without specifying which text came first, supported Amezúa's view and offered a possible motive for Cervantes's belatedly fusing two otherwise separate entities: by joining together the *Casamiento* and the *Coloquio* Cervantes was able to disclaim direct authorship and establish authorial distance between himself and his characters. In 1972 Vicente Cabrera threw his support behind the separate-text argument by noting that in the dedication of his *Novelas ejemplares* to the conde de Lemos Cervantes made reference to twelve—not eleven—short stories.[14]

Yet another voice in the chorus comes from Julio Rodríguez-Luis, who in 1980 signaled the mutual independence of the two novellas and the fact that they can be read separately.

> A mi ver . . . la necesidad de explicar . . . la relación entre ambas novelas subraya su independencia mutua, o cómo, de no existir el epílogo de la historia de su matrimonio en que cuenta Campuzano a Peralta que escuchó y puso por escrito el curioso coloquio, la existencia de una novela no implica en modo alguno la de la anterior o de la siguiente. (1:212 n. 1)[15]

> [To my way of thinking . . . the need to explain . . . the relationship between these two novellas underscores their mutual dependence, which is to say that if the epilogue of Campuzano's story of his marriage did not exist (the part in which he himself informs Peralta that he has overheard and made a transcript of the curious canine conversation), the existence of one novella would in no way imply the existence of another story, whether previous or subsequent to it.]

Amezúa's original argument has been accepted and brought to complete development in two more recent publications of note. In a 1973 article Ruth El Saffar flatly declared the *Casamiento* to be of no particular interest, except for the fact that it represents a reworking of the *Coloquio*, which she says was written at an earlier point, probably in 1605 at Valladolid.[16] The reason why these two stories continue to hold our interest today, she adds, is the fact that Cervantes, by combining the two stories, created a literary and psychological masterpiece: "With the addition of the *Casamiento*, the *Coloquio* becomes part of a larger story about the recovery of an author, through literature, from illness and disgrace" (455). El Saffar's final judgment is that "the *Casamiento* transforms the *Coloquio* from an unfinished dialogue into a work of art" (466).

The separate-text theory received yet another boost in 1981 when José

María Pozuelo Yvancos demonstrated that the two stories are completely separate entities within a larger design and that the *Casamiento* does *not* serve as a frame for the *Coloquio*.[17] Pozuelo Yvancos argues convincingly that they are parallel cases of narrative incrustation, each story having its own introductory narrative frame (432). I shall have more to say about Pozuelo's theory at a later point.

Somewhere between the polar positions staked out by the Casalduero and Amezúa camps lies a middle ground of scholars who cannot seem to decide on which side of the question they wish to fall. One such critic is Alan Soons, who tried in 1961-62 to split the difference by calling the combined *Casamiento* and *Coloquio* a double novel. Another is Peter N. Dunn, who in 1973 referred to the paired stories as a "meta-novela," a study of the relationship between life and fiction, plus a discussion of novelistic technique.[18]

Cervantes and the Picaresque

There can be no denying the affinity of Cervantes's *Casamiento* and *Coloquio* to the picaresque genre. When we consider the shady conduct of both Ensign Campuzano and his slippery bride, followed by the account Berganza renders of his adventures with a series of low-life masters, we cannot avoid the sense that Cervantes's stories are closely following the trail blazed by *Lazarillo de Tormes* (1554) and Mateo Alemán's *Guzmán de Alfarache* (1599). The critic who has written the most complete and penetrating study of the *Casamiento/Coloquio*, Alban K. Forcione, leaves no doubt as to his belief that Cervantes had Alemán's work in mind as he designed and penned the dogs' colloquy.[19]

For his part, Juan Bautista Avalle-Arce calls the *Coloquio* "the most revolutionary of Cervantes's approaches to the picaresque genre."[20] Avalle-Arce proceeds to list some of the many parallels that can be drawn between the lives of Berganza and Guzmán: their birth in Seville, their early victimization at the hands of a scheming woman, a brief turn at procurement *(alcahuetería)*, frequent moral or critical digressions that creep into their autobiographical account, and their eventual decision to repent and live a moral life (598–99). Nonetheless, Cervantes never viewed the picaresque as a polished literary form, says Avalle-Arce, but rather as a genre in development—"algo decididamente *haciéndose*" (600) [something decidedly in the act of becoming]. Which is not to say that Cervantes accepted every element of Alemán's model. Among the factors in *Guzmán* that Avalle-Arce believes Cervantes rejected on ideological grounds was its strict adherence to the autobiographical format; Alemán's prototype saddled the protagonist with tainted bloodlines that overpower all other social and cultural factors in determining his conduct as an adult. As Avalle-Arce reminds us, "[D]eterminism was simply something unthinkable to the creator of Don Quixote" (601).

In Avalle-Arce's view, *Lazarillo* established the autobiographical format—which the critic calls its systolic movement, the contraction of reality—as the norm for the picaresque genre. Alemán accepted *Lazarillo*'s canons and then proceeded to transgress against them, particularly with regard to the sheer volume of material he elected to include in his narration. Cervantes, in turn, rejected *Guzmán*'s voluminous flamboyance in favor of *Lazarillo*'s original narrative economy, adding a diastolic movement by opening up his narration to accommodate more than a single point of view, e.g., Cipión's pithy interjections. It is indeed unfortunate, Avalle-Arce notes at the close of his argument, that posterity chose to follow Alemán's picaresque model, not Cervantes's (601–2).

As I mentioned earlier, Blanco Aguinaga also noticed the similarity of Cervantes's *Coloquio* to Alemán's masterpiece, but chose to emphasize the points on which they parted company. He makes special note of their distinct narrative techniques—a priori in *Guzmán*, a posteriori in the *Coloquio*—and the fact that the Cipión figure is unlike anything to be found in the picaresque.[21] The lack of a preamble, the forward-looking attitude of Berganza, and the open ending are other nonpicaresque elements in the *Coloquio* that Blanco Aguinaga holds up for praise (334–35). The cumulative weight of all these nonpicaresque elements in the *Coloquio* eventually cause the Spanish scholar to wonder if Cervantes might in fact have been parodying *Guzmán* in his canine colloquy (333).

For Gonzalo Sobejano there is no doubt as to the picaresque nature of the *Coloquio*; Berganza is cut from the same mold as Guzmán, including his penchant for moralizing digressions. The major difference is found in their attitude toward evil: Berganza's reaction to the malefactors he encounters is always one of revulsion, while Guzmán's is not.[22] As a final note regarding Cervantes's curious choice of the prose dialogue as the format for his most famous picaresque work, I would like to repeat an observation made by Roberto González Echeverría in an article about Cervantes's decision to enter the marginal literary field of the picaresque:

> Like the picaro Cervantes accepted the values of society and pretended as best he could to live by them. The new novel, as it emerged then, was appropriately a marginal form of writing without substantial antecedents in the classical tradition. It was a combination of rhetorical molds, a simulacrum of other texts with social acceptance. The picaresque lacked an official model; therefore it mimicked real, official documents to render effective its "performance" of the functions of society's texts. Be-

cause it has no prescribed form, the novel often must pretend to be a nonliterary document. It can appear as a *relación*, the report of a scientific expedition, as history, a correspondence, a police report, a chronicle, a memoir, and so on. One fruitful way to study the history of the novel and its relation to society would be to take notice of what it pretends to be throughout the centuries. Is not Cervantes suggesting [in the *Coloquio*] that the novel mimicks whatever kind of text a given society invests with power at a certain point in history?[23]

IRONY AND ESTEFANÍA

As we have already seen in the examination of *Rinconete y Cortadillo (R/C)*, *El celoso extremeño (ZE)*, and *El licenciado Vidriera (LV)*, any discussion of Cervantes's "realistic" novellas cannot overlook or underestimate the significant role that irony plays in their telling. The same is true in the case of the *Casamiento/Coloquio*. Julio Rodríguez-Luis (1984) notes that the denouement of the *Casamiento* is steeped in irony insofar as Campuzano is intelligent enough to realize that he has been brought to ruination by his own *locura*, i.e., his shallow materialistic values.[24] I would suggest that it is irony, rather than any so-called realism, that links these two stories with *R/C*, *ZE*, and *LV*; and it is the same irony that separates these five entries from the more conventional "idealistic" narratives in Cervantes's collection. The protagonists in all five of these stories come to frustrating or tragic ends because they have a weak value system or put too much faith in certain conventional beliefs. In the end they find, to their sorrow, that their values have no substance and their beliefs are ill-founded.

Rodríguez-Luis signals one ironic event in particular from the *Casamiento* that most critics have passed over without comment: Campuzano's fainting spell on a church bench, a fortuitous occurrence that prevents him from taking immediate vengeance—which had clearly been his plan—upon Estefanía for her humiliating deceit. The critic notices the similarity of this case with the one in *ZE* when Carrizales suffers a similar immobilizing attack under almost identical circumstances. In both cases, observes Rodríguez-Luis, the unexpected seizure prevents the protagonist from taking bloody revenge on his wife, thereby making possible a nonviolent conclusion of the story (2:47).[25]

The Spanish scholar goes on to make a strong case for the moral redemption of Doña Estefanía de Caicedo's character; in eyes of this critic Doña Estefanía is not an unsympathetic character, but rather a frank and intelligent woman, a model housekeeper and a loving wife (2:48). Nor should we assume that Rodríguez-Luis stands alone in holding this benevolent opinion of the clever woman who manages to hoodwink the greedy and scheming Campuzano. He merely echoes the sentiments expressed several years before (1970) by Manuel Lloris, who in his impassioned defense of Estefanía calls her the only character who manages to give the story a measure of pathos and deep humanity";[26] similarly, he terms her case "the story of a tragic and grotesque attempt by an unhappy woman seeking social redemption" (20).

The projection of positive qualities upon Estefanía allows Rodríguez-Luis to argue for her ultimate redemption on the grounds that she presumably had every serious intention of remaining with Campuzano, even after the discovery of her fraudulent actions.[27] The major strengths of this story, says this critic, are the psychological depth of its main characters and the spontaneity (i.e., unconventionality) of their reactions to the forces and events that confront them. On the basis of the attractiveness of Estefanía's character and the sweetly ironic denouement of the *Casamiento*, Rodríguez-Luis calls this work "the most *exemplary* of all the *Novelas*" (2:51).

The Witch Cañizares

Of all the characters who appear in the *Casamiento/Coloquio*, the one who has most intrigued the critics over the years has been the witch Cañizares, whose drug-induced reverie in the presence of Berganza constitutes the central episode of the dog's story and the turning point in his life. In recent years a number of critics have offered a variety of theological examinations of the Cañizares episode and its significance.

In 1984 Stephen Boyd, drawing largely from the works of El Saffar and Forcione, presented a Christian exegesis of Cervantes's final two novellas. In Boyd's view, the *Casamiento* is no more than the account of a sinner's conversion,[28] which is essentially El Saffar's judgment in her 1976 study of the two stories in question. When the newly disabused Campuzano stares into his vacant trunk, "open like an empty tomb," he experiences a kind of interior, spiritual death from which he will not recover until he has heard the story of Cañizares (2).

Boyd's explanation of the trunk scene is not unlike Forcione's analysis: "Like Cañizares . . . the Ensign is spiritually dead, and, as he gazes upon the coffin that awaits his corpse, he is forced to ponder the implications of his sinfulness and his mortality."[29] Once it moves past the image of the trunk, however, Boyd's interpretation of the *Coloquio* takes a decidedly allegorical turn. Cañizares's descent into sorcery and witchcraft is viewed as merely a symbolic representation of the nature of sin. i.e., the enslavement of the will by some evil force.[30] Boyd also parts company with most critics in his explanation of the eerie story Cañizares tells Berganza about the witch Camacha. Camacha is said to have transformed two newborn babies into dogs, promising that they would regain their human form only when the arrogant are humbled and the oppressed are exalted. Instead of following the lead of most critics in treating Berganza's narration as a dream, i.e., as the subconscious product of Campuzano's tortured psyche, Boyd prefers to treat Cañizares's account as a real event. The transmutation of men into dogs and their return to human form is, for Boyd, an allegory for the fall and redemption of man (6). Berganza and Cipión are seen to represent man as a sentient animal, as a rational being who experiences a constant tension between his primitive "adamic" nature and his renewed spiritual nature (7).

In Boyd's interpretation Campuzano's life begins to turn around when he awakens to the realization that his past sinful behavior was caused by his enslavement to sensual gratification. His initial reaction to Estefanía's deception, we are reminded, had been one of despair, followed by a thirst for vengeance. The nadir of his spiritual journey is reached when, unable to take revenge upon his tormentor, the ensign retreats to a local church, where he commits himself to the care of the Blessed Virgin and falls into a deep sleep. His experiences at the hospital are part of his recovery (8–9). Cervantes's point in composing the *Casamiento/Coloquio*, says Boyd, is to show that higher truths cannot be grasped intellectually. Moral enlightenment is a process, a procedure in which the reader himself is involved, even as he reads (9).

A narrower, but equally interesting, theological interpretation of the Cañizares episode is provided in a 1986 essay by Anthony Cárdenas.[31] This critic considers the *Coloquio* to be a comment on the Dominicans and their struggle against the Catharist (or Albigensian) heretics in the thirteenth century. In Berganza's fateful encounter with Cañizares, the canine moralist represents St. Dominic, founder of the Dominican Order, as he receives the "confession" of an old witch who stands for the all the demonic forces the Catholic Church (and its Inquisition) set out to combat.[32] The element of *desengaño* enters when Berganza comes to realize that he is not St. Dominic, that he cannot change a fundamentally unjust society. Like Lazarillo at the end of his story, Berganza learns to be content with his service to Mahudes and the gift of human speech.[33]

Yet another attempt at interpreting Cañizares's role in the *Coloquio* was made in 1991 by Carroll B. Johnson, who chooses to view the story in an artistic, rather than moralistic, light.[34] For Johnson, the last of the *Novelas ejemplares* is the story of a former soldier, i.e., a man of arms, trying to become a man of letters by showing his manuscript to his friend, the licenciate Peralta, a professional man of letters (9). In this interpretation the all-important Cañizares episode acquires a sociopolitical significance that most scholars have previously ignored or passed over in silence. Johnson reminds us that in Cervantes's day potion-brewing witches were persecuted for being (1) powerful, liberated women; (2) positive models for a feminine (as opposed to oppressively masculine) culture; and (3) a genuine threat to the established order by virtue of being serious competitors of the new (masculine-dominated) science of medicine (12–13).

During the Cañizares episode, says Johnson, we have two competing discourses: the dogs' masculine-gendered speech (portraying the witch as a hideous and evil sorceress) versus the old woman's completely feminine one (21).[35] In Johnson's view, just as Don Quixote's eloquent defense of imaginative literature manages to deflate the pompous ranting of the canon of Toledo's tirade against that kind of literary fare (*DQ* 1, chap. 50), so too does Cañizares's alternate discourse in the *Coloquio* disqualify the two dogs as spokesmen for Cervantes on the subject of witchcraft. Johnson's ultimate conclusion is that "We are left, as usual, where Cervantes so often leaves us, with nagging unresolved (and probably unresolvable) questions of ambiguity and multiple perspectives, an unresolvable dialectic of competing voices" (22).

Narrative Structure

When it comes to a discussion of the narrative structure of the *Coloquio*, either with or without the preceding *Casamiento*, there is little agreement among the critics as to what the definitive arrangement is. Aside from Casalduero's general observations about fugal movements, the first genuine attempt at a structural analysis of these stories is that of Oldřich Bělič (1966). For this critic the key to understanding the *Coloquio* is to recognize that Cervantes's dialogic account of Berganza's psychological and moral evolution from a "naive puppy" to a "mature philosopher" is artfully rendered through the principle of symmetry, both thematic and structural.[36]

With regard to the formal arrangement of episodes, Bělič calls the first four adventures—which by his count make up 49.2 percent of the story—Berganza's apprenticeship in what Bělič terms "la escuela de la vida" [the school of life]. The central episode of Berganza's experiences with the witch Cañizares constitutes another 25.2 percent of the dialogue and signals a profound attitudinal change in the protagonist; the final four episodes—the remaining 25.6 percent—serve simply to confirm the lessons learned earlier (10).

episodes #1–4	episode #5	episodes #6–9
49.2%	25.2%	25.6%

From a thematic standpoint, again Bělič finds an antithetical symmetry in the arrangement of episodes: adventures one and nine are at opposite poles of the spectrum of evil and good, with all the intermediary episodes arranged according to the principle of gradation (11). The first and fifth episodes are special landmarks on the road Berganza takes toward understanding the problem of evil in this world, the first portraying Berganza's initial experience with an evil master, the fifth representing the absolute nadir of his moral depravity. Episodes six through nine show him gradually ascending from the depths of despair to a kind of spiritual rebirth under Mahudes (12).

Bělič also considers the *Coloquio* a social satire. The various episodes are generally seen to alternate between the light "cuadros de costumbres" and more ponderous (and sometimes allegorical) condemnations of official governmental practices, a form that Bělič calls "sátira estatal" [governmental satire]. According to Bělič episodes one (the butcher), three (the merchant), six (the Gypsies), and eight (the poet) are of the lighter variety; numbers two (the shepherds), four (the constable), and seven (the Morisco) are of the more serious type; adventures five (the drummer; the witch) and nine (the crazy inmates at the hospital; the government official who refuses to listen) are a mixture of the two.

For Vicente Cabrera the fundamental elements of the *Coloquio* are grouped in clusters of three.[37] In his 1972 article Cabrera observes three distinct planes of reality: Cervantes facing Campuzano and Peralta; the ensign and the licentiate facing the talking dogs; and Berganza and Cipión against the world they critique (51). Similarly, the combined stories, when viewed as a single entity, can be seen to consist of three major parts: a prologue (the *Casamiento*), a "parte general" (the *Coloquio*), and a concluding epilogue. Each of these sections, in turn, has a different theme: the first deals with deception among individuals, the second with deceit in human society as a whole, the third with literary trickery, as represented by Campuzano's manuscript (54–55). In a subsequent study (1974), Cabrera observes yet another triad: the three stages through which Peralta, the reader of the Campuzano's manuscript, is seen to pass. He moves from an absolute refusal to believe that two canines have had a conversation, through a period of vacillation between belief and incredulity, to a final stage in which he suspends all judgment in the matter.[38]

Cabrera also comments on what he considers the remarkable synchrony we observe in the behavior of the two friends. The critic makes special note of a pair of occasions in which the lawyer and the soldier-turned-author are seen to act in perfectly complementary ways. At the precise moment when Peralta opens the manuscript to begin reading—the start of his recovery *(desengaño)*—we are told that Campuzano goes off to take a nap on a nearby bench. His mind will be temporarily disconnected, so to speak, while his friend's is engaged in evaluating the document he has written. In the second instance the ensign awakens at the very moment when his friend's reading (and moral disabusement) is completed: "El acabar el *Coloquio* el licenciado y el despertar el Alférez fue todo a un tiempo" (2:359) ['The licentiate finished the *Colloquy* and the ensign woke up at the same time'] (4:157).[39] Cervantes's point here, Cabrera says, is to show how and why the two friends are able to go off at the end united in their shared *desengaño*, not separated by it.[40]

Yet another analysis of the structure of the combined *Casamiento/Coloquio* was produced in 1981 by José María Pozuelo Yvancos. Borrowing heavily from the theories of Mikhail Bakhtin and Gérard Genette, Pozuelo Yvancos offered a very thorough examination of the combined stories and the five *registros* or narrative levels that he observes at work in them. This critic demonstrates convincingly that, contrary to what Casalduero and others have asserted over the years, the *Casamiento* is not simply a frame tale for the *Coloquio*, but rather a completely separate entity, with its own narrative frame.[41] Pozuelo Yvancos's design is summarized in table 5.1.

Table 5.1

Narrator	Medium	Narratee
	Register 1. Frame for the *Casamiento*	
Cervantes	description and dialogue between Campuzano and Peralta at the extreme ends of the combined *Casamiento/Coloquio*	The Reader
	Register 2. The *Casamiento*]	
Campuzano	oral and written versions of the story of his failed marriage	Peralta
	Register 3. Frame for the *Coloquio*	
Campuzano	introduction to the text of the overheard conversation between the two dogs	Peralta
	Register 4. The *Coloquio*	
Berganza	oral and written versions of his life story	Cipión
	Register 5. Cañizares's Story[42]	
Cañizares	extraordinary events of her experiences with Camacha	Berganza

Narrative Style

Aside from the matter of the arrangement of the various narrative and dialogic parts of these combined stories, the fundamental critical question about the *Casamiento/Coloquio*'s form has to do with the various narrative rhythms Cervantes employs in their telling. I have alluded at an earlier point to Forcione's view that the *Coloquio* is told on two narrative planes: one (Berganza's life story), derived from the picaresque novel; the other (Berganza and Cipión's critical discussion and commentary), based on the Lucianic dialogue.[43] Forcione's says such a literary hybrid naturally requires Cervantes to include in his narrative subject matter and satirical techniques appropriate to each genre and "to alter radically the rhythm of his narration, vary its tonalities, and endow its narrator with a protean capacity for shape-changing that goes well beyond the notorious powers of accommodation and disguise which one encounters in the picaresque hero" (26).

The stylistic phenomenon that Forcione observes behind the satire of the *Coloquio* is an ingenious, if highly unusual, plan that the critic refers to as a "deliberate cultivation of formlessness." The reader is obliged to wade through a series of intrusive elements (constant interruptions, annoying repetitions, needless regressions and qualifications, etc.) designed to interfere with his desire to arrive at some satisfactory explanation of Berganza and Cipión's sudden and miraculous acquisition of the power of human speech. Forcione states that Cervantes's intention was to compel his reader to experience a sense of narrative disintegration as he is confronted with "an artistic creation that was outrageously and *self-consciously unartistic*" (37, original emphasis preserved).

Forcione offers a memorable example of Cervantes's penchant for assembling disparate narrative rhythms. He describes Berganza's story of his life with the constable as being initially "a quickly paced dramatic narrative which moves with no interference toward a climactic scene of farce" (31). But then Cervantes abandons that fast-paced anecdotal technique in favor of the dramatic devices that he employed so successfully in the 1605 *Don Quixote* and his one-act comic *entremeses*. The episode of the constable *(alguacil)* ends with a tumultuous scene of confusion and suspicion brought about by the sudden disappearance of the Breton's trousers; chaos reigns as the criminal plot disintegrates into a torrent of abusive railing and bitter exclamations of mutual distrust. Here comic stereotypes abound, particularly in the inflated protestations of nobility and spotless bloodlines from the innkeeper's wife; her rhetorical excesses are marked by her mutilation of the Spanish tongue and her hysterical invocation of certain Latin phrases to be found in her certificate of nobility *(hidalguía)* (31).

What should be clear from all of the above is that in his coupling of the *Casamiento* with the *Coloquio* Cervantes was drawing upon a wide range of literary traditions and models for a work he intended to be a literary and critical tour de force. Let us now examine these two stories, first as separate entities, then as complementary parts of an ingenious plan.

El casamiento engañoso

One of the first things we note about *El casamiento engañoso* is that its basic structure differs remarkably from that of the other stories in *Novelas ejemplares*. Rather than begin in medias res as many of the so-called idealistic novellas do, or at the beginning—as was the case with the three novellas with links to the Porras Manuscript: *Rinconete y Cortadillo (R/C), El celoso extremeño (ZE),* and *El licenciado Vidriera (LV)*—this story opens at the very conclusion of the action: the moment when a weak and wobbly Ensign Campuzano stumbles out of the Hospital of the Resurrection in Vallodolid and runs into his old friend, Peralta. The narration then leaps back in time while the ensign reconstructs for Peralta the series of peculiar events that have conspired to bring him to such a gravely debilitated physical state. From the very title of the work and from the description of Campuzano's physical condition in the opening paragraph it would appear that the element of surprise is not of paramount importance in this story:

> un soldado que, por servirle su espada de báculo y por la flaqueza de sus piernas y amarillez de su rostro. . . . Iba haciendo pinitos y dando traspiés, como convalesciente. (2:281)

> [a soldier using his sword as a walking stick. . . . He staggered and stumbled as if not fully recovered from an illness.] (4:67)

No attempt is made to disguise the fact that the ailing ensign has been devastated by a foolish marriage to some deceitful woman. This detail is revealed early on by Campuzano himself:

> salgo de aquel hospital, de sudar catorce cargas de bubas que me echó una mujer que esgogí por mía, que non debiera. (2:282)

> [. . . I have just come out of that hospital where I have sweated out a dozen or so sores from the clap given to me by a woman whom I took to be mine when I should not have done so.] (4:67)

5 / *El casamiento engañoso* and *El coloquio de los perros*   255

However, this apparent frankness on Campuzano's part is ultimately deceptive; Cervantes has reserved one small but significant surprise for the very end, as we shall see. The final narrative order of the *Casamiento* is shown in schema 29.

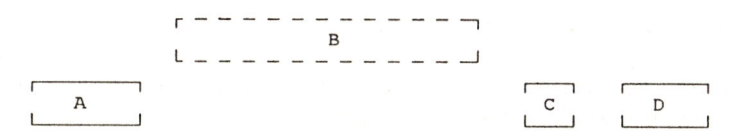

Schema 29. *El casamiento engañoso*

A = Introduction
B = Flashback narrative of Campuzano
C = Moral commentary of Peralta and Campuzano
D = Introduction to the *Coloquio*

In the chronological scheme, however, sections A and B exchange places (schema 30).

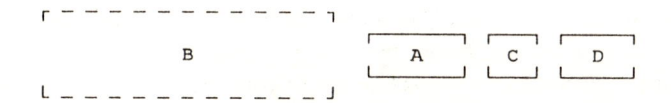

Schema 30. *El casamiento engañoso*

With regard to theme, this story deals with the closely related topics of hypocrisy, the universal conflict in human society between appearances and reality, and the general caution contained in the old saying about *ir por lana y volver trasquilado* (going forth to shear a sheep and coming back as the one shorn). The evidence of showy facades is present everywhere in this story; if the lady in question makes an initial grand display of her gaudy rings, Campuzano himself plays the game with his colorful military uniform and gold chain:

> Estaba yo entonces bizarrísimo, con aquella gran cadena que vuesa merced debió de conocerme, el sombrero con plumas y cintillo, el vestido de colores, a fuer de soldado, y tan gallardo a los ojos de mi locura, que me daba a entender que las podía matar en el aire. (2:283–84)
>
> [At that time, I myself was rather flash, wearing that big chain that you have seen on me, a hat with feathers and hatbands, a coloured jacket, as

befits a soldier, and so splendid was I in the eyes of my own delusion, that
I believed I could have any woman I wanted.] (4:69)

In a similar vein, the ensign informs us that his lady friend's companion approaches another soldier under the pretext of asking him to carry certain letters to her "cousin" in Flanders, but he realizes from the start that the intended recipient is her current lover.

The ensign's lady, whose name is Estefanía, baits the hook with her mysterious air (she refuses to uncover her face during their first encounter), the pale skin of her hands, and her soft, sensual voice—"pues tenía un tono de habla tan suave que se entraba por los oídos en el alma" (2:284) ['for she had a tone of voice so soft that it entered the ear and reached the soul'] (4:69). After a courtship that lasts not much more than a week, the two are married and Campuzano moves with all his worldly possessions into a comfortable house ("una casa muy bien aderezada") that she has led him to believe is hers.

The reader must, from all the clues Cervantes has scattered about the early pages of his narrative, realize that Estefanía's representation of herself and her financial situation is nothing but a great sham. The fragile tissue of her lies begins to disintegrate six days later when someone named Doña Clementa suddenly appears at her door and claims the house belongs to her. Estefanía calms the fears of her new husband with a fairly flimsy explanation: she says Doña Clementa is attempting to trick a certain suitor into proposing marriage to her by claiming that house as her own; things will return to normal as soon as Clementa convinces him to marry her, she asserts. What the reader surely suspects—and what the ensign *ought* to realize—is that Estefanía is attributing to her friend the very same scam she has been perpetrating on him. Blinded by his own greed, Campuzano fails to recognize his own precarious situation in the scenario his wife has constructed.

In the end he is left homeless, penniless, and afflicted with a venereal disease that will cause him to lose all of his hair and then have to undergo twenty days of treatment in a hospital. The ensign can take consolation only from the fact that his deceitful bride will find herself equally embarrassed when she learns that all the flashy gold chains with which she has absconded are virtually worthless. This final piece of information is virtually the only surprise Cervantes has reserved for the final pages.

The *Casamiento engañoso* is, then, something of a *cuento engañoso*. The narrator pretends to reveal all in the opening pages, but such turns out to be not quite the case. The reader is seduced, in effect, just as Campuzano has been. The casual onlooker is deceived into believing that he is able to glimpse the objective reality of the situation from Campuzano's very subjective account of the events. But when the last piece of the picture is finally put into place, the reader realizes that he, too, has been "had." As it turns out, Campuzano's losses are not nearly so great as he has led Peralta—and Cervantes has led his reading public—to believe.

All in all, this is a masterful display of Cervantes's talents as a storyteller and manipulator of plot: the opening description of the pathetically enfeebled ensign immediately draws us into the tale; Campuzano's carefully crafted account of his entrapment—with an abundance of verbal clues to add spice to the narration and deceive us into thinking we are more clever than the foolish protagonist—distracts the reader's attention while Cervantes sets up the final punch line. The coup de grâce is then administered painlessly, almost as an afterthought, a throwaway line to finish off the joke.

The characterization in this story is likewise first-rate, which is sometimes difficult to achieve in a story overflowing with unsavory types. In virtually every other novella in the collection we can find at least one morally upright character worthy of our admiration or sympathy, but the vast majority of critics believe this not to be the case here, although both Lloris and Rodríguez-Luis have attempted to make a case in defense of Estefanía. What is remarkable is that in the *Casamiento*, a story that abounds in hypocrites and sleazy con-artists, Cervantes somehow finds a way to temper the stinging social criticism he delivers. The self-deprecating humor with which Campuzano tells his tale renders him, if not quite lovable, perhaps somewhat less loathsome than he might have been in the hands of a less skillful narrator. He pays the full price for his stupidity, greed, and shortsightedness, but he is seen to emerge a better man for the experience.

EL COLOQUIO DE LOS PERROS

If one were to attempt to present a schematic representation of the chain of Berganza's adventures, one might profitably consider Bělič's outline as a model (schema 31).

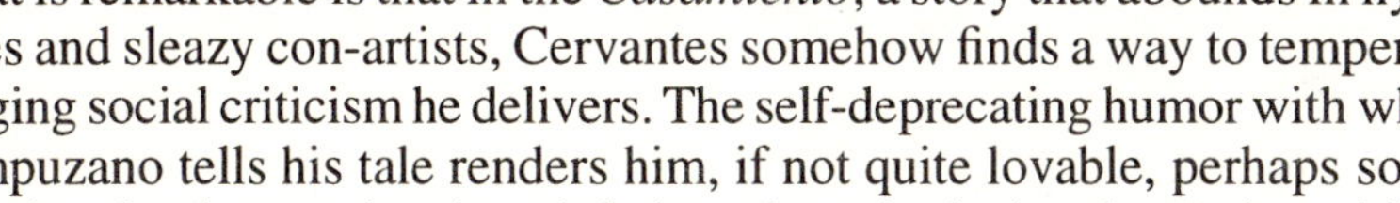

| A | B | C | D | E | F | G | H | I |

«———— 49.2% ————» «—— 25.2% ——» «—— 25.6% ——»

Schema 31. *El coloquio de los perros*

A = the butcher
B = the shepherds
C = the Sevillian merchant

D = the constable
E = the drummer and the witch
F = the Gypsies
G = the Morisco farmer
H = the poet and theater manager
I = with Mahudes at the hospital

A simpler and more accurate design for the *Coloquio* was suggested by Ruth El Saffar in her critical study of that work (1976).[44] El Saffar depicts Berganza's story as consisting of "clusters" of episodes, which can be grouped according to the scheme (39-41) shown in schema 32.

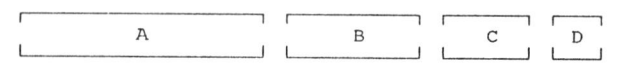

```
┌──────────────┐  ┌──────┐  ┌──────┐  ┌──┐
│      A       │  │  B   │  │  C   │  │ D│
└──────────────┘  └──────┘  └──────┘  └──┘
```

Schema 32. *El coloquio de los perros*

A. The Heart of Society: masters who "contribute directly to the financial interests that dominate Seville":
    1. the butcher (rural-outside)
    2. the shepherds (rural-outside)
    3. the rich merchant (urban-inside)
    4. the constable (urban-inside)

B. Parasites: social types "rejected by society and living off what they can take from it"; they demonstrate how deception and greed operate to undermine spiritual values both consciously (the drummer) and unconsciously (the witch).
    5. the drummer (urban-inside)
    6. the witch (rural-outside)

C. Outsiders: social groups who are excluded from the center of commercial and social power:
    7. the Gypsies (rural-outside)
    8. the Moor (rural-outside)
    9. the poet (urban-inside)
    10. the theater manager (urban-inside)

D. The Good Mahudes: he represents the *spiritual* order of reality, standing in contrast to the social/material order that dominates the first ten episodes. Here Berganza comes in contact with the following persons:
    1. the idealists: a poet, an alchemist, a mathematician and a professional consultant *(arbitrista);*
    2. the rich and powerful who lack spiritual values: the chief magistrate *(corregidor)* and the rich lady with a yapping lapdog.

5 / *El casamiento engañoso* and *El coloquio de los perros*   259

In the first cluster Cervantes is attacking the hypocrisy of the most powerful members of Spanish society, including the Jesuits (episode three), regarding whom El Saffar says Berganza has an ambiguous attitude (49) that renders any subsequent praise of them ironic (46). I prefer to see the narrator's attitude as having conflicting feelings toward them. There can be no ambiguity or uncertainty about the praise that Cervantes, through Berganza, offers for the Jesuit order or their teaching methods. Any ambivalence attributed here would have to be found in Cervantes's reaction to the Jesuits' complicity in assisting wealthy New Christians to advance in certain delicate social areas. El Saffar notes that this episode could be a representation of the Jewish *converso* issue and the distasteful practice of investigating lineages that prevailed in sixteenth-century Spanish society (48). The Sevillian merchant in the *Coloquio* is probably a rich New Christian and the Jesuits are clearly helping him prepare his sons to ascend the socioeconomic ladder. If we are looking for some symbolic meaning for the events that transpire at the school, the dog could be said to represent the tainted family bloodlines that had to be kept under wraps (i.e., locked up at home) if the family hoped to avoid social embarrassment.[45]

The episodes in the first cluster become increasingly more complex in structure at the same time that Berganza grows progressively more disillusioned and his moral stature increases with each new master.[46] We observe Berganza moving steadily from the role of passive observer to one of active opposition to the hypocrisy he encounters in the world. With the butcher Berganza is simply an unwitting accomplice; with the shepherds, he becomes a victim of their crooked scheme; with the African housekeeper, he strives to expose her immoral sexual activities; and with the constable we see Berganza take full charge of exposing his corrupt master's hypocritical—and profitable—subversion of the justice system in Seville (55–56).

The second cluster, which El Saffar calls "linking" episodes, is the structural center of Berganza's experiences, even though the adventures with the drummer and the witch Cañizares take place roughly three-fourths of the way through the *Coloquio*. As many have noted, Berganza's descent into the world of witchcraft and sorcery in these episodes represents the absolute low point of his moral and spiritual development.

El Saffar observes that in the final cluster of adventures the episodes become progressively shorter (78). The Gypsies are said to represent the creative impulse that may be lacking in the rest of Spanish society; they are also thieves who honor neither church nor king (71). The Moriscos, as represented by the Moorish farmer, are portrayed on the one hand as hard workers, on the other as false Christians, miserly hoarders and given to procreating at an unhealthy rate. All in all, says El Saffar, Cervantes seems to prefer the chaotic impulses of the Gypsies to those of the hardworking

Moriscos (73–74). In the episode of the poet Cervantes has an opportunity to satirize some contemporary notions of verisimilitude, and with the theater manager he gets to vent some of his frustrations about the success of his rival, Lope de Vega (76).

The final cluster of Berganza's adventures while in the employ of Mahudes presents a number of indelible examples of mankind's misguided search for absolute truths. The poet is ignorant and ill-educated but dedicated to his craft, although he often mispronounces words and makes false attributions (80). The alchemist in search of the philosopher's stone that will turn all base metals into gold, the mathematician seeking the fixed point, and the *arbitrista* or suggestion maker with a wild scheme to reduce the national debt are all, like Berganza, persons in search of truth in a world that refuses to divulge it (80–81).

Cervantes is less sanguine about the behavior of political figures and the idle rich. The chief magistrate *(corregidor)* is deaf to Berganza's cries for reform. The official says he cannot understand Berganza's practical solution for dealing with the problem of venereal disease among prostitutes in Valladolid and has the complaining animal beaten and expelled (81–82). Similarly, Berganza has to suffer the offensive yapping of a highborn woman's lapdog, a poke at certain disagreeable loudmouths who depend upon the power and position of their patrons to shield them from the retribution they would otherwise face from the victims of their verbal assaults (82).

As for the link between the *Casamiento* and the *Coloquio*, El Saffar's ultimate judgment is that the canine colloquy is simply a dream story that reflects the real-life story that precedes it. Consequently, the story told by Berganza mirrors precisely the Ensign's futile search for a place in upper society (84).

THE COMBINED TEXTS

Having studied the *Casamiento* and the *Coloquio* as separate entities, let us now examine how the combined *Casamiento/Coloquio* fits into Cervantes's overall artistic scheme for his *Novelas ejemplares*. As I have demonstrated on two separate occasions, Cervantes was fond of telling stories in sets of four modules.[47] In Part One of *Don Quixote*, for example, in many instances a single story would be told from four different points of view (Marcela and Grisóstomo), in four distinct stages of development (Cardenio/Luscinda; Fernando/Dorotea), or through an accumulation of plot reversals adding up to four separate actions *(El curioso impertinente)*. In the second part of his masterwork Cervantes turned his attention to the device of telling stories in layers, usually four in number, each of which served as a commentary on the layer immediately below it. This is most noticeable in episodes of the Cave of Montesinos and Maese Pedro's puppet show, about which I shall comment at length below. Suffice it to say that I find the same principle of quadernity at work in the combined *Casamiento/Coloquio*.

The structure of the *Coloquio* itself is quite simple: Berganza narrates the story of his life while Cipión comments on the content and style—mostly the latter—of the narration. However, the transcript of the dogs' conversation does not stand alone; it is joined to the preceding *Casamiento*, in what appears to have been a fortuitous late inspiration. At some point prior to publication Cervantes decided to join these two stories for what I perceive to be two different, though related, reasons. The first was a desire to provide a proper introduction for his prose dialogue; the second—an even more significant decision, as we shall see—was to add two new layers of comment to the story's original pair of critical strata, thereby doubling the effect he was attempting to produce. And once again each critical layer of the *Coloquio* is designed to provide a commentary on the style and content of the narrative presented in the section immediately below it. Cervantes's ultimate scheme for the novella was to produce a narrative spiral that first descends and then ascends through four distinct planes of relation.

At the point of entry (level A) there is the Licenciado Peralta, who in the frame tale reads and comments on the written narrative of Ensign Campuzano; immediately below that, on level B, we have listener Campuzano recording the conversation of the miraculously endowed canines and also offering his own opinions regarding the verisimilitude of the events he has witnessed and recorded. Leaving the frame tale, we enter the text of the colloquy itself at level C; here speaker/narrator Berganza recounts his picaresque adventures to listener/critic Cipión, who continually interrupts to inject his own critical opinions about the content of the narration and the manner in which it is delivered. The bottom level (D) is reached when the witch Cañizares, in the course of one of her reveries, relates to a somewhat incredulous Berganza a rather bizarre tale about some children who were turned into dogs by a sorceress's incantation. We have already noted that this strange tale of demonic forces and implied metempsychosis lies at the linear midpoint of Cervantes's novella and represents, literally and figuratively, the core of his labyrinthine narrative.

Having descended through three layers before reaching this core, the narration begins to ascend again after the witch has finished her incredible account. Back on level C Berganza comments as to whether Cañizares's strange prophecy may somehow be responsible for the faculty of speech with which he and Cipión have suddenly been blessed. He then continues with his life story and concludes his account with how he came to enter the service of the good Mahudes at the hospital in Valladolid and miraculously received there the power of speech. Cervantes brings the tale to a swift conclusion by returning the reader to the outside world, where Campuzano remarks about his own reaction to what he has overheard (level B), and Peralta comments on the general verisimilitude of the ensign's written account (level A). The narration itself can therefore be diagrammed linearly (L = Listener; N = Narrator) in descending and ascending segments (schema 33).

A = Peralta (L); Campuzano (N)
B = Campuzano (L); Berganza & Cipión (N)
C = Cipión (L); Berganza (N)
D = Berganza (L); Cañizares (N)

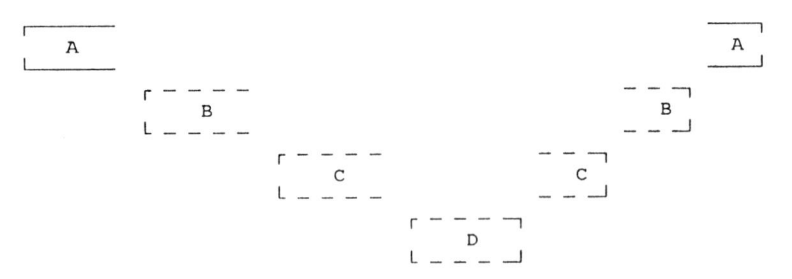

Schema 33. *El casamiento engañoso/El coloquio de los perros*

From a purely chronological standpoint, however, the order of the various parts would be precisely the reverse of the narrative sequence (schema 34).

D	C	B	A
Cañizares's Monologue	Berganza's Life Story	Dialog betw. Berg. & Cip.	Campuzano's Manuscript

Schema 34. *El casamiento engañoso/El coloquio de los perros*

This is not the only occasion on which Cervantes opted to create such a peculiar narrative structure within his fiction; his decision here to link the two stories and thereby add two more levels of critical discourse is very much akin to his belated creation of the Moorish historian Cide Hamete Benengeli at the beginning of chapter 9 of the 1605 *Quixote*.[48] With this ingenious insertion he was able not only to interpose between himself and the reader a straw man, a target for critical barbs in the person of a so-called original historian (and a conveniently unreliable one, at that), but also the additional figures of a Morisco translator and a Spanish editor. The revised plan for the novel would permit each of these contributors to—and therefore partial authors of—the novel to avail himself of a number of opportunities to comment on the verisimilitude, decorum, and other literary attributes of the book *as it was being written*. In so doing, Cervantes invented an ingenious format that would allow him to write an experimental novel and to comment simultaneously about some of the outmoded literary precepts he was *pretending* to invoke in the course of its composition. He realized that there would be more room for the kind of critical debate he wanted to inject if the narrator could be made visible to the reader, extremely fallible, and somewhat insecure about his critical judgment. Once he decided to write a novel about how one ought to write a novel, he was *obliged* to create a bogus author like Cide Hamete. Appending the figures of the translator and the editor was still another stroke of genius, a carefully calculated move designed to provide additional layers of critical reflection and grist for the mill of his ongoing debate.

To judge from the dates of publication of the respective works, it is safe to assume that the multilayered narrative device as we find it in the *Quixote* antedates its use in the *Coloquio*. It is also worth noting that Cervantes utilized the technique of layered critical commentary on various occasions and in both parts of his masterpiece, as George Haley was the first to document.[49] Haley's cogently argued thesis focuses on the parallel relationships that exist between a series of characters involved in the grand-scale composition of Don Quixote's story and the participants in the puppeteer Maese Pedro's relatively fragmentary *retablo* in *Don Quixote,* Part Two. Haley shows that Cervantes's decision to separate his novel into four narrative levels, each one with a different narrator and audience, in chap. 9 of Part One is echoed again precisely and in microcosm in Part Two during the adventure of the Maese Pedro's puppet show (chaps. 25–26).

The narrators who would ordinarily speak or write in the first person (Cervantes and Ginés de Pasamonte, respectively) choose instead to hide behind new identities (the created roles of Cide Hamete and Maese Pedro) that enable them to render their creations in the less-subjective third person. Proceeding on down the list, we observe that Maese Pedro's young assistant mirrors the role of Cide Hamete's translator and the second author/editor (who function as one) at the third narrative level. The fourth and final component is the actual transmission of the narrative to the intended audience (the reader of the novel; those gathered to witness the *retablo*). Haley's observations can be summarized as shown in table 5.2.

Table 5.2

Narrative Levels	In the Quijote as a whole	In the Maese Pedro episode
A. The Hidden Author	Cervantes	Ginés de Pasamonte
B. The Fictional Author	Cide Hamete	Maese Pedro
C. The Intermediary Agent of Transmission	the Translator & Second Author	the Assistant
D. The Intended Audience	the Reader	the Onlookers

Unfortunately, Haley's ingenious analogue, for all its theoretical correctness, cannot be applied directly to the *Coloquio*. The dogs' colloquy operates under a slightly different narrative plan: there is no "hidden narrator," for example. The final story in the *Novelas* does, however, revive the author's practice of utilizing multiple layers of critical commentary. With regard to its structural pattern, the *Coloquio* is more akin to the Cave of Montesinos episode than to any other, as we shall see.

In chapter 24 of Part Two of his masterpiece, Cervantes again presents four distinct layers of narration: (A) the translator and the editor—two voices which often alternate at the same critical level—declare that they will let stand (B) the marginal comments of Cide Hamete regarding the credibility of (C) Don Quixote's solemn declaration to Sancho regarding the truthfulness of (D) his testimony about the events that took place in the Cave of Montesinos.

Working backwards, then, we find the following layers of narration. At the core (level D) we find Don Quixote's rather fantastic account of conversations he had with various chivalric figures during his visit to the enchanted underworld. Immediately atop this (level C) we have Sancho's understandably skeptical reaction to what he has heard. Moving onto the supratextual plane, we encounter at level B the marginal comments of the doubting Moorish historian regarding the dubious veracity of the adventure he himself has just recorded. And finally, at the topmost layer (A), there are the remarks of the book's hypercritical translator and editor, who have opted with some misgivings to publish the entire record and let the reader decide for himself whether or not to believe Don Quixote's story.

Correspondingly, at the core (D) of the *Coloquio* there is the utterly incredible tale told by the witch Cañizares about certain demonic forces that have changed human babies into puppies. Above this, at level C, we have Berganza's expression of complete disbelief at what he has just heard from the old hag's lips. As we ascend to the supratextual zone we encounter Campuzano's marginal expressions of doubt regarding the truthfulness of the dialogue he himself has transcribed (level B). The story ends with Peralta's begrudging acceptance of his companion's transcript (level A). Table 5.3 illustrates how each of the four levels of the Cave of Montesinos episode corresponds precisely with a similar narrative plane in the *Coloquio*.

Table 5.3

Cave of Montesinos	*Coloquio*
A: Surface Level: Ambivalence of the translator and editor and their decision to let the text stand.	Peralta's tepid acceptance of the text in its present form.
B: Second Level: Cide Hamete's comments in the margin about the dubious nature of the episode he has recorded.	Campuzano's openly expressed doubts about the veracity of what he has written.
C: Third Level: Sancho's skeptical reaction to Don Quixote's strange tale.	Berganza's incredulity in the face of what Cañizares has just narrated.
D: Core: Don Quixote's curious account of his encounter with various chivalric heroes in the Cave.	Cañizares's bizarre story of revenge and witchcraft in Toledo.

It is no mere coincidence that Cervantes should choose characters like Campuzano and Peralta to be his commentators on the *Coloquio*, or that the unfortunate ensign should ultimately find himself in an untenable Quixote-like position. In the preceding frame story, the *Casamiento*, Campuzano tells a similarly incredible tale about a contrived counterfeit marriage that has inevitably backfired on him. At the end of Campuzano's narration Peralta demonstrates a reasonably skeptical attitude toward the ensign's story. Asked now to read an even more fantastic tale about two talking dogs, Peralta declares that he is not prepared to believe *anything* from Campuzano's lips—or pen, for that matter. The ensign is obliged to admit that this second story is also quite strange, that he himself had difficulty believing it, even as it was unfolding, and indeed had at first believed it to be a dream. Upon reflection, however, he has concluded that on his own he could not have imagined or invented such a voluminous amount of incredible dialogue, so he affirms that the dogs really *did* speak that night.

The compromise reached at the close of the *Coloquio*, besides effectively replicating the denouement of the Cave of Montesinos adventure, in many ways also echoes the theme of history versus fiction we saw in the judgments made by the priest and Fernando regarding *El curioso impertinente* and the Cautivo's story, respectively. Peralta dismisses Campuzano's transcript of the dogs' colloquy as fiction *(fingido)*, but praises it for being well composed and urges the ensign to continue with the promised second part. Campuzano insists that the entire account is true (i.e., history), but the more sophisticated Peralta refuses to accept it as anything but fiction. In the end they decide not to dispute any further as to whether the dogs actually spoke or not—precisely the same judgment rendered by the translator and editor regarding the plausibility of the Cave of Montesinos episode. All roads, it would seem, lead from the *Coloquio* back to the *Quixote*.

Turning now to the thematic reason for Cervantes's linking the *Casamiento* to the *Coloquio*, let us consider the hypothesis advanced by Ruth El Saffar in 1973.[50] El Saffar proposes that the *Casamiento* is actually a subsequent reworking of the *Coloquio*, one which was intended to cast some light on the dogs' dialogue and transform its meaning, just as Part Two of the *Quixote* represents a revaluation of Part One (455). In her view, the fusion of these two tales allows the lesser story, the dogs' colloquy, to become part of a greater and more meaningful whole. The process requires an otherwise implausible conversation to be incorporated into a broader and much more credible tale about the narrator's moral and physical recovery—or resurrection, if we consider the symbolic nature of the hospital's name—from the illness, alienation and disgrace that have recently plagued his life.[51]

Just as Haley views the Maese Pedro episode as an analogue of the narrative scheme for *Don Quixote* as a whole, El Saffar sees the purgative effect of the woeful Ensign's combined experiences in the two novellas as an echo of the Mad Hidalgo's equally unsettling adventure in the subterranean enchanted world he found at the bottom of the Cave of Montesinos. She points out that both the ensign and Don Quixote are suffering, alienated, and intensely disoriented individuals at the moment they begin their respective adventures (464). Consequently, they are obliged to descend in their dreams to a nether world where they will undergo an intense spiritual transformation that will initiate their journey back to good physical and mental health.[52]

El Saffar demonstrates furthermore that each man's experience in these episodes is bipartite, consisting of one realistic and one fantastic encounter, but recounted in a different order. The first part of Don Quixote's cave adventure (the meeting with Montesinos, Durandarte, Belerma, et al. in a centuries-long state of suspended animation) is utterly implausible, while the second portion (the unexpected encounter with the enchanted Dulcinea and her asking him to lend her six *reales*) has a decidedly realistic tone. Campuzano's ordeal runs in the opposite direction: it opens with a clearly picaresque story about his disastrous courtship and marriage to the cunning Estefanía (he winds up broke and with a bad case of syphilis), then closes with his dreamlike encounter with two chatty canines (451–65).

El Saffar finds each narrator's queer experience to represent a fortuitous liberation from lingering patterns of action that have caused his intense feelings of failure and alienation (456). Moreover, through the process of verbalizing their hallucinatory adventures, both Don Quixote and Campuzano actually begin the long journey to recovery. The critic convincingly argues that Cervantes must have decided at some late point (ca. 1612–13) to fuse the *Coloquio* to the *Casamiento* so as to replicate, thematically at least, the Cave of Montesinos episode (460). In this new arrangement, the ensign's act of transcribing the dreamlike colloquy is supposed to inspire his subsequent purgative confession to Peralta about his ill-conceived marriage.

There remains a nagging question about Cervantes's narrative technique: why has he opted to present the events of these two stories out of their normal chronological sequence? Regrettably, the El Saffar article does not concern itself with such issues. The answer can be found, I believe, by examining a special quirk in Cervantes's style and his marked preference for a particular storytelling strategy.

We have already observed that the combined *Casamiento* and *Coloquio* reprise the practice of constructing multiple levels of narration and criticism that Cervantes established earlier in the *Quixote*. The same device of layered critical commentary provides us with an important clue as to why Cervantes, upon deciding to combine these two tales, chose to begin in medias res, rather than simply narrate the events in their natural chronological order. The simplest linking arrangement would have dealt exclusively with Campuzano. Section A would have portrayed him in the painful process of courting, wedding, and finally losing the shifty Estefanía. The action in the next section (B) would have taken place at the Hospital of the Resurrection, where the woeful ensign would have experienced his hallucinatory descent into the realm of conversing canines. The final portion (C) would have left the linking element (the transcription of the dialogue) for the very end, thereby vitiating the most artistic aspect of the undertaking (schema 35).

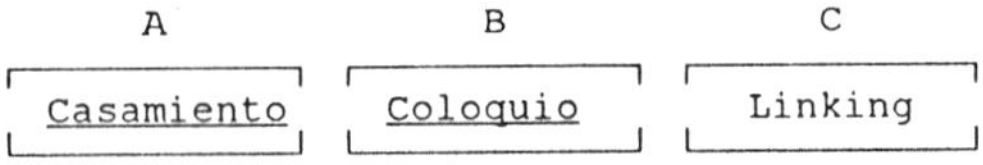

268   THE CRUCIBLE CONCEPT

```
       A              B              C
  ┌─────────┐   ┌─────────┐   ┌─────────┐
  │Casamiento│   │ Coloquio │   │ Linking  │
  └─────────┘   └─────────┘   └─────────┘
```

Schema 35. *El casamiento engañoso/El coloquio de los perros*

Moreover, such a bare-bones structure would have presented a *Coloquio* that featured only the bottom three narrative levels (Campuzano eavesdropping on the dogs' conversation, Cipión listening to Berganza's story, Berganza witnessing Cañizares's grotesque reverie). The topmost level, the role of the Licenciado Peralta as reader of and commentator on Campuzano's manuscript, would have been lost, which then would have made it difficult for Cervantes to point to the moral lesson that El Saffar says the ensign and the reader were supposed to extract from these two closely related experiences. The all-important catalyst Cervantes designed to infuse moral exemplariness into this new arrangement is the sympathetic ear—and later, the acquiescing eyes—of Peralta. In the course of recounting to the licenciado the bizarre particulars of these two unusual experiences, the narrating ensign is forced to confront the unpleasant truth about his own previous comportment, draw the proper moral conclusions, and pledge himself to a serious reform of his personal conduct.

The decision to consider the *Casamiento* and the *Coloquio* as a single hybrid unit necessarily imposes new artistic roles upon them. While it is true that in such a scheme the largely descriptive *Casamiento* is transformed into a "frame" for the purely dialogic *Coloquio*, there are other subtle changes that have not always been appreciated by the critics. Most notable among these is the fact that, while in their original form the two stories have occupied the narrative foreground in the reader's attention, the new arrangement forces both of them into the background, where their function now is to provide analeptic recapitulations or "flashback" accounts of past events. In a purely structural sense, then, these two stories have moved from present to past narrative time. The new arrangement of these two major narrative blocks, along with the sections of text that connect them, is as in schema 36.

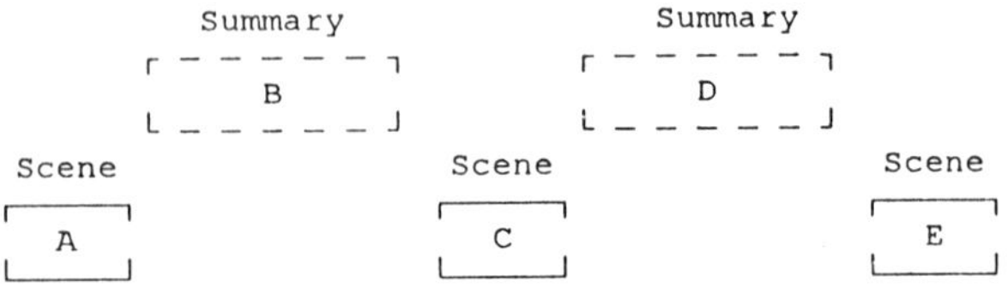

```
              Summary            Summary
           ┌ ─ ─ ─ ─ ┐         ┌ ─ ─ ─ ─ ┐
           │    B    │         │    D    │
           └ ─ ─ ─ ─ ┘         └ ─ ─ ─ ─ ┘
   Scene              Scene              Scene
  ┌─────┐           ┌─────┐            ┌─────┐
  │  A  │           │  C  │            │  E  │
  └─────┘           └─────┘            └─────┘
```

Schema 36. *El casamiento engañoso/El coloquio de los perros*

A = Campuzano meets Peralta outside the hospital
B = Campuzano's story of his *casamiento engañoso*
C = Peralta begins to read the manuscript Campuzano has written
D = Text of the *Coloquio de los perros*, as penned by Campuzano
E = Peralta's comments

The chronological ordering of the same events is quite different, however (schema 37).

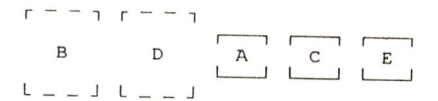

```
   ┌ ─ ─ ┐  ┌ ─ ─ ┐   ┌───┐ ┌───┐ ┌───┐
     B        D        A     C     E
   └ ─ ─ ┘  └ ─ ─ ┘   └───┘ └───┘ └───┘
```

Schema 37. *El casamiento engañoso/El coloquio de los perros*

Thematic considerations aside, Cervantes's creation of the listening licenciado is a sparkling demonstration of the author's technical virtuosity: Peralta's presence at the fourth level as a commentator on all that is narrated below him illustrates Cervantes's intense commitment to greater technical sophistication and structural complexity in his novellas. Cervantes realized that by appending the dreamlike dogs' colloquy to the more realistic account of Campuzano's deceitful marriage he could reproduce, thematically at least, a situation akin to the one Don Quixote faced in the cave.

But Cervantes also understood that certain technical adjustments would have to be made in order to maintain the four-tiered structure of his model(s) from the *Quixote*. Most notable was the need to invert the chronological order of some of the events in the combined stories. He would begin with the ensign's emergence from the hospital (which comes very close to the end of the chronological sequence) and then fuse the overheard *Coloquio* to the previous *Casamiento* by means of the mediating figure of Peralta, who would hear the first story and read the other. To add the desired fourth level of critical commentary, Cervantes employed once again the analeptic "flashback" device of which, to judge from the frequency with which he uses it in the other tales of *Novelas ejemplares*, he was so obviously fond.

Cervantes's Plan

With regard to a more general plan for uniting the *Casamiento* and the *Coloquio*, it would have made perfect sense for Cervantes to fuse these two separate stories in order to provide a reasonable frame for a text that purports to be the transcript of a canine conversation. Both stories deal with a common theme: hypocrisy. And from a psychological standpoint, the devastating embarrassment Campuzano suffers at the hands of Estefanía in the *Casamiento* is certainly cause enough to explain the strange reverie he later experiences and records in the *Coloquio*. But there is yet another level of meaning here. The fusion of these two disparate elements also serves a critical/theoretical purpose in that it allows Cervantes to represent perfectly the complexity of artistic creation and the interdependence of the author and his reader.

In her 1974 study of Cervantes's *novelas*, Ruth El Saffar alludes to the theoretical implications of the combined *Casamiento/Coloquio* when she points out that Campuzano represents the author while his friend Peralta assumes the role of the reader. Together they represent the two parts of the creative process, i.e., the cooperative effort that is required if works of fiction are to achieve the level of verisimilitude that neo-Aristotelian critics demanded of them.[53] El Saffar offers no comment at all about the role of the hypercritical Cipión in the process, but I would suggest that the second dog's role in the *Coloquio* is to give concrete form to the haunting voice of literary theorists in the author's ear as they continually interrupt the creative process in an attempt to constrain the writer's creative instincts and force him to compose in accordance with established literary precepts.

The consensus of these conservative theorists, most notably Torquato Tasso, was that the plausibility of a fictional work depended entirely upon internal factors, i.e., whatever empirical data—usually of a historical, geographic, or scientific nature—the author could provide to convince the sophisticated reader of the text's veracity. Cervantes, beginning with *Don Quixote*, dedicated much of his literary production to demonstrating a radically new notion: that verisimilitude depended upon both internal and external elements. For the Spanish writer, the quality of the artist's representation always works in conjunction with whatever the reader is willing to accept as believable; and the ultimate verisimilitude of a fictional work will perforce be determined by the "cooperative effort" between the author and his reader that El Saffar signaled.

But even as Cervantes insists upon a harmonious effort on the part of the writer and his reader, he also appears to be doing everything in his power to discourage their cooperation. This is the observation made in 1992 by B. W. Ife when he notes that fictional author Campuzano takes great pains to warn Peralta that the transcript he has provided is even more incredible than the bizarre story he has just told of his failed marriage.[54] This unusual disclaimer is designed by Cervantes to call Peralta's attention—and ours—to the highly improbable nature of what is about to be recounted (39). As Ife remarks, had his intention been to accentuate the verisimilitude of the *Coloquio*, Cervantes might reasonably have made some reference to the long literary tradition of talking animals (40). The fact that he eschews this tactic indicates that Cervantes had some other purpose in mind.

According to Ife, Cervantes prefaces the dialogue by having the author of the *Coloquio* impugn his own work's believability; then he presents the dog's conversation verbatim, with absolutely no authorial intrusion that might distract the reader from the protagonists' actual words. The next step is to remove the author entirely from the scene while Peralta reads the manuscript: Cervantes moves Campuzano off to a nearby bench where he slumbers long enough to allow his friend to absorb the text without any authorial interference. The purpose of all this, says Ife, is to confront Peralta with a pure, unadulterated text of the dogs' conversation. In short, the licenciado is placed in the unique position of being able to function as both reader and critic, two very distinct roles, at the same time (41).

As any critic is expected to do, Peralta strives to suspend his skepticism about a canine conversation until he has read all of Campuzano's manuscript. Having completed his reading, Peralta proceeds to issue two apparently self-contradictory statements. First he dismisses the colloquy as totally fictitious *(fingido)*; then he praises the literary artifact as well put together *(bien compuesto)* and urges his friend to proceed with the second part, Cipión's story. Cervantes's point here, according to Ife, is that the credibility of a work of fiction has nothing to do with its internal verisimilitude. It's a matter of the author's skill and the willingness of the reader to be convinced (41).

Ife's analysis helps to explain two things: why Cervantes wrote the *Coloquio* as a prose dialogue, without any authorial intervention; and why he chose to combine it with the *Casamiento*. Cervantes needed a prefatory piece that would provide a critical level (or platform, if you will) from which to pass judgment on the dialogue that would follow. The *Casamiento* was also the perfect introduction to the *Coloquio* because the story of Campuzano's deceitful marriage was so bizarre that it would automatically cast him in the role of an unreliable narrator for the *Coloquio*. (This is not unlike his earlier decision to make the source of *Don Quixote* a Moorish—therefore mendacious and untrustworthy—historian.) The combined *Casamiento* and *Coloquio* provided Cervantes with the perfect vehicle from which to comment on the twin questions of credibility and verisimilitude.[55]

As for Cervantes's reasons for undertaking such a daunting task, we should consider the explanation offered by Edwin Williamson in 1989: that Cervantes disliked Alemán's narrative package and wished to offer the public an alternative to *Guzmán de Alfarache*.[56] In Williamson's view, Alemán's novel is based on the assumption that the value of literature is dependent upon the virtue of the implied author, the newly repentant Guzmán (113). Any semblance of moral uprightness in the *Coloquio* is immediately compromised by the fact that its protagonists are canines and its author an unreliable scoundrel. Unlike Alemán, Cervantes has constructed his picaresque piece so as to leave his reader free to embrace or reject the story that Campuzano relates (121–22).

In 1980 Robert V. Piluso proposed that the figure of the highly literate licentiate was designed to represent the ideal critical reader, not only for the *Coloquio* but indeed for the entire *Novelas ejemplares*.[57] In his final evaluation of the text, Peralta can be viewed as a model critic because he wisely chooses to apply broad aesthetic norms (i.e., the quality of Campuzano's literary fabrication and the artful devices he employs) over narrow empirical, historical, or scientific criteria:

> —Señor Alférez, no volvamos más a esa disputa. Yo alcanzo el artificio del *Coloquio* y la invención, y basta. (2:359)

> [Ensign, sir, let's not get involved in that again. I see the art of the *Colloquy* and its invention and that is enough.] (4:157)

If there is some artistic purpose behind Cervantes's elaborate plan to fuse the *Casamiento* with the *Coloquio*, it is to demonstrate that a skillful author—as Campuzano certainly is in this case—will be able to create an interesting and plausible story out of virtually any subject matter, even something as absurd as a conversation between two dogs.

THE *COLOQUIO* AND THE PROLOGUE

Among the first to suggest a link between the *Coloquio* and Cervantes's prologue to *Novelas ejemplares* was Alan Soons.[58] I would concur on stylistic grounds: the peculiar layering technique Cervantes employs in each of these entities is remarkably similar. Let us examine this technique more closely.

The entire first paragraph of Cervantes's prefatory remarks to the *Novelas* is dedicated to the fabrication of a traditional, but totally fictitious, third-person portrait of the author, as it might have been written by a friend of the author: "Este que véis aquí . . ." (1:51) ['This man you see here . . .'] (1:3). In this hypothetical introduction the *subject* of the prologue (hereafter referred to as the prologuist) becomes in fact the *object* of another writer's work. But the prologuist (a stand-in for Cervantes) suddenly abandons the project and dismisses as futile all such efforts:

> Porque pensar que dicen puntualmente la verdad los tales elogios, es disparate, por no tener punto preciso ni determinado las alabanzas ni los vituperios. (1:51)

[For it is foolish to imagine that such eulogies tell the exact truth, as praise and vituperation have no fixed abode.] (1:3)

In the second paragraph the prologuist begins to compose his own prologue, this time in the first person and with the emphasis placed where he feels it truly belongs: on the uplifting content of the stories to be found within. Here we find the prologuist referring to the text's sweet expressions seasoned with reason and Christian discourse ("requiebros amorosos . . . tan honestos y tan medidos con la razón y discurso cristiano"), to the delicious and wholesome fruit that can be harvested from the collection as a whole and from each single entry ("el sabroso y honesto fruto que se podría sacar, así de todas juntas, como de cada una de por sí"), and to the honest and agreeable exercise that is provided within ("los ejercicios honestos y agradables") (1:51–52).

The point to be made here is that Cervantes's prologue is in many ways an overture that announces the author-reader and speaker-listener relationships that will eventually be presented in the *Coloquio*. Just as Cipión will critique the oral history of his companion Berganza, and as Peralta will peruse the manuscript of his friend Campuzano, here we find the prologuist in the "readerly" role of passing judgment on what his friend has written about him and his work.[59]

In view of the fact that prologues are generally composed at or toward the end of the creative process, it seems reasonable to imagine that Cervantes would have penned his foreword shortly before submitting his manuscript to the printer, at which point he would already have known that the dialogue between Berganza and Cipión was the final entry in his anthology. The introductory essay functions, in a sense, as both prologue and sequel to the canine colloquy. When Peralta and Campuzano exit the stage at the conclusion of the *Coloquio*, they are in fact returning the reader to the curious exchange that took place between prologuist and his artist friend in the prologue. This circular pattern is yet another demonstration of Cervantes's conscious design for his unique collection of short stories.

Conclusion: The Arrangement of the *Novelas exemplares*

Despite the well-intentioned efforts of so many critics to devise some sort of scheme or plan behind the ordering of Cervantes's twelve novellas, I do not believe that a truly satisfactory explanation has yet been offered for the peculiar arrangement the author ultimately chose. The separation of the dozen stories into "realistic" and "idealistic" categories is entirely too simplistic, in my view. It is doubtful that the celebrated Spanish writer would have agreed with such a broad categorization of his literary creations. Cervantes's *novelas* were not only *ejemplares*, but *experimentales* as well. Far more palatable to me is the idea that Cervantes may have arranged his exemplary tales with an eye toward their respective themes and narrative structures. To summarize what I consider a more workable plan for ordering his collection of short works of narrative fiction, I offer the following thumbnail sketches:

1–2. *La gitanilla* and *El amante liberal*: two nearly identical "trial and redemption" novels about the need of the male partner to overcome his feelings of jealousy. They are linked successfully, despite a clear redundancy in theme, because they utilize two radically different narrative plans. The narrative form of *Gitanilla* is rather unremarkable, but *Amante* is clearly an imitation of the classical Byzantine adventure novel and features a perfectly symmetrical narrative structure, with two mirror-image halves balanced on the fulcrum of a central event.

3. *Rinconete y Cortadillo*: a comic parody of the picaresque style, borrowed from the Porras MS for an experiment in verbal *autorretrato*. As an exercise in dialogue, this is a masterpiece; from a structural standpoint, however, it is a most unremarkable work, consisting merely of a series of successive scenes presented without any notable narrative artifice.

4. *La española inglesa*: another "trial and redemption" tale touching on the matter of jealousy. Like *Amante*, this story borrows heavily from the Greek romance tradition and exhibits a carefully balanced structure, but here Cervantes employs two virtually identical narrative halves, each one devoted to the resolution of a different problem.

5. *El licenciado Vidriera*: another experimental novella, combining the standard narrative format with that of the *emblema*; Cervantes's original story is constructed around a core of apothegms and witticisms, which he probably took from the collected sayings of Juan Farfán as presented originally in the Porras MS. Structurally, it employs a very straightforward narrative style to recount, in strict chronological order, the most significant events in the life of the protagonist.

6. *La fuerza de la sangre*: still another "trial and redemption" story, but now with the emphasis on religious imagery; jealousy is *not* a factor in this tale, although passion (as incited by great physical beauty) is. Like the preceding *Amante* and *Española inglesa*, this story features a balanced structure with two mirror-image halves flanking a highly dramatic central event.

7. *El celoso extremeño*: probably placed here for contrast with the previous tale, this story—adapted from the anonymous original that appeared in the Porras MS—is more concerned with jealousy than with passion or physical beauty. The moral lesson is centered around the importance of forgiveness in human relationships. As was the case with the other *novelas* inspired by the Porras source document *(R/C* and *LV)*, the narrative structure here is quite prosaic and strictly chronological.

8. *La ilustre fregona*: a comic version of the "trial and redemption" theme introduced earlier in *La gitanilla*. The narrative scheme of the earlier story is virtually replicated in this entry, with one notable deviation: at a strategic point Cervantes opts to split the main narrative into two parallel threads—one serious, one comic—so as to be able to follow the separate but simultaneous adventures of his two young protagonists.

9–10. *Las dos doncellas* and *La señora Cornelia*: two very similar "honor" tales that deal with theme of romantic passion and jealousy. For prose narratives these stories are remarkably dramatic in tone; they also share the same basic narrative structure: divided into three "acts" or narrative blocks, they feature alternating sections of scene and summary in the early episodes.

11–12. *El casamiento engañoso* and *El coloquio de los perros*: from a structural standpoint, these are two totally disparate stories, but Cervantes manages to blend them with great success by capitalizing on their common theme (recovery/redemption) and their mutual preoccupation with the question of literary verisimilitude. More practical reasons for joining these fables can also be adduced: Cervantes fused them to create a total of four different narrative planes, each commenting on the one immediately below it, as he had done on several occasions in *Don Quixote*. He also expected the former to serve as the frame tale for the latter, which contains only dialogue. The combined *Casamiento/Coloquio* is arguably Cervantes's finest short story from the standpoint of design and execution.

With regard to the sequencing of the stories, I find two major groupings: the first eight stories form one block, the last four comprise another. A pair of very similar "trial and redemption" narratives, *Gitanilla* (#1) and *Fregona* (#8), serve as the opening and closing brackets for the first group. The same kind of plot scheme can be found in the second, fourth, and sixth positions *(Amante, Española inglesa,* and *Fuerza),* but these three stories also feature a more artistic design: a narrative plan that divides the story into symmetrical halves. Interspersed with this trio of complicated narratives we find in the third, fifth, and seventh positions three simple stories, the only entries in the collection that do not interrupt the action of the main plotline with flashbacks or any other kind of analeptic insertion: *R/C, LV,* and *ZE*. In comparison with the rest of the tales in Cervantes's *Novelas*, these stories exhibit a remarkably simple narrative design, a characteristic that, in combination with the fact that all three have a connection with the Porras manuscript, leads me to suspect that they may not originally have been of Cervantes's invention.

When we arrive at the final four novellas in the collection, we notice the emergence of new themes and different narrative patterns. The final four entries are grouped in pairs: *Doncellas* is linked, both thematically and structurally, with the following *Cornelia*, while the *Casamiento* is physically fused with the *Coloquio* to form a composite entity, the preceding narrative serving as an introduction to and frame for the dialogue that follows.

If we observe the collection solely from the standpoint of theme, schema 38 can be used to represent the arrangement of the twelve tales in *Novelas ejemplares*.

1	2	3	4	5	6	7	8	9	10	11	12
A	A		A		A		A				
		B		B		B					
								C	C		
										D	D

Schema 38

A = "Trial and redemption" stories; in this set of original narratives Cervantes presents the concept of life as a crucible. *(Gitanilla, Amante, Española inglesa, Fuerza, Fregona)*

B = Stories taken from or inspired by the Porras manuscript. *(R/C, LV, ZE)*
C = Intrigues of honor and romance. *(Doncellas, Cornelia)*
D = Psychological studies that also engage in some form of literary criticism. *(Casamiento, Coloquio)*

If, however, one considers narrative structure to be the organizing principle behind the arrangement of these stories, a slightly different—yet totally compatible—scheme emerges (schema 39).

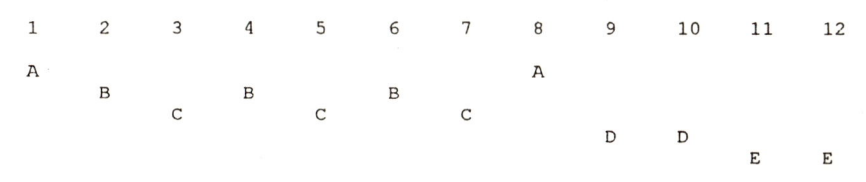

```
1    2    3    4    5    6    7    8    9    10   11   12
A                                       A
     B         B         B
          C         C         C
                                             D    D
                                                       E    E
```

Schema 39

A = Stories that consist primarily of a series of scenes, with a pair of key summaries inserted at strategic points toward the end to bring about an anagnorisis and/or sharp reversal of the action. *(Gitanilla, Fregona)*
B = Perfectly balanced narratives presented in two symmetrical parts; the second half is conceived as either an identical or mirror-image replication of the first. These stories employ various combinations of scene, summary, and ellipsis to achieve their structural symmetry. *(Amante, Española inglesa, Fuerza)*
C = Straightforward narratives that utilize simple combinations of scene and ellipsis; no analeptic summary is used at all. *(R/C, LV, ZE)*
D = Highly dramatic stories that begin in medias res and then make frequent use of summaries for exposition or to introduce fresh plot complications; these summaries are often inserted at strategic points to break up a single long scene. *(Doncellas, Cornelia)*
E = Complex narratives created by fusing two otherwise unrelated stories, then constructing around them an artificial narrative frame. The result is unique: a two-part story built upon alternating blocks of scene and summary. *(Casamiento* and *Coloquio)*

This new arrangement yields considerable insight into whatever plan Cervantes may have had in mind when he organized these novellas as he did. He obviously intended to open with a pair of "trial" stories that would illustrate the same moral lesson (that jealous feelings must be overcome before one is ready for marriage) in two very different ways. The leadoff tale, *La gitanilla*, is a slow-moving narrative which features strong characterization over plot complication. The two main personalities develop slowly before the reader's eyes while the action moves at a leisurely and rather straightforward fashion. There is a revelation at the end which is more startling to the characters themselves than to the reader, who has been amply prepared in advance by the narrator to learn that the little Gypsy girl is really the daughter of aristocrats.

The same theme is reprised in the next tale, *El amante liberal*, but this time with the emphasis on fast action and clever twists in the plot rather than on polished character development. The narrative thread moves continually back and forth in time and space as the lovers Leonisa and Ricardo gradually succeed in establishing a firm relationship. The happy denouement turns not on any startling revelation of fact but rather on a remarkable change in attitude on the part of Ricardo, who suddenly realizes that he will never be able to claim Leonisa's affection until he sets her free to make her own choice of a mate. In effect, then, the first two tales of *Novelas ejemplares* tell substantially the same story and make the same moral point but accomplish their goal through the use of two very different narrative patterns, as shown in schemas 40 and 41.

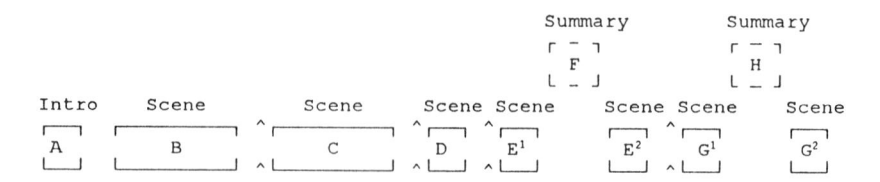

Schema 40. *La gitanilla*

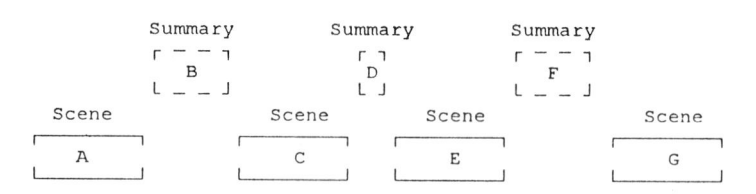

Schema 41. *El amante liberal*

We note here the symmetry that is achieved by striking a perfect balance between two identically structured halves divided at the midpoint by a poetic interlude (section D) that serves as the narrative pivot on which the action turns.

The tone shifts dramatically—and hilariously—downward as we move on to the third story in the lineup, the picaresque parody *Rinconete y Cortadillo*. Although *R/C* marks a refreshing change of pace in the collection, the story of two would-be *pícaros* has no real plot to speak of; it presents us instead with a static but richly humorous portrait of the Sevillian underworld ruled by the comically demonic ringleader, Monipodio. The story opens at an inn outside Seville (A), where we are introduced to the two main characters and continues within the city itself, where the two urchins are brought to the nerve center of Sevillian crime, the house of Monipodio (B). Here they are initiated into the rogues' syndicate, but only after being introduced to and interrogated by as strange a collection of misfits as have ever been presented in Hispanic literature. The narrative ends abruptly without either the presentation or resolution of any situation or set of circumstances that might even loosely be termed a plot. There is no great quest, no ordeal; there are no interesting flashbacks. In fact, there is hardly any forward movement of any sort. The "story" merely consists of two consecutive scenes that fit together rather loosely (schema 42).

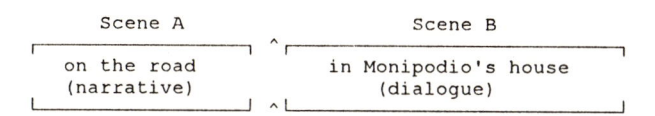

```
         Scene A                    Scene B
    ┌──────────────┐           ┌──────────────────┐
    │ on the road  │           │in Monipodio's house│
    │  (narrative) │           │    (dialogue)    │
    └──────────────┘           └──────────────────┘
```

Schema 42. *Rinconete y Cortadillo*

Despite the practically nonexistent plot and the rather pedestrian construction of the tale, *R/C* is considered one of Cervantes's best-executed comic pieces, and deservedly so, for the piece contains some of the most refreshing and hilarious dialogues and monologues to be found in any literature of the time. As I remarked in *Cervantes: Pioneer and Plagiarist*, Spain's greatest writer uses *R/C* to experiment with the technique of literary self-portrait *(autorretrato)*. Instead of devoting a lot of space to a verbal description of the characters by the narrating voice (as is the case in the Porras version of this story), Cervantes eschews the descriptive passage in favor of clever and revealing monologues delivered by the characters themselves, speeches in which they—through a curious collage of logical and syntactical inconsistencies—provide the reader with an unforgettable image of their unique personalities and often bizarre physical attributes.

At first glance, it may seem very difficult to justify the inclusion of *R/C* as part of a collection of "exemplary" tales. There really are no socially righteous characters to be found in its pages, and goodness certainly cannot be said to triumph at the end. The reader is left to ponder what, if any, moral message can be drawn from this very strange but lighthearted tale about life in the Sevillian *hampa* where dim-witted thieves, warmhearted streetwalkers and crafty card-sharpers abound. The story's hidden exemplariness can be extracted only by taking into account the unmistakably ironic tone that permeates the work from start to finish. The entire novella is an exercise in the technique of reductio ad absurdum in which the real world is stood on its head and the most undignified denizens of the underworld are miraculously endowed with the pompous and frivolous social values of their aristocratic contemporaries.

With the fourth story, *La española inglesa*, Cervantes returns us again to the higher world of literary romance and the familiar themes of beauty and jealousy. This story is longer and more complex in its construction than the previous two "trial and redemption" narratives; the carefully balanced structure of *Amante* is repeated in *La española inglesa*, where we observe the existence of two nearly identical halves, each one containing a separate trial for the hero, Ricaredo (schema 43).

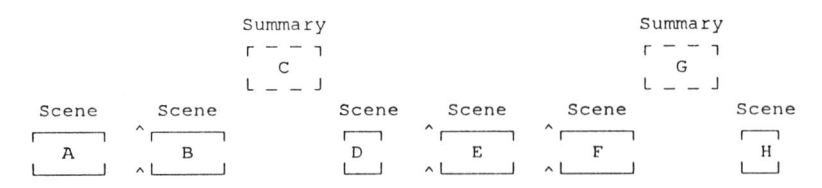

```
                    Summary                          Summary
                    ┌ ─ ─ ┐                          ┌ ─ ─ ┐
                       C                                G
                    └ ─ ─ ┘                          └ ─ ─ ┘
  Scene     Scene      Scene     Scene     Scene      Scene
 ┌─────┐  ┌─────┐    ┌─────┐  ┌─────┐    ┌─────┐    ┌─────┐
 │  A  │  │  B  │    │  D  │  │  E  │    │  F  │    │  H  │
 └─────┘  └─────┘    └─────┘  └─────┘    └─────┘    └─────┘
```

Schema 43. *La española inglesa*

In the first half the young hero is obliged to prove his worthiness to marry the lovely Spanish lass, Isabela; in the process he also manages to reunite her with her natural parents, who have not seen or heard from her since she was kidnapped by Ricaredo's father seven years before. The second part of the story involves a test of Ricaredo's constancy after Isabela is poisoned and her beauty is seriously marred; the main project here is that of reuniting the two lovers after they have been separated for two years by circumstances beyond their control.

The realistic/novelistic pattern returns with the direct and slow-paced *El licenciado Vidriera*. The fifth *novela* is an ironic fictional biography of a man who is entirely too intelligent for his own good. The brilliant and witty Tomás Rodaja/Rueda is ultimately driven from the royal court by an unappreciative society and forced to pursue a military career, a perilous calling to which he had never felt any attraction and for which he had always felt ill-suited. The principal section of Cervantes's narrative consists of a series of roughly sixty witty pronouncements, apothegms, and commentaries that fall from the mouth of the (temporarily) mad protagonist and touch upon a wide variety of recognizable social types. Some of the remarks are favorable, but the great majority of them are of a caustic nature, which therefore renders them wickedly amusing. Here again, as with *R/C*, the structure is simple, direct, and straightforward, eschewing the use of flashback narratives entirely.

The story opens (A) with the encounter of the young protagonist, here called Tomás de Rodaja, with two well-to-do young students who offer to bring him to Salamanca, where he will be employed as their valet and provided with a university education at the same time. The second section (B) is concerned with the next stage of Tomás's intellectual formation, his travels—always as a noncombatant—on the European continent with his friend Captain Valdivia. The third and longest narrative division (C) deals with Tomás's return to Salamanca to complete his studies, his graduation, and a subsequent madness resulting from a potion administered by a scorned female acquaintance. It is during this period of his life that the eccentric Tomás, called Vidriera (the Man of Glass) in honor of his peculiar mania, gains a large measure of renown for his witty aphorisms, dozens of which are included in the text. The final part (D) tells of Tomás's miraculous recovery, then of his disillusioning discovery that the public esteemed his utterances only when they were voiced by an ostensibly deranged individual. The story concludes with his reluctant decision to seek a career in the military, where, as Tomás Rueda, he meets an ironic albeit heroic fate on the battlefields of Flanders (schema 44).

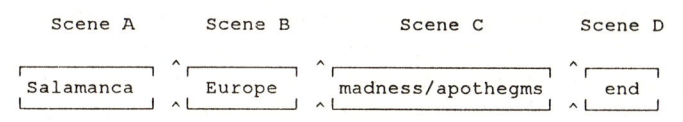

```
    Scene A          Scene B          Scene C          Scene D
  ┌──────────┐    ┌──────────┐    ┌──────────────────┐    ┌──────┐
  │ Salamanca│    │  Europe  │    │madness/apothegms │    │ end  │
  └──────────┘    └──────────┘    └──────────────────┘    └──────┘
```

Schema 44. *El licenciado Vidriera*

A second but equally valid representation of the same story would simply distinguish between the direct criticism Vidriera makes of specific members and stations in society during his madness and the condemnation of society as a whole that is implied in the highly ironic account of his life. In this second scheme, the story is not divided into narrative sections but viewed instead as a continuum (A); the long series of witty sayings and apothegmatic comments (B) represents a change to the direct method of attack, but remains structurally inseparable from the rest of the tale (schema 45).

It is my contention that the collection of clever aphorisms in the third section is yet another connection with the long-lost Porras manuscript. We know that certain sections of Porras's codex contained the collected witticisms

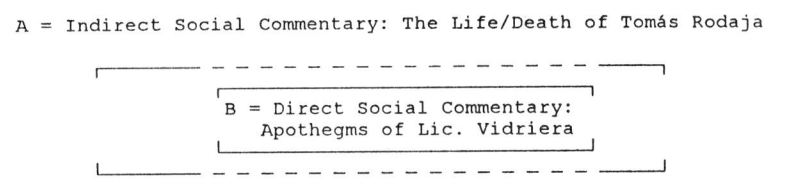

```
A = Indirect Social Commentary: The Life/Death of Tomás Rodaja
┌─────────────────────────────────────┐
│  ┌───────────────────────────────┐  │
│  │  B = Direct Social Commentary: │  │
│  │     Apothegms of Lic. Vidriera │  │
│  └───────────────────────────────┘  │
└─────────────────────────────────────┘
```

Schema 45. *El licenciado Vidriera*

("cuentos, agudezas y genialidades") of a well-known orator of the time, Juan Farfán, plus similar clever commentaries ("chistes, prontitudes y ocurrencias") attributed to other celebrated Sevillian wags. Insofar as he never duplicates the apothegmatic technique in any other of his short narratives, it strikes me as probable that the innovative Cervantes may have on this occasion borrowed still another section from the Porras text—just as he did in the cases of *Rinconete* and *El celoso extremeño*—for the central core of material he would need for an experiment in the development of a new kind of fictional hybrid, a cross between the traditional novella and the new emblematic format that was becoming so popular in the early 1600s.

The sixth item, *La fuerza de la sangre*, returns to the original "trial and redemption" motif, this time with a distinctively theological tone. This story is charged with a religious symbolism that is noticeably absent from the earlier novellas of the same stripe. The theme is a familiar one: the deleterious effect great physical beauty can have on the human psyche. But instead of returning to the hackneyed motif of jealousy *(celos)*, Cervantes focuses on the related issue of uncontrolled male ardor and the damage that can result from excessive and unrestrained sexual passion: rape. Because of Cervantes's extremely optimistic view regarding God's design for the world as we know it, this potentially disastrous situation is eventually brought to a happy and socially acceptable conclusion: the malefactor miraculously recognizes the error of his ways and freely opts to marry his victim and restore her honor.

With regard to structure, once again we note the curiously balanced scheme featured earlier in *Amante* and *Española inglesa*. Like *Amante*, this story is neatly divided into two virtually identical halves sitting astride a dramatic central event (Luisico's life-threatening accident) that serves as a fulcrum for their balancing act (schema 46).

The final narrative derived from the Porras codex is *El celoso extremeño* (*ZE*), which is found in the seventh position in the collection. As was the case with *R/C* and *LV*, the events of this story are told in chronological order, without any recapitulation in flashback form. The story consists of only two parts: (A) the brief prehistory of Felipo Carrizales's prodigal youth

CONCLUSION 283

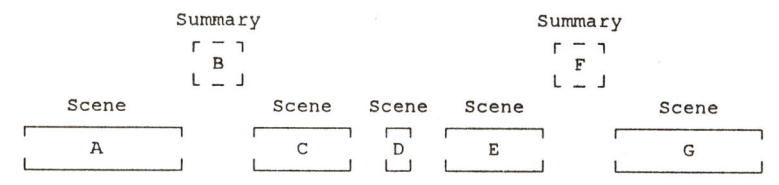

```
           Summary                          Summary
           ┌ ─ ┐                            ┌ ─ ┐
             B                                F
           └ _ ┘                            └ _ ┘
  Scene            Scene   Scene   Scene            Scene
┌─────────┐      ┌───────┐ ┌─┐ ┌───────┐          ┌─────────┐
│    A    │      │   C   │ │D│ │   E   │          │    G    │
└─────────┘      └───────┘ └─┘ └───────┘          └─────────┘
```

Schema 46. *La fuerza de la sangre*

and his eventual return from the New World as a rich, old, and extremely jealous *indiano* in search of a young bride; and (B) the step-by-step account of the young rogue Loaysa's scheme to penetrate the elaborate defenses of Carrizales's fortress of a house and to seduce the old man's teenage bride.

The first part is presented in an a priori style of narration not found anywhere else in Cervantes's short fiction: we are told early on about the old man's extremely jealous nature, a factor from which all his subsequent bizarre actions can be deduced and therefore seem perfectly natural and consistent. Little or no imaginative effort on the part of the reader is required. The longer second part is presented in the usual a posteriori fashion: no advance information is given as to how Loaysa will attempt to breach Carrizales's tight security network or whether he will actually succeed in achieving his goal; the reader must work his way through the story along with the narrator (schema 47).

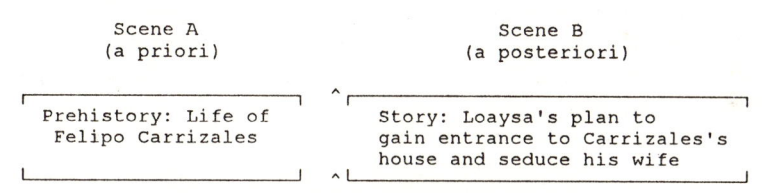

```
        Scene A                        Scene B
      (a priori)                    (a posteriori)

┌────────────────────────┐    ┌──────────────────────────────┐
│  Prehistory: Life of   │    │ Story: Loaysa's plan to      │
│   Felipo Carrizales    │    │ gain entrance to Carrizales's│
│                        │    │ house and seduce his wife    │
└────────────────────────┘    └──────────────────────────────┘
```

Schema 47. *El celoso extremeño*

It is my contention that the focus of Cervantes's version of *ZE* is not on Carrizales's excessive watchfulness over his bride—as critics have generally assumed—but rather on the old man's final forgiveness of Leonora's transgression. As the title of the story indicates, jealousy is indeed the major theme in the earlier Porras version: old Carrizales's sexual insecurity comes to have fatal consequences when he discovers his wife in bed with young Loaysa. In his 1613 version, however, Cervantes makes two changes that alter significantly the meaning of the story. First and most importantly, he allows Leonora to honor her marriage vows and spurn Loaysa's sexual entreaties. Secondly, although Carrizales still goes to his grave convinced of his wife's unfaithfulness, Cervantes lets the reader know that the young girl is in fact innocent of the charges against her. Consequently, the gratuitous absolution that Carrizales offers on his deathbed is suddenly infused with a poignancy and an ironic quality that were totally absent in the original. Cervantes's cleverly conceived denouement manages to elevate the moral character of both spouses at the same time that it provides a moral lesson that could be considered truly Christian.

Equally ironic is the fact that, although the title of the story announces a jealousy theme, the female protagonist's physical charms never actually serve as a motivating factor or provocation for the actions of the amorous males who pursue her. This is totally at variance with the established pattern of Cervantes's other novellas. The original version of *ZE* would appear to have been conceived by an author far less sophisticated than Cervantes, one who did not share the great novelist's Neoplatonic worldview in which physical beauty is viewed as a reflection of corresponding moral and spiritual wholesomeness. I submit that Cervantes must have recognized the potential of the Porras *ZE* and realized that, by carrying out a small number of skillful alterations, he could enhance the exemplarity of the original and render it worthy of inclusion among his collection of *novelas ejemplares*. Lengthy descriptions of the bride's physical beauty would not be essential to the development of the plot or to the moral message he wished to impart, so he left the original intact on that point. As for Cervantes's reasons for placing this tale where he did in the collection, I believe that he did so as a complement to the preceding *Fuerza*, which, although primarily concerned with the potentially evil consequences of overpowering physical attractiveness, was also about Christian forgiveness: Leocadia's willingness to pardon—and then marry—the man who raped her.

The last in the series of "trial and redemption" novellas is found in the eighth spot. *La ilustre fregona* takes a relatively lighthearted approach to the crucible concept; it therefore contrasts sharply with the more serious and even symbolic treatment the subject received in the preceding "trial" stories. The themes of jealousy, beauty, and rape are reprised once again, but now in a minor key, without the gravity or intensity that characterized the earlier narratives.

Structurally speaking, *Fregona* strongly resembles *La gitanilla*, deviating from the lead story's pattern only in section C, where the narrative splits into two parallel plot threads, C^1 and C^2, during the period when the two central figures agree to go their separate ways (schema 48).

The narrator is obliged to split his vision here as he strives to relate the simultaneous adventures of Avendaño at the inn and Carriazo in town. Although the bifurcated linear projection of *Fregona*'s plot appears nowhere

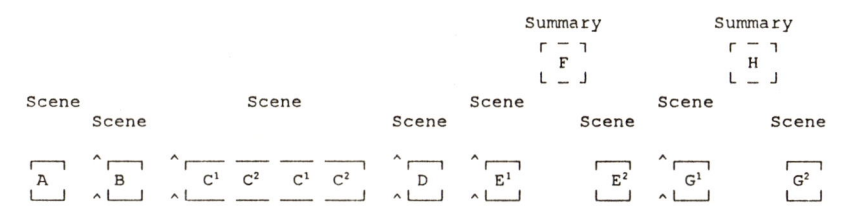

```
                                    Summary            Summary
                                    ┌ ─ ┐              ┌ ─ ┐
                                      F                  H
                                    └ ─ ┘              └ ─ ┘
  Scene           Scene           Scene           Scene
          Scene           Scene           Scene           Scene
  ┌─┐      ┌─┐     ┌──┬──┬──┬──┐     ┌─┐   ┌─┐     ┌─┐     ┌─┐      ┌─┐
   A        B      C¹  C²  C¹  C²     D    E¹       E²     G¹       G²
  └─┘     ^└─┘    ^└──┴──┴──┴──┘    ^└─┘  ^└─┘     └─┘    ^└─┘      └─┘
```

Schema 48. *La ilustre fregona*

else in *Novelas ejemplares*, we should note its similarity to the technique employed by Cide Hamete Benengeli in Part Two of the *Quixote* when he devotes alternate chapters to the adventures of first Don Quixote at the Duke's castle, then Sancho on the "island" of Barataria.

As we reach the final four stories in the collection, we observe a move away from the "trial and redemption" motif that has dominated the first eight novellas. The ninth and tenth tales, *Las dos doncellas* and *La señora Cornelia*, resurrect the omnipresent themes of jealousy and passion that played such an important role in the early stories and the *comedia nueva* of Lope de Vega (i.e., as vices easily aroused by great physical beauty). But now the popular issue of family honor replaces the trial motif as the chief motivating force.

The relationship between these two romantic narratives is approximately the same one we observed earlier between *Gitanilla* and *Amante*. They are variations on the same theme, two complementary approaches to the same basic story idea. *Doncellas* takes a more direct approach and features a much more tightly controlled plot, with little or no extraneous complication to distract the reader as the tale moves toward a swift resolution of the double-edged problem faced by the two heroines: how to restore the honor Teodosia and Leocadia have lost at the hands of the fickle Marco Antonio. The plot moves through three distinct phases, each in a different locale (schema 49).

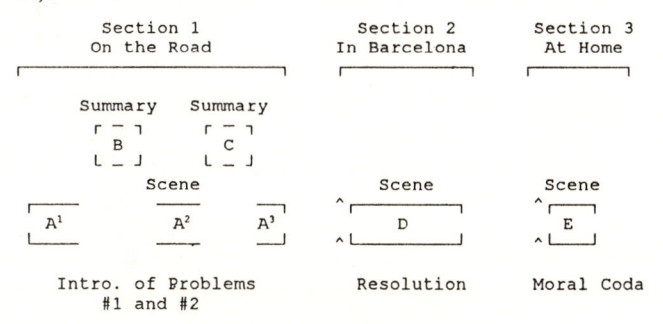

```
         Section 1              Section 2         Section 3
         On the Road            In Barcelona      At Home
      ┌─────────────────┐     ┌──────────┐      ┌──────────┐

         Summary   Summary
         ┌ ─ ┐     ┌ ─ ┐
           B         C
         └ ─ ┘     └ ─ ┘
                    Scene           Scene             Scene
      ┌──┐   ┌──┐   ┌──┐           ┌──────┐         ┌──────┐
       A¹    A²     A³               D                 E
      └──┘   └──┘   └──┘          ^└──────┘        ^└──────┘

      Intro. of Problems          Resolution        Moral Coda
          #1 and #2
```

Schema 49. *Las dos doncellas*

The same general pattern is repeated in *La señora Cornelia*. As we note in schema 50, the action again takes place in three stages, but there are twice as many plot complications.

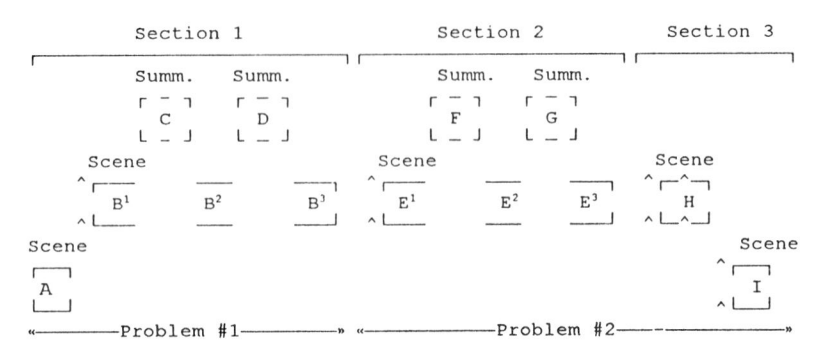

```
                Section 1                              Section 2                  Section 3
         ┌───────────────────────┐         ┌───────────────────────┐         ┌─────────────┐
           Summ.        Summ.                Summ.        Summ.
           ┌ ─ ┐        ┌ ─ ┐                ┌ ─ ┐        ┌ ─ ┐
             C            D                    F            G
           └ _ ┘        └ _ ┘                └ _ ┘        └ _ ┘
           Scene                              Scene                            Scene
           ^┌───┐                             ^┌───┐                           ^┌─^─┐
            B¹         B²         B³          E¹         E²         E³          H
           ^└───┘                             ^└───┘                           ^└─^─┘
   Scene                                                                                Scene
   ┌───┐                                                                                ^┌───┐
     A                                                                                    I
   └───┘                                                                                ^└───┘
   «─────────Problem #1─────────»   «─────────Problem #2─────────»
```

Schema 50. *La señora Cornelia*

In composing these two stories it appears that Cervantes was attempting to popularize in prose fiction the kind of family-honor intrigue that Lope had so successfully exploited on the stage. *Doncellas*, which mirrors the adventures of Dorotea and Luscinda from the 1605 *Quixote*, employs a relatively simple narrative structure, while *Cornelia* exhibits a more baroque, fugal arrangement.

The last two stories in the collection are the most firmly linked of all. The main characters from *El casamiento engañoso*, Peralta and Campuzano, become peripheral entities—but essential ones, from the standpoint of their critical remarks—in *El coloquio de los perros*, which follows it immediately.

Both stories are a curious blend of social and literary criticism. The commentary on social issues is at all times obvious; the literary issues are occasionally more difficult to fathom, but they, too, are present in both tales. For example, on the surface the *Casamiento* appears to be solely about the vice of hypocrisy, relating as it does the history of two unscrupulous lovers who manage to deceive one another by entering under false pretenses into a mutually unrewarding marital arrangement. The artful manner in which the story is told, however, reveals a hidden substratum of literary commentary as well. In telling his tale of mutual deceptions, the narrator Campuzano also lulls us into believing that we have all the essential information at our disposal. As the story draws to a close and the surprising final piece of information is revealed, the reader suddenly realizes that he, too, has been hoodwinked. Cervantes demonstrates here that deception, although potentially disastrous in social situations, can often be a positive and essential element in effective storytelling.

With regard to structure, the *Casamiento* consists principally of Ensign Campuzano's flashback account to his friend Peralta of his catastrophic marital adventure (B), with a brief preceding introduction (A) and a short concluding moral coda (C) for balance. The last few pages are not related at all to the ensign's woeful experience, but rather serve as an introduction to the *Coloquio* that follows (D) (see schema 51).

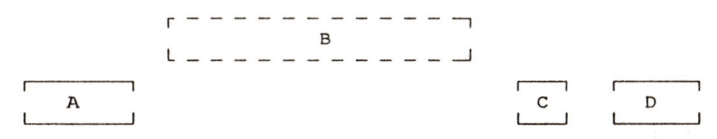

Schema 51. *El casamiento engañoso*

The *Coloquio*, which in tone and format resembles López Pinciano's *Philosophía antigua poética*, is openly concerned with literary issues. The dialogue between Cipión and Berganza tends to alternate between social and literary commentary. Berganza relates a series of personal anecdotes about the various masters he has served—often with mordant criticism of the individuals or certain social institutions with whom he has had contact—while Cipión repeatedly interrupts to critique Berganza's storytelling technique or to add his own views on the social issues raised. The story is told on four distinct levels, each one involving a different narrator-listener tandem; at each of the top three levels they discuss the verisimilitude or credibility of what has been related on the level immediately below. This is a reprise of the layered-criticism technique used by Cervantes at several points in the *Quixote*.

The combined *Casamiento/Coloquio* is a perfectly balanced narrative. Beginning at the topmost level (A), the narrative presents Peralta listening to Campuzano's report of his failed marriage; the story then descends slowly through a pair of intermediate levels (Campuzano overhearing Berganza and Cipión's conversation at level B; Cipión listening to Berganza's oral history at level C) until it reaches the netherworld inhabited by the Toledan witch Cañizares (D). This woman's strange reverie constitutes the bottom layer and functions as the structural midpoint of the story. After the witch concludes her account of demonic doings, the narration spirals back upward until it emerges again at the top with Peralta and Campuzano (schema 52).

Cervantes wisely opted to save his best and most innovative work for the end of his collection. I find it totally appropriate that, in a compilation

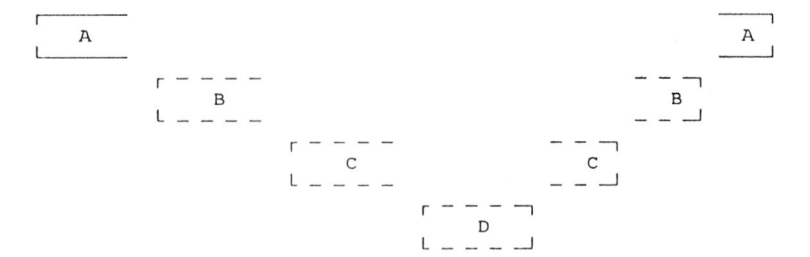

Schema 52. *El casamiento engañoso/El coloquio de los perros*

such as this, the final two tales should deal with the art of storytelling itself, and that the closing story should complete the circle by leading the reader back to the Prologue that introduces the anthology.

In conclusion, let me reiterate my belief that the traditional division of the *Novelas ejemplares* along the lines of "realistic" and "idealistic" tales is only superficially accurate. I have offered in this book a new theoretical approach to the reading of Cervantes's 1613 collection of short stories, one which will, I hope, inspire literary scholars to consider both the themes Cervantes introduced in his novellas and the innovative narrative techniques he used in crafting them.

Notes

INTRODUCTION

1. Ruth El Saffar, "Persiles' Retort: An Alchemical Angle on the Lovers' Labors." *Cervantes* 10, no. 1 (Spring 1990): 23.
2. Cervantes's clear preference for the feminine traits of Teodosia over the masculine attributes of Leocadia in *Las dos doncellas* is entirely consistent with the theory advanced by Ruth El Saffar, who proposes that Cervantes becomes a clear advocate of feminine psychological attributes as the basis for emotional stability in his late (post–1610) fiction. See Ruth El Saffar, *Beyond Fiction: The Recovery of the Feminine in the Novels of Cervantes* (Berkeley: University of California Press, 1984).
3. Ruth El Saffar, *Novel to Romance: A Study of Cervantes's "Novelas ejemplares"* (Baltimore: The Johns Hopkins University Press, 1974), 83.
4. Ibid., 13–29.
5. E. C. Riley, "Cervantes: A Question of Genre," in *Mediaeval and Renaissance Studies on Spain and Portugal in Honour of P. E. Russell*, ed. F. W. Hodcroft, D. G. Pattison, R. D. F. Pring-Mill, and R. W. Truman (Oxford: Society for the Study of Mediaeval Languages and Literature, 1981), 69–85.
6. Gonzalo Sobejano, "Sobre tipología y ordenación de las 'Novelas elemplares' (Artículo-reseña)," *Hispanic Review* 46, no. 1 (Winter 1978): 68–69.
7. E. Michael Gerli, "Romance and Novel: Idealism and Irony in *La gitanilla*," *Cervantes* 6, no. 1 (Spring 1986): 38.
8. See Riley, "Question of Genre," 76–77. Riley lists thirteen different properties of the prose romance that are most aptly applied to Cervantes's works:

1. The romance is either an adventure story or a love story, frequently a combination of the two.
2. The action normally involves a voyage, quest, or trial.
3. The romance is more akin to the myth than to the novel.
4. Supernatural elements are neither prohibited nor limited.
5. There are no empirical norms when it comes to matters of chronological order or geographic precision.
6. The main characters have been simplified, psychologically. Heroes and heroines are to some degree idealized; they are endowed with material gifts like physical beauty, youth, noble lineage, and family wealth; they also possess spiritual qualities like moral virtue and intelligence. They are, in effect, the crème de la crème of the aristocracy, and are often turned into psychological archetypes, symbols, or allegorical figures.

7. The moral issues are also simplified; and although virtue usually triumphs, a happy ending is not essential.

8. In the longer romances, a series of interwoven narratives may be introduced to provide a change of pace; some of these secondary tales may, in fact, be completely detachable from the main action.

9. The course of action and the final resolution of the characters' problems are governed by sudden changes of fortune and unforeseen revelations. Although modern readers would consider such improbable reversals to be merely instances of blind luck or heavy-handed authorial manipulation, Cervantes's contemporaries would have viewed them as examples of the curious workings of Divine Providence presiding over human events and giving meaning to human existence.

10. The stories often seem dreamlike, especially in instances of having one's secret dreams come true.

11. The narrative tends to employ an elevated verbal style.

12. The descriptive passages are often characterized by profuse, sensual, and visually graphic details.

13. The romance is excessively style-conscious, in the sense that it tends to reflect the taste and sensibility of the historical moment in which it is written; this explains why certain romances soon lose their appeal and fall out of favor.

9. Unless otherwise specified, all references to the *Novelas ejemplares* will be taken from Harry Sieber, ed., *Novelas ejemplares*, by Miguel de Cervantes, 2 vols. (Madrid: Cátedra, 1980–81). The accompanying English translations are from B. W. Ife, ed., *Exemplary Novels*, by Miguel de Cervantes Saavedra, 4 vols. (Warminster, England: Aris & Phillips, 1992).

10. Elias L. Rivers, "On the Prefatory Pages of *Don Quixote*, Part II." *Modern Language Notes* 76 (1960): 215. I am grateful to my friend and colleague Catherine Davis Vinel for pointing out the ironic tone of these prefatory paragraphs.

11. Gerli, "Idealism and Irony," 30.

12. Francisco Rodríguez-Marín, *La ilustre fregona, novela de Miguel de Cervantes Saavedra* (Madrid: Revista de Archivos, Bibliotecas y Museos, 1917), x.

13. William C. Atkinson, "Cervantes, el Pinciano, and the *Novelas ejemplares*," *Hispanic Review* 16 (July 1948): 194.

14. Joaquín Casalduero, *Sentido y forma de las "Novelas ejemplares"* (Madrid: Gredos, 1962), 28–30.

15. El Saffar, *Novel to Romance*, 84–85.

16. Sobejano, "Sobre tipología," 73.

17. Riley, "Question of Genre," 77–78.

18. Alban K. Forcione, *Cervantes and the Humanist Vision: A Study of Four "Exemplary Novels"* (Princeton: Princeton University Press, 1982), 27.

19. Julio Rodríguez-Luis, *Novedad y ejemplo de las "Novelas" de Cervantes*, 2 vols. (Madrid: Porrúa-Turanzas, 1980–84), 1:11–12.

20. Albert A. Sicroff, "The Demise of Exemplarity in Cervantes' *Novelas Ejemplares*," in *Hispanic Studies in Honor of Joseph H. Silverman*, ed. Joseph V. Ricapito (Newark, Del.: Juan de la Cuesta, 1988), 345–60.

21. L. A. Murillo, "Narrative Structures in the *Novelas ejemplares*: An Outline," *Cervantes* 8, no. 2 (Fall 1988): 231–50.

22. Nicholas Spadaccini and Jenaro Talens, "Cervantes and the Dialogic World," in *Cervantes's "Exemplary Novels" and the Adventure of Writing*, ed. Michael Nerlich and Nicholas Spadaccini (Minneapolis: The Prisma Institute/University of Minnesota Press, 1989), 205–45.

23. Jean Canavaggio, *Cervantes*, trans. J. R. Jones (New York: Norton, 1990), 254.

24. Seymour Chatman, *Story and Discourse: Narrative Structure in Fiction and Film* (Ithaca, N.Y.: Cornell University Press, 1978).

25. See Gérard Genette, *Narrative Discourse: An Essay in Method* (Ithaca, N.Y.: Cornell University Press, 1980).

26. Ibid., 47–67.

Chapter 1. Cervantes and the Crucible of Love

1. The theme of jealousy (*celos*), so common in Spanish Golden Age literature, is a constant one in the *Novelas ejemplares*. I believe that Cervantes's interest in romantic complications and the various problems associated with the phenomenon of male jealousy was the principal reason for including *El celoso extremeño* among the stories collected in the 1613 work. I have argued previously (*Cervantes: Pioneer and Plagiarist*, 1982) that *El celoso extremeño* was probably not Cervantes's own invention, but rather an anonymous tale discovered by the great writer—probably in the Porras manuscript—reconstituted to reflect Cervantes's own artistic and moral standards, and then published as his own in the *Novelas ejemplares*. Certain aspects of the original had to be expunged and/or altered to conform to Cervantes's rather unconventional views on the subject of jealousy and revenge; this would explain the less verisimilar but more morally upright comportment of Carrizales's bride in the published version versus the adulterous behavior she is guilty of in the Porras account. Cervantes apparently felt a strong attraction to the theme announced in the title and decided to rework the material to suit his own artistic and moral values.

2. Avalle-Arce, "*La Gitanilla*," *Cervantes* 1, nos. 1–2 (Fall 1981): 15; Frank Pierce, "*La gitanilla*: A Tale of High Romance," *Bulletin of Hispanic Studies* 54, no. 4 (October 1977): 285; Hart, "Versions of Pastoral in Three *Novelas ejemplares*," *Bulletin of Hispanic Studies* 58, no. 4 (October 1981): 284; Ter Horst, "Une saison en enfer: *La gitanilla*," *Cervantes* 5, no. 2 (Fall 1985): 89, 105; Gerli, "Romance and Novel: Idealism and Irony in *La gitanilla*," *Cervantes* 6, no. 1 (Spring 1986): 37.

3. S. F. Boyd, "The Mystery of Cervantes' *La gitanilla*," *Forum for Modern Language Studies* (St. Andrews, Scotland) 17, no. 4 (October 1981): 312.

4. Gerli, "Romance and Novel," 30–31.

5. Ibid., 38.

6. Unless otherwise specified, all citations from Cervantes's novellas are taken from Harry Sieber, ed., *Novelas ejemplares*, by Miguel de Cervantes, 2 vols. (Madrid: Cátedra, 1980–81). The accompanying English translations are from B. W. Ife, ed., *Exemplary Novels*, by Miguel de Cervantes Saavedra, 4 vols. (Warminster, England: Aris & Phillips, 1992).

7. L. J. Woodward, "*La gitanilla*," in *Cervantes: Su obra y su mundo: Actas del I Congreso Internacional sobre Cervantes*, ed. Manuel Criado de Val (Madrid: EDI-6, 1981), 446.

8. Félix Martínez-Bonati, "Forms of Mimesis and Ideological Rhetoric in Cervantes's *La gitanilla*," in *Textual Analysis: Some Readers Reading*, ed. Mary Ann Caws (New York: Modern Language Association of America, 1986), 64–73.

9. Woodward, "*La gitanilla*," 447.

10. Isaías Lerner, "Marginalidad en las novelas ejemplares, I: *La gitanilla*," *Lexis* 4, no. 1 (July 1980): 48–49.

11. Casalduero, *Sentido y forma*, 59; Forcione, *Cervantes and the Humanist Vision*, 136–37; Ricapito, *Cervantes's "Novelas Ejemplares": Between History and Creativity*, Purdue Studies in Romance Literatures 10 (West Lafayette, Ind.: Purdue University Press, 1996), 34.

12. Gerli, "Romance and Novel," 35; Resina, "Laissez faire y reflexividad erótica en *La gitanilla*," *MLN* 106, no. 2 (March 1991): 261; Sánchez, "Theater within the Novel: Mass Audience and Individual Reader in *La gitanilla* and *Rinconete y Cortadillo*," in Nerlich and Spadaccini, eds., *Cervantes's "Exemplary Novels,"* 73–98.

13. Rodríguez-Luis, *Novedad y ejemplo*, 1:110–13.

14. Francisco Márquez Villanueva, "La buenaventura de Preciosa." *Nueva Revista de Filología Hispánica* 34, no. 2 (1985–86): 759–68.

15. Boyd, "The Mystery," 315–20.

16. Lerner, "Marginalidad," 52.

17. The significance of the first encounter of Preciosa and the page-poet is signaled by Cervantes's use of direct quotes to record their conversation. The fact that the verbal exchange is recorded verbatim indicates, according to one critic, that the mysterious stranger is destined to be one of the principal characters of the story; the strategy is designed to pique the reader's interest in her future negotiations with the young man. We should contrast this with the immediately preceding scene, the conversation between the admiring Teniente and a crowd of people who had gathered to enjoy Preciosa's curbside performance, where the actual verbal exchange is not repeated directly. On this occasion, the narrator, not wishing to give primary speaking roles to purely secondary characters, achieves the desired effect by summarizing their remarks, leaving the reader with only the final effect of the discussion, i.e., the favorable impression that Preciosa creates when she performs. See Wolfgang Kayser, *Interpretación y análisis de la obra literaria*, trans. M. D. Mouton and V. G. Yebra (Madrid: Gredos, 1958), 238–40.

18. Karl-Ludwig Selig, "Concerning the Structure of Cervantes' *La gitanilla*," *Romanistisches Jahrbuch* 13 (1962): 273–76; Casalduero, *Sentido y forma*, 58; Güntert, "*La gitanilla* y la poética de Cervantes." *Boletin de la Real Academia Española* 52 (1972): 108, 124; El Saffar, *Novel to Romance*, 101; Pierce, "*La gitanilla*: A Tale of High Romance," 285; Anne E. Wiltrout, "Role Playing and Rites of Passage: *La ilustre fregona* and *La gitanilla*," *Hispania* 64, no. 3 (1981): 398; Spieker, "Preciosa y poesía: sobre el concepto cervantino de la poesía y la estructura de *La gitanilla*," *Explicación de Textos Literarios* 4, no. 2 (1975–76): 220; Forcione, *Humanist Vision*, 218.

19. William H. Clamurro, "Value & Identity in 'La gitanilla,'" *Journal of Hispanic Philology* 14, no. 1 (Autumn 1989): 48.

20. Rodríguez-Luis, *Novedad y ejemplo*, 1:122–23.

21. Alban K. Forcione, *Cervantes, Aristotle and the "Persiles"* (Princeton: Princeton University Press, 1970), 306–19.

22. Pierce, "*La gitanilla*: A Tale of High Romance," 291.

23. Ter Horst, "Une saison en enfer," 95 n. 9.

24. Wiltrout, "Role-Playing," 395.

25. Lesley Lipson, "'La palabra hecha nada': Mendacious Discourse in *La gitanilla*," *Cervantes* 9, no. 1 (Spring 1989): 35–53.

26. These very perceptive remarks were made in a paper which Prof. Krummrich delivered at a 1982 NEH Seminar and has generously placed at my disposal: "Tentative Notes toward an Article on *La gitanilla*," 14.

27. Thomas R. Hart, *Cervantes' Exemplary Fictions: A Study of the "Novelas ejemplares"* (Lexington: University Press of Kentucky, 1994), 33.

28. Wiltrout, "Role Playing," 399.

29. Krummrich, "Tentative Notes," 16.

30. Clamurro, "Value and Identity," 53.

31. Lerner, "Marginalidad," 53.

32. Casalduero, *Sentido y forma*, 77.

33. El Saffar, *Novel to Romance*, 101.

34. Forcione, *Humanist Vision*, 215.
35. Casalduero, *Sentido y forma*, 65.
36. Resina, "Laissez faire," 272.
37. Rodríguez-Luis, *Novedad y ejemplo*, 1:130–31. The critic goes on to suggest that Clemente may represent none other than Cervantes himself: a failed poet whose career is aborted by events beyond his own control. Rodríguez-Luis also notes that the initials of two of the page-poet's various aliases, S[ancho] and C[lemente], are the reverse of the author's own C[ervantes] S[aavedra] (1:132).
38. As I shall point out in a later section of this study, this is the same type of stylistic contrast Cervantes draws in the story of the Capitán Cautivo (*Don Quixote* 1, chaps. 39–41). The action-packed trials of the Christian captive Ruy Pérez de Viedma play out rapidly, very much in accord with the rhythms of the traditional Byzantine romance; conversely, the intense clash of emotions aboard ship between the hero's future wife Zoraida and her father, Agi Morato, is portrayed with the deliberate, decidedly more character-oriented narrative technique of the modern novel.
39. Sánchez, "Theater within the Novel," 88.
40. Catherine Davis Vinel, "Multi-genred Texts in Cervantes's *Novelas ejemplares*" (Master's thesis, University of South Carolina, 1993), 5–37.
41. Lipson, "'La palabra hecha nada,'" 36.
42. Carroll B. Johnson, "De economías y linajes en 'La Gitanilla,'" *Mester* 25, no. 1 (Spring 1996): 41.
43. Ibid., 39.
44. Clamurro, "Value and Identity," 59–60.
45. Wiltrout, "Role Playing," 388.
46. Hart, *Cervantes' Exemplary Fictions*, 38.
47. Rodríguez-Luis, *Novedad y ejemplo*, 1:149.
48. A contrary judgment is made by Julio Rodríguez-Luis, who considers the design of *La gitanilla* to be the fundamentally dramatic one, since it reserves for the final scene the revelation of the various characters' true human qualities. The true origins of the heroine Preciosa provide a convenient, last-minute solution to the various problems that have arisen, but they play no role whatsoever in determining the course of events within the story itself. Costanza's prehistory, on the other hand, has a profound effect on certain other characters in the story and is worthy of more detailed presentation in the final pages. Consequently, *La ilustre fregona*, despite sharing virtually the same narrative design as its predecessor, is seen to be less theatrical than *Gitanilla*, conforming more to the traditions and norms of the fictional prose romance (*Novedad y ejemplo*, 1:164–67).
49. B. W. Ife, "From Salamanca to Brighton Rock: Names and Places in Cervantes' *La ilustre fregona*," in *Essays in Honour of Robert Brian Tate from His Colleagues and Pupils*, ed. Richard A. Cardwell (Nottingham, U.K.: University of Nottingham, Department of Hispanic Studies, 1984), 46–52.
50. Wiltrout, "Role Playing," 388.
51. Rodríguez-Luis, *Novedad y ejemplo*, 1:142.
52. Sieber, ed., *Novelas ejemplares*, 2:21.
53. Juan Bautista Avalle-Arce, introduction to *Cervantes: Three Exemplary Novels* (New York: Dell, 1964), 8.
54. Ibid., 11.
55. Javier Herrero, "Emerging Realism: Love and Cash in *La ilustre fregona*," in *From Dante to García Márquez*, ed. Gene H. Bell-Villada, Antonio Giménez, and George Pistorius (Williamstown, Mass.: Williams College, 1987), 47–59.
56. Ibid., 54–57.
57. Hart, "Versions of Pastoral," 283–85.

58. Robert M. Johnston, "Picaresque and Pastoral in *La ilustre fregona,*" in *Cervantes and the Renaissance*, ed. Michael D. McGaha (Easton, Pa.: Juan de la Cuesta, 1980), 167–77.

59. Ana María Barrenechea, "*La ilustre fregona* como ejemplo de estructura novelesca cervantina," in *Actas del Primer Congreso Internacional de Hispanistas, Celebrado en Oxford del 6 al 11 de Septiembre de 1962*, ed. Frank Pierce and Cyril A. Jones (Oxford: Dolphin, 1964), 199–206.

60. Ibid., 201.

61. Ibid., 201; Rodríguez-Luis, *Novedad y ejemplo*, 1:145.

62. Monique Joly, "Para una reinterpretación de *La ilustre fregona*: Ensayo de tipología cervantina," in *Aureum Saeculum Hispanum: Beiträge zu Texten des Siglo de Oro*, ed. Karl-Hermann Körner and Dietrich Briesemeister (Wiesbaden: Steiner, 1983), 103–16.

63. Thomas Hanrahan, "Cervantes and the Moralists," *Hispania* 73, no. 4 (December 1990): 917.

64. Casalduero, *Sentido y forma*, 193.

65. El Saffar, *Novel to Romance*, 105–6.

66. Wiltrout, "Role Playing," 390–92.

67. Ife, "From Salamanca to Brighton Rock," 51.

68. Barrenechea, "*La ilustre fregona* como ejemplo," 202–3.

69. Joaquín Casalduero, "Notas sobre *La ilustre fregona*," *Anales Cervantinos* 3 (1953): 334.

70. Ife, "From Salamanca to Brighton Rock," 50–52.

71. Casalduero, "Notas," 335.

72. Theresa Ann Sears, *A Marriage of Convenience: Ideal and Ideology in the "Novelas ejemplares"* (New York: Peter Lang, 1993), 46.

73. Jorge Checa, "El *romance* y su sombra: Hibridación genérica en *La ilustre fregona,*" *Revista de Estudios Hispánicos* 25 (1991): 31.

74. Casalduero, *Sentido y forma*, 193; Ife, "From Salamanca to Brighton Rock," 51; Wiltrout, "Role Playing," 389.

Chapter 2. Patterns of Symmetrical Design in *El amante liberal, La fuerza de la sangre,* and *La española inglesa*

An earlier—and much more limited—draft of this chapter was published in 1994. See E. T. Aylward, "Patterns of Symmetrical Design in *La fuerza de la sangre* and *La española inglesa,*" *Crítica Hispánica* 16, no. 2 (1994): 189–203.

1. Casalduero, *Sentido y forma*, 81. A different structure is suggested by Eleodoro J. Febres, who posits a tripartite division: (1) from the opening scene up to the arrival of the Jewish trader at the Cypriot capital with Leonisa in tow; (2) from that point to the finish of the naval battle; and (3) from the battle to the conclusion. See Eleodoro J. Febres, "Forma y sentido de *El amante liberal,*" *Anales Cervantinos* 19 (1981): 93–103.

2. Agustín G. Amezúa y Mayo, *Cervantes, creador de la novela corta española*, 2 vols. (Madrid: Consejo Superior de Investigaciones Científicas, 1956–58): 2:60.

3. Karl-Ludwig Selig, "Some Observations on Cervantes' *El amante liberal,*" *Revista Hispánica Moderna* 40, nos. 1–2 (1978–79): 68.

4. El Saffar, *Novel to Romance*.

5. Gonzalo Díaz Migoyo, "La ficción cordial de *El amante liberal,*" *Nueva Revista de Filología Hispánica* 35, no. 1 (1987): 135.

6. Rodríguez-Luis, *Novedad y ejemplo*, 1:13–30.
7. Guillermo Díaz Plaja, "La técnica narrativa de Cervantes (algunas observaciones)." *Revista de Filología Española* 32 (1948): 259. Febres, "Forma y sentido," 100.
8. Febres, "Forma y sentido," 101.
9. Thomas A. Pabon, "Courtship and Marriage in *El amante liberal*: The Symbolic Quest for Self-Perfectibility," *Hispanófila* 26 (September 1982): 52.
10. Díaz Migoyo, "La ficción cordial," 150.
11. Nina Cox Davis, "The Tyranny of Love in *El amante liberal*," *Cervantes* 13, no. 2 (Fall 1993): 110–11.
12. Louis Combet, *Cervantès ou les incertitudes du désir* (Lyons: Presses Universitaires de Lyons, 1981). Combet tends to overstate the case, but his point about Cervantes's penchant for presenting marriageable males as simpering wimps is well taken.
13. For a brief summary of twentieth-century distaste for *Amante* (versus the popularity it enjoyed in Cervantes's time), see Hart, *Cervantes' Exemplary Fictions*, 41.
14. Jennifer Lowe, "A Note on Cervantes' *El amante liberal*," *Romance Notes* 12 (1971): 400–403.
15. All references to the Cervantes text are taken from Harry Sieber, ed., *Novelas ejemplares*, by Miguel de Cervantes, 2 vols. (Madrid: Cátedra, 1980–81). The accompanying English translations are from B. W. Ife, ed., *Exemplary Novels*, by Miguel de Cervantes Saavedra, 4 vols. (Warminster, England: Aris & Phillips, 1992).
16. For a more detailed discussion regarding the many homosexual and feminine allusions Ricardo makes to his rival Cornelio, see Miguel A. Bello, "Una lectura semántica de *El amante liberal*," *Romance Notes* 24 (1983): 132–36.
17. This is the same fortress whose recapture by the Moors some years later constituted a major section of the Cautivo's Story in *Don Quixote*, Part One.
18. El Saffar, *Novel to Romance*, 146.
19. Díaz Migoyo, "La ficción cordial," 145.
20. Sears, *Marriage of Convenience*, 139.
21. Ibid., 164.
22. M. M. Bakhtin, *Dialogic Imagination: Four Essays*, trans. Caryl Emerson and Michael Holquist, ed. Michael Holquist (Austin: University of Texas Press, 1981), 86ff.
23. See Hart, *Cervantes' Exemplary Fictions*, 53. Hart's observation regarding the ways in which Cervantes deviates from the conventions of the Greek romance has been elaborated in a recent master's thesis by Sharon Eadie Knight, "Cervantes and Heliodorus: Elements of the Greek Romance in *El amante liberal* and *La española inglesa*" (University of South Carolina, 1996). Ms. Knight proposes that while Cervantes emulates in the *Amante* some of the technical aspects of Heliodorus's *Ethiopian History* (e.g., the use of "adventure time" and the visual vividness of important scenes), he also infuses his story with several non-Byzantine elements like plausible psychological development in his protagonists and the portrayal of contemporary sociopolitical issues (e.g., the intense rivalry between European Christians and Muslim Turks in the Mediterranean region). The result is a Cervantine hybrid, a short story that manages to combine the marvelous elements of the traditional Greek romance with an element that would eventually become the hallmark of the modern novel: the realistic representation of contemporary society (80–81).
24. Casalduero, *Sentido y forma*, 150.
25. El Saffar, *Novel to Romance*, 129.
26. Robert V. Piluso, "*La fuerza de la sangre*: un análisis estructural," *Hispania* 47 (1964): 485–90; Karl-Ludwig Selig, "Some Observations on *La fuerza de la sangre*," *MLN* 87, no. 6 (1972): 121–25; Margarita Levisi, "La función de lo visual en '*La fuerza de la sangre*,'" *Hispanófila* 49 (1973): 30–46; David M. Gitlitz, "Symmetry and Lust in Cervantes' *La fuerza de la sangre*," in *Studies in Honor of Everett W. Hesse*, ed. William C. McCrary

and José A. Madrigal (Lincoln, Ne.: Society of Spanish and Spanish-American Studies, 1981), 113–22.

27. El Saffar, *Novel to Romance*, 136–37.
28. Forcione, *Cervantes and the Humanist Vision*, 386–87.
29. Rodríguez-Luis, *Novedad y ejemplo*, 1:69.
30. Casalduero, *Sentido y forma*, 166.
31. Piluso, "Un análisis estructural," 487.
32. Rodríguez-Luis, *Novedad y ejemplo*, 1:58, 68.
33. El Saffar, *Novel to Romance*, 132.
34. Forcione, *Humanist Vision*, 380.
35. El Saffar, *Novel to Romance*, 128.
36. Forcione, *Humanist Vision*, 328.
37. Rodríguez-Luis, *Novedad y ejemplo*, 1:56.
38. Patricia E. Grieve, "Embroidering with Saintly Threads: María de Zayas Challenges Cervantes and the Church," *Renaissance Quarterly* 44, no. 1 (Spring 1991): 86–105.
39. Rodríguez-Luis, *Novedad y ejemplo*, 1:63.
40. Clearly, Cervantes's primitive portrayal of the psychology of rape in *Fregona* and *Fuerza* is inconsistent with the findings of recent scientific research on this ugly social phenomenon. We know now that sexual violations are more about the abuse of power than they are about carnal gratification. Consequently, the modern reader must approach these two novellas with an even greater suspension of disbelief than we would normally accord a work of fiction. It would be wrong, however, to denigrate Cervantes's treatment of this delicate subject, as Grieve has done, for not having a woman's perspective on the issue or because he does not display the enlightened societal attitudes toward sexual misconduct that have evolved in the late twentieth century. Any historical figure must be judged vis-à-vis the social mores of his/her own times. It would be equally unfair to censure George Washington or Thomas Jefferson for having owned African slaves in the eighteenth century.
41. El Saffar, *Novel to Romance*, 128–29.
42. John J. Allen traces the origins of the crucifix-as-witness motif to an old Toledan legend, later utilized by the romantic poet Zorrilla in "A buen juez, mejor testigo," in which a statue of Christ plays the key role. He adds that Gonzalo de Berceo used the crucifix in the same way in *La deuda pagada*. See Allen, "*El Cristo de la Vega* and *La fuerza de la sangre*," *MLN* 83 (1968): 271–75.
43. R. P. Calcraft, "Structure, Symbol and Meaning in Cervantes's *La fuerza de la sangre*," *Bulletin of Hispanic Studies* 58, no. 3 (July 1981): 197–204; Nina M. Scott, "Honor and Family in *La fuerza de la sangre*," in *Studies in Honor of Ruth Lee Kennedy*, ed. Vern G. Williamsen and A. F. Michael Atlee (Chapel Hill, N.C.: Estudios de Hispanófila, 1977), 125–32; Gitlitz, "Symmetry and Lust," 114; Dina de Rentiis, "Cervantes's *La fuerza de la sangre* and the Force of Negation," in Nerlich and Spadaccini, eds., *Cervantes's "Exemplary Novels,"* 157–74.
44. Marcia Welles, "Violence Disguised: Representation of Rape in Cervantes' 'La fuerza de la sangre,'" *Journal of Hispanic Philology* 13, no. 3 (Spring 1989): 242.
45. Grieve, "Embroidering," 95.
46. Scott, "Honor and Family," 131.
47. Calcraft, "Structure, Symbol and Meaning," 201.
48. Rentiis, "The Force of Negation," 166–69.
49. Adriana Slaniceanu, "The Calculating Woman in Cervantes' *La fuerza de la sangre*," *Bulletin of Hispanic Studies* 64, no. 2 (April 1987): 101–10.
50. Edward H. Friedman, "Cervantes's *La fuerza de la sangre* and the Rhetoric of Power," in Nerlich and Spadaccini, eds., *Cervantes's "Exemplary Novels,"* 125–56.

51. Gitlitz, "Symmetry and Lust," 119–21.
52. Welles, "Violence Disguised," 250.
53. Friedman, "The Rhetoric of Power," 154.
54. Catherine Davis Vinel, "Double Discourse in Cervantes's *Novelas ejemplares*," (Ph.D. diss., University of South Carolina, 1994), 222–35.
55. Gitlitz, "Symmetry and Lust," 116.
56. Stacey L. Parker Aronson, "La 'textualización' de Leocadia y su defensa en *La fuerza de la sangre*," *Cervantes* 16, no. 2 (Fall 1996): 71–88.
57. El Saffar, *Novel to Romance*, 150.
58. David Cluff, "The Structure and Theme of *La española inglesa*: A Reconsideration," *Revista de Estudios Hispánicos* 10 (1976): 261.
59. Thomas A. Pabon, "The Symbolic Significance of Marriage in Cervantes' 'La española inglesa,'" *Hispanófila* 63 (1978): 59–66.
60. Rodríguez-Luis, *Novedad y ejemplo*, 1:51.
61. Mercedes Alcázar Ortega, "Palabra, memoria y aspiración literaria en *La española inglesa*," *Cervantes* 15, no. 1 (Spring 1995): 33–45.
62. Carroll B. Johnson, "*La española inglesa* and the Practice of Literary Production," *Viator* 19 (1988): 377–416.
63. Casalduero, *Sentido y forma*, 119.
64. Guillermo Díaz Plaja, "La técnica narrativa de Cervantes (algunas observaciones)." *Revista de Filología Española* 32 (1948): 237–68. In contrast to Casalduero's binary construct for *Española inglesa*, Díaz-Plaja had proposed three narrative phases: (1) a harmonic ascent to happiness; (2) a catastrophic decline; and (3) the grand finale.
65. Jennifer Lowe, "The Structure of Cervantes' *La española inglesa*," *Romance Notes* 9, no. 2 (1968): 287–90.
66. Guido Mancini, "La 'morale' della *Española inglesa*," in *Aspetti e problemi delle letterature iberiche: Studi offerti a Franco Meregalli*, ed. Giuseppe Bellini (Rome: Bulzoni, 1981), 219–36.
67. Díaz-Plaja, "La tècnica narrativa," 262.
68. Cluff, "The Structure and Theme," 265–67.
69. Ibid., 268.
70. Rodolfo Schevill and Adolfo Bonilla, ed., *Novelas ejemplares*, by Miguel de Cervantes Saavedra, 3 vols. (Madrid: Gráficas Reunidas, 1922–25); Georges Hainesworth, *Les "Novelas ejemplares" de Cervantès en France au XVIIe Siècle* (Paris, Champion, 1933); Mack Singleton, "The Date of *La española inglesa*," *Hispania* 30, no. 3 (August 1947): 329–35.
71. Francisco Rodríguez Marín, *El Loaysa de "El celoso extremeño"* (Sevilla: P. Díaz, 1901), 235; cited in El Saffar, *Novel to Romance*, 150 n. 10.
72. Amezúa y Mayo, *Cervantes, creador*, 2:126–27.
73. Singleton, "The Date of *La española inglesa*," 333.
74. Rodríguez-Luis, *Novedad y ejemplo*, 1:31–32, n. 1.
75. Geoffrey Stagg, "The Composition and Revision of 'La española inglesa,'" in *Studies in Honor of Bruce W. Wardropper*, ed. Dian Fox, Harry Sieber, and Robert Ter Horst (Newark, Del: Juan de la Cuesta, 1989), 305–21.
76. El Saffar, *Novel to Romance*, 152–53.
77. Johnson, "The Practice of Literary Production," 384–85.
78. Spain and Portugal were united under a single crown—Spain's—from 1580 to 1665.
79. Cluff, "The Structure and Theme," 263–64.
80. The ploy of using a poisoned piece of fruit to alter radically the life of a story's protagonist can be traced back at least to the Bible and was a popular device in Renaissance

fiction. Cervantes uses it again in the very next tale when he provides a doctored quince to cause the strange madness of the Licenciado Vidriera.

81. El Saffar, *Novel to Romance*, 159.
82. Rodríguez-Luis, *Novedad y ejemplo*, 1:43.
83. Alcázar Ortega, "Palabra, memoria y aspiración literaria," 44.
84. Johnson, "The Practice of Literary Production," 403.
85. Vinel, "Double Discourse," 134.
86. The original ten thousand escudos Isabela is awarded in London (1: 272) are converted into ten thousand *ducados* when they are collected in Seville (1:274). The same is true in Ricaredo's case: the certificate in the amount of sixteen hundred escudos that he has drawn up in Italy is redeemed for the same number of *ducados* in Algiers and later Seville (1:279, 281, 282). According to Bruce W. Wardropper, the value of a *ducado* was slightly higher ($2.00) than that of an escudo ($1.65); if all the escudos received in England were later redeemed in *ducados*, the payee would receive an additional 21.21 percent in the exchange. See Bruce W. Wardropper, *Teatro español del Siglo de Oro* (New York: Scribner's, 1970), 904–5. Jean Canavaggio, on the other hand, reports the value of an escudo (in 1989 gold prices) at $34.00, the gold *ducado* at $36.50 (315). By his reckoning, the resulting bonus would be merely 7.35 percent. In any case, Cervantes's two protagonists clearly seem to be making a tidy profit in exchanging gold escudos for the same number of *ducados*. See Jean Canavaggio, *Cervantes*, trans. J. R. Jones (New York: Norton, 1990), 315.
87. Casalduero, *Sentido y forma*, 133–34.
88. Stanislav Zimic, "El *Amadís* cervantino: Apuntes sobre *La española inglesa*," *Anales Cervantinos* 25–26 (1987–88): 467–83.
89. María Caterina Ruta, "*La española inglesa*: El desdoblamiento del héroe," *Anales Cervantinos* 25–26 (1987–88): 371–82.
90. Adam Gai, "El cronotopos de *La española inglesa*," *Neophilologus* 9, no. 1 (Jan. 1985): 67–74; Cluff, "The Structure and Theme," 263; Johnson, "The Practice of Literary Production," 402, 405; Sieber, ed., *Novelas ejemplares*, 1:29–30.
91. Casalduero, *Sentido y forma*, 131.
92. Johnson, "The Practice of Literary Production." 403–4.
93. Marsha S. Collins, "Transgression and Transfiguration in Cervantes's *La española inglesa*," *Cervantes* 16, no. 1 (Spring 1996): 54–73.
94. Rodríguez-Luis, *Novedad y ejemplo*, 1:50.
95. Johnson, "The Practice of Literary Production," 408.
96. Catherine Davis Vinel echoes Johnson's economic interpretation of *Española* in her discussion of the story's characters. In Vinel's eye, when Clotaldo abducts Isabel he is representing the old economic order, the aristocrats whose economic and social prosperity is traditionally derived from a combination of plunder and astute matrimonial alliances. Ricaredo, on the other hand, represents a new kind of aristocracy that willingly embraces an alliance with the new, emerging merchant class that was about to take control of Spain's economy. What makes Vinel's analysis especially noteworthy is the daring thematic connection she makes between *La española inglesa* and the preceding *Rinconete y Cortadillo*. In her analysis, Monipodio and Clotaldo are linked by their stodgy economic conservatism, while the enterprising young boys are akin to Ricaredo in their attempt to become members of the new merchant class of Seville. See Vinel, "Double Discourse," 134–35.
97. Gai, "El cronotopos," 67.
98. Zimic, "El *Amadís* cervantino," 471.
99. Sharon Eadie Knight notes that although *La española inglesa* shares at least fifteen plot motifs with the Greek romance, it contains several key elements that set it apart from the Heliodoran model: the heroine is passive, immutable and not of noble lineage; purely

economic interests play a major role in the development of the plot; and the story is set in a distinctly contemporary milieu. See "Cervantes and Heliodorus," 91–97.
  100. Riley, "Question of Genre," 69–85.
  101. Vinel, "Double Discourse," 123.
  102. Collins, "Transgression and Transfiguration," 59.
  103. El Saffar, *Novel to Romance*, 161.
  104. Cluff, "The Structure and Theme," 276.
  105. El Saffar, *Novel to Romance*, 159; Cluff, "The Structure and Theme," 269.
  106. Gai, "El cronotopos," 67–68.
  107. Cluff, "The Structure and Theme," 278.
  108. Manuel da Costa Fontes, "Love as an Equalizer in *La española inglesa*," *Romance Notes* 16 (1975): 742–48.
  109. Sicroff, "The Demise of Exemplarity, 345–60.
  110. Ricapito, *Cervantes's "Novelas Ejemplares,"* 53.
  111. Casalduero, *Sentido y forma*, 130–31.
  112. Cluff, "The Structure and Theme," 280–81.
  113. Vinel, "Double Discourse," 158.

Chapter 3. Porras's Manuscript and the Curious Configuration of *R/C, ZE,* and *LV*

  1. E. T. Aylward, *Cervantes: Pioneer and Plagiarist* (London: Tamesis, 1982).
  2. E. T. Aylward, "Lighten up, Geoffrey!" *Cervantes* 14, no. 1 (Spring 1994): 109–15. This article is a reply to Geoffrey Stagg, "The Refracted Image: Porras and Cervantes," *Cervantes* 4, no. 2 (Fall 1984): 139–53.
  3. Aylward, *Pioneer and Plagiarist*, 13–18.
  4. All citations from the Porras versions of *R/C* and *ZE* are from Rodolfo Schevill and Adolfo Bonilla, ed. *Novelas ejemplares*, by Miguel de Cervantes Saavedra, 3 vols. (Madrid: Gráficas Reunidas, 1922–25); in all cases the names of the editors will precede the page references given in parentheses. All English translations of the Porras version are my own.
  5. All citations from the 1613 Cervantine version of *R/C, ZE,* and *LV* are from Harry Sieber, ed., *Novelas ejemplares*, by Miguel de Cervantes (Madrid: Cátedra, 1980–81); in all cases the editor's name will precede the page references given in parentheses. The accompanying English translations are from B. W. Ife, ed., *Exemplary Novels*, by Miguel de Cervantes Saavedra, 4 vols. (Warminster, England: Aris & Phillips, 1992).
  6. Of the other tales, only *La fuerza de la sangre* fails to leap backward in time at some point; in place of the usual flashback recapitulation, in *Fuerza* Cervantes provides two brief interludes dealing with Rodolfo's comfortable seven-year hiatus in Italy following his rape of Leocadia. The effect is the same: the main action taking place in Toledo (Leocadia's pregnancy, the birth of Luisico, plus the unusual circumstances that serve to bring about the eventual reunion of Leocadia and Rodolfo) is interrupted at carefully designated points to remind the reader of the continued existence of Luisico's natural father and to chronicle the parallel events that have been taking place in Rodolfo's life during his well-advised sabbatical abroad.
  7. The Porras version, which most critics believe to antedate the 1613 account, leaves no doubt as to the wife's adultery. There is no uneasiness provoked here by her silence; Isabela (the bride's name in the earlier version) keeps quiet when confronted because she has no defense at all.

8. Casalduero, *Sentido y forma*, 117–18.
9. Eleodoro J. Febres, "*Rinconete y Cortadillo*: Estructura y otros valores estéticos," *Anales Cervantinos* 11 (1972): 98.
10. Ibid., 100.
11. Hart, "Versions of Pastoral," 290.
12. Ronald G. Keightley, "The Narrative Structure of *Rinconete y Cortadillo*," in *Essays on Narrative Fiction in the Iberian Peninsula in Honour of Frank Pierce*, ed. R. B. Tate (Oxford: Dolphin, 1982) 39–54.
13. Dian Fox, "The Critical Attitude in *Rinconete y Cortadillo*," *Cervantes* 3, no. 2 (Fall 1983): 142.
14. Carroll B. Johnson, "The Old Order Passeth, or Does It? Some Thoughts on Community, Commerce and Alienation in *Rinconete y Cortadillo*," in *On Cervantes: Essays for L. A. Murillo*, ed. James A. Parr (Newark, Del.: Juan de la Cuesta, 1991), 85–104.
15. Casalduero, *Sentido y forma*, 116.
16. Johnson, "The Old Order Passeth," 92.
17. Ibid., 93.
18. Ibid., 94.
19. Frank Pierce, "*Rinconete y Cortadillo*: An Extreme Case of Irony," in *Hispanic Studies in Honour of Geoffrey Ribbans*, ed. Ann L. Mackenzie and Dorothy S. Severin (Liverpool, U.K.: Liverpool University Press, 1992), 55–63; Fox, "The Critical Attitude," 139; Keightley, "Monipodio's Realm," in Cardwell, ed., *Essays in Honour of Robert Brian Tate*, 53–58.
20. Johnson, "The Old Order Passeth," 95.
21. Rodríguez-Luis, *Novedad y ejemplo*, 1:188.
22. Johnson, "The Old Order Passeth," 96–97.
23. Casalduero, *Sentido y forma*, 99.
24. Ibid., 110–11.
25. Domingo Ynduráin Múñoz, "'Rinconete y Cortadillo.' De entremés a novela," *Boletín de la Real Academia Española* 46 (1966): 321–33.
26. Febres, "Estructura y otros valores," 109–10.
27. Karl-Ludwig Selig, "Cervantes' *Rinconete y Cortadillo* and the Two 'Libros de memoria'," *Revista Hispánica Moderna* 40, nos. 3–4 (1978–79): 126–27.
28. Sánchez, "Theater within the Novel," 73–98.
29. Rodríguez-Luis, *Novedad y ejemplo*, 1:189.
30. José Pascual Buxó, "Estructura y lección de *Rinconete y Cortadillo*," in *Lavori Ispanistici*, serie 2 (Florence, Italy: Università degli Studi di Firenze; Facoltà di Magistero, Istituto Ispanico, 1970), 69–96.
31. Keightley, "Narrative Structure," 40–41.
32. El Saffar, *Novel to Romance*, 30.
33. Rodríguez-Luis, *Novedad y ejemplo*, 1:191–92.
34. Vinel, "Double Discourse," 117–18.
35. As Casalduero (*Sentido y forma*, 99) was among the first to note, the Porras version of R/C also contains the seed of an intriguing episode involving one of Monipodio's prostitutes and a drunken foreigner who is comically referred to as "un bretón que hedía a vino y brea a tiro de arcabuz" (Schevill and Bonilla 1:283) [a Breton who reeked of wine and tar from far away]. This miniepisode disappears from the 1613 text of R/C, only to be resurrected as part of the *Coloquio de los perros*. In this new and expanded version, la Cariharta's character is transformed into a streetwalker named la Colindres, but the references to Monipodio and his gang continue.
36. Rodríguez-Luis, *Novedad y ejemplo*, 1:179.

37. Aden W. Hayes makes the same error in judgment about which boy is carrying which weapon. See Aden W. Hayes, "Narrative 'Errors' in *Rinconte y Cortadillo*," *Bulletin of Hispanic Studies* 58, no. 1 (January 1981): 14.
38. Casalduero, *Sentido y forma*, 108.
39. Rodríguez-Luis, *Novedad y ejemplo*, 1:182.
40. Hayes, "Narrative 'Errors,'" 18.
41. Gonzalo Díaz Migoyo, "Lectura protocolaria del realismo en *Rinconete y Cortadillo*," in *Josep María Solà-Solé: Homage, Homenaje, Homenatge (Miscelánea de estudios de amigos y discípulos)*, ed. Antonio Torres-Alcalá, Victorio Agüero, y Nathaniel B. Smith (Barcelona: Puvill, 1984), 2:55–64.
42. Johnson cites a recent biography of Medina-Sidonia written by Peter O'M. Pierson: *Commander of the Armada: The Seventh Duke of Medina-Sidonia* (New Haven: Yale University Press, 1989), 1.
43. Johnson, "The Old Order Passeth, 99.
44. Clorinda Donato, "Leonora and Camila: Female Characterization and Narrative Formula in the Cervantine *Novela*," *Mester* 15, no. 2 (Fall 1986): 13–24.
45. Forcione, *Cervantes and the Humanist Vision*, 31.
46. El Saffar, *Novel to Romance*, 42.
47. A. F. Lambert, "The Two Versions of Cervantes' *El celoso extremeño*: Ideology and Criticism," *Bulletin of Hispanic Studies* 57, no. 3 (July 1980): 219–31.
48. Juan Bautista Avalle-Arce, "*El celoso extremeño*, de Cervantes," in *Homenaje a Ana María Barrenechea*, ed. Lía Schwartz-Lerner and Isaías Lerner (Madrid: Castalia, 1984), 199–205.
49. Maurice Molho, "Aproximación al *Celoso extremeño*," *Nueva Revista de Filología Hispánica* 38, no. 2 (1990): 743–92.
50. For a discussion of other mythological and biblical elements in ZE, see Peter N. Dunn, "Las 'Novelas ejemplares,'" in *Suma Cervantina*, ed. J. B. Avalle-Arce and E. C. Riley (London: Tamesis, 1973), 81–118; Dean W. McPheeters, "Ovid and the Jealous Old Man of Cervantes," in *Estudios literarios de hispanistas norteamericanos dedicados a Helmut Hatzfeld con motivo de su 80 aniversario*, ed. Josep M. Solà-Solé, Alessandro Crisfulli, and Bruno Damiani (Barcelona: Hispam, 1975), 157–65; Manuel Gómez Reinoso, "El mito recurrente en *El celoso extremeño*," in *Festschrift José Cid Pérez*, ed. Alberto Gutiérrez de la Solana and Elio Alba-Buffill (New York: Senda Nueva de Eds., 1981), 281–87; and Kenneth Brown, "Notas sobre los elementos mitológicos, bíblicos y folklóricos en *El celoso extremeño*," in *Studies on Don Quijote and Other Cervantine Works*, ed. Donald W. Bleznick (York, SC: Spanish Literary Publications, 1984), 65–77.
51. Edwin Williamson, "El 'misterio escondido' en *El celoso extremeño*: Una aproximación al arte de Cervantes," *Nueva Revista de Filología Hispánica* 38.2 (1990): 799.
52. Manuel García Martín, "*El celoso extremeño* y su influencia en la comedia del siglo XVII," in *Cervantes: Su obra y su mundo: Actas del I Congreso Internacional sobre Cervantes*, ed. Manuel Criado de Val (Madrid: EDI-6, 1981), 409–21.
53. El Saffar, *Novel to Romance*, 47.
54. Williamson, "El 'misterio escondido,'" 807 n. 18. A similar view is expressed by Stephen H. Lippmann, "Revision and Exemplarity in Cervantes's *El celoso extremeño*," *Cervantes* 6, no. 2 (Fall 1986): 113–21. Lippmann states that ZE ends with Leonora and Carrizales remaining emotionally as far apart as they had been at the beginning of their marriage (115). The negative views of Williamson and Lippmann stand at the opposite end of the critical spectrum from the rosier interpretations of the final confrontation advanced by El Saffar, Lambert, and Forcione.

55. Lambert, "The Two Versions," 227.
56. El Saffar, *Novel to Romance,* 47.
57. Hart, *Cervantes' Exemplary Fictions,* 92.
58. Ibid., 95.
59. Gwynne Edwards, "Los dos desenlaces de *El celoso extremeño,*" *Boletín de la Biblioteca Menéndez Pelayo* 49 (1973): 281–91.
60. Lambert, "The Two Versions," 230–31 n. 30.
61. Charlotte Stern, "*El celoso extremeño*: Entre farsa y tragedia," in *Estudios sobre el Siglo de Oro en homenage a Raymond R. MacCurdy,* ed. Angel González, Tamara Holzapfel and Alfred Rodríguez (Albuquerque: University of New Mexico, Department of Modern and Classical Languages, 1983; Madrid: Cátedra, 1983), 333–42.
62. Alison Weber, "Tragic Reparation in Cervantes' *El celoso extremeño,*" *Cervantes* 4, no. 1 (Spring 1984): 38.
63. Myriam Yvonne Jehenson, "Quixotic Desires or Stark Reality?" *Cervantes* 15, no. 2 (Fall 1995): 31.
64. Eleodoro J. Febres, "*El celoso extremeño*: Estructura y otros valores estéticos," *Hispanófila* 57 (1976?): 7–22. Febres and Casalduero disagree as to the central theme of ZE: Casalduero believes it to be the issue of Leonora's freedom; Febres says it's about jealousy (8).
65. Amezúa y Mayo, *Cervantes, creador,* 2:234.
66. Casalduero, *Sentido y forma,* 175.
67. Febres, "Estructura y otros valores," 9.
68. Americo Castro, "*El celoso extremeño* de Cervantes," in *Hacia Cervantes,* 3d ed., rev. (Madrid: Taurus, 1967), 420–50.
69. Aylward, *Pioneer and Plagiarist,* 80–91.
70. See ibid., 84–90, for a fuller discussion of the question of Carrizales as a substitute for the figure of Philip II, as well as the portrayal of his ominous house as a miniature Escorial. Of special interest in these pages are the comments regarding Cervantes's imaginative use of daylight (i.e., the many ways Carrizales attempts to keep Leonora isolated from it) to symbolize the harsh intellectual and social restrictions Philip II imposed in his post-Tridentine decrees to guard his subjects against the "contamination" of foreign ideas.
71. El Saffar, *Novel to Romance,* 45–47.
72. Francisco J. Sánchez, *Lectura y representación: Análisis cultural de las "Novelas ejemplares" de Cervantes* (New York: Peter Lang, 1993), 114.
73. Hart, *Cervantes' Exemplary Fictions,* 92.
74. Luis Rosales, "La evasión del prójimo o el hombre de cristal," *Cuadernos Hispanoamericanos* 9 (81); (1956): 254.
75. E. Michael Gerli, "La picaresca y *El licenciado Vidriera*: género y contragénero en Cervantes," in *La picaresca: orígenes, textos y estructuras. Actas del I Congreso Internacional sobre la picaresca organizado por el Patronato "Arcipreste de Hita,"* ed. Manuel Criado de Val (Madrid: Fundación Universitaria Española, 1979), 577–87.
76. Rodríguez-Luis, *Novedad y ejemplo,* 1:201.
77. Edward H. Friedman, "Conceptual Proportion in Cervantes' 'El licenciado Vidriera,'" *South Atlantic Bulletin* 39, no. 4 (November 1974): 57.
78. Friedman, "Conceptual Proportion," 58.
79. Ricapito, *Cervantes's "Novelas Ejemplares,"* 72.
80. Rodríguez-Luis, *Novedad y ejemplo,* 1:207.
81. E. C. Riley, "Cervantes and the Cynics: *El licenciado Vidriera* and *El coloquio de los perros,*" *Bulletin of Hispanic Studies* 53, no. 3 (July 1976): 189–99.
82. Forcione, *Humanist Vision,* 245, n. 44; 247.

83. Gwynne Edwards, "Cervantes's 'El licenciado Vidriera': Meaning and Structure," *Modern Language Review* 68 (1973): 559–68.
84. El Saffar, *Novel to Romance,* 51.
85. Eleodoro J. Febres, "*El licenciado Vidriera:* Nuevas indagaciones en cuanto a su estructura y contenido," *Cuadernos Hispanoamericanos* (Madrid) 381 (March 1982): 544–56.
86. Walter Glannon, "The Psychology of Knowledge in *El licenciado Vidriera,*" *Revista Hispánica Moderna* 40, no. 3–4 (1978–79): 86–96.
87. Anthony J. Cascardi, "Cervantes and Skepticism: The Vanishing of the Body," in *Essays on Hispanic Literature in Honor of Edmund L. King,* ed. Sylvia Molloy and Luis Fernández Cifuentes (London: Tamesis, 1983), 23–29.
88. Sieber refers to Narciso Alonso Cortés's conjecture in his 1916 edition of *LV* (p. 30) that Cervantes was possibly referring to the Huguenot disturbances in the French capital during September 1567. See Harry Sieber, ed., *Novelas ejemplares,* by Miguel de Cervantes, 2:51 n. 31.
89. I count 18 out of 32 pages in the Sieber edition devoted to Vidriera's witticisms; Singer estimates his *agudezas* to make up 56 percent of the text. See Armand E. Singer, "Cervantes' *Licenciado Vidriera:* Its Form and Substance," *West Virginia University Philological Papers* 8 (1951): 13–31.
90. Armand E. Singer, "The Sources, Meaning, and the Use of the Madness Theme in Cervantes' *Licenciado Vidriera,*" *West Virginia University Philological Papers* 6 (1949) 31–53; idem, "Form and Substance," 13–31.
91. Otis H. Green, "*El licenciado Vidriera*: Its Relation to the *Viaje del Parnaso* and the *Examen de Ingenios* of Huarte," in *Linguistic and Literary Studies in Honor of Helmut A. Hatzfeld,* ed. Alessandro S. Crisafulli (Washington, D.C.: Catholic University of America Press, 1964), 213–20.
92. Gerli, "La picaresca y *El licenciado Vidriera,*" 587.
93. Daniel L. Heiple, "The Trap of the Fortunate Isles in *El licenciado Vidriera,*" in *Selected Proceedings of the Thirty-Fifth Annual Mountain Interstate Foreign Language Conference,* ed. Ramón Fernández-Rubio (Greenville, S.C.: Furman University, 1987), 185–92.
94. Green, *"El licenciado Vidriera,"* 217.
95. Forcione, *Humanist Vision,* 226.
96. Singer, "Form and Substance," 19–22.
97. Francisco A. de Icaza, *Las "Novelas ejemplares" de Cervantes. Sus críticos, Sus modelos literarios, Sus modelos vivos* (1901; reprint, Ateneo de Madrid, 1916), 169; Narciso Alonso Cortés, prologue to *El licenciado Vidriera,* by Miguel de Cervantes (Valladolid: Imprenta Castellana, 1916), xvi; Casalduero, *Sentido y forma,* 138; Singer, "Sources, Meaning and the Use of the Madness Theme," 42; Singer, "Form and Substance," 17; Anthony Close, "Algunas reflexiones sobre la sátira en Cervantes," *Nueva Revista de Filología Hispánica* 38, no. 2 (1990): 493–511.
98. Singer, "Form and Substance," 17–18).
99. Narciso Alonso Cortés, prologue, xi–xxvi.
100. Amezúa y Mayo, *Cervantes, creador,* 2:174–75.
101. Riley, "Cervantes and the Cynics," 191–92.
102. Forcione, *Humanist Vision,* 237; Daniel L. Heiple, "*El licenciado Vidriera* y el humor tradicional del loco," *Hispania* 66, no. 1 (March 1983): 17–20.
103. Aylward, *Pioneer and Plagiarist,* 14–15.
104. This is particularly true in the case of Vidriera's several scholarly quotations from Classical Latin, for which an *ingenio lego* like Cervantes would probably have required some external scholarly assistance.

CHAPTER 4. *LAS DOS DONCELLAS* AND *LA SEÑORA CORNELIA:*
DRAMATIC ECHOES OF *DON QUIXOTE,* PART ONE

1. It should be added that the documented existence of alternate versions of *Rinconete y Cortadillo* and *El celoso extremeño* in the Porras Manuscript (ca. 1606) has also been used to deny the claim to original authorship by Cervantes. See Aylward, *Pioneer and Plagiarist*.
2. Rodolfo Schevill and Adolfo Bonilla, ed., *Novelas ejemplares*, by Miguel de Cervantes Saavedra, 3 vols. (Madrid: Gráficas Reunidas, 1922–25), 3:393.
3. Casalduero, *Sentido y forma*, 206–8.
4. Amezúa y Mayo, *Cervantes, creador*, 2:326–37.
5. Rachel Frank, "Deceit in Cervantes' *Novelas ejemplares*," *Hispanic Review* 13 (1945): 244–52.
6. Jennifer Thompson, "The Structure of Cervantes' *Las dos doncellas*," *Bulletin of Hispanic Studies* 40 (1963): 144–50.
7. Rodríguez-Luis, *Novedad y ejemplo*, 1:85–86.
8. Geoffrey Stagg, "*La Galatea* and 'Las dos doncellas' to the Rescue of *Don Quixote*, Part II," in Cardwell, ed., *Essays in Honour of Robert Brian Tate*, 125–30.
9. Caroline Schmauser, "Dynamism and Spatial Structure in *Las dos doncellas*," in Nerlich and Spadaccini, eds., *Cervantes's "Exemplary Novels,"* 175–203.
10. Stagg, "*La Galatea* and 'Las dos doncellas,'" 127.
11. All citations from *Las dos doncellas* and *La señora Cornelia* are taken from Harry Sieber, ed., *Novelas ejemplares*, by Miguel de Cervantes, 2 vols. (Madrid: Cátedra, 1980–81); parenthetical documentation will include the abbreviations *DD* or *SC*. The accompanying English translations are from B. W. Ife, ed., *Exemplary Novels*, by Miguel de Cervantes Saavedra, 4 vols. (Warminster, England: Aris & Phillips, 1992).
12. All citations from the *Quijote* are taken from Martin de Riquer, ed., *Don Quijote de la Mancha*, by Miguel de Cervantes, 10th ed., 2 vols. (Barcelona, Juventud, 1984); parenthetical documentation will include the abbreviation *DQ*. The accompanying English translations are my own.
13. Thomas Pabon, "Secular Resurrection through Marriage in Cervantes' *La señora Cornelia, Las dos doncellas* and *La fuerza de la sangre*," *Anales Cervantinos* 16 (1977): 109–24.
14. El Saffar, *Novel to Romance*, 1974).
15. Linda Britt, "Teodosia's Dark Shadow? A Study of Women's Roles in Cervantes' *Las dos doncellas*," *Cervantes* 8, no. 1 (Spring 1988): 39–46.
16. Rodríguez-Luis, *Novedad y ejemplo*, 1:76–77.
17. L. A. Murillo, "Narrative Structures in the *Novelas ejemplares*: An Outline," *Cervantes* 8, no. 2 (Fall 1988): 242.
18. Thompson, "The Structure of Cervantes' *Las dos doncellas*," 150.
19. Casalduero, *Sentido y forma*, 219.
20. Murillo, "Narrative Structures," 243.
21. Schmauser, "Dynamism and Spatial Structure," 196.
22. Rodríguez-Luis, *Novedad y ejemplo*, 1:86.
23. Ricapito, *Cervantes's "Novelas Ejemplares,"* 113.
24. María Zabala-Peña, "Los personajes de *Las dos doncellas*: sus fallos y la necesidad de la peregrinación a Santiago" (Term paper, University of South Carolina, Fall 1992).
25. Sieber, ed., *Novelas ejemplares*, 2:29–31.
26. Casalduero, *Sentido y forma*, 223–24.

27. Amezúa y Mayo, *Cervantes, creador,* 2:359.
28. El Saffar, *Novel to Romance,* 119.
29. Rodríguez-Luis, *Novedad y ejemplo,* 1:87, 1:100ff.
30. Ricapito, *Cervantes's "Novelas Ejemplares,"* 106–11.
31. Gail Bradbury, "Lope, Cervantes, a Marriage Trick and a Baby," *Hispanófila* 28 (Sept. 1984): 11–19.
32. I would like to thank Devon Hanahan for pointing out as many as seventeen different occasions—apart from the four long analeptic passages—throughout *Cornelia* in which some major or minor character recounts for another some significant event or occurrence that will facilitate the reader's task of sorting out and assembling the pieces of *Cornelia*'s complicated plotline. "Narrative Technique in *La señora Cornelia*" (Term paper, University of South Carolina, Fall 1994).
33. Esther Lacadena y Calero, "*La señora Cornelia* y su técnica narrativa," *Anales Cervantinos* 15 (1976): 199–210.
34. Juan Bautista de Avalle-Arce, "La ejemplaridad de una novelita," *Quaderni Ibero-Americani* 78 (December 1995): 5–8.
35. Lacadena y Calero, "*La señora Cornelia* y su técnica narrativa," 209.
36. Peter N. Dunn, "Las 'Novelas ejemplares,'" in *Suma Cervantina,* ed. J. B. Avalle-Arce and E. C. Riley (London: Tamesis, 1973), 109.
37. Avalle-Arce, "La ejemplaridad," 5–8.
38. Sicroff, "The Demise of Exemplarity," 345–60.
39. Pabon, "Secular Resurrection," 113.
40. Bradbury, "Lope, Cervantes, a Marriage Trick and a Baby," 11–19.
41. Catherine Davis Vinel, "Double Discourse in Cervantes's *Novelas ejemplares*" (Ph.D. diss., University of South Carolina, 1994), 205–21.
42. Rodríguez-Luis, *Novedad y ejemplo,* 1:101.
43. Vinel, "Double Discourse," 213–14.
44. El Saffar, *Novel to Romance,* 109–28.

Chapter 5. The Enigmatic Layered Structure of *El casamiento engañoso* and *El colloquio de los perros*

1. Michael Zappala, "Cervantes and Lucian," *Symposium* 33, no. 1 (Spring 1979): 65–82.
2. Antonio Oliver, "La filosofía cínica y el 'Coloquio de los perros,'" *Anales Cervantinos* 3 (1953): 291–307.
3. Amezúa y Mayo, *Cervantes, creador,* 1:422.
4. Zappala, "Cervantes and Lucian," 71.
5. Riley, "Cervantes and the Cynics," 189–99.
6. Casalduero, *Sentido y forma,* 237.
7. Alban K. Forcione, *Cervantes and the Mystery of Lawlessness: A Study of "El casamiento engañoso y El coloquio de los perros"* (Princeton: Princeton University Press, 1984), 126.
8. Blanco Aguinaga, "Cervantes y la picaresca: Notas sobre dos tipos de realismo," *Nueva Revista de Filología Hispánica* 11 (1957): 313–42.
9. Pamela Waley, "The Unity of the *Casamiento engañoso* and the *Coloquio de los perros,*" *Bulletin of Hispanic Studies* 34 (1957): 201–12.
10. L. J. Woodward, "*El casamiento engañoso* y *El coloquio de los perros,*" *Bulletin of Hispanic Studies* 36 (1959): 80–87.

11. Karl-Ludwig Selig, "The Interplay of Form and Point of View in *El casamiento engañoso*," in *Spanische Literatur in Goldenen Zeitalter: Fritz Schalk zum 70 Geburtstag*, ed. Horst Baader and Erich Loos (Frankfurt: Klostermann, 1973), 394–400.

12. Forcione, *Cervantes and the Mystery of Lawlessness*, 17.

13. E. C. Riley, "Cervantes, Freud, and Psychoanalytic Narrative Theory," *Modern Language Review* 88, no. 1 (January 1993): 12.

14. Amezúa y Mayo, *Cervantes, creador,* 2:388; L. A. Murillo, "Cervantes' *Coloqio de los perros,* a Novel-Dialogue," *Modern Philology* 58 (February 1961): 175; Vicente Cabrera, "Nuevos valores de 'El casamiento engañoso' y 'El coloquio de los perros,'" *Hispanófila* 45 (1972): 49 n. 2.

15. Rodríguez-Luis, *Novedad y ejemplo.*

16. Ruth El Saffar, "Montesinos' Cave and the *Casamiento engañoso* in the Development of Cervantes' Prose Fiction," *Kentucky Romance Quarterly* 20 (1973): 451–67.

17. José María Pozuelo Yvancos, "Enunciación y recepción en el *Casamiento-Coloquio*," in *Cervantes: Su obra y su mundo: Actas del I Congreso Internacional sobre Cervantes,* ed. Manuel Criado de Val (Madrid: EDI-6, 1981), 423–35.

18. Alan Soons, "An Interpretation of the Form of *El casamiento engañoso y Coloquio de los perros*," *Anales Cervantinos* 9 (1961–62): 203–12; Dunn, "Las 'Novelas ejemplares,'" 118.

19. Forcione, *Cervantes and the Mystery of Lawlessness*, 143, n. 20.

20. Juan Bautista Avalle-Arce, "Cervantes entre pícaros," *Nueva Revista de Filología Hispánica* 38, no. 2 (1990): 591–603.

21. Blanco Aginaga, "Cervantes y la picaresca."

22. Gonzalo Sobejano, "El 'Coloquio de los perros' en la picaresca y otros apuntes," *Hispanic Review* 43, no. 1 (Winter 1975): 25–41.

23. Roberto González Echevarría, "The Life and Adventures of Cipión: Cervantes and the Picaresque," *Diacritics* 10, no. 3 (1980): 15–26.

24. Rodríguez-Luis, *Novedad y ejemplo,* 2:41.

25. The fact that neither Carrizales nor Campuzano is permitted to avenge the dishonor he has suffered at the hands of an offending female is typical of Cervantes's fiction. In *La tía fingida (TF),* a work often attributed to Cervantes, one of the central female figures, a charlatan named Doña Claudia, is subjected to a most humiliating public punishment in the town square of Salamanca. Such a cruel denouement is, in my opinion, decidedly un-Cervantine and an important reason why we should disregard the suggestion that Cervantes may have penned *TF*. I shall have more to say on the subject in an article I am currently preparing for publication.

26. Manuel Lloris, "El casamiento engañoso," *Hispanófila* 39 (May 1970): 16.

27. Rodríguez-Luis, *Novedad y ejemplo,* 2:49.

28. Stephen Boyd, "Sin and Grace in *El casamiento engañoso* y *El coloquio de los perros*," in *What's Past is Prologue: A Collection of Essays in Honour of L. J. Woodward,* ed. Salvador Bacarisse, Bernard Bentley, Mercedes Clarasó, and Douglas Gifford (Edinburgh: Scottish Academic Press, 1984), 1.

29. Forcione, *Cervantes and the Mystery of Lawlessness,* 139.

30. Boyd, "Sin and Grace," 3.

31. Anthony Cárdenas, "Berganza: Cervantes' *Can[is] Domini*," in *Cervantes and the Pastoral,* ed. José J. Labrador Herráiz and Juan Fernández Jiménez (Cleveland: Cleveland State University, Penn State University, Behrend College, 1986), 19–35.

32. The Cathars, a sect of Manichaean dualists who rejected all things material as tools of the devil, were condemned as heretics and eventually exterminated during the Albigensian Crusade of the early 1200s. In Cervantes's time these dissidents were frequently associated—erroneously, as it turns out—with the practice of witchcraft because

the charges against them were similar to the accusations that were later leveled against certain individuals during an epidemic of witchcraft that broke out in the 1300s. The fact that the respective persecutions took place a century apart did not prevent the connection between the Cathars and the practice of witchcraft from being firmly established in the minds of many European Catholics. See Jeffrey Burton Russell, *Witchcraft in the Middle Ages* (Ithaca, N.Y.: Cornell University Press, 1972), 120–24.

33. Cárdenas, "Berganza," 30–31.

34. Carroll B. Johnson, "Of Witches and Bitches: Gender, Marginality and Discourse in *El casamiento engañoso y Coloquio de los perros*," *Cervantes* 11, no. 2 (Fall 1991): 7–25.

35. Michael Nerlich (1989) observes a completely different pair of competing discourses in the *Coloquio*. Nerlich draws a sharp distinction between the respective roles played by the two canine protagonists. On the one hand Cipión is presented as a scholastic who utilizes books as the primary source of his knowledge. He cannot understand or appreciate the antirhetorical—and antischolastic—commentary of his counterpart Berganza, who looks to his own life experience as a guide in his judgments, acts and utterances. See Michael Nerlich, "On the Philosophical Dimension of *El casamiento engañoso* and *El coloquio de los perros*," in Nerlich and Spadaccini, eds., *Cervantes's "Exemplary Novels,"* 247–329.

36. Oldřich Bělič, "La estructura de *El coloquio de los perros*," in *Acta Universitatis Carolinae; Philologica 4 (1966); Romanistica Pragensia IV* (Prague: University of Karlova, 1966), 3–19. In a 1992 article M. J. Thacker disputes Bělič's thesis. Thacker observes no noteworthy improvement or deterioration in either of the dogs during the *Coloquio*. This constancy, says Thacker, is precisely what makes Berganza and Cipión reliable witnesses. See M. J. Thacker, "Cervantes' Exemplary *Pícaros*," in *Hispanic Studies in Honour of Geoffrey Ribbans*, ed. Ann L. Mackenzie and Dorothy S. Severin, *Bulletin of Hispanic Studies Special Homage Volume* (1992): 47–53.

37. Cabrera, "Nuevos valores."

38. Vicente Cabrera, "El sueño del alférez Campuzano," *Nueva Revista de Filología Hispánica* 23 (1974): 388–91.

39. Unless otherwise specified, all citations from *El casamiento engañoso* and *El coloquio de los perros* are taken from Harry Sieber, ed., *Novelas ejemplares*, by Miguel de Cervantes, 2 vols. (Madrid: Cátedra, 1980–81). The accompanying English translations are from B. W. Ife, ed., *Exemplary Novels*, by Miguel de Cervantes Saavedra, 4 vols. (Warminster, England: Aris & Phillips, 1992).

40. Cabrera, "El sueño del alférez Campuzano," 390–91.

41. Pozuelo Yvancos, "Enunciación y recepción en el *Casamiento-Coloquio*," 432.

42. According to Genette, registers 1 and 3 would be considered *heterodiegetic* narratives, i.e., told in the *third person,* from a point of view lying outside the actual story. Conversely, registers 2, 4, and 5, because they are autobiographical (told in the *first person* and focused from within the story), are called *homodiegetic* narratives.

43. Forcione, *Cervantes and the Mystery of Lawlessness*, 24.

44. Ruth El Saffar, *Cervantes: A Critical Study of "El casamiento engañoso" and "El coloquio de los perros"* (London: Grant & Cutler, 1976).

45. Forcione observes that El Saffar's judgments here follow the lead of Maurice Molho in claiming that "the Jesuits are subtly shown to be in collusion with the *converso* merchants in their efforts to 'buy' clean genealogies" (*Cervantes and the Mystery of Lawlessness*, 151–52 n. 12). El Saffar portrays Cervantes as an opponent of such subversive scheming on the part of the Jesuits, while Forcione casts him as a supporter of the order's efforts to foment greater social mobility in Spanish society. In view of Cervantes's known opposition to so many of the conventional beliefs of his contemporaries, I find Forcione's view more plausible.

46. El Saffar, *Critical Study,* 44–45.

47. E. T. Aylward, "The Device of Layered Critical Commentary in *Don Quixote* and *El coloquio de los perros*," *Cervantes* 7, no. 2 (Fall 1987): 57–69. See also E. T. Aylward, *Towards a Revaluation of Avellaneda's "False Quixote"* (Newark, Del.: Juan de la Cuesta, 1989), 63–70. Many of the observations I made in these earlier studies are reproduced in this chapter with the generous permission of the publishers.

48. The technique of multiple layers or planes of commentary is used again toward the close of book 1 of the *Persiles*, at a point when several narrators are engaged in telling their life stories to a critical audience.

49. George Haley, "The Narrator in *Don Quijote*: Maese Pedro's Puppet Show," *MLN* 80 (1965): 145–65.

50. El Saffar, "Montesinos' Cave," 455.

51. Forcione appears to concur with El Saffar at one point; he observes that the *Casamiento* is an independent confession framing and maintaining a subordinate one (i.e., the core episode of Cañizares's revelations about witchcraft). Forcione views the frame tale's elaborate set of imaginative correspondences as a link with the second story's episode of the Toledan witch (*Cervantes and the Mystery of Lawlessness*, 135). At a later point he parts company with El Saffar, labeling the *Casamiento* a powerful counterforce to the narrative movement of the *Coloquio*, which he declares to be the more dominant of the two stories (146).

52. Forcione, disagreeing, prefers to interpret the Cave of Montesinos adventure as a parody of the romance conventions of anagnorisis, an ironic treatment of the descent and recognition themes so prevalent in the romantic tradition. These same conventions later reappear in the *Coloquio* during Berganza's grotesque encounter with Cañizares (*Cervantes and the Mystery of Lawlessness*, 48–49). In Forcione's view, the theme of Don Quixote's descent into the cave is man's adversarial relationship with time and its unpleasant consequences (e.g., mortality and decay). Quixote is confronted in his dream with the fact of man's inescapably transitory nature and the ultimate futility of his own dreams of immortality. The *Coloquio*, on the other hand, is said to deal with the moral theme of demonic powers in conflict with divine purposes (51–55).

53. El Saffar, *Novel to Romance*, 81–82.

54. B. W. Ife, *Lectura y ficción en el Siglo de Oro: Las razones de la picaresca* (Barcelona: Edición Crítica, 1992).

55. Fred Abrams, supporting an idea originally advanced by Emile Charles in his work, *Michel de Cervantes: Sa vie, son temps, son oeuvre politique et littéraire* (Paris, 1866), states that the name Berganza points to Cervantes himself. If we suppress the fourth and eighth letters of the dog's name (*g* and *a*), says Abrams, we get the following anagrammatic sequence: Berganza » Beranz » Zerban » Cervan[tes]. The same process can be seen at work with Cipión's name: Cipión » Pincio » Pinci[an]o. If Abrams's theory is correct, it might be said that what Peralta is reading is a conversation between Cervantes and López Pinciano.

56. Edwin Williamson, "Cervantes as Moralist and Trickster: The Critique of Picaresque Autobiography in *El casamiento engañoso y El coloquio de los perros*," in *Essays on Hispanic Themes in Honour of Edward C. Riley*, ed. Jennifer Lowe and Philip Swanson (Edinburgh: Department of Hispanic Studies, University of Edinburgh, 1989), 104–26.

57. Robert V. Piluso, "El papel mediador del narrador en dos *novelas ejemplares* de Cervantes," in *Actas del Sexto Congreso Internacional de Hispanistas celebrado en Toronto del 22 al 26 de agosto de 1977*, ed. Alan M. Gordon and Evelyn Rugg (Toronto: Department of Spanish and Portuguese, University of Toronto, 1980), 571–74.

58. Soons, "An Interpretation of the Form," 209.

59. I wish to thank my colleague Catherine Davis Vinel for her valuable suggestions regarding Cervantes's prologue and its relationship to the *Coloquio*.

Works Cited

General Literary Criticism

Bakhtin, M. M. *The Dialogic Imagination: Four Essays*. Translated by Caryl Emerson and Michael Holquist. Edited by Michael Holquist. Austin: University of Texas Press, 1981.

Chatman, Seymour. *Story and Discourse: Narrative Structure in Fiction and Film*. Ithaca, N.Y.: Cornell University Press, 1978.

Genette, Gérard. *Narrative Discourse: An Essay in Method*. Ithaca, N.Y.: Cornell University Press, 1980.

Kayser, Wolfgang. *Interpretación y análisis de la obra literaria*. Translated by M. D. Mouton and V. G. Yebra. Madrid: Gredos, 1958.

Editions of Cervantes's Works

Cervantes, Miguel de. *Don Quijote de la Mancha*. Edited by Martín de Riquer. 10th ed. 2 vols. Barcelona: Juventud, 1984.

———. *Novelas ejemplares*. Edited by Harry Sieber. 2 vols. Madrid: Cátedra, 1980–81.

Cervantes Saavedra, Miguel de. *Exemplary Novels*. Edited by B. W. Ife. 4 vols. Warminster, England: Aris & Phillips, 1992.

———. *Novelas ejemplares*. Edited by Rodolfo Schevill and Adolfo Bonilla. 3 vols. Madrid: Gráficas Reunidas, 1922–25.

On Cervantes and/or the *Novelas ejemplares*

Amezúa y Mayo, Agustín G. *Cervantes, creador de la novela corta española*. 2 vols. Madrid: Consejo Superior de Investigaciones Científicas, 1956–58.

Apráiz y Sáenz del Burgo, Julián. *Estudio histórico-crítico sobre las Novelas ejemplares de Cervantes*. Vitoria: Domingo Sar, 1901.

Atkinson, William C. "Cervantes, el Pinciano, and the *Novelas ejemplares*." *Hispanic Review* 16 (July 1948): 189–208. Reprinted in *Critical Essays on Cervantes*, edited by Ruth El Saffar, 123–39. Boston: G. K. Hall, 1986.

Avalle-Arce, Juan Bautista. Introduction to *Cervantes: Three Exemplary Novels*. New York: Dell, 1964.

Aylward, E. T. *Cervantes: Pioneer and Plagiarist*. London: Tamesis, 1982.

———. "Lighten up, Geoffrey!" *Cervantes* 14, no. 1 (Spring 1994): 109–15.

———. "Patterns of Symmetrical Design in *La fuerza de la sangre* and *La española inglesa*." *Crítica Hispánica* 16, no. 2 (1994): 189–203.

———. *Towards a Revaluation of Avellaneda's "False Quixote."* Newark, Del.: Juan de la Cuesta, 1989.

Bataillon, Marcel. "Cervantès penseur d'après le livre d'Americo Castro." *Revue de la littérature comparée* 8 (1933): 318–38.

Canavaggio, Jean. *Cervantes*. Translated by J. R. Jones. New York: Norton, 1990.

Casalduero, Joaquín. *Sentido y forma de las "Novelas ejemplares."* 1943. Madrid: Gredos, 1962.

Cascardi, Anthony J. "Cervantes and Skepticism: The Vanishing of the Body." In *Essays on Hispanic Literature in Honor of Edmund L. King*, edited by Sylvia Molloy and Luis Fernández Cifuentes, 23–29. London: Tamesis, 1983.

Castro, Américo. "La ejemplaridad de las novelas cervantinas." *Nueva Revista de Filología Hispánica* 2, no. 4 (1948): 319–32.

———. *Hacia Cervantes*. 3d rev. ed., Madrid: Taurus, 1967.

———. *El pensamiento de Cervantes*. Madrid: Hernando, 1925.

Close, Anthony. "Algunas reflexiones sobre la sátira en Cervantes." *Nueva Revista de Filología Hispánica* 38, no. 2 (1990): 493–511.

Combet, Louis. *Cervantès ou les incertitudes du désir*. Lyons: Presses Universitaires de Lyons, 1981.

Criado de Val, Manuel. *Análisis verbal del estilo. Indices verbales de Cervantes, de Avellaneda y del autor de "La tía fingida."* Madrid: Consejo Superior de Investigaciones Científicas, 1953.

Crooks, Esther J. "The Influence of Cervantes in France in the Seventeenth Century." *The Johns Hopkins Studies in Romance Literatures and Languages*, extra vol. 4 (1931).

Díaz Plaja, Guillermo. "La técnica narrativa de Cervantes (algunas observaciones)." *Revista de Filología Española* 32 (1948): 237–68. Reprinted in *Conferencias desarrolladas con motivo del IV centenario del nacimiento de Cervantes*, 21–25. Barcelona, 1949.

Drake, Dana B. *Miguel de Cervantes Saavedra: A Critical Bibliography*. Vol. 1: The *Novelas ejemplares*. Blacksburg, Va.: Virginia Polytechnic Institute, 1968.

Dunn, Peter N. "Las 'Novelas ejemplares.'" In *Suma Cervantina*, edited by J. B. Avalle-Arce and E. C. Riley, 81–118. London: Tamesis, 1973.

El Saffar, Ruth. *Beyond Fiction: The Recovery of the Feminine in the Novels of Cervantes*. Berkeley: University of California Press, 1984.

———. *Novel to Romance: A Study of Cervantes's "Novelas ejemplares."* Baltimore: The Johns Hopkins University Press, 1974.

———. "Persiles' Retort: An Alchemical Angle on the Lovers' Labors." *Cervantes* 10, no. 1 (Spring 1990): 17–33.

Entwistle, William J. "Cervantes, the Exemplary Novelist." *Hispanic Review* 9 (1941): 103–9.

Fernández de Avellaneda, Alonso [pseud.]. Prologue to *Don Quijote de la Mancha*. Edited by Martín de Riquer. 3 vols. Clásicos Castellanos 174–76. Madrid: Espasa-Calpe, 1972.

Fernández de Navarrete, Martín. "Vida de Miguel de Cervantes." In *Obras de Miguel de Cervantes*, 1:i–cvi. Paris: Baudry, 1861.

Fitzmaurice-Kelly, James. Introduction to *The Exemplary Novels*, by Miguel de Cervantes. Glasgow: Gowans & Gray, 1902.

Forcione, Alban K. *Cervantes, Aristotle and the "Persiles."* Princeton: Princeton University Press, 1970.

———. *Cervantes and the Humanist Vision: A Study of Four "Exemplary Novels."* Princeton: Princeton University Press, 1982.

Frank, Rachel. "Deceit in Cervantes' *Novelas ejemplares*." *Hispanic Review* 13 (1945): 244–52.

Hainsworth, G[eorges]. "Les nouvelles exemplaires de Cervantès en Italie." *Bulletin Hispanique* 31 (1929): 143–47.

———. *Les "Novelas ejemplares" de Cervantès en France au XVIIe Siècle*. Paris: Champion, 1933. Reprint, New York: Burt Franklin, 1971.

———. "Cervantès en France—à propos de quelques opinions récentes." *Bulletin Hispanique* 24 (1932): 128–44.

Hart, Thomas R. *Cervantes' Exemplary Fictions: A Study of the* Novelas ejemplares. Lexington: University Press of Kentucky, 1994.

———. "Versions of Pastoral in Three *Novelas ejemplares*." *Bulletin of Hispanic Studies* 58, no. 4 (October 1981): 283–91.

Hatzfeld, Helmut. "Thirty Years of Cervantes Criticism." *Hispania* 30 (1947): 321–28.

Herrero-García, Miguel. "Una hipótesis sobre las *Novelas ejemplares*." *Revista Nacional de Educación* (Madrid) 96 (1950): 33–37.

Icaza, Francisco A. de. *Las "Novelas ejemplares" de Cervantes: Sus críticos, Sus modelos literarios, Sus modelos vivos*. 1901. Reprint, Ateneo de Madrid, 1916.

———. *Supercherías y errores cervantinos puestos en claro*. Madrid: Renacimiento, 1917.

Knight, Sharon Eadie. "Cervantes and Heliodorus: Elements of the Greek Romance in *El amante liberal* and *La española inglesa*." Master's thesis, University of South Carolina, 1996.

McLean, Malcolm D. "Marital Problems in the Works of Cervantes." *Library Chronicle* (University of Texas) 3 (1948): 81–89.

Menéndez y Pelayo, Marcelino. "Cultura literaria de Miguel de Cervantes y elaboración del *Quijote*." In *Estudios y discursos de crítica histórica y literaria. Edición nacional de las obras completas de Menéndez Pelayo*, 6:323–56. Madrid: Consejo Superior de Investigaciones Científicas, 1941.

Meregalli, Franco. "Le *Novelas ejemplares* nello svolgimento della personalità de Cervantes." *Letterature Moderne* 10 (1960): 334–51.

Murillo, L. A. "Narrative Structures in the *Novelas ejemplares*: An Outline." *Cervantes* 8, no. 2 (Fall 1988): 231–50.

Ortega y Gasset, José. *Meditaciones del Quijote*. Madrid: Residencia de Estudiantes, 1914.

Pabon, Thomas. "Secular Resurrection through Marriage in Cervantes' *La señora Cornelia, Las dos doncellas* and *La fuerza de la sangre*." *Anales Cervantinos* 16 (1977): 109–24.

Pellicer, Juan Antonio. "Vida de Miguel de Cervantes Saavedra." In *El ingenioso hidalgo don Quijote de la Mancha*, 1:cxli–clvi. Madrid: Gabriel de Sancha, 1797.

Pfandl, Ludwig. *Geschichte der spanischen National-literatur in ihrer Blützeit*. Freiburg in Breisgau: Herder, 1929.

Pierce, Frank. "Reality and Realism in the Exemplary Novels." *Bulletin of Hispanic Studies* 30 (1953): 134–42.

Piluso, Robert V. *Amor, matrimonio y honra en Cervantes.* New York: Las Americas Publishing Company, 1967.

Ricapito, Joseph V. *Cervantes's "Novelas Ejemplares": Between History and Creativity.* Purdue Studies in Romance Literatures 10. West Lafayette, Ind.: Purdue University Press, 1996.

Riley, E. C. "Cervantes: A Question of Genre." In *Mediaeval and Renaissance Studies on Spain and Portugal in Honour of P. E. Russell*, edited by F. W. Hodcroft, D. G. Pattison, R. D .F. Pring-Mill, and R. W. Truman, 69–85. Oxford: Society for the Study of Mediaeval Languages and Literature, 1981. A Spanish version of this article appears as "Cervantes: Una cuestión de género," in *El "Quijote" de Cervantes*, trans. Mercedes Juliá, ed. George Haley (Madrid: Taurus, 1980), 37–51.

———. "Cervantes and the Cynics: *El licenciado Vidriera* and *El coloquio de los perros.*" *Bulletin of Hispanic Studies* 53, no. 3 (July 1976): 189–99.

Rivers, Elias L. "On the Prefatory Pages of *Don Quixote*, Part II." *Modern Language Notes* 76 (1960): 214–21.

Rodríguez-Luis, Julio. Estudio preliminar. In *Novelas ejemplares*, by Miguel de Cervantes, 1:7–58. Madrid: Taurus, 1983.

———. *Novedad y ejemplo de las "Novelas" de Cervantes.* 2 vols. Madrid: Porrúa-Turanzas, 1980–84.

Sánchez, Francisco J. *Lectura y representación: Análisis cultural de las "Novelas ejemplares" de Cervantes.* New York: Peter Lang, 1993.

———. "Theater within the Novel: Mass Audience and Individual Reader in *La gitanilla* and *Rinconete y Cortadillo.*" In *Cervantes's "Exemplary Novels" and the Adventure of Writing*, edited by Michael Nerlich and Nicholas Spadaccini, 73–98. Minneapolis: The Prisma Institute/University of Minnesota Press, 1989.

Schevill, Rudolph. *Cervantes.* New York: Duffield, 1919.

Schevill, Rudolph, and Adolfo Bonilla. Introduction to the *Novelas ejemplares*, by Miguel de Cervantes. Madrid: Schevill and Bonilla, 1925.

Sears, Theresa Ann. *A Marriage of Convenience: Ideal and Ideology in the "Novelas ejemplares."* New York: Peter Lang, 1993.

Sicroff, Albert A. "The Demise of Exemplarity in Cervantes' *Novelas ejemplares.*" In *Hispanic Studies in Honor of Joseph H. Silverman*, edited by Joseph V. Ricapito, 345–60. Newark, Del.: Juan de la Cuesta, 1988.

Sieber, Harry. Introduction to the *Novelas ejemplares*, by Miguel de Cervantes. Madrid: Cátedra, 1981.

Sobejano, Gonzalo. "Sobre tipología y ordenación de las 'Novelas elemplares' (Artículo-reseña)." *Hispanic Review* 46, no. 1 (Winter 1978): 65–75.

Sordo, Enrique. "Notas al margen. Realidad y ficción de las *Novelas ejemplares.*" *Cuadernos de literatura* 3 (1948): 271–83.

Stagg, Geoffrey. "The Refracted Image: Porras and Cervantes." *Cervantes* 4, no. 2 (Fall 1984): 139–53.

Tieck, Johann Ludwig. *Schriften.* Vol 11. Berlin: Reimer, 1929.

Turkevich, Ludmilla Buketoff. *Cervantes in Russia.* Princeton: Princeton University Press, 1950.

Wardropper, Bruce W. *Teatro español del Siglo de Oro.* New York: Scribner's, 1970.

Wiltrout, Ann E. "Role Playing and Rites of Passage: *La ilustre fregona* and *La gitanilla*." *Hispania* 64, no. 3 (1981): 388–99.

Vinel, Catherine Davis. "Double Discourse in Cervantes's *Novelas ejemplares*." Ph.D. diss., University of South Carolina, 1994. Abstract in *Dissertation Abstracts International* 54 (1995): DA9517316.

———. "Multi-genred Texts in Cervantes's *Novelas ejemplares*." Master's thesis, University of South Carolina, 1993.

ON *LA GITANILLA*

Avalle-Arce, Juan Bautista. "*La Gitanilla*." *Cervantes* 1, nos. 1–2 (Fall 1981): 9–17.

Boyd, S. F. "The Mystery of Cervantes' *La gitanilla*." *Forum for Modern Language Studies* (St. Andrews, Scotland) 17, no. 4 (October 1981): 312–21.

Clamurro, William H. "Value & Identity in 'La gitanilla.'" *Journal of Hispanic Philology* 14, no. 1 (Autumn 1989): 43–60.

Gerli, E. Michael. "Romance and Novel: Idealism and Irony in *La gitanilla*." *Cervantes* 6, no. 1 (Spring 1986): 29–38.

Güntert, Georges. "*La gitanilla* y la poética de Cervantes." *Boletín de la Real Academia Española* 52 (1972): 107–34.

Johnson, Carroll B. "De economías y linajes en 'La Gitanilla.'" *Mester* 25, no. 1 (Spring 1996): 31–48.

Krummrich, Philip. "Tentative Notes toward an Article on *La gitanilla*." Paper presented at the NEH Summer Seminar on Cervantes at the Newberry Library, Chicago, Ill., August 1982.

Lerner, Isaías. "Marginalidad en las novelas ejemplares, I: *La gitanilla*." *Lexis* 4, no. 1 (July 1980): 47–59.

Lipson, Lesley. "'La palabra hecha nada': Mendacious Discourse in *La gitanilla*." *Cervantes* 9, no. 1 (Spring 1989): 35–53.

Márquez Villanueva, Francisco. "La buenaventura de Preciosa." *Nueva Revista de Filología Hispánica* 34, no. 2 (1985–86): 741–68.

Martínez-Bonati, Félix. "Forms of Mimesis and Ideological Rhetoric in Cervantes's *La gitanilla*." In *Textual Analysis: Some Readers Reading*, edited by Mary Ann Caws, 64–73. New York: Modern Language Association of America, 1986.

Pierce, Frank. "*La gitanilla*: A Tale of High Romance." *Bulletin of Hispanic Studies* 54, no. 4 (Oct. 1977): 283–95.

Resina, Joan Ramón. "Laissez faire y reflexividad erótica en *La gitanilla*." *MLN* 106, no. 2 (March 1991): 257–78.

Selig, Karl-Ludwig. "Concerning the Structure of Cervantes' *La gitanilla*." *Romanistisches Jahrbuch* 13 (1962): 273–76. See also *Die romanische Novelle*, 214–19. Darmstadt: Wissenschaftliche, 1976.

Spieker, Joseph B. "Preciosa y poesía: Sobre el concepto cervantino de la poesía y la estructura de *La gitanilla*." *Explicación de Textos Literarios* 4, no. 2 (1975–76): 213–20.

Ter Horst, Robert. "Une saison en enfer: *La gitanilla*." *Cervantes* 5, no. 2 (Fall 1985): 87–127.

Woodward, L. J. "*La gitanilla*." In *Cervantes: Su obra y su mundo: Actas del I Congreso Internacional sobre Cervantes*, edited by Manuel Criado de Val, 445–51. Madrid: EDI-6, 1981.

On *El amante liberal*

Bello, Miguel A. "Una lectura semántica de *El amante liberal*." *Romance Notes* 24 (1983): 132–36.

Davis, Nina Cox. "The Tyranny of Love in *El amante liberal*." *Cervantes* 13, no. 2 (Fall 1993): 105–24.

Díaz Migoyo, Gonzalo. "La ficción cordial de *El amante liberal*." *Nueva Revista de Filología Hispánica* 35, no. 1 (1987): 129–50.

Febres, Eleodoro J. "Forma y sentido de *El amante liberal*." *Anales Cervantinos* 19 (1981): 93–103.

Lowe, Jennifer. "A Note on Cervantes' *El amante liberal*." *Romance Notes* 12 (1971): 400–403.

Pabon, Thomas A. "Courtship and Marriage in *El amante liberal*: The Symbolic Quest for Self-Perfectibility." *Hispanófila* 76 (September 1982): 47–52. This article appeared originally as "Viajes de peregrinos: La búsqueda de la perfección en *El amante liberal*," in *Cervantes: Su obra y su mundo: Actas del I Congreso Internacional sobre Cervantes*, ed. Manuel Criado de Val (Madrid: EDI-6, 1981, 317–75.

Selig, Karl-Ludwig. "Some Observations on Cervantes' *El amante liberal*." *Revista Hispánica Moderna* 40, nos. 1–2 (1978–79): 67–71.

On *Rinconete y Cortadillo*

Buxó, José Pascual. "Estructura y lección de *Rinconete y Cortadillo*." In *Lavori Ispanistici*, serie 2, 69–96. Florence, Italy: Università degli Studi di Firenze; Facoltà di Magistero, Istituto Ispanico, 1970.

Díaz Migoyo, Gonzalo. "Lectura protocolaria del realismo en *Rinconete y Cortadillo*." In *Josep María Solà-Solé: Homage, Homenaje, Homenatge (Miscelánea de estudios de amigos y discípulos)*, edited by Antonio Torres-Alcalá, Victorio Agüero y Nathaniel B. Smith, 2:55–64. Barcelona: Puvill, 1984.

Febres, Eleodoro J. "*Rinconete y Cortadillo*: Estructura y otros valores estéticos." *Anales Cervantinos* 11 (1972): 97–111.

Fox, Dian. "The Critical Attitude in *Rinconete y Cortadillo*." *Cervantes* 3, no. 2 (Fall 1983): 135–47.

Hayes, Aden W. "Narrative 'Errors' in *Rinconete y Cortadillo*." *Bulletin of Hispanic Studies* 58, no. 1 (January 1981): 13–20.

Johnson, Carroll B. "The Old Order Passeth, or Does It? Some Thoughts on Community, Commerce and Alienation in *Rinconete y Cortadillo*." In *On Cervantes: Essays for L. A. Murillo*, edited by James A. Parr, 85–104. Newark, Del.: Juan de la Cuesta, 1991.

Keightley, Ronald G. "Monipodio's Realm." In *Essays in Honour of Robert Brian Tate from His Colleagues and Pupils*, edited by Richard A. Cardwell, 53–58. Nottingham, U.K.: University of Nottingham, Department of Hispanic Studies, 1984.

———. "The Narrative Structure of *Rinconete y Cortadillo*." In *Essays on Narrative Fiction in the Iberian Peninsula in Honour of Frank Pierce*, edited by R. B. Tate, 39–54. Oxford: Dolphin, 1982.

Pierce, Frank. "*Rinconete y Cortadillo*: An Extreme Case of Irony." In *Hispanic Studies in Honour of Geoffrey Ribbans*, edited by Ann L. Mackenzie and Dorothy S. Severin, 55–63. Liverpool: Liverpool University Press, 1992.

Selig, Karl-Ludwig. "Cervantes" *Rinconete y Cortadillo* and the Two 'Libros de memoria.'" *Revista Hispánica Moderna* 40, nos. 3–4 (1978–79): 126–27.

Yndurráin Múñoz, Domingo. "'Rinconete y Cortadillo': De entremés a novela." *Boletín de la Real Academia Española* 46 (1966): 321–33.

On *La española inglesa*

Alcázar Ortega, Mercedes. "Palabra, memoria y aspiración literaria en *La española inglesa*." *Cervantes* 15, no. 1 (Spring 1995): 33–45.

Cluff, David. "The Structure and Theme of *La española inglesa*: A Reconsideration." *Revista de Estudios Hispánicos* 10 (1976): 261–81.

Collins, Marsha S. "Transgression and Transfiguration in Cervantes's *La española inglesa*." *Cervantes* 16, no. 1 (Spring 1996): 54–73.

Costa Fontes, Manuel da. "Love as an Equalizer in *La española inglesa*." *Romance Notes* 16 (1975): 742–48.

Gai, Adam. "El cronotopos de *La española inglesa*." *Neophilologus* 9, no. 1 (January 1985): 67–74.

Johnson, Carroll B. "*La española inglesa* and the Practice of Literary Production." *Viator* 19 (1988): 377–416.

Lowe, Jennifer. "The Structure of Cervantes' *La española inglesa*." *Romance Notes* 9, no. 2 (1968): 287–90.

Mancini, Guido. "La 'morale' della *Española inglesa*." In *Aspetti e problemi delle letterature iberiche: Studi offerti a Franco Meregalli*, edited by Giuseppe Bellini, 219–36. Rome: Bulzoni, 1981.

Pabon, Thomas A. "The Symbolic Significance of Marriage in Cervantes' 'La española inglesa.'" *Hispanófila* 63 (1978): 59–66.

Ruta, María Caterina. "*La española inglesa*: El desdoblamiento del héroe." *Anales Cervantinos* 25–26 (1987–88): 371–82.

Singleton, Mack. "The Date of *La española inglesa*." *Hispania* 30, no. 3 (August 1947): 329–35.

Stagg, Geoffrey. "The Composition and Revision of 'La española inglesa.'" In *Studies in Honor of Bruce W. Wardropper*, edited by Dian Fox, Harry Sieber and Robert Ter Horst, 305–21. Newark, Del.: Juan de la Cuesta, 1989.

Zimic, Stanislav. "El *Amadís* cervantino: Apuntes sobre *La española inglesa*." *Anales Cervantinos* 25–26 (1987–88): 467–83.

On *El licenciado Vidriera*

Alonso Cortés, Narciso. Prologue to *El licenciado Vidriera*, by Miguel de Cervantes. Valladolid: Imprenta Castellana, 1916.

Edwards, Gwynne. "Cervantes's 'El licenciado Vidriera': Meaning and Structure." *Modern Language Review* 68 (1973): 559–68.

Febres, Eleodoro J. "*El licenciado Vidriera*: Nuevas indagaciones en cuanto a su estructura y contenido." *Cuadernos Hispanoamericanos* (Madrid) 381 (March 1982): 544–56.

Friedman, Edward H. "Conceptual Proportion in Cervantes' 'El licenciado Vidriera.'" *South Atlantic Bulletin* 39, no. 4 (November 1974): 51–59.

Gerli, E. Michael. "La picaresca y *El licenciado Vidriera:* Género y contragénero en Cervantes." In *La picaresca: orígenes, textos y estructuras: Actas del I Congreso Internacional sobre la picaresca organizado por el Patronato "Arcipreste de Hita,"* edited by Manuel Criado de Val, 577–87. Madrid: Fundación Universitaria Española, 1979.

Green, Otis H. "*El licenciado Vidriera*: Its Relation to the *Viaje del Parnaso* and the *Examen de Ingenios* of Huarte." In *Linguistic and Literary Studies in Honor of Helmut A. Hatzfeld*, edited by Alessandro S. Crisafulli, 213–20. Washington, D.C.: Catholic University of America Press, 1964.

Glannon, Walter. "The Psychology of Knowledge in *El licenciado Vidriera*." *Revista Hispánica Moderna* 40, nos. 3–4 (1978–79): 86–96.

Heiple, Daniel L. "*El licenciado Vidriera* y el humor tradicional del loco." *Hispania* 66, no. 1 (March 1983): 17–20.

———. "The Trap of the Fortunate Isles in *El licenciado Vidreira*." In *Selected Proceedings of the Thirty-Fifth Annual Mountain Interstate Foreign Language Conference*, edited by Ramón Fernández-Rubio, 185-92. Greenville, S.C.: Furman University, 1987.

Rosales, Luis. "La evasión del prójimo o el hombre de cristal." *Cuadernos Hispanoamericanos* 9, no. 81 (1956): 253–81.

Singer, Armand E. "Cervantes' *Licenciado Vidriera*: Its Form and Substance." *West Virginia University Philological Papers* 8 (1951): 13–31.

———. "The Sources, Meaning, and the Use of the Madness Theme in Cervantes' *Licenciado Vidriera*." *West Virginia University Philological Papers* 6 (1949): 31–53.

ON *LA FUERZA DE LA SANGRE*

Allen, John J. "*El Cristo de la Vega* and *La fuerza de la sangre*." *MLN* 83 (1968): 271–75.

Calcraft, R. P. "Structure, Symbol and Meaning in Cervantes's *La fuerza de la sangre*." *Bulletin of Hispanic Studies* 58, no. 3 (July 1981): 197–204.

Friedman, Edward H. "Cervantes's *La fuerza de la sangre* and the Rhetoric of Power." In *Cervantes's "Exemplary Novels" and the Adventure of Writing*, edited by Michael Nerlich and Nicholas Spadaccini, 125–56. Minneapolis: The Prisma Institute/University of Minnesota Press, 1989.

Gitlitz, David M. "Symmetry and Lust in Cervantes' *La fuerza de la sangre*." In *Studies in Honor of Everett W. Hesse*, edited by William C. McCrary and José A. Madrigal, 113–22. Lincoln, Ne.: Society of Spanish and Spanish-American Studies, 1981.

Grieve, Patricia E. "Embroidering with Saintly Threads: María de Zayas Challenges Cervantes and the Church." *Renaissance Quarterly* 44, no. 1 (Spring 1991): 86–105.

Levisi, Margarita. "La función de lo visual en 'La fuerza de la sangre.'" *Hispanófila* 49 (1973): 30–46.

Parker Aronson, Stacey L. "La 'textualización' de Leocadia y su defensa en *La fuerza de la sangre*." *Cervantes* 16, no. 2 (Fall 1996): 71–88.

Piluso, Robert V. "*La fuerza de la sangre:* Un análisis estructural." *Hispania* 47 (1964): 485–90.

Rentiis, Dina de. "Cervantes's *La fuerza de la sangre* and the Force of Negation." In *Cervantes's "Exemplary Novels" and the Adventure of Writing*, edited by Michael Nerlich and Nicholas Spadaccini, 157–74. Minneapolis: The Prisma Institute/University of Minnesota Press, 1989.

Scott, Nina M. "Honor and Family in *La fuerza de la sangre*." In *Studies in Honor of Ruth Lee Kennedy*, edited by Vern G. Williamsen and A. F. Michael Atlee, 125–32. Chapel Hill: Estudios de Hispanófila, 1977.

Selig, Karl-Ludwig. "Some Observations on *La fuerza de la sangre*." *MLN* 87, no. 6 (1972): 121–25.

Slaniceanu, Adriana. "The Calculating Woman in Cervantes' *La fuerza de la sangre*." *Bulletin of Hispanic Studies* 64, no. 2 (April 1987): 101–10.

Welles, Marcia. "Violence Disguised: Representation of Rape in Cervantes' 'La fuerza de la sangre.'" *Journal of Hispanic Philology* 13, no. 3 (Spring 1989): 240–52.

On *El celoso extremeño*

Avalle-Arce, Juan Bautista. "*El celoso extremeño*, de Cervantes." In *Homenaje a Ana María Barrenechea*, edited by Lía Schwartz-Lerner and Isaías Lerner, 199–205. Madrid: Castalia, 1984.

Brown, Kenneth. "Notas sobre los elementos mitológicos, bíblicos y folklóricos en *El celoso extremeño*." In *Studies on Don Quijote and Other Cervantine Works*, edited by Donald W. Bleznick, 65–77. York, S.C.: Spanish Literary Publications, 1984.

Castro, Américo. "*El celoso extremeño* de Cervantes." In *Hacia Cervantes*, 3d rev. ed., 420–50. Madrid: Taurus, 1967.

Donato, Clorinda. "Leonora and Camila: Female Characterization and Narrative Formula in the Cervantine *Novela*." *Mester* 15, no. 2 (Fall 1986): 13–24.

Edwards, Gwynne. "Los dos desenlaces de *El celoso extremeño*." *Boletín de la Biblioteca Menéndez Pelayo* 49 (1973): 281–91.

Febres, Eleodoro J. "*El celoso extremeño*: Estructura y otros valores estéticos." *Hispanófila* 57 (1976): 7–22.

Gómez-Reinoso, Manuel. "El mito recurrente en *El celoso extremeño*." In *Festschrift José Cid Pérez*, edited by Alberto Gutiérrez de la Solana and Elio Alba-Buffill, 281–87. New York: Senda Nueva de Eds., 1981.

Jehenson, Myriam Yvonne. "Quixotic Desires or Stark Reality?" *Cervantes* 15, no. 2 (Fall 1995): 26–39.

Lambert, A. F. "The Two Versions of Cervantes' *El celoso extremeño*: Ideology and Criticism." *Bulletin of Hispanic Studies* 57, no. 3 (July 1980): 219–31.

Lippmann, Stephen H. "Revision and Exemplarity in Cervantes's *El celoso extremeño*." *Cervantes* 6, no. 2 (Fall 1986): 113–21.

McPheeters, Dean W. "Ovid and the Jealous Old Man of Cervantes." In *Estudios literarios de hispanistas norteamericanos dedicados a Helmut Hatzfeld con motivo de su 80 aniversario*, edited by Josep M. Solà-Solé, Alessandro Crisfulli, and Bruno Damiani, 157–65. Barcelona: Hispam, 1975.

Molho, Maurice. "Aproximación al *Celoso extremeño*." *Nueva Revista de Filología Hispánica* 38, no. 2 (1990): 743–92.

Rodríguez Marín, Francisco. *El Loaysa de "El celoso extremeño."* Sevilla: P. Díaz, 1901.

Stern, Charlotte. "*El celoso extremeño*: Entre farsa y tragedia." In *Estudios sobre el Siglo de*

Oro en homenage a Raymond R. MacCurdy, edited by Angel González, Tamara Holzapfel and Alfred Rodríguez, 333–42. Albuquerque: University of New Mexico, Department of Modern and Classical Languages, 1983. Madrid: Cátedra, 1983.

Weber, Alison. "Tragic Reparation in Cervantes' *El celoso extremeño*." *Cervantes* 4, no. 1 (Spring 1984): 35–51.

Williamson, Edwin. "El 'misterio escondido' en *El celoso extremeño*: Una aproximación al arte de Cervantes." *Nueva Revista de Filología Hispánica* 38, no. 2 (1990): 793–815.

On *La ilustre fregona*

Barrenechea, Ana María. "*La ilustre fregona* como ejemplo de estructura novelesca cervantina." In *Actas del Primer Congreso Internacional de Hispanistas, Celebrado en Oxford del 6 al 11 de Septiembre de 1962*, edited by Frank Pierce and Cyril A. Jones, 199–206. Oxford: Dolphin, 1964.

Casalduero, Joaquín. "Notas sobre *La ilustre fregona*." *Anales Cervantinos* 3 (1953): 331–39.

Checa, Jorge. "El *romance* y su sombra: hibridación genérica en *La ilustre fregona*." *Revista de Estudios Hispánicos* 25 (1991): 29–47.

Hanrahan, Thomas. "Cervantes and the Moralists." *Hispania* 73, no. 4 (December 1990): 906–20.

Herrero, Javier. "Emerging Realism: Love and Cash in *La ilustre fregona*." In *From Dante to García Márquez*, edited by Gene H. Bell-Villada, Antonio Giménez, and George Pistorius, 47–59. Williamstown, Mass.: Williams College, 1987.

Ife, B. W. "From Salamanca to Brighton Rock: Names and Places in Cervantes' *La ilustre fregona*." In *Essays in Honour of Robert Brian Tate from His Colleagues and Pupils*, edited by Richard A. Cardwell, 46–52. Nottingham, U.K.: University of Nottingham, Department of Hispanic Studies, 1984.

Johnston, Robert M. "Picaresque and Pastoral in *La ilustre fregona*." In *Cervantes and the Renaissance*, edited by Michael D. McGaha, 167–77. Easton, Pa.: Juan de la Cuesta, 1980.

Joly, Monique. "Para una reinterpretación de *La ilustre fregona*: Ensayo de tipología cervantina." In *Aureum Saeculum Hispanum: Beiträge zu Texten des Siglo de Oro*, edited by Karl-Hermann Körner and Dietrich Briesemeister, 103–16. Wiesbaden: Steiner, 1983.

Rodríguez-Marín, Francisco. *La ilustre fregona, novela de Miguel de Cervantes Saavedra*. Madrid: Revista de Archivos, Bibliotecas y Museos, 1917.

On *Las dos doncellas*

Britt, Linda. "Teodosia's Dark Shadow? A Study of Women's Roles in Cervantes' *Las dos doncellas*." *Cervantes* 8, no. 1 (Spring 1988): 39–46.

Schmauser, Caroline. "Dynamism and Spatial Structure in *Las dos doncellas*." In *Cervantes's "Exemplary Novels" and the Adventure of Writing*, edited by Michael Nerlich and Nicholas Spadaccini, 175–203. Minneapolis: The Prisma Institute/University of Minnesota Press, 1989.

Stagg, Geoffrey. "*La Galatea* and 'Las dos doncellas' to the Rescue of *Don Quixote*, Part II." In *Essays in Honour of Robert Brian Tate from His Colleagues and Pupils*, edited

by Richard A. Cardwell, 125–30. Nottingham, U.K.: University of Nottingham, Department of Hispanic Studies, 1984.
Thompson, Jennifer. "The Structure of Cervantes' *Las dos doncellas*." *Bulletin of Hispanic Studies* 40 (1963): 144–50.
Zabala-Peña, María. "Los personajes de *Las dos doncellas:* Sus fallos y la necesidad de la peregrinación a Santiago." Term paper, University of South Carolina, Fall 1992.

On *La señora Cornelia*

Avalle-Arce, Juan Bautista de. "La ejemplaridad de una novelita." *Quaderni Ibero-Americani* 78 (December 1995): 5–8.
Bradbury, Gail. "Lope, Cervantes, a Marriage Trick and a Baby." *Hispanófila* 82 (September 1984): 11–19.
Hanahan, Devon. "Narrative Technique in *La señora Cornelia*." Term paper, University of South Carolina, Fall 1994.
Lacadena y Calero, Esther. "*La señora Cornelia* y su técnica narrativa." *Anales Cervantinos* 15 (1976): 199–210.

On *El casamiento engañoso* and *El coloquio de los perros*

Abrams, Fred. "Cervantes' Berganza-Cipion Anagrams in *El coloquio de los perros*." *Names* 24 (1976): 325–26.
Avalle-Arce, Juan Bautista. "Cervantes entre pícaros." *Nueva Revista de Filología Hispánica* 38, no. 2 (1990): 591–603.
Aylward, E. T. "The Device of Layered Critical Commentary in *Don Quixote* and *El coloquio de los perros*." *Cervantes* 7, no. 2 (Fall 1987): 57–69.
Bělič, Oldřich. "La estructura de *El coloquio de los perros*." In *Acta Universitatis Carolinae, Philologica 4 (1966). Romanistica Pragensia IV*, 3–19. Prague: University of Karlova, 1966.
Blanco Aguinaga, Carlos. "Cervantes y la picaresca. Notas sobre dos tipos de realismo." *Nueva Revista de Filología Hispánica* 11 (1957): 313–42.
Boyd, Stephen. "Sin and Grace in *El casamiento engañoso* y *El coloquio de los perros*." In *What's Past is Prologue: A Collection of Essays in Honour of L. J. Woodward*, edited by Salvador Bacarisse, Bernard Bentley, Mercedes Clarasó, and Douglas Gifford, 1–9. Edinburgh: Scottish Academic Press, 1984.
Cabrera, Vicente. "Nuevos valores de 'El casamiento engañoso' y 'El coloquio de los perros.'" *Hispanófila* 45 (May 1972): 49–58.
———. "El sueño del alférez Campuzano." *Nueva Revista de Filología Hispánica* 23 (1974): 388–91.
Cárdenas, Anthony. "Berganza: Cervantes' *Can[is] Domini*." In *Cervantes and the Pastoral*, edited by José J. Labrador Herráiz and Juan Fernández Jiménez, 19–35. Cleveland: Cleveland State University, Penn State University, Behrend College, 1986.
El Saffar, Ruth. *Cervantes: A Critical Study of "El casamiento engañoso" and "El coloquio de los perros."* London: Grant & Cutler, 1976.
———. "Montesinos' Cave and the *Casamiento engañoso* in the Development of Cervantes' Prose Fiction." *Kentucky Romance Quarterly* 20 (1973): 451–67.

Forcione, Alban K. *Cervantes and the Mystery of Lawlessness: A Study of "El casamiento engañoso y El coloquio de los perros."* Princeton: Princeton University Press, 1984.

González Echevarría, Roberto. "The Life and Adventures of Cipión: Cervantes and the Picaresque." *Diacritics* 10, no. 3 (1980): 15–26.

Haley, George. "The Narrator in *Don Quijote*: Maese Pedro's Puppet Show." *MLN* 80 (1965): 145–65.

Ife, B. W. *Lectura y ficción en el Siglo de Oro: Las razones de la picaresca.* Barcelona: Edición Crítica, 1992.

Johnson, Carroll B. "Of Witches and Bitches: Gender, Marginality and Discourse in *El casamiento engañoso y Coloquio de los perros.*" *Cervantes* 11, no. 2 (Fall 1991): 7–25.

Lloris, Manuel. "El casamiento engañoso." *Hispanófila* 39 (May 1970): 15–20.

Murillo, L. A. "Cervantes' *Coloquio de los perros*, a Novel-Dialogue." *Modern Philology* 58 (February 1961): 174–85.

Nerlich, Michael. "On the Philosophical Dimension of *El casamiento engañoso* and *El coloquio de los perros.*" In *Cervantes's "Exemplary Novels" and the Adventure of Writing*, edited by Michael Nerlich and Nicholas Spadaccini, 247–329. Minneapolis: The Prisma Institute/University of Minnesota Press, 1989.

Oliver, Antonio. "La filosofía cínica y el 'Coloquio de los perros.'" *Anales Cervantinos* 3 (1953): 291–307.

Piluso, Robert V. "El papel mediador del narrador en dos *novelas ejemplares* de Cervantes." In *Actas del Sexto Congreso Internacional de Hispanistas celebrado en Toronto del 22 al 26 de agosto de 1977*, edited by Alan M. Gordon and Evelyn Rugg, 571–74. Toronto: Department of Spanish and Portuguese, University of Toronto, 1980.

Pozuelo Yvancos, José María. "Enunciación y recepción en el *Casamiento-Coloquio.*" In *Cervantes: Su obra y su mundo: Actas del I Congreso Internacional sobre Cervantes*, edited by Manuel Criado de Val, 423–35. Madrid: EDI-6, 1981.

Riley, E. C. "Cervantes, Freud, and Psychoanalytic Narrative Theory." *Modern Language Review* 88, no. 1 (January 1993): 1–14.

Russell, Jeffrey Burton. *Witchcraft in the Middle Ages.* Ithaca, N.Y.: Cornell University Press, 1972.

Selig, Karl-Ludwig. "The Interplay of Form and Point of View in *El casamiento engañoso.*" In *Spanische Literatur in Goldenen Zeitalter: Fritz Schalk zum 70 Geburtstag*, edited by Horst Baader and Erich Loos, 394–400. Frankfurt: Klostermann, 1973.

Sobejano, Gonzalo. "El 'Coloquio de los perros' en la picaresca y otros apuntes." *Hispanic Review* 43, no. 1 (Winter 1975): 25–41.

Soons, Alan. "An Interpretation of the Form of *El casamiento engañoso y Coloquio de los perros.*" *Anales Cervantinos* 9 (1961–62): 203–12.

Thacker, M. J. "Cervantes' Exemplary *Pícaros.*" In *Hispanic Studies in Honour of Geoffrey Ribbans*, edited by Ann L. Mackenzie and Dorothy S. Severin. *Bulletin of Hispanic Studies Special Homage Volume* (1992): 47–53.

Waley, Pamela. "The Unity of the *Casamiento engañoso* and the *Coloquio de los perros.*" *Bulletin of Hispanic Studies* 34 (1957): 201–12.

Williamson, Edwin. "Cervantes as Moralist and Trickster: The Critique of Picaresque Autobiography in *El casamiento engañoso y El coloquio de los perros.*" In *Essays on Hispanic Themes in Honour of Edward C. Riley*, edited by Jennifer Lowe and Philip Swanson, 104–26. Edinburgh: Department of Hispanic Studies, University of Edinburgh, 1989.

Woodward, L. J. "*El casamiento engañoso* y *El coloquio de los perros*." *Bulletin of Hispanic Studies* 36 (1959): 80–87.

Zappala, Michael. "Cervantes and Lucian." *Symposium* 33, no. 1 (Spring 1979): 65–82.

Index of Critics Cited

Abrams, Fred: on the name Berganza as a pseudonym for Cervantes, 308n. 55

Alcázar Ortega, Mercedes: on *La española inglesa*, 138; on *La fuerza de la sangre*, 127

Allen, John J.: on the origins of the crucifix-as-witness motif in *La fuerza de la sangre*, 296n. 42

Alonso Cortés, Narciso: on Huguenot disturbances in Paris (in *El licenciado Vidriera*), 303n. 88; on *El licenciado Vidriera*, 201

Amezúa y Mayo, Agustín G.: on *El amante liberal*, 95; on the *Casamiento* and *Coloquio* as separate entities, 243–44; on *El celoso extremeño*, 30, 182; on *El coloquio de los perros*, 241; on *Las dos doncellas*, 209; on *La española inglesa*, 132–33; on *El licenciado Vidriera*, 202; on *La señora Cornelia*, 226

Apráiz y Sáenz del Burgo, Julián: on the *Novelas* in general, 30

Atkinson, William C.: on the *Novelas* in general, 20, 30

Avalle-Arce, Juan Bautista: on *El celoso extremeño*, 178; on *El coloquio de los perros*, 245–46; on *La gitanilla*, 42, 65; on *La ilustre fregona*, 74; on *El licenciado Vidriera*, 190; on *La señora Cornelia*, 231–32, 235

Aylward, E. T.: on *El celoso extremeño*, 176–77, 183, 282–84; on Cervantes's treatment of the theme of jealousy, 291n. 1; on *El licenciado Vidriera*, 203, 281–82; on the Porras Manuscript, 152–54; on the portrayal of Philip II in *El celoso extremeño*, 302 n. 70; on *Rinconeta y Cortadillo*, 165–67, 279–80

Bakhtin, M. M.: on the chronotype for the adventure novel of ordeal, 108

Barrenechea, Ana María: on *La ilustre fregona*, 76, 82

Bataillon, Marcel: on the *Novelas* in general, 30

Bĕlič, Oldřich: on the episodic arrangement of *El coloquio de los perros*, 250–51, 257

Bello, Miguel A.: on homosexual and feminine allusions to Cornelio in *El amante liberal*, 295n. 16

Blanco Aguinaga, Carlos: on *El coloquio de los perros*, 246; on the combined *Casamiento* and *Coloquio*, 242

Boyd, S[tephen] F.: on *El coloquio de los perros*, 248–49; on *La gitanilla*, 49

Bradbury, Gail: on *La señora Cornelia*, 228–29, 235

Britt, Linda: on *Las dos doncellas*, 219–20

Buxó, José Pascual: on *Rinconete y Cortadillo*, 161

Cabrera, Vicente: on the *Casamiento* and *Coloquio* as separate entities, 244; on *El coloquio de los perros*, 251–52

Calcraft, R. P.: on *La fuerza de la sangre*, 113, 120

Canavaggio, Jean: on the *Novelas* in

general, 29; on the value of Spanish coins in the seventeenth century, 298 n. 86
Cárdenas, Anthony: on *El coloquio de los perros,* 249
Casalduero, Joaquín: on *El amante liberal,* 94–95, 99; on *El celoso extremeño,* 170–71, 182; on the combined *Casamiento* and *Coloquio,* 242; on *Las dos doncellas,* 208–9, 222; on *La española inglesa,* 127–28, 132, 139–40, 149; on *La fuerza de la sangre,* 109–10; on *La gitanilla,* 48, 51, 62, 65; on *La ilustre fregona,* 81, 83, 92; on *El licenciado Vidriera,* 201; on the *Novelas* in general, 20–22, 30; on *Rinconete y Cortadillo,* 156–57, 160; on *La señora Cornelia,* 226
Cascardi, Anthony J.: on *El licenciado Vidriera,* 192
Castro, Américo: on *El celoso extremeño,* 30; on the *Novelas* in general, 30
Chatman, Seymour: on five ways of representing narrative time vs. story time, 32
Checa, Jorge: on the central theme of *El celoso extremeño,* 302 n. 64; on the combined *Casamiento* and *Coloquio,* 242; on the episode of the Breton sailor in the Porras Manuscript, 300 n. 35; on *La ilustre fregona,* 91
Cluff, David: on *La española inglesa,* 132, 140, 142, 146, 148–49; on *La fuerza de la sangre,* 125, 129–32
Collins, Marsha S.: on *La española inglesa,* 143, 145
Combet, Louis: on *El amante liberal,* 98; on Cervantes's generally unfavorable representation of young males, 295 n. 12
Costa Fontes, Manuel da: on *La española inglesa,* 148–49
Criado de Val, Manuel: on the Porras Manuscript, 152
Crooks, Esther J.: on the *Novelas* in general, 30

Davis, Nina Cox: on *El amante liberal,* 96
Díaz Migoyo, Gonzalo: on *El amante liberal,* 95–96, 107; on *Rinconete y Cortadillo,* 169

Díaz-Plaja, Guillermo: on *La española inglesa,* 128–29; on the *Novelas* in general, 30; on the structure of *La española inglesa,* 297 n. 64
Donato, Clorinda: on *El celoso extremeño,* 172
Drake, Dana B.: on the *Novelas* in general, 29
Dunn, Peter N.: on the combined *Casamiento* and *Coloquio,* 245; on *La señora Cornelia,* 234

Edwards, Gwynne: on *El celoso extremeño,* 181; on *El licenciado Vidriera,* 190–92
El Saffar, Ruth: on *El amante liberal,* 95, 104; on the *Casamiento* and *Coloquio* as separate entities, 244; on *El celoso extremeño,* 177, 179–80; on Cervantes's opinion of the Jesuits, 307 n. 45; on Cervantes's presentation of feminine psychological attributes, 289 n. 1; on *El coloquio de los perros,* 248, 258–60; on the combined *Casamiento* and *Coloquio,* 266–67, 270; on *Las dos doncellas,* 219; on *Las dos doncellas* and *La señora Cornelia,* 238; on *La española inglesa,* 125, 133–34, 137, 146; on *La fuerza de la sangre,* 109–12; on *La gitanilla,* 51, 62, 65; on *La ilustre fregona,* 81; on *El licenciado Vidriera,* 192; on the link between the *Casamiento* and the *Coloquio,* 308 n. 51; on the *Novelas* in general, 11, 15, 18, 22–24; on *Rinconete y Cortadillo,* 161–62; on *La señora Cornelia,* 226
Entwhistle, William J.: on the *Novelas* in general, 30

Febres, Eleodoro J.: on *El amante liberal,* 96; on *El celoso extremeño,* 182; on the central theme of *El celoso extremeño,* 302 n. 64; on *El licenciado Vidriera,* 190, 192; on *Rinconete y Cortadillo,* 156, 160; on the structure of *El amante liberal,* 294 n. 1
Fernández de Avellaneda, Alonso [pseud.]: on the *Novelas* in general, 30
Fernández de Navarrete, Martín: on the *Novelas* in general, 30

Fitzmaurice-Kelly, James: on *El celoso extremeño*, 30; on *El licenciado Vidriera*, 30; on the *Novelas* in general, 30
Forcione, Alban K.: on the Cave of Montesinos episode (vs. El Saffar), 308n. 52; on *El celoso extremeño*, 173–76; on Cervantes's opinion of the Jesuits, 307n. 45; on *El coloquio de los perros*, 245, 253–54; on the combined *Casamiento* and *Coloquio*, 243; on *La fuerza de la sangre*, 110; on *La gitanilla*, 48, 51–52, 63, 65; on *El licenciado Vidriera*, 190, 195–96, 202–3; on the link between the *Casamiento* and the *Coloquio*, 308 n. 51; on the *Novelas* in general, 24–25
Fox, Dian: on *Rinconete y Cortadillo*, 159
Frank, Rachel: on *Las dos doncellas*, 209
Friedman, Edward H.: on *La fuerza de la sangre*, 120; on *El licenciado Vidriera*, 189–90

Gai, Adam: on *La española inglesa*, 140, 144, 146
Genette, Gérard: on *analepse* (flashback technique), 32; on heterodiegetic vs. homodiegetic narratives, 307n. 42
Gerli, E. Michael: on *La gitanilla*, 42, 65; on *El licenciado Vidriera*, 189, 195; on the *Novelas* in general, 16, 18–19
Gitlitz, David M.: on *La fuerza de la sangre*, 109, 113, 120
Glannon, Walter: on *El licenciado Vidriera*, 190, 192
González Echeverría, Roberto: on *El coloquio de los perros*, 246–47
Green, Otis H.: on *El licenciado Vidriera*, 30, 195, 203
Grieve, Patricia E.: on Cervantes's treatment of the subject of rape, 296 n. 40; on *La fuerz de la sangre*, 111, 115
Güntert, Georges: on *La gitanilla*, 51

Hainesworth, Georges: on *La española inglesa*, 132; on *El licenciado Vidriera*, 30; on the *Novelas* in general, 30

Haley, George: on the layered structure of the *Quixote*, 263–64
Hanahan, Devon: on the frequency of secondary narratives in *La señora Cornelia*, 305n. 32
Hanrahan, Thomas: on *La ilustre fregona*, 80
Hart, Thomas R.: on *El celoso extremeño*, 181, 187; on *La gitanilla*, 42, 60; on *La ilustra fregona*, 74; on *Rinconete y Cortadillo*, 156; on twentieth-century distaste for *El amante liberal*, 295 n. 13
Hatzfeld, Helmut: on the *Novelas* in general, 30
Hayes, Aden W.: on *Rinconete y Cortadillo*, 169
Heiple, Daniel L.: on *El licenciado Vidriera*, 190, 195, 202
Herrero, Javier: on *La ilustra fregona*, 74
Herrero-García, Miguel: on the *Novelas* in general, 30

Icaza, Francisco A. de: on *El licenciado Vidriera*, 201; on the *Novelas* in general, 30
Ife, B. W.: on the combined *Casamiento* and *Coloquio*, 270–71; on *La ilustre fregona*, 71, 82, 84, 92

Jehenson, Myriam Yvonne: on *El celoso extremeño*, 182
Johnson, Carroll B.: on the biography of the duke of Medina-Sidonia, 301 n. 42; on *El coloquio de los perros*, 249–50; on *La española inglesa*, 134, 138–40, 143–44, 149; on *La fuerza de la sangre*, 127; on *La gitanilla*, 65–66; on *Rinconete y Cortadillo*, 157–58, 169–70
Johnston, Robert M.: on *La ilustre fregona*, 74
Joly, Monique: on *La ilustre fregona*, 79

Kayser, Wolfgang: on the use of direct quotes vs. narrative summaries in *La gitanilla*, 292 n. 17
Keightley, Ronald G.: on *Rinconete y Cortadillo*, 157, 159, 161
Knight, Sharon Eadie: on Cervantes's

deviation from Greek romance conventions in *El amante liberal*, 295 n. 23; on Cervantes's deviation from Greek romance conventions in *La española inglesa*, 298–99 n. 99

Krummrich, Philip: on *La gitanilla*, 59, 62

Lacadena y Calero, Esther: on *La señora Cornelia*, 229–30, 232–33
Lambert, A. F.: on *El celoso extremeño*, 178, 180–81
Levisi, Margarita: on *La fuerza de la sangre*, 109
Lippmann, Stephen H.: on the ending of *El celoso extremeño*, 301 n. 54
Lipson, Lesley: on *El coloquio de los perros*, 249–50; on *La gitanilla*, 52, 65
Lloris, Manuel: on *El casamiento engañoso*, 248

Mancini, Guido: on *La española inglesa*, 128–29
McLean, Malcolm D.: on *El celoso extremeño*, 30
Menéndez y Pelayo, Marcelino: on the *Novelas* in general, 30; on *Rinconete y Cortadillo*, 156
Meregalli, Franco: on the *Novelas* in general, 30
Molho, Maurice: on *El celoso extremeño*, 178
Murillo, L. A.: on the *Casamiento* and *Coloquio* as separate entities, 244; on *Las dos doncellas*, 220, 222; on the *Novelas* in general, 26–28

Nerlich, Michael: on *El coloquio de los perros*, 307 n. 35

Oliver, Antonio: on the classical influences upon Cervantes, 240–41
Ortega y Gasset, José: on the *Novelas* in general, 30

Pabon, Thomas A.: on *El amante liberal*, 96; on *Las dos doncellas*, 215; on *La española inglesa*, 126–27; on *La señora Cornelia*, 235
Parker Aronson, Stacey L.: on *La fuerza de la sangre*, 124

Pellicer, Juan Antonio: on the *Novelas* in general, 30
Pfandl, Ludwig: on *El celoso extremeño*, 30; on *Rinconete y Cortadillo*, 156
Pierce, Frank: on *La gitanilla*, 42, 51; on the *Novelas* in general, 30; on *Rinconete y Cortadillo*, 159
Piluso, Robert V.: on *La fuerza de la sangre*, 109–10; on Licenciado Peralta as the ideal critical reader, 272
Porras Manuscript, the, 152–56, 160, 162, 164–67, 169–71, 173–74, 176, 203, 205; changes made in the text of *El celoso extremeño*, 184–88; the original ending for *El celoso extremeño*, 177–81
Pozuelo Yvancos, José María: on the *Casamiento* and *Coloquio* as separate entities, 245; on *El coloquio de los perros*, 252–53

Rentiis, Dina de: on *La fuerza de la sangre*, 114, 120
Resina, Joan Ramón: on *La gitanilla*, 48, 63
Ricapito, Joseph V.: on *La española inglesa*, 149; on *La gitanilla*, 48; on *El licenciado Vidriera*, 189–90; on *La señora Cornelia*, 228
Riley, E. C.: on Cervantes's ambivalence toward "romance" conventions, 145; on *El coloquio de los perros* and *El licenciado Vidriera*, 241–42; on the combined *Casamiento* and *Coloquio*, 243; on *El licenciado Vidriera*, 190, 202; on the *Novelas* in general, 25; on the thirteen properties of the prose romance, 289–90 n. 8.
Rivers, Elias L.: on the Introduction to the 1615 *Quixote*, 18
Rodríguez-Luis, Julio: on *El amante liberal*, 95–96; on the *Casamiento* and *Coloquio* as separate entities, 244; on *El casamiento engañoso*, 247–48; on *Las dos doncellas*, 210, 220, 223–24; on *La española inglesa*, 127, 137, 143; on the figure of the failed poet in *La gitanilla*, 294 n. 37; on *La fuerza de la sangre*, 110–11; on *La gitanilla*, 48, 63; in *El licenciado Vidriera*, 189; on

Rodríguez-Luis *(continued):*
the *Novelas* in general, 25; on *Rinconete y Cortadillo,* 159, 161, 163, 167–69; on *La señora Cornelia,* 226–28; on the theatricality of *La gitanilla* and *La ilustra fregona,* 294n. 48
Rodríguez-Marín, Francisco: on *El celoso extremeño,* 30; on *La española inglesa,* 132; on *El licenciado Vidriera,* 30; on the *Novelas* in general, 20
Rosales, Luis: on *El licenciado Vidriera,* 188
Russell, Jeffrey Burton: on the Catharist heresy, 306–7n. 32
Ruta, María Caterina: on *La española inglesa,* 139

Sánchez, Francisco J.: on *El celoso extremeño,* 186; on *La gitanilla,* 48, 64; on *Rinconete y Cortadillo,* 161
Schevill, Rudolph: on *El licenciado Vidriera,* 30; on the *Novelas* in general, 30
Schevill, Rudolph, and Adolfo Bonilla: on *Las dos doncellas,* 208; on *La española inglesa,* 132; on the *Novelas* in general, 30
Schmauser, Caroline: on *Las dos doncellas,* 210, 223
Scott, Nina M.: on *La fuerza de la sangre,* 113, 119
Sears, Theresa Ann: on *El amante liberal,* 107–8; on *La ilustre fregona,* 90
Selig, Karl-Ludwig: on *El amante liberal,* 95; on the combined *Casamiento* and *Coloquio,* 243; on *La fuerza de la sangre,* 109; on *La gitanilla,* 51; on *Rinconete y Cortadillo,* 161
Sicroff, Albert A.: on *La española inglesa,* 149; on the *Novelas* in general, 26; on *La señora Cornelia,* 235
Sieber, Harry: on *La española inglesa,* 140; on *La ilustre fregona,* 73; on *La señora Cornelia,* 235
Singer, Armand E.: on *agudezas* as a major portion of *El licenciado Vidriera's* text, 303n. 89; on *El licenciado Vidriera,* 30, 190, 195–96, 201
Singleton, Mack: on *La española inglesa,* 132–33

Slaniceanu, Adriana: on *La fuerza de la sangre,* 120
Sobejano, Gonzalo: on *El coloquio de los perros,* 246; on the *Novelas* in general, 15–16, 18–19, 24
Soons, Alan: on the *Coloquio's* link with the prologue to the *Novelas,* 272–73; on the combined *Casamiento* and *Coloquio,* 245
Sordo, Enrique: on *El celoso extremeño,* 30
Spadaccini, Nicholas, and Jenaro Talens: on the *Novelas* in general, 28–29
Spieker, Joseph B.: on *La gitanilla,* 51
Spitzer, Leo: on *El celoso extremeño,* 30
Stern, Charlotte: on *El celoso extremeño,* 182

Ter Horst, Robert: on *La gitanilla,* 42, 52
Thacker, M. J.: vs. Bělič on *El coloquio de los perros,* 307n. 36
Thompson, Jennifer: on *Las dos doncellas,* 209, 214–15, 219–21
Tieck, Johann Ludwig: on the *Novelas* in general, 30
Turkevich, Ludmilla Buketoff: on the *Novelas* in general, 30

Vinel, Catherine Davis: on Archimboldo's *The Vegetable Gardener,* 236; on economic connections between *La española inglesa* and *Rinconete y Cortadillo,* 298n. 96; on *La española inglesa,* 138, 145, 150; on *La fuerza de la sangre,* 121; on *La gitanilla,* 64; on *La señora Cornelia,* 236–37

Waley, Pamela: on the combined *Casamiento* and *Coloquio,* 242
Wardropper, Bruce W.: on the value of Spanish coins in the seventeenth century, 298n. 86
Weber, Alison: on *El celoso extremeño,* 182
Welles, Marsha S.: on *La fuerza de la sangre,* 115, 120
Williamson, Edwin: on *El celoso extremeño,* 178, 180; on the combined *Casamiento* and *Coloquio,* 271
Wiltrout, Ann E.: on *La gitanilla,* 51–52; on *La ilustre fregona,* 81, 92

Woodward, L. J.: on the combined *Casamiento* and *Coloquio,* 242–43; on *La gitanilla,* 44

Ynduráin Múñoz, Domingo: on *Rinconete y Cortadillo,* 160

Zabala-Peña, María: on *Las dos doncellas,* 304n. 24

Zappala, Michael: comparing Lucian, Erasmus, and Cervantes, 240–41

Zimic, Stanislav: on *La española inglesa,* 139, 144